THE  TIMES
ANCIENT
CIVILIZATIONS

THE TIMES

ANCIENT CIVILIZATIONS

Edited by Hugh Bowden

TIMES BOOKS
London

First published in 2002 by
TIMES BOOKS
HarperCollins*Publishers*
77-85 Fulham Palace Road
Hammersmith, London W6 8JB

Printed and bound in Italy by Editoriale Johnson SpA, Bergamo

British Library Cataloguing in Publication Data. A catalogue record for this book is available from the British Library.

ISBN 0 0071 0859 1

Editorial Direction
Philip Parker

Editorial
Ceire Clark

Design
Kathryn Gammon

Cartographic Direction and Design
Martin Brown

Cartography
Cosmographics, Watford, England

Additional cartography and Illustrations
Andras Bereznay
Mel Pickering, Contour Publishing

Place-names consultant
Pat Geelan

Subject Index
Chris Howse

The publishers would also like to thank the following: Fiona Screen; El. Morati and Dr. Nikolaos Kaltsas, National Archaeological Museum of Athens; Ruth Janson, Brooklyn Museum; Derek Welsby, British Museum; Maria de Pascale, British Museum Photographic Service; Elizabeth Morgan, Dept. of Oriental Antiquities, British Museum; Herma Chang, Dept. of West Asian Antiquities, British Museum; Janet Larkin, Dept. of Coins and Medals, British Museum; Allan Scollan, Dept of Greek and Roman Antiquities, British Museum; Andreas Klostermaier; E.F. Legner

Contributors

GENERAL EDITOR

Hugh Bowden
Lecturer in Ancient History
King's College London

Daud Ali
Lecturer in Early Indian History
School of Oriental and
African Studies, University of London

Richard Alston
Lecturer in Classics
Royal Holloway, University of London

Isabel Anderton

Elizabeth Baquedano
Lecturer
Birkbeck College, University of London

Joe Cribb
Deputy Keeper
Department of Coins and Medals
The British Museum

Carol Michaelson
Assistant Keeper
Department of Oriental Antiquities
The British Museum

Justin Morris
Curator of South Asian Archaeology
Department of Oriental Antiquities
The British Museum

Margaret Oliphant

Caroline Orwin

Julia Shaw
Junior Research Fellow
Merton College
Oxford University

StJohn Simpson
Assistant Keeper
Department of the Ancient Near East
The British Museum

Michael Willis
Curator
Department of Oriental Antiquities
The British Museum

Contents

PART I The Basis of Civilization

PART II Age of Bronze c. 3000–1000 BC

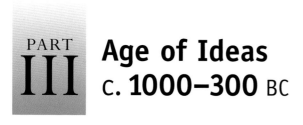

PART V — Age of Transformation c. AD 250–750

PART VI — Ancient Civilizations of the New World

Introduction

What does 'Ancient Civilizations' mean? How ancient? What counts as civilized? These are questions to which there can be no definitive answers, but this book aims to challenge some traditional views and to demonstrate newer ways of answering them.

One approach to defining 'civilization' is to produce a list of features that a society must possess, such as urbanism, literacy and metal-working, or perhaps a certain kind of social organization. These are important areas, which are discussed in Part One, but terms like 'urbanism' are not simple, and there are societies without literacy or without knowledge of metallurgy that must be recognized as civilizations. A useful idea for making sense of the development of societies is 'complexity'. This is not something that societies either have or lack, but a continuum. Not all societies develop in the same way, so there can be no one way of defining complexity, or identifying it in the archaeological record. As a result the decisions about starting points for this book may seem arbitrary, but the aim is to illustrate the variety of civilizations in the ancient world as well as their antiquity.

The choice of endpoint is more deliberate, and also more controversial. The western approach to the past has tended to see the fall of the Roman empire in the west a little before AD 500 as marking the end of the ancient world. This view, in which the Christian Roman empire is replaced, after a period of uncertainty, by a Christian Medieval world, that then lays the foundation for the modern triumph of the west, is a distortion of history, even in Europe, and makes still less sense in the rest of the world. Above all it vastly underestimates the effect of the rise of Islam. By around AD 750, little more than a century after the death of Muhammad, Islamic armies had travelled the length of the Mediterranean, and were fighting in southern France, beneath the walls of Constantinople and on the borders of China. Given the continuing importance of Islam throughout the world today, its rise seems the point to mark the division between the ancient and the modern worlds.

The book is organized in a series of sweeps across the old world, moving from west to east. Part Two traverses the terrain three times, looking at what are known as the early, middle and late bronze ages. After that Parts Three, Four and Five each make a single sweep. The aim is to illustrate how different parts of the world developed at the same time, as well as showing how each area changed through time. Part Six covers central and south America, whose civilizations developed independently of the old world. It would be entirely arbitrary to end this section around AD 750, so it carries the story on until European contact in the early 16th century.

Some civilizations produced historians who have provided accounts of their own past. Others produced documents from which such narratives can be reconstructed. Still others produced nothing of this sort, and have left only material remains for archaeologists to interpret. This variety of evidence is inevitably reflected in the descriptions of ancient civilizations in this book. For some we have the names of rulers, the dates of battles, and the other elements of history; for others we can say nothing about individuals or events, and must talk of other things. As well as guiding the reader through the world's ancient civilizations, the book aims to display the various ways in which they have been and are being explored.

Hugh Bowden
March 2002

Chronology

AFRICA/AMERICAS	EUROPE	WEST ASIA	INDIA AND CHINA

AFRICA/AMERICAS

c. **3100 BC** Unification of Egypt

2686 BC Beginning of Old Kingdom in Egypt

2613–2494 BC Fourth Dynasty Pharaohs, builders of the Great Pyramids

2181 BC End of the Old Kingdom in Egypt

2023 BC Beginning of Middle Kingdom in Egypt

1720 BC End of Middle Kingdom in Egypt

c. **1648-1540 BC** Hyksos rule in Egypt

1550 BC Accession of Ahmose marks the start of the New Kingdom in Egypt

EUROPE

c. **1900 BC** Beginning of First Palace Period in Crete

c. **1700 BC** Destruction of First Palaces in Crete. Knossos becomes dominant centre in Crete

c. **1628 BC** Eruption of volcano on Thera (Santorini)

c. **1500 BC** Destruction of New Palaces in Crete; Mycenaean occupation of Crete.

WEST ASIA

c. **2900 BC** Start of Early Dynastic period in Mesopotamia

2340 BC Accession of Sargon of Agade

2112 BC Accession of Ur-Nammu of Ur

2004–1595 BC Old Babylonian Period in Mesopotamia

1813–1781 BC Reign of Shamshi-adad I of Assyria

1792–1750 BC Reign of Hammurabi of Babylon

c. **1650 BC** Beginning of Hittite state

1595 BC Hittite raid on Babylon
1595–1155 BC Kassite rule in Babylon

INDIA AND CHINA

c. **3800–3200 BC** Pre-early Harappan period in India

c. **3200–2600 BC** Early Harappan period

c. **2600–2500 BC** Early-Mature Harappan period

c. **2000 BC** Beginning of post-urban period in Harappan orbit
c. **2000–1600 BC** Erlitou cuture in China

c. **1900–1300 BC** Harappan Transition
c. **1900–1300 BC** Mature Harappan
c. **1900–1300 BC** Post-urban Harappan

c. **1800 BC** Compilation of early hymns of Rig Veda, and beginning of influence of Indo-Aryan speaking groups

c. **1600–1400 BC** Erligang culture in China

c. **1500 BC** Composition of Rig Veda Samhita complete
c. **1500–1400 BC** Beginnings of bronze technology in China

AFRICA/AMERICAS	EUROPE	WEST ASIA	INDIA AND CHINA
			c. 1500–1050 BC Shang Dynasty
			c. 1400–1200 BC First evidence of Chinese script from Shang capital at Anyang
			1400–1050 BC Yinxu culture (Anyang)
1352–1336 BC Reign of Akhenaten			
		1363–1330 BC Reign of Ashur-uballit I of Assyria	
1336–1327 BC Reign of Tutankhamun			
		1344–1322 BC Reign of Hittite King Suppiluliuma I	
1279–1213 BC Reign of Ramesses II	**c. 1300 BC** Destruction of palace at Knossos		
1209 BC Egyptians fight Sea People in the Delta			
	c. 1200 BC Destruction of Mycenaean palaces in Greece	**c. 1200 BC** Collapse of Hittite empire	**c. 1200 BC** Ritual deposit of bronzes at Sanxingdui, Sichuan
c. 1200 BC San Lorenzo, oldest Olmec site flourishing			**c. 1200 BC** Tomb of Queen Fu Hao, Anyang
c. 1200–200 BC Chavin cultures flourishing in the Andes			**c. 1200 BC** Late post-urban period (Indus)
			c. 1200 BC Shift of power towards Gangetic Valley area
		1176 BC Egyptians fight Sea People in Levant	
1069 BC End of the New Kingdom in Egypt			**c. 1100 BC–800 BC** Addition of late hymns in Rig Veda ('Late Vedic' period)
			c. 1100 BC Appearance of iron in association with Painted Grey Ware in Gangetic Valley
		1114–1076 BC Reign of Tiglath-pileser I of Assyria	**c. 1100 BC** Late Vedic literature (Dharmasras, Baudhayana, Gautama)
			c. 1100 BC Rise of settlement hierarchy in Ganges Valley
		c. 1000 BC Foundation of Kingdom of Israel	**1050–771 BC** Western Zhou dynasty
		900–600 BC Urartu is a major power in Eastern Anatolia	**c. 900 BC** A 'ritual revolution' affecting use of bronze vessels in China
	c. 900 BC Earliest Etruscan communities emerge		**c. 900–600 BC** Composition of *Shujing, Book of Songs*
		883–859 BC Reign of Ashurnasirpal II of Assyria	
	c. 800 BC Beginning of Phoenician settlement in western Mediterranean		

770–400 BC

AFRICA/AMERICAS	EUROPE	WEST ASIA	INDIA AND CHINA
742–654 BC Egypt under Nubian rule	**c. 750 BC** Beginning of Greek settlement in Italy and Sicily	**704–681 BC** Reign of Sennacherib of Assyria **668–627 BC** Reign of Ashurbanipal of Assyria	**770–476 BC** Spring and Autumn period
664–525 BC 26th (Saïte) dynasty rule Egypt	**c. 655–585 BC** Period of Tyranny in Corinth	**625–605 BC** Reign of Nabopolassar of Babylon marks end of Neo-Assyrian empire and creation of Neo-Babylonian empire **612 BC** Nineveh destroyed by Babylonians	
	c. 600 BC Beginning of urbanization in Rome	**604–562 BC** Reign of Nebuchadnezzar II of Babylon	**c. 600 BC** Invention of porcelain **589 BC** Construction of the Grand Canal, linking the Yangzi to the North China Plain
		597 BC Capture of Jerusalem by Babylonians	
	c. 560–510 BC Period of Tyranny in Athens	**559 BC** Accession of Cyrus the Great of Persia marks beginning of Achaemenid empire	**c. 551–479 BC** Life of Confucius
		c. 550 BC Achaemenid annexation of northwest India. Associated with urbanization at Charsadda and Taxila **539 BC** Conquest of Babylon by Cyrus of Persia	**c. 550 BC** Appearance of fortified capitals in Gangetic Valley in association with Northern Black Polished Ware **c. 550 BC** Appearance of uninscribed, punch-marked coins in India
525 BC Persian invasion of Egypt		**530 BC** Death of Cyrus the Great of Persia **521–486 BC** Reign of Darius I of Persia	**539–538 BC** Earliest dated cave at Dunhuang, and flourishing of trans Asiatic 'Silk Route' **c. 535–500 BC** Xie He, author of the 'Six Laws of painting'
	c. 508/7 BC Reforms of Cleisthenes create Athenian democracy		**c. 500 BC** First coinage in Zhou China **500–400 BC** Growth of 'Pure land' tradition of Buddhism
			493–c. 460 BC Building of the main Tanyao caves at Yungang, Shanxi province
	c. 480–479 BC Persian invasion of Greece		**c. 486 BC** Birth of Buddha
			476–221 BC Warring States period
	c. 431–404 BC Peloponnesian War in Greece		**c. 406–c. 345 BC** Gu Kaizhi, Jin dynasty painter
	c. 406–366 BC Tyranny of Dionysius I in Syracuse		**c. 400 BC** Rise of Magadhan imperialism under Nanda dynasty
c. 400 BC Iron-working amongst Nok culture in Nigeria			

AFRICA/AMERICAS	EUROPE	WEST ASIA	INDIA AND CHINA
			c. 400–200 BC Composition of *Daode jing* (*The Way and its Power*): a Daoist text
	c. 395 BC Rome sacked by Gauls		**c. 365–309 BC** Wang Xizhi, Jin dynasty calligrapher
		334 BC Invasion of Persian empire by Alexander the Great	**338 BC** Earliest dated Buddha image in China
	338 BC Athens and Thebes defeated by Philip of Macedon at Chaeronea	**330 BC** Alexander the Great defeats Darius III and becomes King of Persia	
	336 BC Accession of Alexander the Great	**c. 326–325 BC** Invasion of Alexander the Great and formation of Hellenistic colonies in the northwest area, ruled from Syria	
323 BC Ptolemy I takes control of Egypt		**323 BC** Death of Alexander the Great	**c. 321 BC** Beginning of the 'Pan Indian State' under the Mauryan emperor, Chandragupta I
			c. 310 BC Accession of Chandragupta Maurya
			c. 303 BC Treaty with Seleucus (Mauryans)
c. 300 BC Abandonment of Olmec site at La Venta			**c. 300 BC** Beginning of fully fledged urbanism beyond the Gangetic Valley region
			c. 300 BC Silk first used as painting and writing surface
			c. 273–236 BC Further expansion of the Mauryan empire under Ashoka
	264–241 BC First Punic War between Rome and Carthage. Rome ends up in control of Sicily		
264 BC Romans sack Carthage	**238 BC** Rome seizes Corsica and Sardinia from Carthage	**247 BC** Beginning of Parthian Era	
c. 250 BC First occupation at Jenne-jeno in Mali	**225 BC** Romans begin conquest of Cisalpine Gaul		
	221–179 BC Reign of Philip V of Macedon		**221 BC** Qin Shi Huangdi unites China
	218–201 BC Second Punic War between Rome and Carthage		
	211 BC Death of Archimedes in siege of Syracuse		**210 BC** Qin Shi Huangdi dies
			206 BC–AD 9 Western Han dynasty
			c. 186 BC–168 BC Tombs 1-3 at Mawangdui
			c. 185 BC Fall of Mauryans
		171–138 BC Reign of Mithradates I of Parthia	
	146 BC Romans sack Carthage		
	146 BC Romans sack Corinth		
		133 BC Kingdom of Pergamum bequeathed to Rome	
	121 BC Roman province of Narbonensis created in southern Gaul		**c. 122 BC** Tomb of King of Nanyue at Guangzhou

113 BC–AD 319

AFRICA/AMERICAS	EUROPE	WEST ASIA	INDIA AND CHINA
			c. **113** BC Tomb of Liu Sheng and Dou Wan and Mancheng
			c. **100** BC–AD **100** Invention of paper in China
	91–89 BC Social War between Rome and the Italians followed by extension of Roman citizenship throughout Italy		
	58–49 BC Julius Caesar campaigns in Gaul		
	44 BC Death of Julius Caesar **43** BC Death of Cicero	c. **4** BC–AD **33** Life of Jesus	
	31 BC Battle of Actium: Octavian (Augustus) in sole control of the Roman Empire		
c. **30** BC Death of Cleopatra VII. Roman annexation of Egypt	**AD 14** Death of Augustus		AD **9**–AD **23** Wang Mang interregnum (Xin dynasty) AD **25**–AD **220** Eastern Han dynasty c. AD **30** Accession of Kujula Kadphises begins Kushan hegemony c. AD **80** Accession of Vima Takto, conqueror of India
	AD 43 Roman invasion of Britain		
	AD 79 Pompeii destroyed by eruption of Vesuvius	**AD 115** Roman sack of Ctesiphon under Trojan	AD **100** Creation of stone tombs as focus of ancestral cults in China c. AD **100** Buddhism established in Chinese capital
c. AD **100** The rise of Aksum. c. AD **100** Start of Classic Period in Mexico (to c. AD 900) c. AD **100**–c. AD **600** Moche culture in the Andes			c. AD **127** Accession of Kanishka I, patron of Buddhism
c. AD **200**–c. AD **270** Aksum actively involved in the affairs of the South Arabian states (Himyar, Saba, Hadhramawt and Qataban)			c. AD **147** Shrines of the Wu family, Shandon province c. AD **175** Confucian classics carved in stone by imperial order, forming a state-supported ideological canon
		AD **213–224** Reign of Artabanus V, last Parthian King AD **224** Crowning of Ardashir I at Ctesiphon	AD **193** Earliest written evidence for Buddhist images in China
c. AD **250** Start of Classic Period in Mayan areas	AD **235–284** Period of rapid turn-over of Roman emperors AD **259–274** Gallic empire' of Posthumus and Tetricus	c. AD **231** Sasanian conquest of Kushan Bactria AD **260–272** Palmyrene empire of Odenathus and Zenobia	AD **220** Last Han emperor abdicates AD **220** Chinese script systematized under the Qin dynasty
c. AD **270** Issue of Aksumite coinage begins under Endubis c. AD **290–373** Life of Athanasius of Alexandria	AD **284–305** Reign of Diocletian AD **312–337** Reign of Constantine		AD **304** Hsiungnu invade China; China fragments to AD 589 AD **319–320** Beginning of Gupta Era
		AD **347–407** Life of John Chrysostom	c. AD **360** Fall of Kushans

AFRICA/AMERICAS

C. AD 333 Traditional date for Aksumite conversion to Christianity

AD 354–430 Life of Augustine of Hippo

AD 439 Vandals invade Roman North Africa

C. AD 500 Monte Albán is Zapotec capital
C. AD 500 Substantial settlement at Gao on Upper Niger
C. AD 500–900 Tiahuanaco culture flourishing
C. AD 520 Aksumite invasion of Himyar to avenge persecution of Himyarite Christians

AD 533 Belisarius conquers Vandal kingdom
C. AD 533 Tikal defeated by lowland Maya states

C. AD 700 Decline of Aksum
C. AD 700 Monte Albán abandoned
C. AD 700 Kingdom of Chimu in the Andes
C. AD 900 Collapse of Huari culture
C. AD 900–1521 Post-Classic Mayan period
C. AD 900–1220 Toltec period in Mexico
C. AD 1325 Aztecs arrive in Valley of Mexico
C. AD 1438 Inca capital established at Cusco
C. AD 1440 Period of Aztec expansion begins
AD 1519–21 Spanish conquest of the Aztec kingdom
AD 1524 Spanish enter Yucatán peninsula
AD 1532 Spanish conquest of the Inca empire

EUROPE

AD 342–419 Life of Jerome
AD 361–363 Reign of Julian
AD 378 Battle of Adrianople
AD 379–395 Reign of Theodosius I, last emperor of both Western and Eastern Roman Empire
AD 410 Visigothic sack of Rome under Alaric
AD 476 Romulus Augustulus, last emperor of Western Roman empire deposed

AD 493–526 Gothic state of Theodoric in Italy
AD 527–565 Reign of Justinian
AD 536 Belisarius captures Rome

AD 590–604 Pope Gregory the Great

AD 732 Battle of Poitiers

WEST ASIA

AD 410 The Seleucia Synod and the foundation of the Persian Church

AD 540 Sasanian sack of Antioch

AD 614 Sasanian sack of Jerusalem

AD 622 The *Hijra*; Beginning of Islamic Era

AD 632 Death of Muhammad

AD 636–7 Arab conquest of Syria and Iraq
AD 637 Arab sack of Ctesiphon

AD 632–661 Period of Orthodox Caliphs
AD 651 Death of Yazdgard III, the last Sasanian ruler

AD 661–750 Umayyad Caliphate
AD 750 Abbasid Caliphate established

INDIA AND CHINA

AD 385–413 Reign of Chandragupta II

AD 477–500 Reign of Budhagupta

AD 589-618 Sui Dymasty reunites China
AD 630 Tang Dynasty begins (to AD 906)

C. AD 630 Harsa is defeated by the Calukya king Pulakesin II
AD 630–643 Huan Tsang visits India in search of religious books

AD 641 Harsa sends envoy to Tang court in China
AD 642 Badami is sacked by the Pallavas

AD 711 Arabs conquer Sindh

AD 751 Battle of Talas River
AD 752 Ras rakua king Dantidurga overthrows the Calukya empire

The Basis of Civilization

The study of civilizations is the concern of historians, archaeologists and anthropologists. Written documents, the remains of material culture, comparative evidence from contemporary cultures all provide clues about the origins and development of ancient civilization.

Civilizations grew in different ways, but some questions can be asked of all of them, even if the current state of knowledge may not always produce satisfactory answers. How did the people support themselves? What tools and weapons did they use? How were their communities organized? What records did they keep?

Examining these questions first will help us to understand why civilizations emerged when and where they did, and also tell us something about their diversity.

The **Origins** of **Civilization**

Complex societies, the societies generally described as 'civilizations', emerged in various parts of the world at different times. Some of the circumstances that led to their emergence were repeated in several places, but others were unique to single region.

The trigger for the creation of complex societies was the concentration of the population of a region in a smaller area, so that settlements larger than villages could be established. The domestication of plants and animals led inevitably to the concentration of populations in the most fertile areas, and this is why the valleys of slow-flowing rivers were often the cradles of civilizations. Examples include the Yangtze, the Indus and the Tigris and Euphrates. In Africa the desiccation of the desert appears to have encouraged this process: in the fourth millennium BC in Egypt; and around 1000 BC in the case of the inland delta of the Upper Niger. In most of these cases, but not in West Africa, the development of irrigated agriculture, which allowed the production of enough food to support a section of the population not directly involved in agriculture, is seen as a key factor in the creation of socially stratified societies. However, not all civilizations emerged in this way. Minoan Crete, for example, and the civilizations of the New World, did not rely on irrigation. In these cases it may be that the concentration of resources in geographically defined areas (such as the Oaxaca Valley in Mexico) allowed the populations of those areas to develop into more complex communities.

THE 'SPREAD OF CIVILIZATIONS'

Historians have talked about the 'spread of civilizations' but this is not a simple notion. The elements of civilization cannot be transferred wholesale from one area to another. However, it is clear that communication between different regions did much to stimulate social developments. Craft goods, in particular metalwork, were spread by trade and other forms of exchange, and these would acquire the status of prestige objects. Possession of such things, or control of access to them, by one section of a community was a stimulus for the development of stratified societies, with powerful rulers or ruling elites. As well as goods, technological innovations such as metallurgy, the use of writing and military techniques also spread along exchange routes. In many cases it is still a

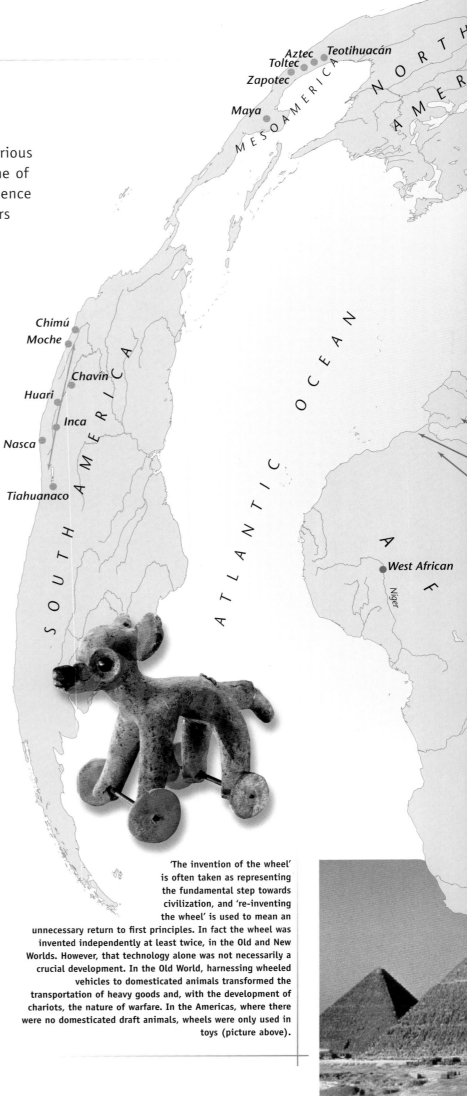

'The invention of the wheel' is often taken as representing the fundamental step towards civilization, and 're-inventing the wheel' is used to mean an unnecessary return to first principles. In fact the wheel was invented independently at least twice, in the Old and New Worlds. However, that technology alone was not necessarily a crucial development. In the Old World, harnessing wheeled vehicles to domesticated animals transformed the transportation of heavy goods and, with the development of chariots, the nature of warfare. In the Americas, where there were no domesticated draft animals, wheels were only used in toys (picture above).

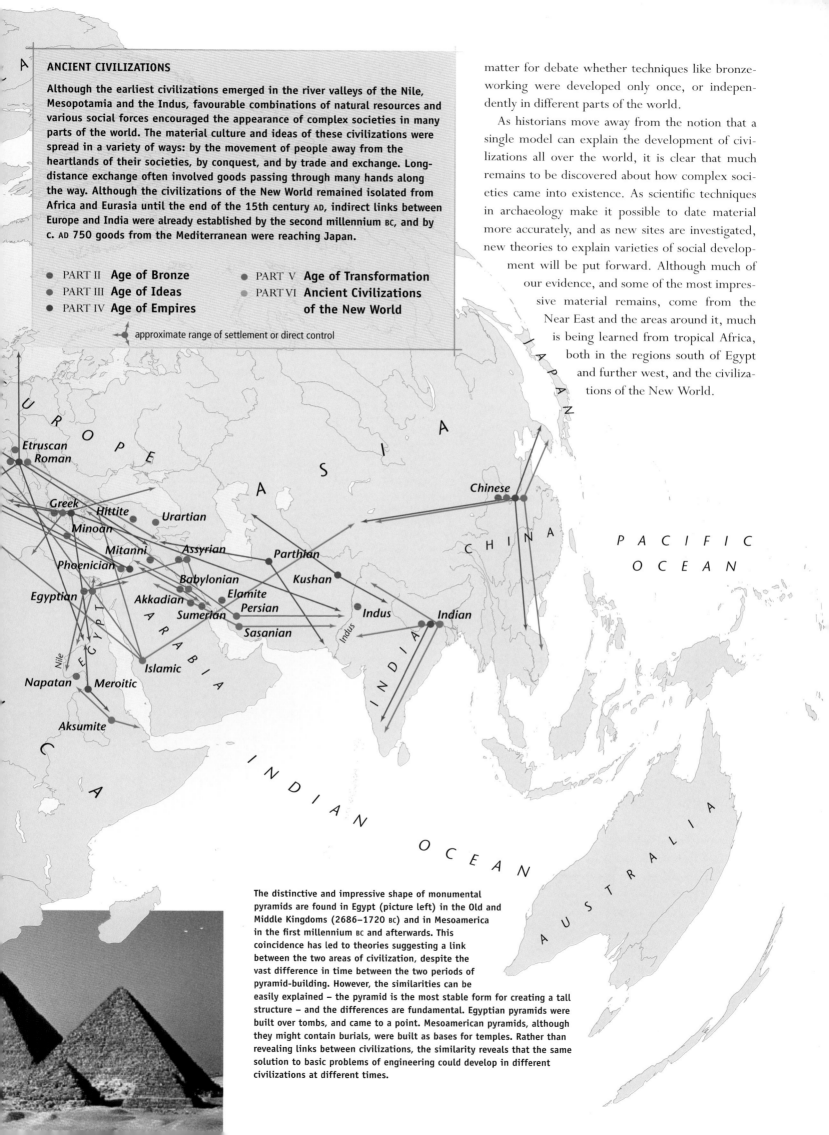

ANCIENT CIVILIZATIONS

Although the earliest civilizations emerged in the river valleys of the Nile, Mesopotamia and the Indus, favourable combinations of natural resources and various social forces encouraged the appearance of complex societies in many parts of the world. The material culture and ideas of these civilizations were spread in a variety of ways: by the movement of people away from the heartlands of their societies, by conquest, and by trade and exchange. Long-distance exchange often involved goods passing through many hands along the way. Although the civilizations of the New World remained isolated from Africa and Eurasia until the end of the 15th century AD, indirect links between Europe and India were already established by the second millennium BC, and by c. AD 750 goods from the Mediterranean were reaching Japan.

- ● PART II **Age of Bronze**
- ● PART III **Age of Ideas**
- ● PART IV **Age of Empires**
- ● PART V **Age of Transformation**
- ● PART VI **Ancient Civilizations of the New World**

←◆→ approximate range of settlement or direct control

matter for debate whether techniques like bronze-working were developed only once, or independently in different parts of the world.

As historians move away from the notion that a single model can explain the development of civilizations all over the world, it is clear that much remains to be discovered about how complex societies came into existence. As scientific techniques in archaeology make it possible to date material more accurately, and as new sites are investigated, new theories to explain varieties of social development will be put forward. Although much of our evidence, and some of the most impressive material remains, come from the Near East and the areas around it, much is being learned from tropical Africa, both in the regions south of Egypt and further west, and the civilizations of the New World.

The distinctive and impressive shape of monumental pyramids are found in Egypt (picture left) in the Old and Middle Kingdoms (2686–1720 BC) and in Mesoamerica in the first millennium BC and afterwards. This coincidence has led to theories suggesting a link between the two areas of civilization, despite the vast difference in time between the two periods of pyramid-building. However, the similarities can be easily explained – the pyramid is the most stable form for creating a tall structure – and the differences are fundamental. Egyptian pyramids were built over tombs, and came to a point. Mesoamerican pyramids, although they might contain burials, were built as bases for temples. Rather than revealing links between civilizations, the similarity reveals that the same solution to basic problems of engineering could develop in different civilizations at different times.

Agriculture and **Metallurgy**

The domestication of plants was a prerequisite of all ancient societies. Barley and emmer (a kind of wheat) were first domesticated in the Levant around 8000 BC. Rice-based agriculture started about a thousand years later in China, and by around 3000 BC maize was being cultivated in the Americas and types of millet in West Africa. At the same time pulses and root crops were also domesticated. The organization needed for extensive irrigation systems in turn shaped the development of more sophisticated societies.

In fertile river valleys irrigation could be used to increase crop yield, either by relying on the natural inundation by the Nile floods, or by the construction of canals, as happened in Mesopotamia. The need to organize large numbers of people to create and maintain irrigation systems is seen as one of the driving forces behind the civilizations of the great river valleys. In areas where irrigation was not used, such as Bronze Age Greece, palaces or temples appear to have acted as centres for the collection and redistribution of agricultural produce.

The domestication of animals was also an important element in the development of societies in the old world. Although pigs were generally bred to be eaten, sheep and goats were herded for their wool and dairy products. Cattle were also sometimes used for dairy production, but more commonly as traction animals, as were horses and donkeys. Domesticated animals, along with other agricultural produce, were also used in religious sacrifices. It appears to be a feature of sacrifice in many societies that the

Terracotta relief from Locri in southern Italy, showing Persephone and Dionysus, 5th century BC (below left). Agriculture in the Mediterranean was based around the triad of grain, grapes and olives, which provided the majority of the Mediterranean diet. The imp-ortance of agriculture in Greek life is indicated by its cent-rality in religion. Persephone, who is shown holding a stalk of wheat, was closely associated with cereals, and Dionysus, here holding a wine-cup and a vine, was associated with wine. The myths associated with both deities involved death and rebirth, and were concerned with the civilizing power of agriculture and the liberating power of wine.

victims were animals that had been involved in the agricultural process. It is striking that in Mexico, where there were no domesticated animals (except perhaps turkeys), human sacrifice was regularly practiced.

METAL-WORKING

The use of metals by the earliest societies is the basis for the traditional division of prehistory into its main stages – the Stone, Bronze and Iron Ages (see glos-

Atlantic Ocean

Mt Gabriel

Baltic Sea

E U R O P E

Dnieper

R U S S I

4th millennium BC

Río Tinto

Mitterberg

3rd/4th millennium BC

Rudna Glava

5th millennium BC

Volga

Ura

Ajbunar

Black Sea

Kozlu

Aegean

Caucasus Mts.

Caspian Sea

Sea

Taurus Mts.

Crete

Mediterranean Sea

1st/2nd millennium BC

Mazorayeh

Chale Ghe

4th millennium BC

Timna

Euphrates

S a h a r a

4th millennium BC

6th millenniu

1st/2nd millennium BC

A R A B I A

Niger

Nile

Red Sea

Persian Gulf

A F R I C A

20

Congo

sary: *chronological divisions*). Although this scheme does not fit all parts of the world, it brings out the importance of metal-working in the development of civilization.

All ancient civilizations used metals, but in some parts of the world the technology for producing and working them developed further than in others. Naturally occurring metals, in particular gold, but also copper and very occasionally iron, could be worked by cold hammering. This technique was good for producing decorative work, but gold and copper were too soft to be of much practical use. In the New World, where gold-working developed in the Andes and was later introduced to Mexico, stone tools and weapons continued to be used until European contact.

The techniques of smelting copper were developed in the fifth millennium BC in the Balkans and the Near East, but it was the combining of copper with tin to create the much harder alloy bronze that made possible the creation of metal tools and

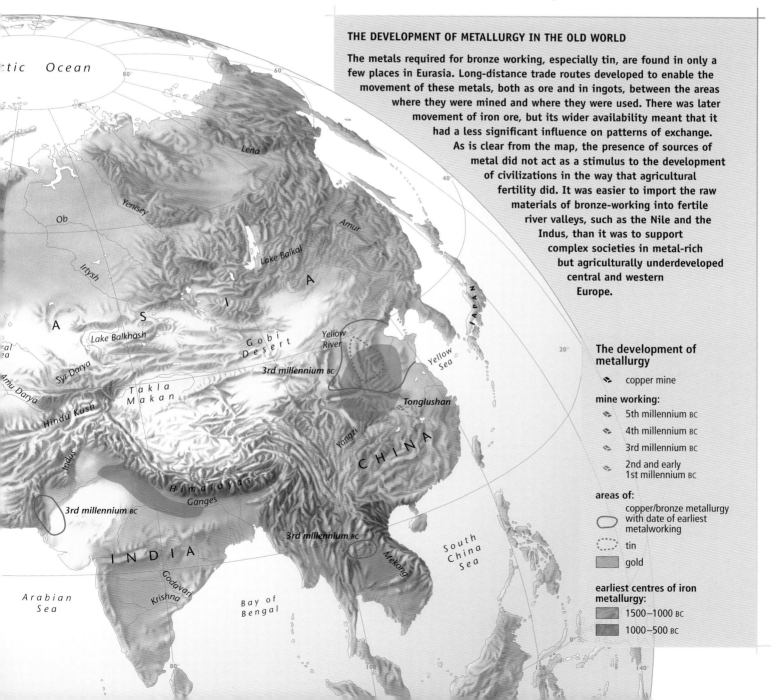

Model scene of cattle being counted from the tomb of Meketre at Thebes, c. 1990 BC (above). Domesticated cattle were valuable for a number of purposes. Cows provided milk for the manufacture of dairy products, while oxen were used as draft animals, for ploughing as well as transport; cattle also provided meat and leather. Cattle ownership was an indication of wealth: placing such models in tombs – a practice found outside Egypt as well – was a way of displaying the status of the man being buried.

weapons. These weapons increased the agricultural efficiency and the military effectiveness of the early cities of the Near East. Bronze was also used in Shang China, and the differences in the technologies suggest that it developed independently, although this is disputed.

Copper and tin ores are found in relatively few places, and it has been argued that control of the supply of metals was a source of power for the Bronze Age elite. Producing workable iron from ore was a more difficult process, but once it was mastered it made possible harder tools and sharper, stronger weapons from a much more widely available ore. Once again Chinese technology developed in its own way, with the use of cast iron.

THE DEVELOPMENT OF METALLURGY IN THE OLD WORLD

The metals required for bronze working, especially tin, are found in only a few places in Eurasia. Long-distance trade routes developed to enable the movement of these metals, both as ore and in ingots, between the areas where they were mined and where they were used. There was later movement of iron ore, but its wider availability meant that it had a less significant influence on patterns of exchange. As is clear from the map, the presence of sources of metal did not act as a stimulus to the development of civilizations in the way that agricultural fertility did. It was easier to import the raw materials of bronze-working into fertile river valleys, such as the Nile and the Indus, than it was to support complex societies in metal-rich but agriculturally underdeveloped central and western Europe.

The development of metallurgy

- copper mine

mine working:
- 5th millennium BC
- 4th millennium BC
- 3rd millennium BC
- 2nd and early 1st millennium BC

areas of:
- copper/bronze metallurgy with date of earliest metalworking
- tin
- gold

earliest centres of iron metallurgy:
- 1500–1000 BC
- 1000–500 BC

Cities, Rulers and Writing

Cities and writing are often taken as two of the basic elements of any civilization. Both are found in Mesopotamia at an early period, and both also developed independently in China and Mesoamerica, and possibly elsewhere. However, there is a great variety in the forms and functions of cities and also in the uses to which writing was first put. This reflects the diversity of social organization in the ancient world.

I n Mesopotamia and several other parts of the world numbers of urban centres appeared at about the same time, and these are thought to represent the centres of independent city-states (see glossary), which shared a common culture, but competed with each other. City-states do not seem to have emerged in Egypt, and it is uncertain whether this form of social organization existed in China or in the Andes. In most other parts of the world, however, this may have been the earliest stage of state formation, and in some cases it remained the basic political and economic unit for many centuries. Some city-states, such as Rome, Babylon or Teotihuacán in Mexico, were able to transform themselves into the centres of large empires.

It is unlikely that a single form of government developed in all early civilizations. Although monarchy was the most widespread form of government in the ancient world, the city-states of the Mediterranean in the first millennium BC had assemblies at which all citizens could vote on important issues. This kind of primitive democracy may well have existed earlier in other parts of the world, although it is clear that even in these cases power remained in the hands of

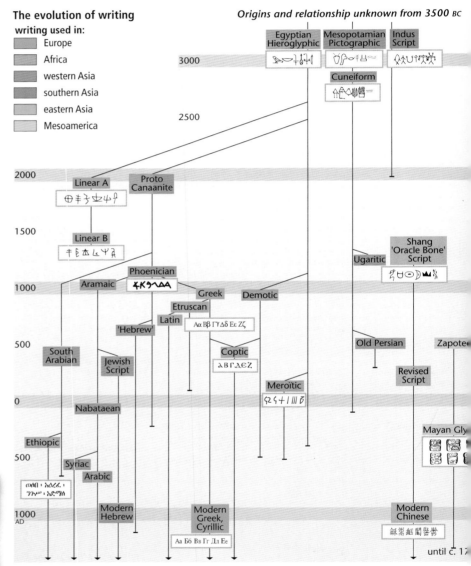

The evolution of writing

writing used in:
- Europe
- Africa
- western Asia
- southern Asia
- eastern Asia
- Mesoamerica

Origins and relationship unknown from 3500 BC

Seal from Mohenjo-Daro, third millennium BC (left). These seals are thought to record the names or titles of merchants. Although the Indus script has not been deciphered, most of the surviving examples have been found in places associated with trade and exchange. Many seal stones of this sort, combining images and writing, have been found in the Indus civilization, in Mesopotamia and in Minoan Crete. Some scholars have argued that writing itself developed out of the use of seals impressed in clay to record quantities and types of goods.

Writing appeared independently in at least three different parts of the world: the Near East, China and Mexico. The relationships between the earliest scripts of Egypt, Mesopotamia and India are not certainly established, especially because it is difficult to estimate how long the use of writing pre-dates the earliest surviving examples. The diagram (above) indicates the probable relationships between scripts. These relationships can be different from those between the languages they are used to represent: Greek, for example, was first written down in the Bronze Age using Linear B, but when literacy re-emerged in Greece centuries later, a version of the Phoenician alphabet was used.

the elite. The organization of space in cities can indicate something of their political structure: in more consensual societies rich and poor live together in mixed residential areas, and the rich draw their support from their neighbourhoods.

RELIGION AND RITUAL

Religion was a fundamental element of all ancient societies. However, the image of communities dominated by powerful religious groups or ruled by priest-kings, using their position to keep the mass of the population in submission, is not supported by evidence. Political, military and religious power always went together, and rulers were expected to maintain good relations with the gods as well as guarding the safety and prosperity of the community. Each city had its own gods and goddesses, and the size and wealth of its temples was seen to reflect their power and prestige. By investing wealth in religious buildings and rituals cities could unite their populations and display their strength.

THE ORIGINS OF WRITING

The origins of writing are difficult to identify, but it is clear that writing was used for different purposes in different societies. In Mesopotamia, Egypt and the Indus cities its earliest function appears to have been administrative, with the earliest examples usually found inscribed on pottery, or on wet clay, recording quantities of goods. In Shang China, writing is first used for divination, with questions inscribed on tortoise shells or the shoulder-blades of cattle, known as 'oracle bones'. When the alphabet was first used in Greece in the eighth century BC, its uses were less utilitarian: examples include lines of poetry inscribed on pots, and abecedaria (the alphabet, or part of it, written out) given as dedications to the gods. Not all societies developed systems of writing: the civilizations of the Andes flourished without writing, and there is no evidence for it in West Africa before contact with Islam (see glossary: *writing systems*).

URUK:

Uruk (plan below) was one of the earliest cities of Mesopotamia, and the oldest Mesopotamian writing tablets were found there. Its form is typical of early cities, not only in Mesopotamia but also in other parts of the world. The city was dominated by the ceremonial complex of Eanna, and its associated religious sanctuaries. This ritual centre is described near the beginning of the Epic of Gilgamesh, composed in the later third millennium BC: 'Behold its outer wall, whose cornice is like copper, peer at the inner wall, which none can equal! Seize upon the threshold, which is from of old! Draw near to Eanna, the dwelling of Ishtar, which no future king, no man, can equal. Go up and walk on the walls of Uruk, inspect the base terrace, examine the brickwork: is not its brickwork of burnt brick? Did not the Seven lay its foundations?'

The Emperor Marcus Aurelius sacrificing in Rome, AD 176 (above). Roman emperors were members of all the major priestly colleges in Rome, and also held the position of Pontifex Maximus (Chief Priest). In this relief Marcus Aurelius is shown dressed as a priest and engaged in a sacrifice in the centre of the city of Rome. The relief was part of a triumphal arch erected to celebrate his victories in Germany, and emphasizes the role of the emperor as both military and religious leader of Rome. This combination of functions was the usual situation in ancient societies, and is frequently illustrated in the public representations of rulers.

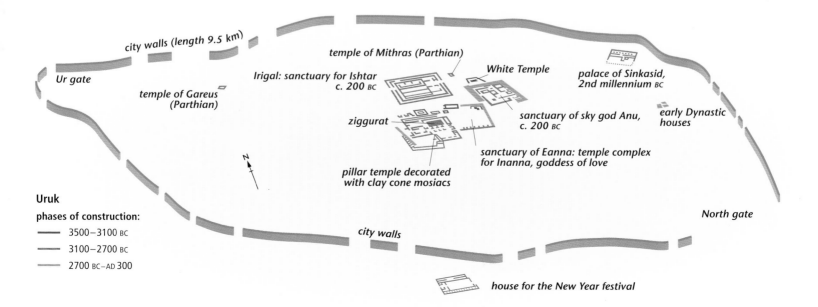

city walls (length 9.5 km)

temple of Mithras (Parthian)

Ur gate

Irigal: sanctuary for Ishtar c. 200 BC

White Temple

palace of Sinkasid, 2nd millennium BC

temple of Gareus (Parthian)

ziggurat

sanctuary of sky god Anu, c. 200 BC

early Dynastic houses

pillar temple decorated with clay cone mosaics

sanctuary of Eanna: temple complex for Inanna, goddess of love

N

Uruk

phases of construction:

— 3500–3100 BC

— 3100–2700 BC

— 2700 BC–AD 300

city walls

North gate

house for the New Year festival

Age of Bronze
c. 3000–1000 BC

An Egyptian slave prepares beer, from a tomb at Giza.

The first cities appeared in Mesopotamia towards the end of the fourth millennium BC. In the next two thousand years, civilizations grew up, flourished and collapsed in Asia, Africa and Europe. They shared the use of bronze technology and writing, and were characterized by urban settlements with prominent ceremonial centres, but each developed its own distinctive patterns of social organization.

In Egypt periods of prosperity and imperial ambition, when the whole of the land was united under a single ruling dynasty, alternated with periods of disunity and weakness. In contrast, in Mesopotamia there was constant competition between rival cities, each trying to achieve regional domination. This competition reached its height in the period between 1600 and 1200 BC, when the Levant became the battleground between the imperial powers of Mesopotamia, Anatolia and Egypt.

The detailed organization of the palace societies of the Aegean in Europe and the urban centres of the Indus region remains mysterious, as the scripts in which they wrote are undeciphered. Both show signs of strong central organization, and both had well established trade links with the Near East. Meanwhile, in China after 1500 BC a powerful state emerged along the Yellow River with its own distinctive bronze-working practices.

Old Kingdom Egypt: The Age of the Pyramids, c. **3100–2023** BC

Throughout its history, the importance of the the river Nile to the land and the people of Ancient Egypt cannot be over-estimated. An Egyptian hymn, which pays homage to the river, describes it as: 'Food provider, bounty maker – who creates all that is good'. In a land of virtually no rainfall the Nile provided water and food as well as transport and without the river the entire region would be a desert. The harnessing of its annual floods made possible a civilization that was to last for over 25 centuries.

E gypt's ancient history spans 3,000 years and for convenience is divided into several phases, principally Old, Middle and New Kingdoms, which are in turn divided into 31 dynasties.

According to tradition, Upper and Lower Egypt were united around 3100 BC under Menes, possibly the same person as Narmer, who is associated with the founding of Memphis. Although it is impossible to trace events precisely, it seems likely that the tradition of unification actually represents a conquest of the Delta by southern rulers.

Great changes took place in the late prehistoric period, when monumental buildings were erected and, most importantly, the first writing occurred. The beginnings of the Early Dynastic period (c. 3100 BC) saw the foundation of the future state, as irrigation works were extended and a centralized system of administration was developed. Burial customs became increasingly complex and the Step Pyramid at Saqqara, the first such structure, was built.

The great pyramids built at Giza were constructed for the succeeding 4th Dynasty rulers. Although they are now stripped of their fine stone facings and gilded cap stones, they are still an extraordinary technological feat. The monumental size of these pyramids clearly indicates the dominance of the pharaoh, who acted as an intermediary between the gods and mankind. Their construction is also evidence of the degree of state organization that the Egyptians had achieved.

At the nearby capital of Memphis, strategically placed at the junction of the Nile and its delta, there was a centralized government with a well-organized bureaucracy. Under its aegis, the peasants, who made up most of the country's population, were employed on the ambitious building projects during the Nile's annual flood. They were always liable for labour service as, in theory, the land on which they lived and worked for the rest of the year belonged to the king. The state also organized trade with the Levant for precious woods and oil and there were regular mining, quarrying and trading expeditions to Sinai, the Eastern Desert and to Nubia.

The nobles who formed part of the court were traditionally buried in *mastaba* (bench-shaped) tombs surrounding the Pyramids, symbolizing their relationship to the ruler. Under the 5th Dynasty the royal tombs became smaller as the power of the Pharaoh diminished; increasingly the nobles chose to

The Greek historian Herodotus described Egypt as 'the gift of the river'. The kingdom of the pharaohs grew up in the fertile valley of the Nile below the first cataract at Elephantine (map right). The kingdom was traditionally divided into the 'two lands': Lower Egypt, the area of the Nile Delta, with its capital at Memphis; and Upper Egypt, with its capital at Thebes. The river facilitated communication north and south, while trade routes linked the Nile with the Red Sea and with the oases that guarded Egypt's western flank.

The Narmer palette (above) portrays the king as the archetypal warrior who unites the two lands. Narmer wears the red crown of Lower Egypt and inspects the battlefield; on the reverse (top) he wears the white Upper Crown of Egypt. The palette also contains very early hieroglyphic pictograms.

Situated on the edge of the desert to the west of the Nile, the pyramids at Giza are amongst the most famous monuments in the world. Like all Egyptian pyramids, each of those at Giza forms part of a substantial complex (plan right) containing a valley temple, causeway, mortuary temple and smaller pyramids of the queens, all surrounded by the *mastaba* tombs of priests and officials. The Great Pyramid of Khufu, the largest at Giza, is over 147 metres high and dates from c. 2540 BC. Despite elaborate security measures, including rubble blockings and granite portcullises, all the Old Kingdom pyramids were broken into and ransacked, probably before 2000 BC.

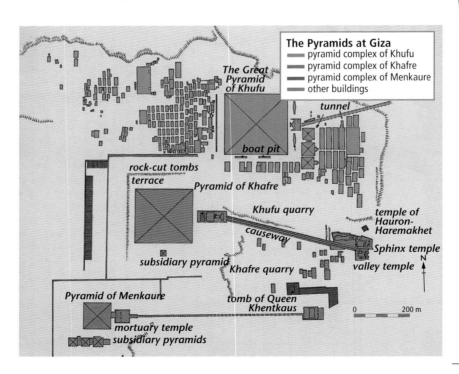

The Pyramids at Giza
- pyramid complex of Khufu
- pyramid complex of Khafre
- pyramid complex of Menkaure
- other buildings

The Great Pyramid of Khufu

tunnel

boat pit

rock-cut tombs
terrace

Pyramid of Khafre

Khufu quarry

temple of Hauron-Haremakhet

causeway

Sphinx temple

subsidiary pyramid

Khafre quarry

valley temple

N

Pyramid of Menkaure

tomb of Queen Khentkaus

0   200 m

mortuary temple
subsidiary pyramids

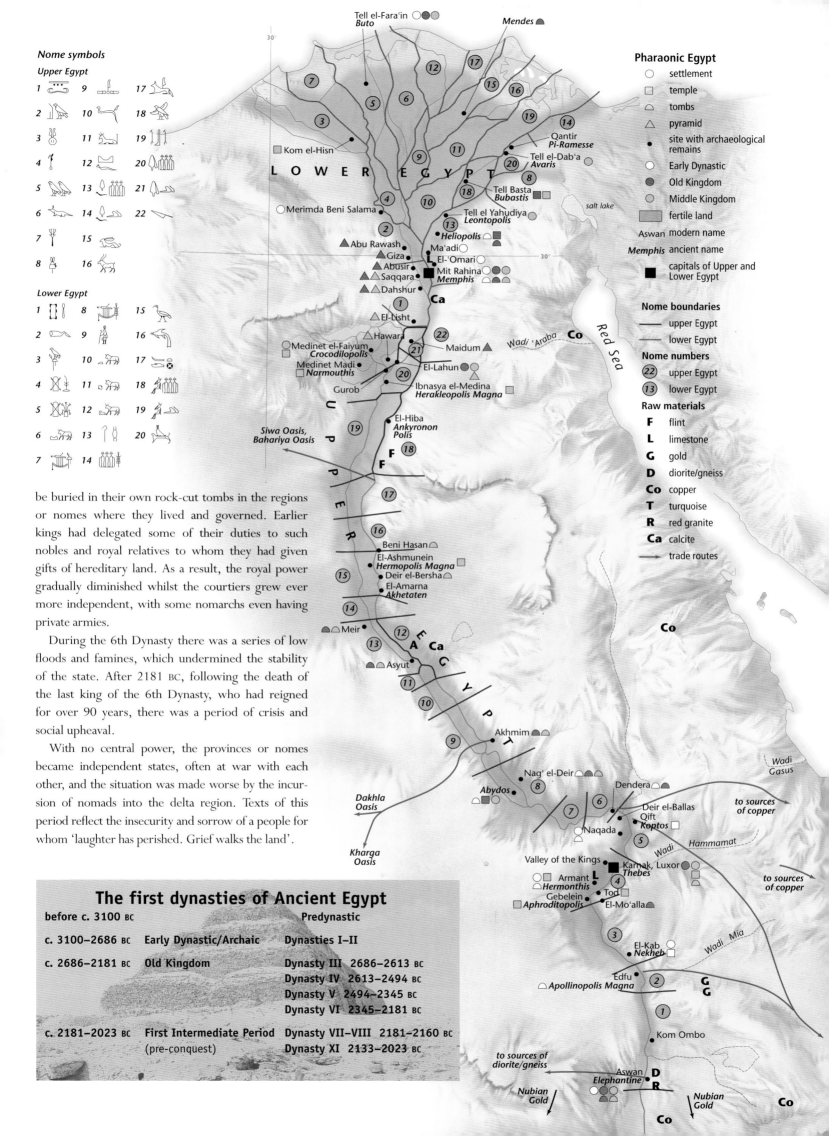

Nome symbols

Upper Egypt

1 ... 9 ... 17 ...
2 ... 10 ... 18 ...
3 ... 11 ... 19 ...
4 ... 12 ... 20 ...
5 ... 13 ... 21 ...
6 ... 14 ... 22 ...
7 ... 15 ...
8 ... 16 ...

Lower Egypt

1 ... 8 ... 15 ...
2 ... 9 ... 16 ...
3 ... 10 ... 17 ...
4 ... 11 ... 18 ...
5 ... 12 ... 19 ...
6 ... 13 ... 20 ...
7 ... 14 ...

Pharaonic Egypt

○ settlement
□ temple
△ tombs
△ pyramid
• site with archaeological remains
○ Early Dynastic
● Old Kingdom
○ Middle Kingdom
▨ fertile land
Aswan modern name
Memphis ancient name
■ capitals of Upper and Lower Egypt

Nome boundaries
— upper Egypt
— lower Egypt

Nome numbers
㉒ upper Egypt
⑬ lower Egypt

Raw materials
F flint
L limestone
G gold
D diorite/gneiss
Co copper
T turquoise
R red granite
Ca calcite
→ trade routes

be buried in their own rock-cut tombs in the regions or nomes where they lived and governed. Earlier kings had delegated some of their duties to such nobles and royal relatives to whom they had given gifts of hereditary land. As a result, the royal power gradually diminished whilst the courtiers grew ever more independent, with some nomarchs even having private armies.

During the 6th Dynasty there was a series of low floods and famines, which undermined the stability of the state. After 2181 BC, following the death of the last king of the 6th Dynasty, who had reigned for over 90 years, there was a period of crisis and social upheaval.

With no central power, the provinces or nomes became independent states, often at war with each other, and the situation was made worse by the incursion of nomads into the delta region. Texts of this period reflect the insecurity and sorrow of a people for whom 'laughter has perished. Grief walks the land'.

The first dynasties of Ancient Egypt

before c. 3100 BC		Predynastic
c. 3100–2686 BC	Early Dynastic/Archaic	Dynasties I–II
c. 2686–2181 BC	Old Kingdom	Dynasty III 2686–2613 BC
		Dynasty IV 2613–2494 BC
		Dynasty V 2494–2345 BC
		Dynasty VI 2345–2181 BC
c. 2181–2023 BC	First Intermediate Period	Dynasty VII–VIII 2181–2160 BC
	(pre-conquest)	Dynasty XI 2133–2023 BC

Map labels:

Tell el-Fara'in / *Buto*, Mendes, Kom el-Hisn, LOWER EGYPT, Merimda Beni Salama, Qantir / *Pi-Ramesse*, Tell el-Dab'a / *Avaris*, Tell Basta / *Bubastis*, Tell el Yahudiya / *Leontopolis*, salt lake, *Heliopolis*, Ma'adi, El-'Omari, Mit Rahina / *Memphis*, Abu Rawash, Giza, Abusir, Saqqara, Dahshur, El-Lisht, Hawara, Ca, Medinet el-Faiyum / *Crocodilopolis*, Medinet Madi / *Narmouthis*, Gurob, Maidum, El-Lahun, Ibnasya el-Medina / *Herakleopolis Magna*, Wadi 'Araba, Co, Red Sea, El-Hiba / *Ankyronon Polis*, Siwa Oasis, Bahariya Oasis, UPPER EGYPT, Beni Hasan, El-Ashmunein / *Hermopolis Magna*, Deir el-Bersha, El-Amarna / *Akhetaten*, Meir, Asyut, Akhmim, Nag' el-Deir, *Abydos*, Dendera, Deir el-Ballas, Qift / *Koptos*, Naqada, Wadi Hammamat, Wadi Gasus, to sources of copper, Valley of the Kings, Karnak, Luxor / *Thebes*, Armant / *Hermonthis*, Gebelein, Tod, *Aphroditopolis*, El-Mo'alla, El-Kab / *Nekheb*, Edfu / *Apollinopolis Magna*, Wadi Mia, Kom Ombo, Aswan / *Elephantine*, Nubian Gold, to sources of diorite/gneiss, Dakhla Oasis, Kharga Oasis, to sources of copper

Sumer and Akkad,
Mesopotamia: c. 2900–2004 BC

Following the development of urban life in southern Mesopotamia in the fourth millennium BC, several small city-states had emerged in the fertile alluvium between the Tigris and Euphrates rivers by c. 2900 BC. It is from this time that written evidence appears and some kind of history can be reconstructed. During the succeeding half millennium, known as the Early Dynastic period (c. 2900–2340 BC), the city-state was the dominant political organization.

For the earliest period written evidence about Mesopotamia is sparse and even later, when more abundant, is unevenly distributed. On the other hand, the material remains are plentiful and increase as the cities expanded.

The term 'Sumer and Akkad', although first recorded at the end of this period, only came into regular use from the time of the Empire of Agade (2340–2159 BC). It did not refer to defined political units, but to the plain of southern Mesopotamia, perhaps with reference to its cultural and linguistic diversity. Sumerian, unrelated to any known language, was first expressed in pictographic script on clay tables c. 3300 BC and evolved into cuneiform; it died out in the spoken form early in the second millennium BC, although it remained a language of scholarship. Akkadian, which is Semitic, became the dominant language of Mesopotamia and was written in cuneiform, adapted from Sumerian.

Each Early Dynastic city-state had a supreme ruler controlling resources and institutions and some included several towns. Lying relatively close to each other, the cities were surrounded by uncultivated grazing lands, which served as a buffer between then, but over which conflict developed, as populations grew and the demand for land increased. Indeed, the Early Dynastic cities, surrounded by large defensive walls, seem almost constantly to have been at war with each other, their soldiers fighting with bronze weapons and using four-wheeled war-chariots drawn by onagers.

The fortunes of these city-states, such as Kish, Lagash, Ur and Umma, fluctuated as they struggled with each other and constantly changed alliances.

Mesopotamia occupies a key position (map below) on lines of communication and trade routes. Southern Mesopotamia has no sources of metals, and the need to ensure the supply of bronze and other goods including timber was an important stimulus to military campaigns and imperialism. Although the rulers of Agade and Ur gained new control over large territories, they did not establish new imperial identities to replace loyalty to individual cities.

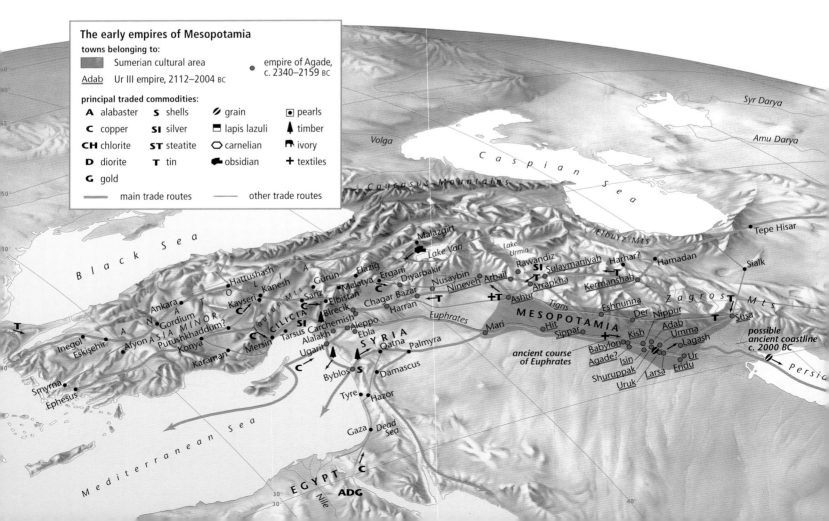

The early empires of Mesopotamia

towns belonging to:

Sumerian cultural area

Adab   Ur III empire, 2112–2004 BC

• empire of Agade, c. 2340–2159 BC

principal traded commodities:

A alabaster	**S** shells	grain	pearls
C copper	**SI** silver	lapis lazuli	timber
CH chlorite	**ST** steatite	carnelian	ivory
D diorite	**T** tin	obsidian	textiles
G gold			

main trade routes   other trade routes

This is thought to have been reflected in the Sumerian King List. Whilst the king list seems to be reliable for the later phases of Sumerian history, its validity for the Early Dynastic period has been questioned. It is possible that its compilation reflects the need for legitimation of the rulers under whom it was executed, and that it should be seen as depicting an idea of reality, rather than an accurate account of a remote past.

THE EMPIRE OF AGADE

Ultimately, Lugalzagessi, the ruler of Umma, took the title King of the Land of Sumer, heading a short-lived confederation of cities, which ended in conquest by Sargon of Agade, c.2340 BC. This was the first successful attempt at centralization of power in Mesopotamia and brought all the cities of Sumer and Akkad under the control of one dynasty. Thereafter, the alternation of strong centralized political control, interspersed with periods of turmoil, becomes a characteristic feature of Mesopotamian history.

According to legend, Sargon, a foundling, became cup-bearer to the King of Kish, whom he overthrew. He conquered Mesopotamia and extended his domains to North Syria and Elam (SW Iran). Agade, his newly founded capital, perhaps in the vicinity of Baghdad, has not yet been found. There was a deliberate policy of centralization and Agade

Bronze head of Sargon (2340–2284 BC) from Nineveh (opposite left). One tradition relates that he began his career as cup-bearer to the King of Kish. Yet he became one of the world's earliest empire-builders. He defeated the Sumerian ruler Lugalzagessi of Uruk, seizing all southern Mesopotamia and achieved conquests as far afield as northern Syria, southern Anatolia and Elam in western Persia. His armies were formidable: an inscription records that '5,400 men eat bread daily before him'.

Urban populations in Mesopotamia grew during the Early Dynastic period (map right) with 80 per cent of the population living in cities. Shuruppak, for example, had a population of 14–30,000 by 2600 BC.

A clay administrative table from Ur III (below) impressed with the scribe's seal. It depicts a goddess leading a worshipper and on the reverse lists ploughmen employed by the state with the quantities of land assigned to them as wages.

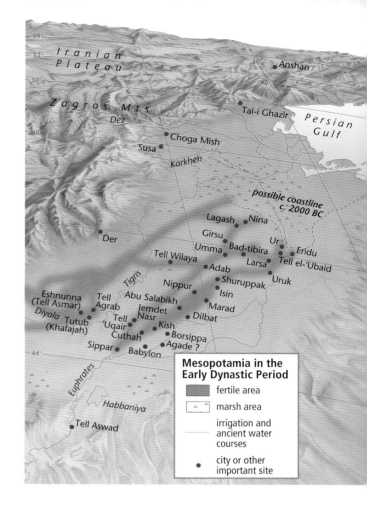

Mesopotamia in the Early Dynastic Period

- fertile area
- marsh area
- irrigation and ancient water courses
- • city or other important site

became the main centre of production and trade. Under his grandson, Naram-Sin, the empire reached its apogee. However, around 2000 BC internal and external pressures, exacerbated by attacks from the Gutians, led to the disintegration of the empire and a return to inter-city rivalries.

The Third Dynasty of Ur (2112–2004 BC), founded by the Sumerian warrior king Ur-Nammu emerged victorious and strongly reasserted the concept of political unity under a single ruler, the model set by the empire of Agade. State organization was highly centralized and there was a century of prosperity before the imperial structure collapsed. The final onslaught came from the Elamites, who sacked the city and carried off its king. In the words of the *Lamentations over the Destruction of Ur*: 'Elam, like a swelling flood wave, left only the spirits of the dead. In Ur [people] were smashed as if they were clay pots.'

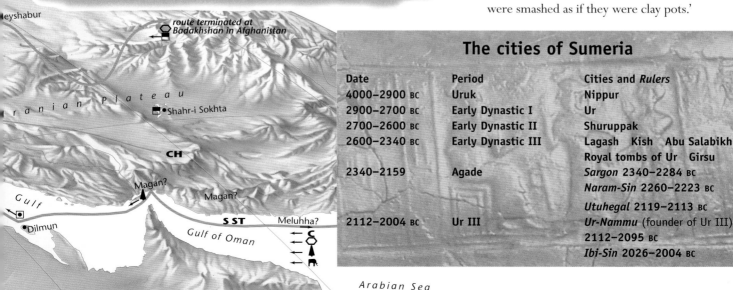

The cities of Sumeria

Date	Period	Cities and *Rulers*
4000–2900 BC	Uruk	Nippur
2900–2700 BC	Early Dynastic I	Ur
2700–2600 BC	Early Dynastic II	Shuruppak
2600–2340 BC	Early Dynastic III	Lagash Kish Abu Salabikh
		Royal tombs of Ur Girsu
2340–2159	Agade	*Sargon 2340–2284 BC*
		Naram-Sin 2260–2223 BC
		Utuhegal 2119–2113 BC
2112–2004 BC	Ur III	*Ur-Nammu* (founder of Ur III)
		2112–2095 BC
		Ibi-Sin 2026–2004 BC

Arabian Sea

Sumer: The First Cities
C. **2900–2004** BC

The development of urban life in southern Mesopotamia was probably the result of several interacting factors, most notably a reliable food supply from both irrigation farming and the wild resources of the marshes; as a result, population increased and some specialization of labour was required. This in turn seems to have led to the emergence of large-scale institutions for food storage and distribution. Linked to this was the need for record keeping and the development of writing, c. 3300 BC.

A votive statue of Gudea (c.2150–c. 2125 BC), ruler of Lagash (right). Gudea restored a number of the city temples, and placed statues of himself within them. This rebuilding and his patronage of the priesthood are celebrated in the 'Cylinders of Lagash'. Gudea's hands are folded in a traditional gesture of greeting and prayer.

The complete absence of stone and metals in Mesopotamia encouraged contacts with neighbouring regions (Northern Iraq, Syria, Turkey and Elam). In this connection, the recent discovery of a large urban site c. 4000 BC at Tell Hamoukar in north-eastern Syria raises many new questions including, for instance, where such civilization first developed.

By the early third millennium BC, urbanism was well established and between c. 2800 and c. 2400 BC a highly developed Sumerian city life is well attested at a number of sites, most of which were situated on branches of the Euphrates. Each city came under the protection of a particular god who dwelt in its temple, such as Zababa, a war god, at Kish. The most important religious centre of the Sumerians, Nippur, contained the main temple of Enlil, god of the sky and head of the pantheon. Part of the city was dominated by his temple complex, which was not only a religious centre but also a wealthy and self-sufficient organization and an important part of the economy. In the temple schools, the scribal elite

A crown of gold leaves (below) from the Royal Tombs of Ur. The wealthy burials of the rulers and their entourages in royal tombs preserve an image of courtly life at Ur. The ladies wore intricate headdresses and jewellery fashioned of gold, silver and semi-precious stones; cosmetics, toilet-boxes and wooden chests have also been found in the graves. All these objects reveal the skill and innovation of Sumerian craftsmen in techniques such as metal casting, engraving and riveting.

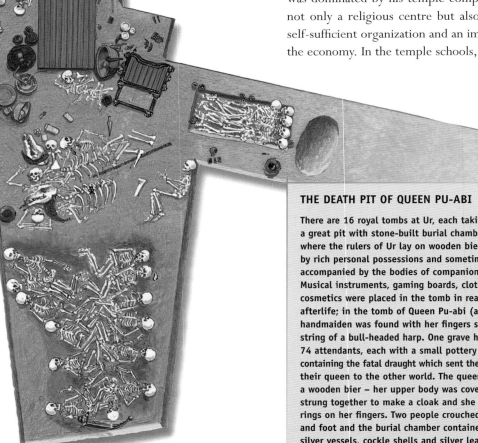

THE DEATH PIT OF QUEEN PU-ABI

There are 16 royal tombs at Ur, each taking the form of a great pit with stone-built burial chambers at one end, where the rulers of Ur lay on wooden biers, surrounded by rich personal possessions and sometimes accompanied by the bodies of companions and servants. Musical instruments, gaming boards, clothes and cosmetics were placed in the tomb in readiness for the afterlife; in the tomb of Queen Pu-abi (above), a handmaiden was found with her fingers still on the string of a bull-headed harp. One grave held as many as 74 attendants, each with a small pottery cup possibly containing the fatal draught which sent them to accompany their queen to the other world. The queen herself lay on a wooden bier – her upper body was covered with beads strung together to make a cloak and she wore ten gold rings on her fingers. Two people crouched at her head and foot and the burial chamber contained gold and silver vessels, cockle shells and silver leaf.

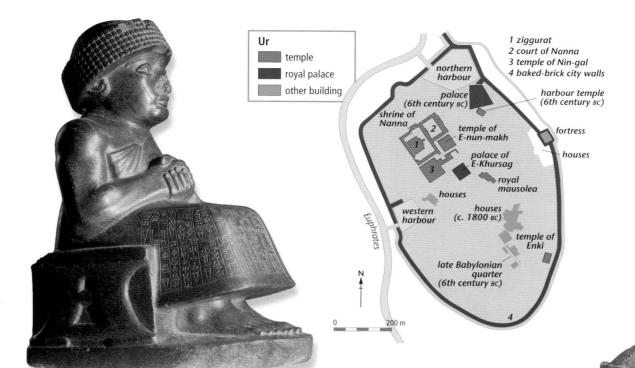

Ur

- temple
- royal palace
- other building

1 ziggurat
2 court of Nanna
3 temple of Nin-gal
4 baked-brick city walls

northern harbour

palace (6th century BC)

shrine of Nanna

temple of E-nun-makh

palace of E-Khursag

harbour temple (6th century BC)

fortress

houses

royal mausolea

houses

western harbour

houses (c. 1800 BC)

temple of Enki

Euphrates

late Babylonian quarter (6th century BC)

N

0   200 m

4

Like many Mesopotamian cities of its day, the centre of Ur (plan left) was dominated by a sacred enclosure containing temples; the most famous of these was a three-storeyed ziggurat. Food for the god was prepared in a kitchen within the precinct. To the south of the sacred enclosure lay the burial area of the kings of Ur. Still further south lay an area of private houses of c. 1800 BC. They were built largely of mud-brick and arranged around an open courtyard.

The helmet of Meskalandu from Ur (below). The helmet is fashioned from a single sheet of gold.

was trained in the complexities of the cuneiform script and to be the future administrators; at Ur under the Third Dynasty (2112–2004 BC), they formed a huge and efficient bureaucracy, producing vast and detailed records.

The temple precincts were sacred areas, and so they were regularly rebuilt. The resulting mounds, or tells, are highly visible and have attracted archaeologists since excavations began. Several sites are known primarily from excavations of temples with relatively little known about the cities which once surrounded them. The large role the temples seem to have played may simply reflect the available evidence. Indeed, recent work on one of the temple archives suggests that the estates of the various deities were the property of the ruler and his family and that the earlier theory of a Sumerian theocracy was based on a faulty interpretation of texts.

Little is known about the political administration of these cities or about the early Sumerian kingship. This institution seems to have developed from the time when war leaders were appointed as strong men by councils of elders, to direct others in battles and various disputes with neighbouring territories. The title designating king, *lugal*, means 'great man' and may go back to this original function, which in time became permanent. There is no certainty as to what distinguishes other titles used for rulers from each other; these are *en* and *ensi*, which roughly translate as lord and governor.

TRADE AND WARFARE

As a result of the frequent warfare between the cities, military equipment became well developed and included war-chariots and bronze spears, shields and helmets. There are several examples of such equipment in Sumerian iconography, such as on a stela of Eannatum of Lagash. The contents of the Royal Tombs of Ur (c. 2500–1700 BC) included a number of weapons, items of military apparel and equipment. The tombs also had rich and numerous objects of gold, silver, lapis lazuli and other precious stones, such as carnelian. These finds indicate not only the wealth of the Sumerians and a high level of craftsmanship, but also show that they had access to metals for weapons and tools and to precious raw materials required for the production of luxury items. Lapis lazuli, for instance, came from Afghanistan along trade routes through Iran. Objects identical to those known from the Indus Valley were also found in the Royal Tombs, suggesting trading links with that region.

Minoan Crete
c. **2000–1500** BC

The earliest civilization in Europe appeared in Crete early in the second millennium BC. There was some contact between Crete and civilizations further east, in particular with Egypt and the Levant, and aspects of Cretan social organization resemble practices in the Near East. However the mountainous terrain of Crete and the islands north of it was unlike the alluvial plains of Egypt or Mesopotamia, and Minoan civilization, as it developed on Crete, was very different in form.

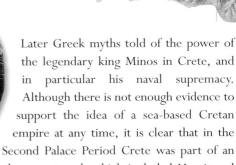

The earliest town-like settlements in the Aegean are found in the Cycladic islands, but a more complex form of social organization emerged on Crete in the so-called First Palace Period (c. 1900–1700 BC). Crete at this time appears to have been divided into at least five regions, including areas centred on Knossos, Phaistos and Mallia, each with its own 'palace'. The palaces were usually built with courtyards to their west containing large storage pits, and this suggests that the palaces had an important role in redistributing agricultural produce. They may also have had a ritual purpose, like the cities of the Near East in the Bronze Age. There is no evidence of powerful individual rulers or ruling families, and the detailed organization remains unknown.

These first palaces all appear to have suffered damage or destruction around 1700 BC. Many explanations have been offered for this phenomenon, including fire or earthquakes, but it seems unlikely that a single natural disaster could have affected palaces over so wide an area. Subsequent developments on Crete suggest that the palaces could have been destroyed in a series of wars which left Knossos the dominant power on the island.

THE SECOND PALACE PERIOD

The palaces at Knossos, Phaistos and Mallia were re-built, and other new ones constructed after 1700 BC, although in the Second Palace Period the whole island appears to have been ruled from Knossos. The new palaces imitated Knossos in their form, but lacked its decorative frescoes, which suggests that they were subordinate to it. Yet Crete was not a very centralized society. The existence of 'villas', smaller administrative centres, indicates a more devolved administration, headed by a ruling elite rather than a single monarch. The frescoes at Knossos and the villas around it, which depict aspects of life on Crete, reveal no interest in military matters. Crete had systems of fortification, but the rulers of the island appear not to have emphasized this side of their power, and the palaces were not fortified.

Three different systems of writing are known from Crete in the First and Second Palace periods. None has been deciphered. The Phaistos disc (top), of c. 1700 BC, is a unique example of a form of printed document: symbols were pressed into both sides of a disc of soft clay in a spiral, starting at the edge. The disc was then fired to create a document that would last. The disc was probably brought to Crete, possibly from southwest Anatolia; the text on the disc uses 45 different symbols and the script is therefore probably a syllabary. Two other scripts were widely used in Crete in the period c. 2000–1500 BC. Examples of a 'pictographic' or 'hieroglyphic' script (bottom right) have been found at Knossos, Phaistos and Mallia, mainly on seal stones. The most widespread script is Linear A (bottom far right), found mainly inscribed on clay tablets. These were not deliberately fired, and were not intended as permanent records. Linear A tablets have been found outside Crete, on Melos, Keos and Thera. The script is a syllabary, and it is related to the later Linear B script which was used to write a form of Greek in the 13th century BC (see page 40).

Later Greek myths told of the power of the legendary king Minos in Crete, and in particular his naval supremacy. Although there is not enough evidence to support the idea of a sea-based Cretan empire at any time, it is clear that in the Second Palace Period Crete was part of an exchange network which included Ugarit and Egypt in the eastern Mediterranean, and documents from these places mention Kaphtor or Keftiu, thought to refer to Minoan Cretans. Minoan power in this period did extend beyond Crete with the establishment of a settlement on the island of Cythera south of the Peloponnese, and its influence was felt in the Peloponnese and the central Aegean. In the town of Akrotiri on Thera (modern Santorini), frescoes have been found like those from Knossos. In 1628 BC a massive eruption of the island's volcano covered the town in ash and debris, which helped to preserve the frescoes. Although it was once thought that this eruption was responsible for the destruction of Minoan civilization, it seems in fact to have had little effect on Crete – even the inhabitants of Akrotiri appear to have had enough warning to evacuate the town.

The Second Palace Period on Crete came to an end c. 1500 BC, when all the palaces except Knossos were destroyed. A number of explanations have been put forward to explain the immediate circumstances of these destructions, but it is clear that in their aftermath Crete found itself under the control of new rulers from mainland Greece (see page 40).

MINOAN CRETE

Minoan Crete was dominated by its palaces (map below). In the First Palace Period these were probably independent, each controlling its own hinterland, but after c. 1700 BC the whole island may have been administered from Knossos, and have had a hierarchy of administrative sites, with the palaces acting as regional centres and supported by 'villas' spread throughout the island. Important religious activity took place at cave and peak sanctuaries in the countryside, and there must have been important links between these sanctuaries and the palaces: the peak sanctuaries generally appeared at the same time as the First Palaces, and some were modified at the time of the construction of the Second Palaces. Animal sacrifice seems to have taken place at the caves, but not at peak sanctuaries, though there is evidence of bonfires. Dedications of animal figurines and other cult objects have been found at both.

major use in First Palace Period only
- ● other centres
- ▲ peak sanctuaries
- ☊ cave sanctuaries
- ◆ other sanctuaries

major use in First and Second Palace Periods
- ■ large palaces
- ▪ small palaces or villas
- ● other centres
- • other sites
- ▲ peak sanctuaries
- ☊ cave sanctuaries
- ◆ other sanctuaries

major use in Second Palace Period only
- ■ large palaces
- ▪ small palaces or villas
- ● other centres
- • other sites

- **H** finds of Hieroglyphic writing
- ◉ find of printed text (Phaistos disk)
- **A** finds of Linear A tablets
- **A** finds of other Linear A inscriptions

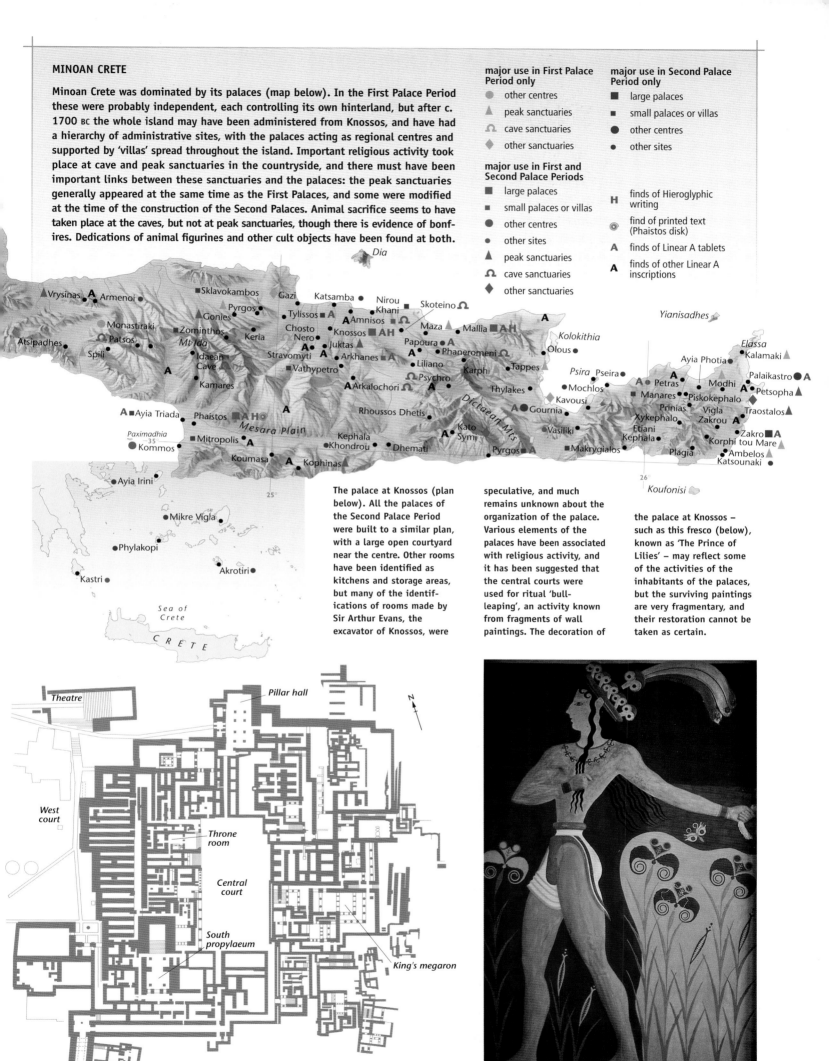

The palace at Knossos (plan below). All the palaces of the Second Palace Period were built to a similar plan, with a large open courtyard near the centre. Other rooms have been identified as kitchens and storage areas, but many of the identifications of rooms made by Sir Arthur Evans, the excavator of Knossos, were speculative, and much remains unknown about the organization of the palace. Various elements of the palaces have been associated with religious activity, and it has been suggested that the central courts were used for ritual 'bull-leaping', an activity known from fragments of wall paintings. The decoration of the palace at Knossos – such as this fresco (below), known as 'The Prince of Lilies' – may reflect some of the activities of the inhabitants of the palaces, but the surviving paintings are very fragmentary, and their restoration cannot be taken as certain.

The Palace of Knossos

0   25 m

Egypt: The Middle Kingdom and the Hyksos 2023–1550 BC

The Middle Kingdom was the 'classical' phase of Egyptian civilization, seemingly a period of great political strength and unity, particularly in the 12th Dynasty. It was a time when literature flowered; the works of this period were seen as a model for later ages. Rich documentary sources, including records from Memphis and papyri from the Fayyum, help to give a picture of a powerful and stable government and administration, king and court, state and society.

Following the political fragmentation and the troubles of the First Intermediate Period, which lasted for about 150 years until 2023 BC, the country was re-unified under Mentuhotep of Thebes, a strong ruler who restored order and consolidated the country's borders. He expelled the Asiatics from the delta, campaigned against the Libyans and nomads of the east, sent trading expeditions to Syria and Palestine and in Nubia levied a tribute and made the trading routes safe again. Under the succeeding rulers of the 11th Dynasty (2023–1963 BC), Egyptian ships sailed to Punt – probably Ethiopia – for incense and quarrying expeditions were led to the Wadi Hammamat. The reign of Mentuhotep IV, the last ruler of this dynasty, ended in turmoil.

For some 200 years from 1991 BC the country prospered under the able and energetic rulers of the 12th Dynasty. The first of these pharaohs, Amenemhet I, moved the court to Itj-towy in the north, which became the seat of government. Thebes, however, continued to be very important as a dynastic centre and was known as the 'southern city' to distinguish it from the northern 'residence.' These rulers of the 12th Dynasty built their pyramids in the Fayyum, where they under-

took a major project of land drainage, which greatly increased available agricultural land.

As in the Old Kingdom, the vizier continued to be the most important and powerful official next to the king. Taxes supported the court and its projects and tight control was exercised in their collection. At this time there seems to have been a shift in certain aspects of kingship, as reflected in the sculpture and literature; thus royal statues were much larger than formerly and give an impression of great strength; the king was now seen as hero and warrior.

MIDDLE KINGDOM CULTURE

The Middle Kingdom produced great works of Egyptian literature, including songs lamenting the brevity and uncertainty of life, and tales such as the *Story of Sinuhe* which describes the activities of a courtier in the reign of Sesostris I (1943–1899 BC), who goes into exile and is ultimately pardoned by the king: 'His majesty said: "He shall not fear, he shall not dread! He shall be a Companion among the nobles." I left the audience-hall, the royal daughters giving me their hands. We went through the great portals, and I was put in the house of a prince. In it were luxuries: a bathroom and mirrors. In it were riches from the

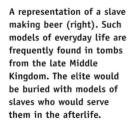

A representation of a slave making beer (right). Such models of everyday life are frequently found in tombs from the late Middle Kingdom. The elite would be buried with models of slaves who would serve them in the afterlife.

Statue of Sesostris III (1862-1844 BC) from Deir el Bahri, to the west of Thebes (right). The 12th dynasty kings campaigned successfully in Nubia, extending Egyptian control below the second cataract, and building a series of major fortresses along the Nile. Sesostris III was the most successful of these kings, and the boundary inscriptions he set up at Semna recount his achievement: 'The living Horus… the King of Upper and Lower Egypt… the Lord of the Two Lands: Sesostris, given life-stability-health forever. Year 16, third month of winter: the king made his southern boundary at Heh: I have made my boundary further south than my fathers, I have added to what was bequeathed me. I am a king who speaks and acts, what my heart plans is done by my arm. One who attacks to conquer, who is swift to succeed, in whose heart a plan does not slumber…'

KINGSHIP IN ANCIENT EGYPT

Mentuhotep

Sesostris III

The Egyptian king or pharaoh played a central role not only in the political overlordship, but also in the religious consciousness of ancient Egypt. He was believed to be the 'living son' of the chief god, Re, and to possess god-like powers himself, including that of ensuring the Nile flooded each year to bring fertility to the lands beside it. Each year the king performed special rituals to ensure the river rose at the correct time. The special regalia which the king wore symbolized his role in the land. These included the red and white double crown which symbolized that he was King of the Two Lands of Egypt. Each pharaoh had several titles, indicating different aspects of his kingship. The cartouches (left) show the birth names (by which we generally refer to them) and the throne names used by contemporaries.

White crown (Upper Egypt)

Red crown (Lower Egypt)

Double crown (The Two Lands)

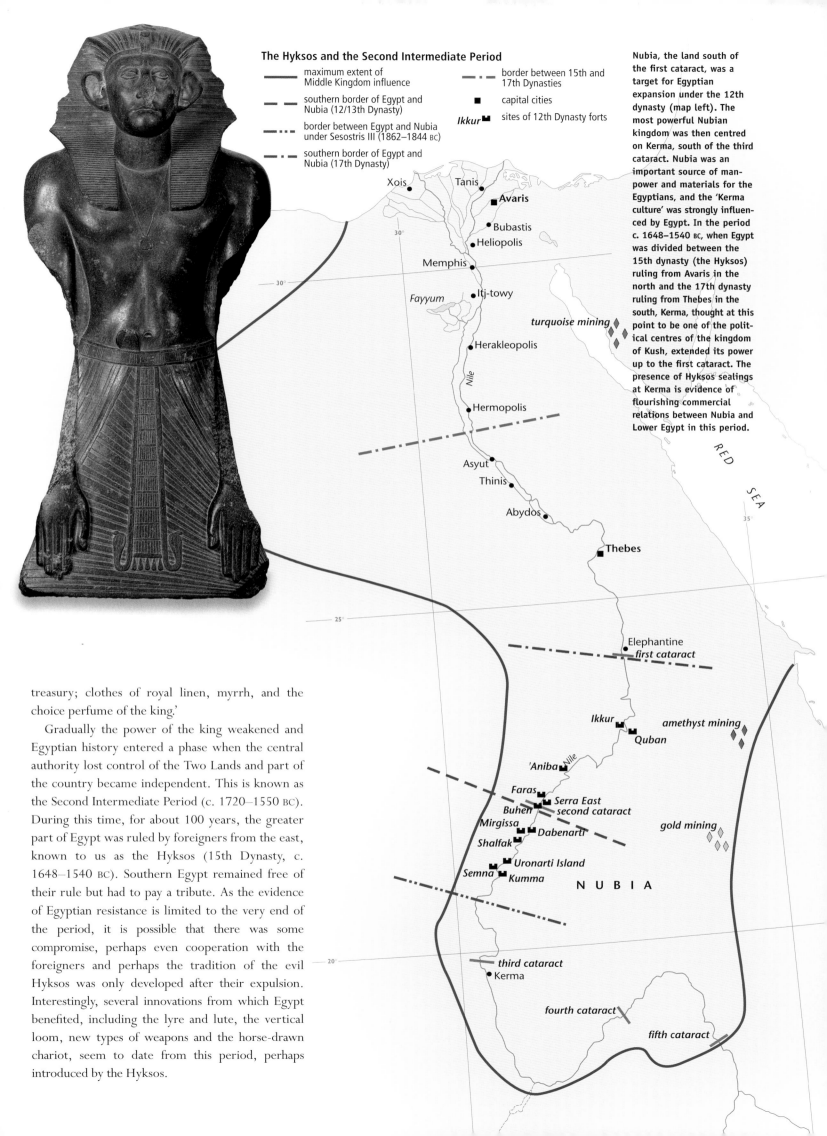

The Hyksos and the Second Intermediate Period

——— maximum extent of Middle Kingdom influence

– – – southern border of Egypt and Nubia (12/13th Dynasty)

–··– border between Egypt and Nubia under Sesostris III (1862–1844 BC)

–·–·– southern border of Egypt and Nubia (17th Dynasty)

–·–·– border between 15th and 17th Dynasties

■ capital cities

Ikkur ■ sites of 12th Dynasty forts

Nubia, the land south of the first cataract, was a target for Egyptian expansion under the 12th dynasty (map left). The most powerful Nubian kingdom was then centred on Kerma, south of the third cataract. Nubia was an important source of man-power and materials for the Egyptians, and the 'Kerma culture' was strongly influenced by Egypt. In the period c. 1648–1540 BC, when Egypt was divided between the 15th dynasty (the Hyksos) ruling from Avaris in the north and the 17th dynasty ruling from Thebes in the south, Kerma, thought at this point to be one of the political centres of the kingdom of Kush, extended its power up to the first cataract. The presence of Hyksos sealings at Kerma is evidence of flourishing commercial relations between Nubia and Lower Egypt in this period.

Xois

Tanis

Avaris

Bubastis

Heliopolis

Memphis

Fayyum

Itj-towy

turquoise mining

Herakleopolis

Nile

Hermopolis

Asyut

Thinis

Abydos

Thebes

RED SEA

Elephantine
first cataract

Ikkur

amethyst mining

Quban

'Aniba *Nile*

Faras

Serra East
Buhen *second cataract*

Mirgissa

Dabenarti

Shalfak

gold mining

Uronarti Island

Semna Kumma

N U B I A

third cataract
Kerma

fourth cataract

fifth cataract

treasury; clothes of royal linen, myrrh, and the choice perfume of the king.'

Gradually the power of the king weakened and Egyptian history entered a phase when the central authority lost control of the Two Lands and part of the country became independent. This is known as the Second Intermediate Period (c. 1720–1550 BC). During this time, for about 100 years, the greater part of Egypt was ruled by foreigners from the east, known to us as the Hyksos (15th Dynasty, c. 1648–1540 BC). Southern Egypt remained free of their rule but had to pay a tribute. As the evidence of Egyptian resistance is limited to the very end of the period, it is possible that there was some compromise, perhaps even cooperation with the foreigners and perhaps the tradition of the evil Hyksos was only developed after their expulsion. Interestingly, several innovations from which Egypt benefited, including the lyre and lute, the vertical loom, new types of weapons and the horse-drawn chariot, seem to date from this period, perhaps introduced by the Hyksos.

Merchant Princes
Mesopotamia **2004–1595** BC

The 400 years following the fall of Ur is known as the Old Babylonian period. This term refers to the form of the Akkadian language in use in southern Mesopotamia at this time, rather than the political situation. What we know of the politics of the period comes largely from documents surviving in a number of archives, most importantly from the city of Mari. They reveal a world of powerful kings competing for power.

The ruling dynasties of several of the cities of the region, including Babylon, Mari and Ashur, have Amorite names. Amorite tribes, speaking a western Semitic language, had been settled in Mesopotamia in the third millennium BC and it would appear that after the collapse of the Ur III empire (see page 28), their leaders took power in a number of cities. In southern Mesopotamia the rulers of Isin took over many of the elements of royal ritual from Ur, but in the period from c. 1900 BC their power was restricted by the expansion of Larsa under its Amorite rulers. Isin was eventually conquered by Rim-Sin I in 1793 BC.

To the north Ashur, independent of Ur since c. 2000 BC, grew powerful in part through its exploitation of long-distance trade and its commercial activities in Anatolia. In 1813 BC Ashur was captured by another Amorite chieftain, Shamshi-Adad I, who went on to create an Assyrian empire controlling much of north Mesopotamia.

THE MARI ARCHIVE

One of the cities captured by Shamshi-Adad was Mari, which regained its independence after Shamshi-Adad's death, when it was recaptured by its former ruler Zimri-Lin. A royal archive found at Mari includes much correspondence between the rulers of the region in the period c. 1800-1760 BC, and without these documents our knowledge of events and of daily life in Mesopotamia would be much poorer. As well as diplomatic letters, the archive contains reports to the rulers about the revelations of seers and prophets, and about legal processes. One such process is the 'river-ordeal', referred to in a number of Mesopotamian legal texts, including the Law Code of Hammurabi. The ordeal required a person accused of wrong-doing

Rival Kings		
Assyria	Shamshi-adad I	1813–1781 BC
Babylon	Sin-muballit	1812–1793 BC
	Hammurabi	1792–1750 BC
Larsa	Rim-Sin I	1822–1763 BC
Isin	Damiq-ilishu	1816–1794 BC
Mari	Yaggid-Lim	1820–1811 BC
	Yahdun-Lim	1810–1795 BC
	Sumu-Yaman	1794–1791 BC
	Yasmah-Addu	1790–1776 BC
	Zimri-Lim	1775–1761 BC

to swim a substantial distance underwater: if they survived they were vindicated. If members of the elite were involved, the inhabitants of their towns and villages might be expected to go through the ordeal on their behalf.

The political rivalries of the time are described clearly in one letter from the Mari archive: 'no king is powerful by himself. 10 or 15 kings follow Hammurabi of Babylon, as many follow Rim-Sin of Larsa, Ibalpiel of Eshnunna and Amutpiel of Qatna,

Although kings of Assyria and Babylon were able briefly to dominate parts of Mesopotamia in the way that Agade and Ur III had done before, these empires were not stable (map right). More long-lasting were the trading networks that developed, which are revealed in documents from the trading settlement at Kanesh, which acted as the centre of Assyrian commercial activity in Anatolia. Assyrian merchants settled in trading quarters on the edges of Anatolian cities and in Northern Mesopotamia, and were able to direct trade over large parts of the Near East.

A detail from a polychrome fresco from the palace at Mari, dating to c. 1800 BC (below). It shows a procession of figures leading sacrificial bulls. The palace-complex covered an area of 3 hectares, and many of its royal apartments, reception rooms and throne rooms were decorated with wall-paintings, sculptures and inlaid work.

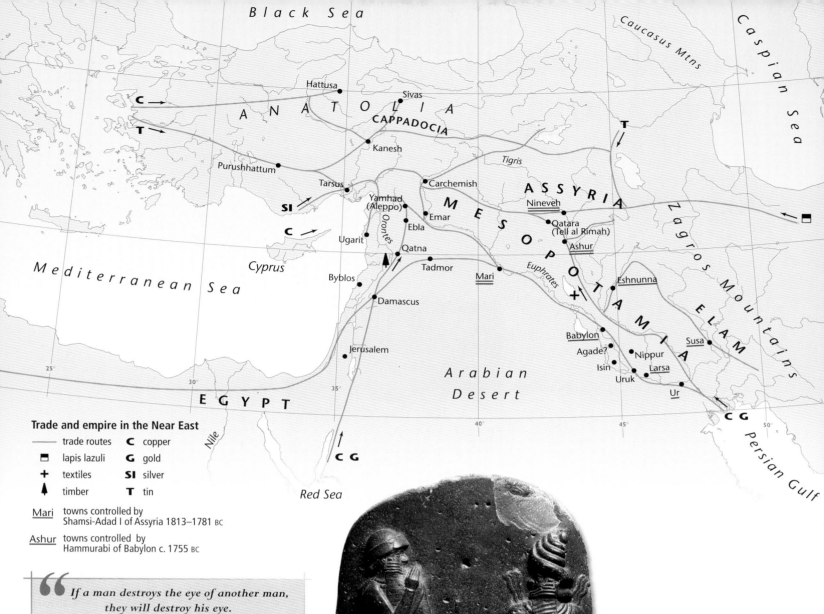

The map shows trade routes, with labels including:

Black Sea · Caucasus Mtns · Caspian Sea · Hattusa · Sivas · ANATOLIA · CAPPADOCIA · Kanesh · Tigris · ASSYRIA · Purushhattum · Tarsus · Carchemish · MESOPOTAMIA · Nineveh · ZagrosMountains · Yamhad (Aleppo) · Emar · Qatara (Tell al Rimah) · Ashur · ELAM · Orontes · Ebla · Ugarit · Qatna · Ashur · Eshnunna · Susa · Mediterranean Sea · Cyprus · Tadmor · Mari · Euphrates · Byblos · Damascus · Babylon · Agade? · Nippur · Susa · Isin · Larsa · Jerusalem · Uruk · Ur · Arabian Desert · EGYPT · Nile · Red Sea · Persian Gulf

Trade and empire in the Near East

— trade routes   **C** copper
■ lapis lazuli   **G** gold
+ textiles   **SI** silver
▲ timber   **T** tin

<u>Mari</u> towns controlled by
Shamsi-Adad I of Assyria 1813–1781 BC

<u>Ashur</u> towns controlled by
Hammurabi of Babylon c. 1755 BC

> *If a man destroys the eye of another man,*
> *they will destroy his eye.*
> *If he breaks the bone of another man,*
> *they will break his bone.*
> *If he destroys the eye of a subordinate or*
> *breaks the bone of a subordinate he shall pay*
> *one mina of silver*
>
> **From the Law Code of Hammurabi**

while 20 kings follow Yarim-Lin of Yamhad.' The importance of Yamhad (modern Aleppo), which has not been excavated, would not otherwise have been suspected. Its position on the trade routes must have been a reason for its success.

Hammurabi of Babylon, from another Amorite dynasty and most famous for his Law Code, was the most successful empire-builder of the period. His city lies below the water table and has not been excavated, but he is known to have built fort-ifications and splendid temples. Documents indicate that his was an efficiently run state with a powerful king, whose officials came from the wealthy land-owning aristocracy. There was much scholarly activity and the first mathematical and geometrical texts appeared in this period.

For the first 30 years of his reign Hammurabi acted as an ally and subordinate of the then more powerful Shamshi-Adad I of Assyria and Rim-Sin of Larsa. The situation changed in 1763 BC, when he took Isin, Uruk, Ur Nippur and Larsa; two years later he gained control over Eshnunna, giving him access to Iran, and in the same year he conquered Assyria. In 1760 BC Mari was captured and Hammurabi now extended his territory westwards. With the final destruction of Eshnunna, Babylon found itself in control of an area comparable to that of the Ur III Empire. Although much of the territory was later lost, it remained an important centre until it was sacked by the Hittites in 1595 BC (see page 42).

The top of a basalt stele containing the Law Code of Hammurabi (left). The relief shows Hammurabi (standing, left) receiving the commission to compile a law code from Shamash, the sun-god and patron of justice. It was probably originally erected in the temple of Shamash at Sippar in the last years of Hammurabi's reign. The code itself was a collection of laws on a range of topics, including fixed prices for a variety of goods. How the code was used in practice is not clear. It was in part a symbol of the king's commitment to justice, and in the epilogue to the laws, Hammurabi writes: 'At the command of the sun-god, the great judge of heaven and earth, may my justice become visible in the land; at the command of Marduk may what I have written find no-one who removes it; in Esagila, which I love, may my name be pronounced with gratitude eternally.'

Indus Civilization
2500–1500 BC

The Indus (or Harappan) civilization covered a large geographical area which is today part of India and Pakistan, with the Indus river and its tributaries as its focus. However, the Indus civilization had a much broader effect on a diverse range of cultures from the Iranian Plateau in the wast down to Gujarat and the Thar desert in the southeast. The civilization developed from small agricultural villages and pastoral camps that were present from around 7000 BC onwards.

Nearly two hundred sites spanning the pre-early, early, mature, and final Harappan periods have been excavated, but three stand out in terms of their size, Mohenjo-Daro, Harappa, and Dholavira. These sites display common features such as a raised mound, a regular network of streets, and drainage, which are also found on a smaller scale at other sites. These urban centres contained buildings of a ceremonial, administrative, and residential nature, and were clearly well planned. The larger houses consisted of a courtyard with a number of rooms arranged around it, whilst the smaller houses consisted of a single room. The houses were constructed of baked bricks of a standard size (28 x 14 x 7 cm). The similarity between settlements in terms of layout and construction, in addition to uniform objects such as stone weights, shows a high degree of standardization indicative of a central political force. Harappa, Mohenjo-Daro, and Dholavira might be considered as 'capital' cities, but other provincial urban settlements also existed, among them Kalibangan, Chanhu-Daro, Amri, and Dabarkot.

INDUSTRY AND TRADE

These large settlements were centres of industrial activity with workshops for potters, stone-workers, metalworkers, bead-workers, and shell-workers. The raw materials for these industrial activities were both exploited locally and imported along established trade and exchange networks which had been in place for several millennia. Finds such as Mesopotamian cylinder seals at Mohenjo-Daro and

An Indus seal (above) found at Mohenjo-Daro. The first three seals were found at Harappa by Sir Alexander Cunningham in 1875. The seals contain writing in an as yet undeciphered script. Up to 400 separate signs have been identified, but progress in determining their meaning has been limited.

Weights from Mohenjo-Daro. These are found in various sizes ranging from those that were lifted via a metal ring to those that measure c. 1 cm^3. They are predominantly made from chert.

Indus seals in Mesopotamia demonstrate maritime trade with that region via the Persian Gulf. In addition, materials such as tin and lapis lazuli would have been imported overland from Afghanistan and Central Asia. Whilst a core region of the Indus civilization developed, settlements in more transitional zones with their origins in the Neolithic also continued to develop in parallel, many located in key geographical locations such as the entrances to mountain passes that would have been used as overland routes by the Indus peoples.

THE INDUS SCRIPT

Perhaps the most intriguing aspect of the Indus Civilization is its script. Despite the existence of 2500 inscriptions, it is as yet undeciphered. It was used only for short inscriptions primarily on seals but also on other small objects. An exception to this is an inscription found at Dholavira which contains characters 37 cm in height. Until this script has been deciphered little will be known about the political structure or religious beliefs of the Indus civilization. However, some symbols and motifs do show tentative relations to later Indian gods and goddesses such as Shiva whilst the large number of female figurines may represent a 'Mother Goddess'.

The mature Harappan period came to an end in about 2000 BC for unknown reasons and the settlement pattern returned to one of agricultural villages and pastoral camps. However, elements of the culture continued to exist until around 1300 BC when the Iron Age began to take shape (see page 54).

Chronology	
Pre-early Harappan	3800–3200 BC
Early Harappan	3200–2600 BC
Early-Mature Harappan Transition	2600–2500 BC
Mature Harappan	2500–1900 BC
Post-urban Harappan	1900–1300 BC

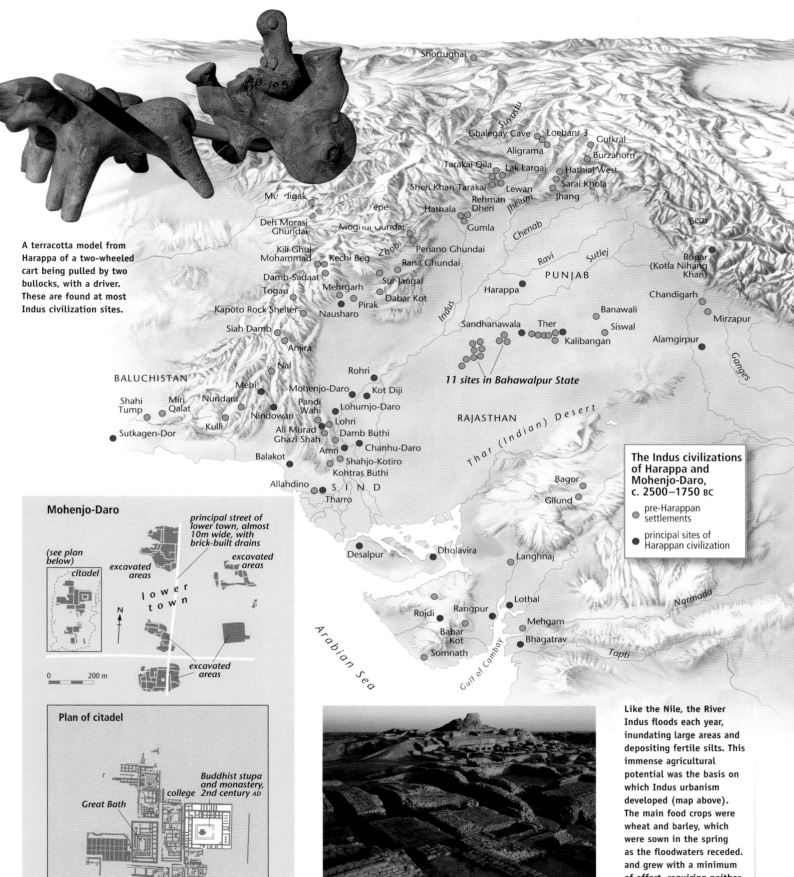

A terracotta model from Harappa of a two-wheeled cart being pulled by two bullocks, with a driver. These are found at most Indus civilization sites.

Shortughai

Suvastu

Ghalegay Cave · Loebanr 3
Aligrama · Gufkral · Burzahom
Tarakai Qila · Lak Largai · Hathial West
Sheri Khan Tarakai · Lewan · Sarai Khola
Rehman Dheri · Jhang

Beas

Mundigak
Tepe
Deh Morasi Ghundai
Moghul Gundai
Hathala
Gumla
Jhelum

Kili Ghul Mohammad · Kechi Beg · Zhob
Periano Ghundai
Rana Ghundai

Ravi · Sutlej

PUNJAB

Harappa

Ropar (Kotla Nihang Khan)

Chandigarh

Mirzapur

Damb-Sadaat
Togau
Mehrgarh
Sur Jangal
Dabar Kot
Pirak
NaTsharo

Chenab

Sandhanawala · Ther · Banawali · Siswal
Kalibangan

Alamgirpur

Ganges

Siah Damb

Anjira

Nal

Rohri

BALUCHISTAN

Mehi

Mohenjo-Daro · Kot Diji

RAJASTHAN

11 sites in Bahawalpur State

Thar (Indian) Desert

Shahi Tump · Miri Qalat · Nundara
Kulli · Nindowari
Pandi Wahi
Lohumjo-Daro
Lohri

Ali Murad · Damb Buthi
Ghazi Shah
Amri · Chanhu-Daro
Balakot · Shahjo-Kotiro
Kohtras Buthi
Allahdino · SIND
Tharro

Sutkagen-Dor

Indus

Bagor
Gilund

Mohenjo-Daro

(see plan below)

citadel

l o w e r   t o w n

principal street of lower town, almost 10m wide, with brick-built drains

excavated areas

excavated areas

excavated areas

N

0   200 m

Desalpur

Dholavira

Langhnaj

Rojdi · Rangpur
Babar Kot
Somnath

Lothal
Mehgam
Bhagatrav

Narmada

Tapti

Arabian Sea

Gulf of Cambay

The Indus civilizations of Harappa and Mohenjo-Daro, c. 2500–1750 BC

○ pre-Harappan settlements

● principal sites of Harappan civilization

Plan of citadel

Buddhist stupa and monastery, 2nd century AD

college

Great Bath

mud-brick embankment (13m wide)

Temple complex

baked-brick tower

N

0   50 m

assembly hall

baked-brick bastions

Covering an area of 60 hectares, Mohenjo-Daro (plan left) was a substantial city, with a population which may have reached 40,000. The lower town was the main residential area, with houses of various sizes divided into nine blocks by regularly laid-out streets. The citadel (picture above) was a religious, ceremonial and administrative centre; the so-called college building may have the residence of a priestly elite. The Great Bath may have been an area set aside for ritual bathing. South of the Great Bath is an area known as the Assembly Hall, which may represent an audience chamber. The city declined around 2000 BC, possibly because of a shift in the course of the River Indus, which left the fields around the city desolate, no longer replenished by the annual flood.

Like the Nile, the River Indus floods each year, inundating large areas and depositing fertile silts. This immense agricultural potential was the basis on which Indus urbanism developed (map above). The main food crops were wheat and barley, which were sown in the spring as the floodwaters receded. and grew with a minimum of effort, requiring neither irrigation nor manuring. Rice was also cultivated at some sites, though it only became an important food plant when settlement spread to the middle and lower Ganges in the second and first millennium BC. A wide range of domestic animals was also kept, including Indian humped cattle, sheep and goats, Indian boar, elephants and possibly camels.

The **Aegean** in the **Late Bronze Age** c. **1500–1200** BC

Around 1500 BC the island of Crete saw a wave of destruction and the establishment in Knossos of rulers from the mainland of Greece. The next three centuries saw great developments in the Aegean world, with the appearance of palaces in the Peloponnese and parts of central Greece. Although influenced by elements of earlier Minoan civilization, these new centres of power, with their Greek-speaking Mycenaean rulers, were a significant new element of the Late Bronze Age world.

In Crete the Mycenaeans seem to have established an area of rule that covered much of the centre and the west of the island, and their influence extended further. Knossos was the centre of their administration, and the Minoan palace continued in use until its destruction in c. 1300 BC. Even after that the presence of Linear B tablets show that it remained an important place. The presence of Linear B tablets at Chania (known as Cydonia in this period and later) suggest that this became an increasingly powerful city, possibly independent from Knossos, or possibly replacing it as the chief centre in Crete.

THE GROWTH OF MYCENAEAN PALACES

The influence of the Mycenaean presence in Crete was eventually felt on the mainland of Greece, where, in the 14th century BC, palaces appeared for the first time. These shared some features with the Minoan palaces found on Crete, but were very different in other ways. The presence of large storage jars, and the large number of inventories found amongst the Linear B tablets, show that, as in Crete, the palaces had important functions in storage and redistribution of agricultural goods. Mycenaean palaces were, however, fortified and at their centre, rather than an open area, there was the main hall of the palace, called by archaeologists the *megaron*. The Linear B tablets from Knossos and Pylos reveal something about the political organization of the palaces: at the top of the hierarchy was the *Wanax* or king, and below him a *Lawagetas*, literally leader of the people, though his function is less clear. Other officials, whose role is uncertain, include *Telestai*, *Koreteres*, *Prokoreteres* and *Qasileis*, the latter apparently headmen of different groups of personnel. There was possibly a class of warriors, the *heqetai*, and of slaves, the *doeroi*. Many of the tablets from Pylos are concerned with land-tenure, and some scholars have suggested that the palaces operated a form of feudalism. However that may be, it is clear that Mycenaean society was very hierarchical, and must have been centrally organized.

Objects found in shipwrecks off the southern coast of Anatolia from the 14th and 13th centuries BC show the wide range of goods being carried around the Aegean

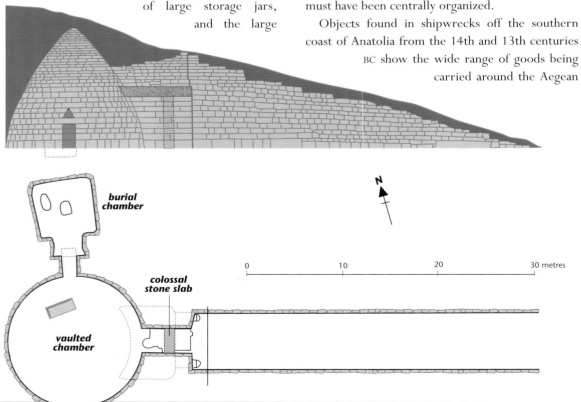

burial chamber

colossal stone slab

vaulted chamber

N

0   10   20   30 metres

The most obvious archaeological features from the Mycenaean period in Greece are the tholos tombs and the palaces (map right). Most of the tholos tombs predate the construction of the palaces on the mainland, and their distribution suggests that in the 15th and early 14th centuries BC there were numerous small communities governed by princes or small ruling groups. With the creation of the palaces these communities might have been absorbed into larger political units. Different areas of the mainland appear to have developed in different ways. The Linear B evidence from Pylos indicates that the palace there controlled a large territory, probably covering most of the southwest Peloponnese. In contrast the Argolid in the northeast Peloponnese contains several palaces and fortified citadels, which suggests that it continued to be made up of a number of competing statelets. Further north, Boeotia was again an area with several fortified centres, while in Attica only the Athenian acropolis shows evidence of defensive walls.

Tombs in Late Bronze Age Greece took a variety of forms, but the most impressive are the large beehive shaped tholos tombs (diagram left), which belong mainly to the 15th and 14th centuries BC. It may be that the design was adopted from Cretan tombs of the Middle Bronze Age, although there is much dispute about this. The tombs would be built into hillsides, or buried in the ground. The masonry was usually of a very high order, and the largest tombs might have diameters of over 14 metres. The corpse would be buried either in the main chamber or in a smaller side chamber, with the main chamber containing grave goods. In some cases horses were killed and buried in the *dromos* (the entrance passage). The tombs were demonstrations of the wealth and power of those buried in them, and again became places of veneration for some of the emerging communities of the eighth century BC.

**The Aegean in the
Late Bronze Age**

- ■ palace settlement
- ● other major fortified settlement
- ○ other settlement
- ▲ tholos tombs
- ✛ sanctuary site
- **B** site with Linear B tablets
- **B** site with stirrup jars
  inscribed with Linear B

Lithares modern name

in this period. These ships were carrying materials from the Aegean, Italy, Cyprus, the Levant, Egypt and Mesopotamia, possibly working on a regular circuit, trading in whatever they could buy and sell; amongst many other things they carried large quantities of copper ingots, and it is clear that metals were an important element in more long-distance trading. Mycenaean pottery has been found throughout the Aegean and the central and eastern Mediterranean, north into Macedonia, south into Egypt, and as far west as Sicily and Sardinia. The spread of pottery is not necessarily evidence of a widespread Mycenaean trading network, as it could have reached these destinations by means of local smaller-scale exchange networks. It does, however, indicate the extent to which the Aegean was part of the wider Near Eastern world in this period.

THE END OF MYCENAEAN RULE

Although there are signs of destructions in a number of palaces at various times in the Late Bronze Age, in around 1200 BC there is evidence of widespread destruction of all the palaces on the Greek mainland. Whatever the causes of this destruction, the communities that emerged in Greece in the following centuries were organized very differently. Only the remnants of fortification walls and tholos tombs were left to remind later Greeks of their Bronze Age past.

A tablet and a stirrup jar inscribed with Linear B script. Linear B is a script adapted from the Cretan Linear A for writing Greek. Examples survive on pottery, where a few words might be written on a jar before it was fired, but longer inscriptions come from clay tablets preserved when the places in which they were used were burned down, accidentally firing the tablets. Linear B tablets are found in centres in mainland Greece as well as Crete, and all the surviving examples date from the 13th century BC. The tablets are administrative documents, and although there is much in them that is unclear, they do provide valuable evidence for the functioning of the Mycenaean palaces, and the social organization of Greece in the last century of the Bronze Age.

The Hittites
1650–1200 BC

Between c. 1650 and c. 1200 BC the Hittites dominated Central Anatolia and neighbouring regions, and for a time successfully challenged Egyptian control of the Levant. The Hittites controlled an empire whose history was marked by successive expansions and contractions, which at times reduced their territory to the environs of Hattusa, their fortified capital north of the Halys in central Anatolia.

Evidence for the very early Hittite period is fragmentary. Their capital Hattusa was originally a Hattic settlement and, although little is known of the Hattic people, their influence on Hittite culture can be seen in both the name of the capital and the country, known as Hatti. Hattic influence can also be seen in ritual and religious symbolism.

The evidence for the formation of the Hittite empire is problematic, as there are no documentary sources for Anatolian history between the end of the Assyrian trading settlements in c. 1800 BC and the appearance of an almost fully formed Hittite state in c. 1650 BC. This latter development is revealed by archives at Hattusa, made up mostly of tablets written in Hittite, an Indo-European language, using an adapted form of cuneiform. The Hittites themselves called the language 'Neshite', that is the language of Kanesh.

THE NATURE OF THE HITTITE EMPIRE

Although we have some information about the Hittite state under its first great ruler, Hattusili I, most of our evidence comes from the Empire period, c. 1420–1200 BC. The empire consisted of a large number of small territories ruled by subject 'kings'. Despite their title, their power was limited,

and they owed their positions entirely to the 'Great King' ruling from Hattusa. His presence was widely felt, and there were royal palaces and storehouses throughout Hittite territory. As the chief religious figure of the state, the Great King led much of Hittite religious activity, including a number of festivals throughout the year.

The king was also the chief commander in war, and all the Hittite rulers led their troops in person. Victories demonstrated not only the might of the king but also the support of the gods of Hatti. They also brought in tribute and new territory for the king to distribute to his loyal followers.

Loyalty to the person of the king was an important element in holding the Hittite empire together. Client-kings were often bound to the king by marriage to a female member of the royal family, so that they, and even more their children, would feel bound to the Hittite heartland. Client rulers would also be expected to raise troops and campaign with the king, and to provide labour and goods as

A libation vase in the form of a lion (above).The image of a lion played an important role in Hittite art, as seen on lion sculptures at Yazilikaya and monumental gate lions at the capital, Hattusa.

Hattusa (plan below) was the capital of the Hittite kingdom from c. 1650 to 1200 BC. The naturally defensive outcrop of Büyükkale was the original core of the city, but as the Hittite Empire expanded the capital was rebuilt. By 1400 BC, both the upper and lower city had been constructed, and in the 13th century BC fortifications were extended and a royal palace built, which housed the archive and which has yielded over 3,000 cuneiform tablets. The walls were punctuated with magnificent gateways, including that known as the Lion Gateway (below left).

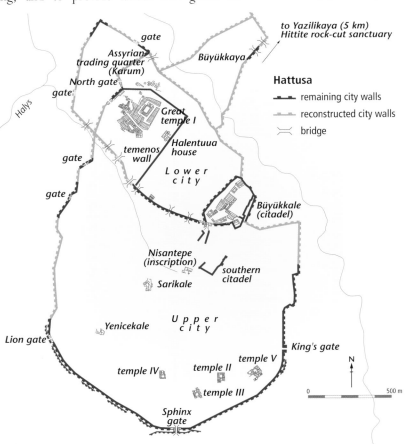

Hattusa

- ▬•▬ remaining city walls
- ▬▬ reconstructed city walls
- ⋈ bridge

to Yazilikaya (5 km)
Hittite rock-cut sanctuary

gate
Assyrian trading quarter (Karum)
Büyükkaya
North gate
gate
Halys
Great temple I
temenos wall
Halentuua house
Lower city
gate
Büyükkale (citadel)
gate
Nisantepe (inscription)
southern citadel
Sarikale
Yenicekale
Upper city
Lion gate
King's gate
temple V
temple IV
temple II
temple III
Sphinx gate

0   500 m

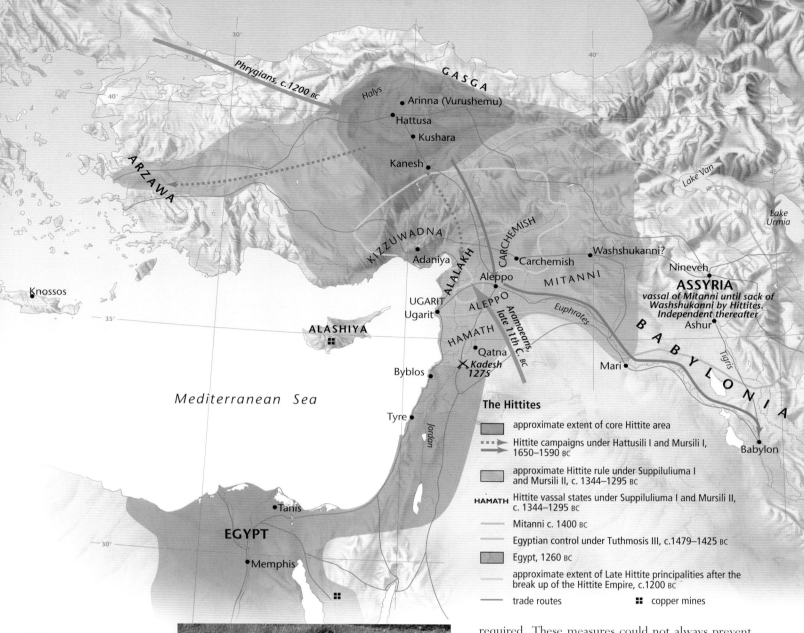

The Hittites

- ▓ approximate extent of core Hittite area
- ⇢ Hittite campaigns under Hattusili I and Mursili I, 1650–1590 BC
- ▓ approximate Hittite rule under Suppiluliuma I and Mursili II, c. 1344–1295 BC
- HAMATH Hittite vassal states under Suppiluliuma I and Mursili II, c. 1344–1295 BC
- Mitanni c. 1400 BC
- Egyptian control under Tuthmosis III, c.1479–1425 BC
- Egypt, 1260 BC
- approximate extent of Late Hittite principalities after the break up of the Hittite Empire, c.1200 BC
- trade routes   copper mines

Map labels: Phrygians, c.1200 BC · GASGA · Halys · Arinna (Vurushemu) · Hattusa · Kushara · Kanesh · ARZAWA · KIZZUWADNA · Adaniya · ALALAKH · CARCHEMISH · Carchemish · Washshukanni? · MITANNI · Lake Van · Lake Urmia · Nineveh · ASSYRIA vassal of Mitanni until sack of Washshukanni by Hittites. Independent thereafter · Ashur · Aleppo · ALEPPO · Ugarit · UGARIT · Knossos · ALASHIYA · HAMATH · Euphrates · Aramaeans, late 11th C. BC · Qatna · Kadesh 1275 · Byblos · Mari · BABYLONIA · Tigris · Babylon · Mediterranean Sea · Jordan · Tyre · Tanis · EGYPT · Memphis

Hittite expansion came in two phases (map above). Hattusili I (1650–1620 BC) consolidated his power in central Anatolia, and his successor Mursili I (1620–1590 BC) took Aleppo and even sacked Babylon. There followed a period of chaos, in which even the capital city Hattusa was lost. Hittite resurgence came under Suppiluliuma I (1344–1322 BC) who conquered Mitanni and took the cities of Ugarit and Carchemish in Syria. His successor, Mursili II (1321–1295 BC), expanded Hittite territory to the west and north. Although 1200 BC saw the collapse of the Hittite empire, a number of 'neo-Hittite' statelets survived in north Syria until around 700 BC.

The Hittite king Tudhaliya IV (1239–1209 BC) shown with the god Sharruma, from the sanctuary at Yazilikaya (right). The depiction of the Hittite king with deities on rock-cut reliefs is characteristic.

required. These measures could not always prevent rivalry between members of the royal family. In the 'Old Kingdom' period, the assassination of Mursili I set off a chain of bloody successions over the next 70 years. Such instability was less evident in the period of the Empire, although Mursili III (1271–1264 BC) was driven into exile by his uncle, who set himself up as Hattusili III (1264–1239 BC).

Despite the building of forts and frontier garrisons, the Hittites were always threatened by hostile neighbours to the north and west. Arzawa, in western Anatolia, was the target of campaigns under Hattusili I (1650–1620 BC) and Mursili II (1321–1295 BC), but in between was sufficiently powerful to conduct a correspondence with the Egyptian kings of the Amarna period (1390–1327 BC). Around 1200 BC, new challenges appeared from the Phrygians to the north-west and the Gasga to the north-east. Until this time, the Hittite kingdom had shown itself to be remarkably resilient, able to reassert itself after periods of anarchy and loss of territory. After 1200 BC, however, the Hittite empire disappeared for ever. This final collapse, still not fully understood, needs to be considered in the context of much wider upheavals throughout the Near East (see page 52).

New Kingdom Egypt
The Imperial Age **1550–1069** BC

Under the pharaohs of the 18th Dynasty, Egypt gained control of Palestine, Syria and Nubia, and became the leading power in the Near East. The expulsion and pursuit of the Hyksos into Palestine by Ahmose (1550–1525 BC), founder of the dynasty, led to the first moves towards control of this area. In Nubia, where rich mines provided the gold of Egypt and whose chieftains had become independent of Egyptian authority, the Middle Kingdom boundaries were once more established.

This New Kingdom saw a dramatic change in Egypt's attitude to warfare and foreign conquest. There was now a full-time and highly professional army. The two-wheeled horse-drawn chariot, perhaps introduced by the Hyksos, was an important weapon and also a key element of royal iconography, which emphasized the king as a warrior, excelling in martial skills. In contrast to earlier periods, the military began to play an important role in the administration and occupied high official positions close to the king. At the new palace of Memphis, the great military campaigns were planned and the soldiers were 'armed before pharaoh'.

CONQUESTS IN NUBIA AND THE LEVANT

An aggressive military and foreign policy was now pursued. Expansion in the early New Kingdom into the Levant and into Nubia originated in attempts to strengthen the boundaries of Egypt against threats from rulers in Asia and Kush. Although in the past there had been frequent raids into Palestine and Nubia – and in the latter case the establishment of forts and long-term garrison – the scale of military operations was now of far greater magnitude, with the standing army almost continuously on campaign.

Control of Nubia was crucial in providing economic support for Egypt and here Amenophis I (1525–1504 BC) further extended the boundary to Semna. The province was administered by 'the King's son of Kush and Overseer of the southern frontier lands', who also served as overlord of the

native Nubian governors. Egyptian domination was symbolized by the construction of walled towns, each with its own temple, which replaced the Middle Kingdom fortresses. Apart from the gold mines of Kush, Nubia was also the source of luxury goods, such as copper, ivory, ebony and skins.

In Asia, Tuthmosis I (1504–1491 BC) campaigned in the Levant and reached the Euphrates, thus bringing Syria and Palestine under Egyptian hegemony; nothing is known about the arrangements, if there were any, for controlling this area. Under Queen Hatshepsut (1479–1458 BC), who acted as a male sovereign, control over Nubia and the Levant seems to have been maintained, thus permitting her nephew and stepson Tuthmosis III (1479–1425 BC) to launch the first of 17 campaigns into the Levant immediately he became sole ruler. He, too, reached the Euphrates and led Egypt into conflict with Mitanni. Egypt's hold over the Levant was not completely secure, however, for there was a serious rebellion in Palestine c. 1416 BC, which was brutally crushed. The situation

Ramesses II in his war chariot at Kadesh (above). The chariot was a key element in the Egyptian arsenal and pharaohs are frequently depicted driving chariots over their enemies.

Ramesses II was intent on stopping Hittite forays in to western Syria and c. 1275 BC marched north, seeking to overwhelm the army of the Hittite king, Muwatallis. At Kadesh on the Orontes the Hittite army was waiting (maps left). The Hittites crossed the river and overran the Egyptian camp on the west bank, whilst another Egyptian division was charged by Hittite chariots. Ramesses managed to regroup and push back the Hittites who took refuge in Kadesh. Both sides subsequently claimed victory.

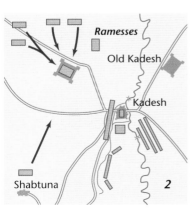

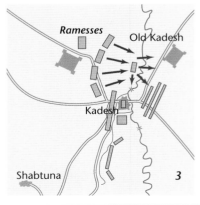

Battle of Kadesh, 10 May 1275 BC

⬛ Egyptian divisions

⬛ Hittite divisions

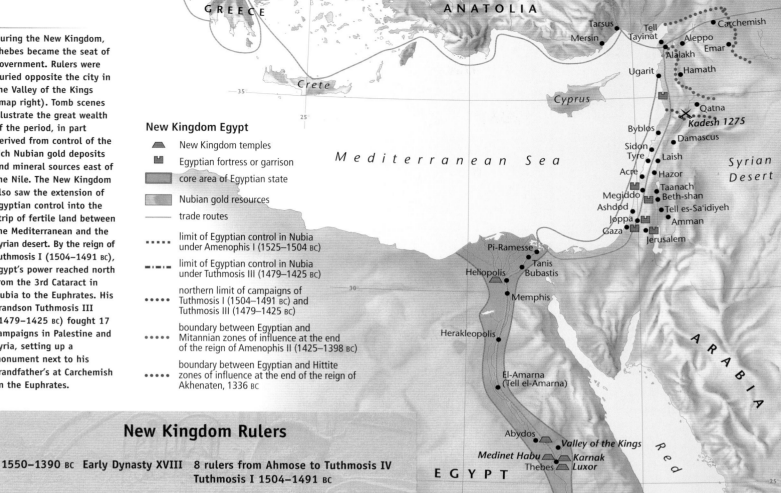

During the New Kingdom, Thebes became the seat of government. Rulers were buried opposite the city in the Valley of the Kings (map right). Tomb scenes illustrate the great wealth of the period, in part derived from control of the rich Nubian gold deposits and mineral sources east of the Nile. The New Kingdom also saw the extension of Egyptian control into the strip of fertile land between the Mediterranean and the Syrian desert. By the reign of Tuthmosis I (1504–1491 BC), Egypt's power reached north from the 3rd Cataract in Nubia to the Euphrates. His grandson Tuthmosis III (1479–1425 BC) fought 17 campaigns in Palestine and Syria, setting up a monument next to his grandfather's at Carchemish on the Euphrates.

New Kingdom Egypt

- New Kingdom temples
- Egyptian fortress or garrison
- core area of Egyptian state
- Nubian gold resources
- trade routes
- ····· limit of Egyptian control in Nubia under Amenophis I (1525–1504 BC)
- —·—·— limit of Egyptian control in Nubia under Tuthmosis III (1479–1425 BC)
- ····· northern limit of campaigns of Tuthmosis I (1504–1491 BC) and Tuthmosis III (1479–1425 BC)
- ····· boundary between Egyptian and Mitannian zones of influence at the end of the reign of Amenophis II (1425–1398 BC)
- ····· boundary between Egyptian and Hittite zones of influence at the end of the reign of Akhenaten, 1336 BC

New Kingdom Rulers

1550–1390 BC	Early Dynasty XVIII	8 rulers from Ahmose to Tuthmosis IV Tuthmosis I 1504–1491 BC
1390–1295 BC	Late Dynasty XVIII (includes Amarna period)	6 rulers from Amenophis III to Horemhab Akhenaten 1352–1336 BC
1295–1187 BC	Dynasty XIX	8 rulers from Ramesses I to Tawosret Ramesses II 1279–1213 BC
1186–1069 BC	Dynasty XX South	10 rulers from Setnakhat to Ramesses XI Ramesses XI 1098–1069 BC

in this region now stabilized, doubtless assisted by the peace made with Mitanni in the reign of Tuthmosis IV (1398–1390 BC). The expansion of the Hittites threatened both Mitanni and Egypt, who sealed their peace by dynastic marriages. This alliance lasted for some 50 years, until Mitanni was defeated and her domains divided between Hatti and Assyria.

Through the tablets in the archive of the royal capital at El-Amarna, details of Egypt's imperial and diplomatic relations can be followed. It has long been assumed that Akhenaten (1352–1336 BC) ignored requests for help from cities in the Levant and lost control of territory there. However, aid was probably sent as the empire was not substantially diminished and indeed even cities near the borders, such as Tyre and Byblos, remained under Egyptian control. There is evidence also that Akhenaten campaigned in the Levant.

The 19th Dynasty rulers, Seti I and Ramesses II tried to expand Egypt's boundaries in Syria, where they came into conflict with the Hittites. In the fifth year of Ramesses II (c. 1275 BC), in a great battle against the Hittites at Kadesh on the Orontes, the outcome was indecisive and the boundaries between the two spheres of influence remained much the same. The subsequent peace treaty, sealed by marriage between the royal houses, was probably prompted by Egypt's problems on its western frontier and for Hatti, the rising power of Assyria. The treaty lasted until the eclipse of the Hittites (see page 42), by which time the west had become a chronic problem for Egypt.

Statue of Ramesses II (1279–1213 BC), wearing the double-crown of Egypt. Although known for his military prowess, in 1269 he made peace with the Hittites, allowing him to concentrate on a vast building programme, including the the vast rock-cut temple at Abu Simbel.

Religion and Society in New Kingdom Egypt 1550–1069 BC

Egypt was at its most wealthy and powerful during the New Kingdom (the 18th to 20th Dynasties) when it controlled an empire reaching from Syria to Nubia. Although in many respects Egyptian society and state remained unchanged and for the majority of the people – the peasants – life continued to be shaped by the eternal cycle of inundation, cultivation, harvest, offerings to the gods and tax collection, expansion to empire profoundly affected Egypt's institutions, economy, society and culture.

For nearly half a millennium Egypt remained a unified state, whatever the vicissitudes of politics or the economy. There are rich documentary sources, and the remains of monuments such as the great temples at Thebes and Abu Simbel, the splendid treasures from the tomb of Tutankhamun and the beautiful sculptures and paintings from Tell el-Amarna give some idea of Egypt's prosperity and the standards of craftsmanship at this time. The wealth from trade, tribute and loot stimulated cultural life, as did closer contact with other countries. The increasing militaristic tone of the inscriptions and iconography is a feature of the New Kingdom period but so too were new fashions in clothing and jewellery and new customs and gods.

As a result of the greater power and resources now at the ruler's disposal, the royal household became much larger and wealthier; from this time the 'great house' (per'ao) – hence 'pharaoh' – became a synonym for 'ruler'. During the reign of Tuthmosis I (1504–1491 BC), the court moved from Thebes to

The antechamber of Tutankhamun's tomb as it was when first opened by the archaeologist Howard Carter in 1922 (below left). Tutankhamun (1336–1327 BC) succeeded to the throne as a boy. During his short reign the worship of the old gods, suppressed by Akhenaten, was restored. His tomb survived largely intact and yielded a fabulous trove of treasures.

Hatshepsut (1479–1458 BC), succeeded to the throne as half-sister and wife of Tuthmosis II. After his short reign, she wielded supreme power during the minority of Tuthmosis III, her step-son. She had statues constructed depicting herself as a male pharaoh and had a lavish funerary temple built at Deir el-Bahri (below right). After her death Tuthmosis III had many of the monuments defaced or destroyed.

Memphis, where a royal palace was built.

At Thebes there were massive building programmes; the provincial shrine of Amun at Karnak became a state temple, continuously enlarged and enhanced. It was the main treasury of the state and here the pharaohs dedicated booty from victorious campaigns. In rock-cut tombs in the Valley of the Kings, a canyon on the west bank opposite Thebes, lavish grave goods were placed with the pharaohs and huge mortuary temples and their complexes were constructed nearby. The queens and princes were buried in neighbouring valleys, as were the nobles, whose tombs were painted with scenes of daily life.

THE AMARNA PERIOD

Amenophis IV (1352–1336 BC) abandoned the worship of Amun, claiming divine guidance from the Aten, or sun disc, and took the name Akhenaten, meaning 'beneficial to the sun disc'. Probably because of opposition to this cult at Thebes, he moved his capital to the newly built city of

The most significant break with Egyptian religious tradition occurred in the reign of Amenophis IV (1352–1336 BC). This pharaoh changed his residence from the temple-city of Amun Re at Thebes and established a new capital at El-Amarna. He promoted the worship of the solar disc, Aten, and forbade the worship of Amun Re and the other gods. He also took the new name of Akhenaten. The religious reform was accompanied by new, more naturalistic styles of art. Here (left) the pharaoh and his family are depicted on a stela with the solar disc of Aten.

Aketaten, 'horizon of the Aten' (El-Amarna), some 300 kilometres north of Thebes. Neither the distinctive naturalistic style of art, nor the revolutionary religious ideas survived the accession of the young Tutankhamun and traditional policies were reasserted during his reign. The most important documentary source for Egypt's relations with its foreign subjects and with neighbouring states, the 'Amarna letters', comes from the site of this short-lived city.

Egypt's foreign territory and political power waned towards the end of the reign of Ramesses II (1279–1213 BC), with battles closer to home, on the Libyan frontier and attacks in the delta by the Sea Peoples. There were also signs of domestic turmoil, with strikes by workers on the royal tombs and the discovery of a plot against the pharaoh's life. After a long period of decline under weak rulers, much of the royal power was usurped by the High Priests of Amun at Thebes and finally, in the reign of Ramesses XI (1098–1069 BC), Egypt was again divided between north and south (see page 76).

THE GODS OF EGYPT

OSIRIS The lord of the gods. He became the first pharaoh, but was killed by his jealous brother Seth. Osiris's wife Isis managed to revive him, but Seth tore the body to shreds. Osiris then became god of the underworld.

HORUS Son of Osiris, and god of the sky. He appears in Egyptian texts with the head of a hawk or in the shape of a hawk. He was the special protector of the pharaohs, who were given the title 'The Living Horus'.

ISIS Wife of Osiris and mother of Horus. She became the principal deity of funeral rites, reflecting her role at her husband Osiris's funeral. She was also represented as the archetypal mother.

ANUBIS Jackal-headed Anubis was the god of embalming and of burial-places. After the death of Osiris, Anubis embalmed his body and created the first mummy. In the underworld, he presided at the weighing of a dead person's heart to determine if their good deeds outweighed the bad.

HATHOR Goddess of women and fertility. She was often represented in the form of a cow.

THOTH The god of wisdom, Thoth bore the head of an ibis. He was traditionally the inventor of writing and in the underworld recorded the names of all the dead whose hearts were weighed.

Osiris

Thoth

Isis

Anubis

Hathor

Horus

Empires and Diplomacy 1600–1200 BC

Between c. 1600 and 1200 BC the major powers of the Near East contended with each other for control of the region by means of war and diplomacy. Much of our knowledge of this period comes from the 'Amarna Letters', a collection of clay tablets containing correspondence between Egyptian rulers of the later 18th Dynasty and their neighbours and vassals. They reveal, amongst other things, the existence of an otherwise little known-power, Mitanni.

The Amarna letters date from the reigns of Amenophis III and IV (Akhenaten) and Tutankhamun (1390–1327 BC). Written in Akkadian, the diplomatic language of the time, in cuneiform script, they include letters from subject princes and cities in the Levant, from Cyprus and from the powers of the region, Assyria, Babylonia, and the Hittites. In the letters we see rulers sending gifts to each other, and sometimes entering into dynastic marriages, such as that between Amenophis III and Taduhepa, daughter of Tushratta of Mitanni, who wrote to his son-in-law: 'I have sent you, as a present to my brother, five chariots and five yoke of horses, and as a present to Taduhepa my sister, I have sent her trinkets of gold, a pair of gold earrings... and goodly stones...' After the death of Amenophis III, Taduhepa was married to his son, Akhenaten.

Little is known about Tushratta's kingdom, Mitanni, before it appears in the historical record in c. 1480 BC, when Parrattarna of Mitanni was in control of Aleppo. By the end of the 15th century BC, Saushtatar had brought Assyria under Mitannian control. Tushratta, who was assassinated in c. 1340 BC, was the last king of an independent Mitanni. His kingdom was destroyed by the Assyrians and Hittites, and a document from the Hittite capital, Hattusa records a treaty in which Tushratta's son Shattiwaza is recognized as the ruler of Mitanni as a Hittite vassal. Archaeology has revealed little of the culture of Mitanni, and its capital, Washshukanni, presumably somewhere in the Khabur valley, has not yet been found.

It was Ashur-uballit I who took advantage of the Hittite attack on Mitanni to turn Assyria from a subject state into one of the leading powers of the area.

The collapse of Mitanni in c. 1340 BC left the Near East divided between rival powers (map above). The fortunes of these competing states were very much determined by the ambitions and qualities of their rulers, and episodes of expansion were generally followed by periods of decline. Finally, in the century after c. 1200 BC, the whole region was transformed by a general crisis which swept away some of the major powers and reduced the others to temporary powerlessness (see page 52).

The city of Ashur (plan left), the centre of the Assyrian state. Building at Ashur dates back to c. 1800 BC, but several major constructions belong to the Middle Assyrian period (c. 1600–1000 BC). Adad-nirari I (1307–1275 BC) and Tukulti-Ninurta I (1244–1208 BC) built their palaces there, although Tukulti-Ninurta also created a short-lived new city across the Tigris. Tiglath-pileser I (1114–1076 BC) records in his annals his restoration of the temples of the city, including the temple of Ishtar.

Bit Akitu

old river bed

temple of Ashur

palace of Tukulti-Ninurta I

temple of Anu-Adad

ziggurat

palace of Adad-Nirari I

Gurgurri Gate (main gate)

residential quarters

temple of Ishtar

temple of Sin-Shamash

Tigris

N

outer wall

west gate

south gate

0   50   100   150   200   250 m

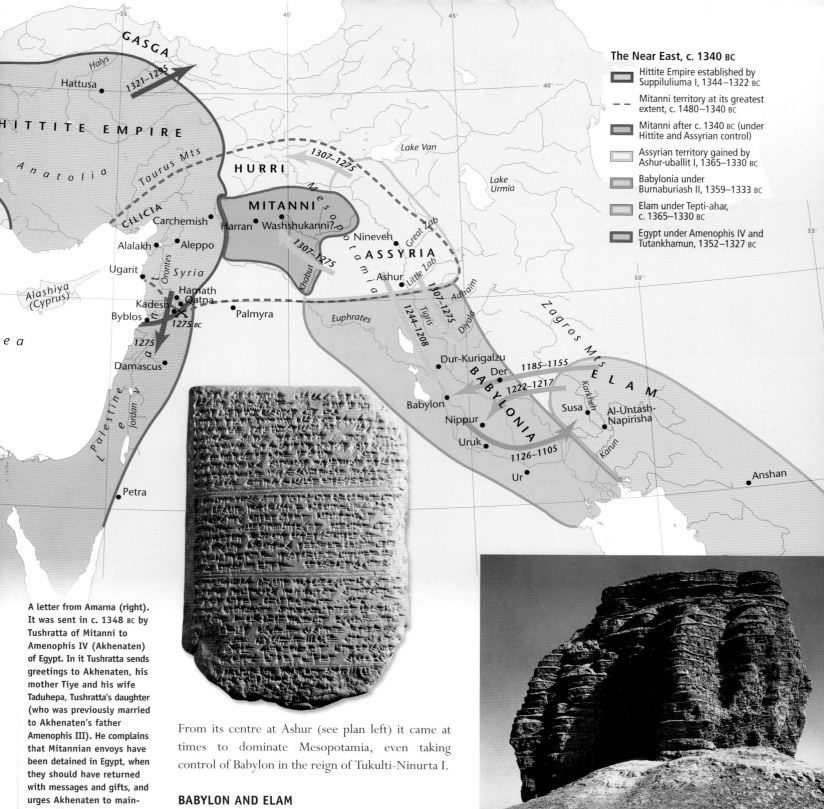

The Near East, c. 1340 BC

- Hittite Empire established by Suppiluliuma I, 1344–1322 BC
- Mitanni territory at its greatest extent, c. 1480–1340 BC
- Mitanni after c. 1340 BC (under Hittite and Assyrian control)
- Assyrian territory gained by Ashur-uballit I, 1365–1330 BC
- Babylonia under Burnaburiash II, 1359–1333 BC
- Elam under Tepti-ahar, c. 1365–1330 BC
- Egypt under Amenophis IV and Tutankhamun, 1352–1327 BC

A letter from Amarna (right). It was sent in c. 1348 BC by Tushratta of Mitanni to Amenophis IV (Akhenaten) of Egypt. In it Tushratta sends greetings to Akhenaten, his mother Tiye and his wife Taduhepa, Tushratta's daughter (who was previously married to Akhenaten's father Amenophis III). He complains that Mitannian envoys have been detained in Egypt, when they should have returned with messages and gifts, and urges Akhenaten to maintain a friendly policy towards Mitanni. The letter is typical of those found at Amarna and reveals the binding together of personal and political matters in the relationships between the rulers of this period.

The ziggurat of Dur-Kurigalzu (far right). The city of Dur-Kurigalzu was built by the Kassite king Kurigalzu I in the early 14th century BC to defend Babylonian access to the Diyala valley from the Assyrians and Elamites. The much-weathered ziggurat still dominates the site, which includes a sanctuary area and, some distance away, the remains of a magnificent palace.

From its centre at Ashur (see plan left) it came at times to dominate Mesopotamia, even taking control of Babylon in the reign of Tukulti-Ninurta I.

BABYLON AND ELAM

After a Hittite raid in c. 1595 BC, Babylon had come under the control of the Kassites, a people of obscure origin, whose rule lasted for 400 years. There is little documentary evidence from this period, although Mesopotamia appears to have been very stable at this time. While some of their customs were distinctive, the Kassites adopted many aspects of Mesopotamian culture and religion. They were noted for their horses and chariots: Burnaburiash II, writing to Akhenaten about problems with Assyria, and requesting help, adds, 'I have sent you… precious stones, 15 pairs of horses, for five wooden chariots…'

To the east of Babylon lay Elam, with its chief cities of Susa and Anshan. In the period after c. 1450 BC Elam became involved in the affairs of Mesopotamia, and when Babylonia came under Assyrian control after 1224 BC the Elamite king Kiden-Hutran (c. 1235–1210 BC) invaded its territory, sacking Der and Nippur. In the following century Shutruk-Nahhunte (1185–1155 BC) captured Babylon itself, installed a puppet ruler, and took the cult-statue of Marduk back with him to Susa. The attack was avenged by the Babylonian king Nebuchadnezzar I (1126–1105 BC), who restored the statue to Babylon, but soon after this records vanish as Babylon and Elam were affected by the general upheaval of the Late Bronze Age (see page 52).

Near Eastern Religions
c. 3000–1000 BC

Religion and ritual played a fundamental role in the lives of Ancient Near Eastern peoples, influencing every aspect of life, from kingship, which was believed to be given by the gods, to the demons responsible for diseases and other misfortunes. To fulfil these varied roles, almost all the religions had extensive pantheons with many deities. Whilst rituals and religious practices can in part be reconstructed, the belief systems which underlay them are less well understood.

The religion of bronze age Mesopotamia and Egypt was polytheistic. Each community had its own gods, with its own local cults and particular cult practices. As cities grew in power, so worship of their gods spread more widely, leading to the development of urban and national pantheons. Amun of Thebes, the city of the 12th and 18th Dynasty Egyptian rulers (some of whose names incorporated that of the god), was identified as the supreme deity of the Egyptian pantheon, but also appears in 5th Dynasty pyramid texts as a primeval deity. In Assyria Ashur, originally the city god of Ashur, became a deity associated with the whole country and an element in the king's name.

Non-human elements were frequently used in depictions of personified deities, as, for instance the rays of light piercing the shoulders of the Mesopotamian sun god Shamash. In Egypt, where animals were particularly associated with gods, a deity might be represented in animal or abstract form, or in

A limestone stele from Ugarit depicting the god Baal with a thunderbolt. Baal was in origin the god of thunder and rain for the people of Canaan. He was also god of fertility – his name means 'lord' and became applied to a wide range of deities throughout the Near East. By the time of the Ugarit tablets, he had become chief of the Canaanite pantheon. His worship was associated with sacred prostitution and was vehemently denounced by Jewish prophets such as Hosea and Jeremiah.

human form with certain animal elements.

In Mesopotamian religious thought the gods shaped the destinies of mankind, individually and collectively. From the evidence of myths and legends, it seems that whilst possessing supernatural powers, the gods were understood to behave like humans, with the same needs and emotions. Beyond the

> *My father gave me heaven, gave me earth,*
> *I, the queen of heaven am I!*
> *Is there one god who can vie with me?*
> *Enlil gave me heaven, gave me earth,*
> *I, the queen of heaven am I!*
> *He has given me lordship,*
> *He has given me queenship,*
> *He has given me battle, given me combat,*
> *And he gave me flood and tempest.*
> *He has placed heaven as a crown,*
> *He has tied the earth as a sandal,*
> *He has fastened the holy me-garment about my body.*
> *Heaven is mine, earth is mine,*
> *In Erech, the Eanna is mine, In Zabalom, the Giguna is mine,*
> *In Nippur, the Duranki is mine, In Ur, the Edilman is mine,*
> *In Girsu, the Eshdam is mine, In Adab, the Eshara is mine,*
> *In Kish, the Hursag Kalama is mine, In Dev, the Amashkuga is mine,*
> *In Akshak, the Anzaka is mine, In Agada, the Ulmash is mine.*
> *Is there one god who can vie with me?*

Self-Laudatory Hymn of
Inanna and Her Omnipotence, 3rd millennium BC

elemental, the attributes and functions of deities could be manifold and complex. Thus Shamash was not only sun god, but also the god of justice and protector of the poor, and was particularly associated with the cities of Sippar and Larsa. The Babylonian goddess of love and war, Ishtar, can be identified with Inanna, a Sumerian fertility goddess, and also with the Canaanite Astarte.

Some of the more distinctive religious practices in this period are to be found in the Levant, although this is one of the least understood parts of the region in the bronze age. While in the rest of the Near East the gods were generally represented more or less anthropomorphically, in Canaanite religion the cult centred on stones, reflecting perhaps a reverence for elemental forces. The Hebrew cult of Yahweh developed into the monotheism of Judaism, where no representation of the god was permitted at all.

CULTS AND FESTIVALS

There were specific cults and festivities for the gods, such as the Akitu or New Year festival at Babylon in honour of Marduk. Animals were sacrificed to secure divine favour and, in Mesopotamia, also for the taking of omens and divination. In certain cultures gods were worshipped in sacred groves or on hilltops, but it was in general temples, the houses of the gods, where they dwelt in the form of divine statues, that were the main religious centres. It was thought that the deity was actually present in its image, so that if carried off, as in times of war, the god remained away until the image was returned. Made of precious materials in special workshops, it was ritually endowed with life. Temple staff, effectively the courtiers of the god, cared for it, dressing and feeding it, singing and playing music.

The general populace seems not to have been permitted entry to the temple, or at any rate not to

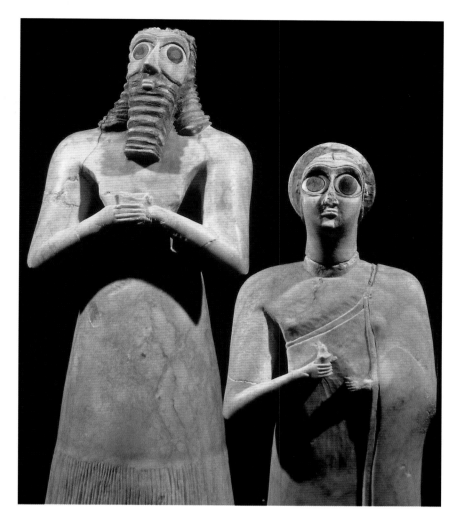

certain parts of it. Doubtless people watched the great processions of the state cults, but it was to their own personal god that they prayed, asking for intercession with other gods or for protection from evil spirits. Prophylactic amulets and clay replicas of gods are widely found, suggesting the importance of the image in personal religion. In Mesopotamia, where the king was the link between the gods and the people they had created to serve them, the ruler was the executive officer of the gods rather than the centre of some cosmic order on earth.

Sumerian sculptures from Tell Asmar, c. 2700–2600 BC. They represent praying male and female statuettes with goblets and may have served as votive offerings left by worshippers.

Shamash, the sun god, (left) and Marduk (right) depicted on a seal from the third millennium BC. Marduk was the creator god of the Babylonians. He is said to have killed the primal dragon goddess Tiamat and created earth and heaven from her corpse. He became the supreme Babylonian deity. Shamash, known to the Sumerians as Utu, was god of the sun and of light, the force which allowed plants to grow and life to flourish. He is the subject of one of the greatest surviving Sumerian hymns 'The Great Hymn to Utu.'

The **Near East** in the
Late Bronze Age c. **1200–1000** BC

The two centuries after 1200 BC saw profound changes in the Near East. Cities and palaces were destroyed throughout the eastern Mediterranean, the Hittite Empire in Anatolia collapsed, and in Mesopotamia the great powers of Assyria and Babylon lost most of their territory. The Iron Age world which emerged from the chaos was characterized by new forms of writing, new materials for tools and weapons, and new forms of social organization. The precise reasons for this collapse remain elusive.

A widespread theory is that the destruction of the eastern Mediterranean cities was the work of raiders known as the 'Sea Peoples', a disparate coalition of islanders and others who moved south east through the Aegean and then to Cyprus and the Levant. The Pharaohs Merneptah and Ramesses III both described battles against people from the sea, and letters written in the city of Ugarit in northern Syria shortly before it was destroyed similarly refer to attacks from the sea. However, while the battles may be a symptom of weakening Egyptian power, they are unlikely to be its sole cause.

Bronze Age political organization was very fragile. Throughout the Near East during this period, power was centralized in the cities and palaces, with kings and their courts controlling almost every aspect of life. The authority of political and military leaders relied on their ability to provide for their subjects: anything that might threaten stability would bring the whole system crashing down. Yet the cities could not control the communities of nomadic pastoralists who lived on the fringes of their territories and who presented a constant threat to the central administrations.

What actually caused the collapse of the political organizations in Greece and Anatolia is not known: earthquakes have been suggested as a problem in Greece, and Egyptian documents indicate that the Hittite Empire suffered a prolonged drought shortly before its collapse. The Mycenaean palaces were destroyed and not reoccupied. In western Anatolia there emerged gradually the new kingdoms of Phrygia, with its centre at Gordion, and Lydia, ruled from Sardis, but little is known of them before the eighth century BC, while further east nomadic groups around Lake Van established the kingdom of Urartu.

THE RISE OF NEW POWERS
The disruption to the supply of bronze that followed the destruction of the Hittite empire must have

had serious consequences for Mesopotamia and Egypt. Deprived of agricultural tools and weapons, the kings were less able to fend off the raids of the nomad pastoralists around their territories. In the 11th century BC these nomads found themselves in possession of the former territories of the Bronze Age's great powers, and began themselves to settle and build cities: in the Levant the Philistines, the Phoenicians and the Israelites became important players in the Iron Age, as did the Medes and the Persians east of the Tigris. The political organization of these new cities was more broadly based than that of their predecessors: soldiers were drawn from a larger proportion of the community, and with military activity came rights as citizens.

Ramesses III described and illustrated his battles against the Sea Peoples on land and sea on the walls of his mortuary temple at Medinet Habu near Thebes (above). Part of the hieroglyphic text is translated on the map (opposite).

A large number of inscribed clay tablets survive from the city of Ugarit, such as this one (left) in the shape of a liver. They cast much light on the religious, social and cultural life of the city, and include letters which provide some evidence of the international situation during the time of Ugarit's prominence, c. 1400–1200 BC.

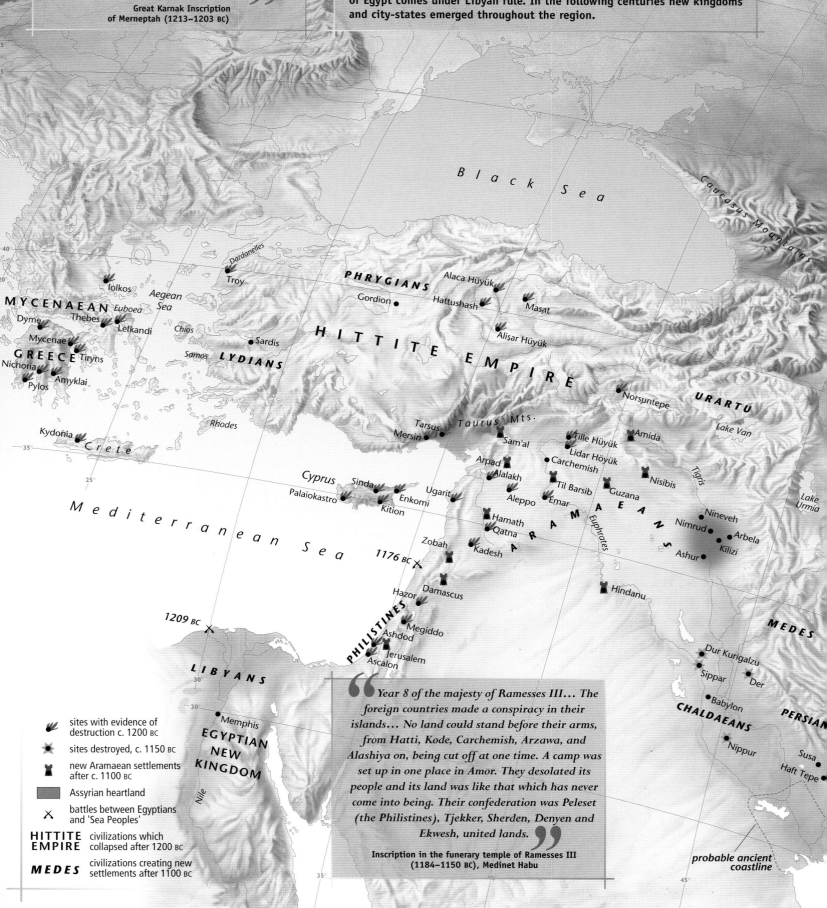

DESTRUCTION AND DISRUPTION IN THE NEAR EAST, 1200–1000 BC

In a brief period around 1200 BC most of the major urban and administrative centres in the eastern Mediterranean were destroyed, and then abandoned. In the next century the territories of Assyria, Babylon and Elam came under attack from Aramaean, Chaldaean and Persian pastoralists, losing control of much of their former possessions. A number of Mesopotamian cities were sacked, and others depopulated. After c. 1050 BC records of events in Assyria and Babylon disappear, evidence of major disruption to the administration of the cities, and at the same time much of Egypt comes under Libyan rule. In the following centuries new kingdoms and city-states emerged throughout the region.

Black Sea

Caucasus Mountains

PHRYGIANS

Dardanelles

Troy

Alaca Hüyük

Gordion

Hattushash

Masat

Aleşar Hüyük

HITTITE EMPIRE

Iolkos

Aegean Sea

MYCENAEAN

Euboea

Dyme

Thebes

Lefkandi

Chios

Sardis

Mycenae

Samos

LYDIANS

GREECE Tiryns

Nichoria

Amyklai

Pylos

Norsuntepe

URARTU

Lake Van

Rhodes

Tarsus *Taurus Mts.*

Amida

Kydonia

Mersin

Sam'al

Tille Hüyük

Crete

Lidar Höyük

Carchemish

Nisibis

Cyprus

Sinda

Arpad

Alalakh

Til Barsib

Guzana

Tigris

Palaiokastro

Enkomi

Ugarit

Aleppo

Emar

Nineveh

Kition

Nimrud

Mediterranean Sea

Hamath

Arbela

Zobah

Qatna

ARAMAEANS

Ashur

Kilizi

1176 BC

Kadesh

Euphrates

Hazor

Damascus

Hindanu

1209 BC

Megiddo

PHILISTINES

Ashdod

Jerusalem

Ascalon

MEDES

Dur Kurigalzu

LIBYANS

Sippar

Der

Memphis

Babylon

EGYPTIAN
NEW
KINGDOM

CHALDAEANS

PERSIANS

Nippur

Susa

Nile

Haft Tepe

*probable ancient
coastline*

Legend

- sites with evidence of destruction c. 1200 BC
- sites destroyed, c. 1150 BC
- new Aramaean settlements after c. 1100 BC
- Assyrian heartland
- ✗ battles between Egyptians and 'Sea Peoples'
- **HITTITE EMPIRE** civilizations which collapsed after 1200 BC
- **MEDES** civilizations creating new settlements after 1100 BC

Post-Indus India
c. 1500–1000 BC

From around 2000 BC, Mohenjo-Daro and other Harappan cities in Baluchistan, Sind and Punjab began to show signs of urban decline. The exact reasons are not known, but a variety of social and environmental explanations have been put forward. These include the drying up of the Indus river system; the breakdown of trading networks with Mesopotamia; and, more controversially, the arrival of Indo-Aryan speaking groups in northwest India.

The post-Harappan period is characterized by a gradual process of 'deurbanization': public architecture and town-planning disappeared; settlements shrank in size and number; long-distance trading networks and specialized craft production declined; whilst material evidence for writing in the form of 'Indus seals' becomes limited, not to appear again until the re-emergence of urbanism well over a thousand years later. At the same time there was a marked redistribution of population towards the upper Gangetic valley region.

ECONOMIC AND CULTURAL DECLINE

The transformation of Harappan culture between 2000 and 1000 BC took a variety of forms in different parts of the Harappan orbit. In the western Punjab, there was a dramatic drop in the number of urban centres, accompanied by the appearance of less sophisticated cultures associated with the 'Cemetery H' phase at Harappa and related sites. In Saurashtra, at sites such as Lothal and Dholavira, the economic infrastructure based on trade and craft production seems to have collapsed. There was a marked reversion to a hunter-gatherer, semi-nomadic existence, and to material forms associated with pre-urban Chalcolithic cultures which had existed alongside the Harappan civilization since at least the third millennium BC. By 1200 BC, many sites in Sindh, Cholistan, Baluchistan and Saurashtra show evidence for complete abandonment. Some scholars attribute this to further climatic and tectonic instability which led to the drying up of the Ghaggar Hakra river.

A somewhat different pattern of urban decline occurred in east Punjab, Haryana and the upper-Ganga Yamuna Doab, which lies at the borders of Harappan influence. There is a massive increase in the number of settlements during the post-Harappan period, which suggests a large-scale reorientation of power towards the eastern regions. The situation in areas beyond the Harappan orbit is quite different again. At sites such as Atranjikhara and Lal Qila in the central Doab, or Chirand in the lower Gangetic valley, cultural development from earlier

Finds of copper artefacts
- ▲ sites of copper hoards
- ● one or two copper artefacts
- △ copper hoards with indefinite location

These copper pieces (below right) came from a hoard of 424 objects found at Gungeria, Madhya Pradesh. This is the largest of over 80 hoards the distribution of which extends from the upper Gangetic valley to Tamil Nadu in the south, and including Haryana, Malwa, and the Deccan. Many of the hoards are associated with a type of pottery known as Ochre Coloured Pottery, which has been linked to the indigenous Chalcolithic cultures of the Ganga valley. This evidence, coupled with similarities to copper objects from Mature Harappan contexts, suggests a chronological range of third to second millennium BC. An independent copper metallurgy tradition dateable to the late fourth millennium BC has been identified at Chalcolithic sites such as Ganeswar in northwest Rajasthan, which appear to have been the major suppliers of copper objects to nearby Harappan cities.

The pattern of urban decline during the second millennium BC extends from the Indus heartland in the northwest to the borders of Harappan influence in the upper Ganga-Yamuna Doab. Beyond this to the east lies an area whose rich agricultural and copper metallurgy traditions were laid down during the earlier Chalcolithic context and continued to flourish independently from the Harappan culture during the post-urban period (maps left and right).

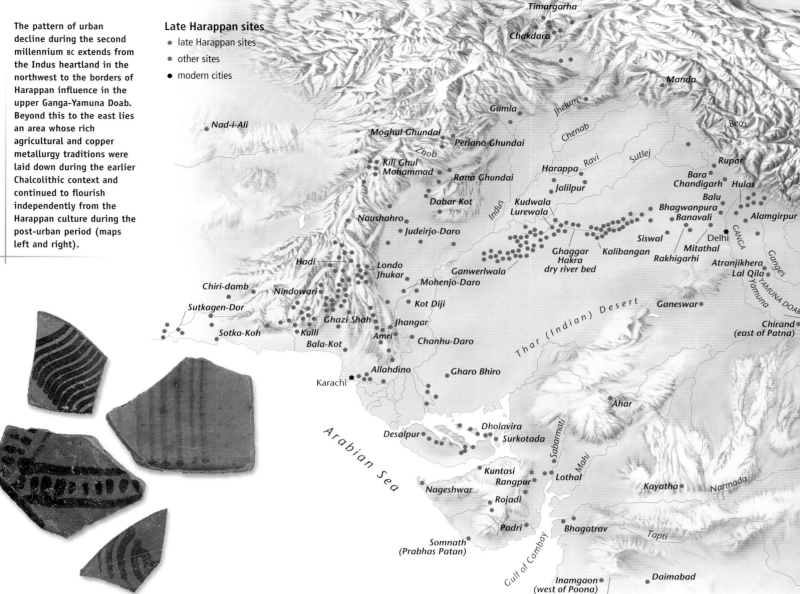

Late Harappan sites

- late Harappan sites
- other sites
- modern cities

Timargarha

Chakdara

Manda

Gumla

Jhelum

Beas

Nad-i-Ali

Moghul Ghundai

Periano Ghundai

Chenab

Zhob

Kili Ghul Mohammad

Rana Ghundai

Harappa

Ravi

Sutlej

Rupar

Bara Chandigarh

Hulas

Jalilpur

Dabar Kot

Kudwala Lurewala

Indus

Balu

Bhagwanpura

Banavali

Alamgirpur

Naushahro

Judeirjo-Daro

Siswal

Delhi

GANGA

Ghaggar Hakra dry river bed

Kalibangan

Mitathal

Rakhigarhi

Atranjikhera

Lal Qila

Ganges

Hadi

Londo Jhukar

Ganwerlwala

Mohenjo-Daro

YAMUNA DOAB

Yamuna

Chiri-damb

Nindowari

Kot Diji

T h a r (I n d i a n) D e s e r t

Ganeswar

Chirand (east of Patna)

Sutkagen-Dor

Ghazi Shah

Kulli

Jhangar

Amri

Chanhu-Daro

Sotka-Koh

Bala-Kot

Allahdino

Gharo Bhiro

Karachi

Ahar

A r a b i a n   S e a

Desalpur

Dholavira

Surkotada

Sabarmati

Mahi

Kuntasi Rangpur

Lothal

Kayatha

Narmada

Nageshwar

Rojadi

Padri

Bhagatrav

Tapti

Gulf of Cambay

Somnath (Prabhas Patan)

Inamgaon (west of Poona)

Daimabad

This finely polished pottery (above), decorated with black geometric designs and known as Painted Grey Ware (PGW), first appears in c. 1100 BC and most frequently comes in the form of deep bowls, dishes and basins. Its distribution extends from the old bed of the river Ghaggar to the Ganga-Yamuna Doab. Its similarity to earlier Painted Red and Black wares found at Chalcolithic sites, helps to challenge theories linking PGW with Indo-Aryan migrations. PGW is most commonly presented as the marker for the Indian Iron Age. Yet it is not until c. 600 BC that iron objects are found in significant numbers, in association with the 'second urbanization' of the early historic period.

Neolithic-Chalcolithic traditions was relatively uninterrupted. The same applies to sites beyond the Harappan influence, such as Kayatha in central India, or Inamgoan in the Deccan, which appear to have independently reached a level of 'incipient agriculture' based on the cultivation of a wide range of crops including rice, wheat, barley, sesame, gram and cotton, and the production and trade of copper objects. This uneven distribution of cultural development has certainly challenged the picture of a homogenous 'dark age' following the downfall of the Harappan civilization, and has forced a reappraisal of the theory that it was only with the introduction of iron technology and wet-rice cultivation that an urban civilization centred upon the Gangetic valley was able to re-emerge in the first half of the first millennium BC.

THE ARYAN MIGRATION THEORY

The theory that at some time between 2000 and 1000 BC, Indo-Aryan-speaking groups entered northwest India in various waves, leading to the gradual assimilation of their language and cultural practices by pre-existing populations, has been hotly debated in recent years. The original 'proof' for this theory was provided by 18th-century comparative linguistics which discovered the link between Sanskrit and other Indo-European languages, and references in the *Rig Veda* to the Aryas, a cultural elite which is described as a frequent participant in migrations and battles. Recently, the Aryan migration theory has been challenged on both archaeological and political grounds. By some, it is rejected as the product of Colonial ideology. Such scholars prefer to see the Aryans as indigenous to the Indus plain. There is also little archaeological evidence to support the idea of an Aryan identity linked on ethnic grounds alone. More generally, theories which link the appearance of iron and Painted Grey Ware in c. 1100 BC with the movement of Indo-Aryan-speaking groups into the Gangetic valley are increasingly regarded as products of outdated 'diffusionist' models which over-emphasized the correlation between material 'cultures' and 'peoples'. Although the Aryas of the *Rig Veda* have not been identified in the archaeological record, the linguistic evidence for the assimilation of Indo-Aryan languages throughout north India cannot be denied. Those who stress the indigenous identity of the Aryans theorize that the Harappans spoke an Indo-Aryan language. These claims, however, remain unproven pending the decipherment of the Harappan script.

Shang China
c.**1500–1050** BC

The Shang were a dynasty of kings who ruled in the middle valley of the Yellow River and are known to later generations of Chinese from accounts in some of the earliest historical texts. Shang China was distinguished from the preceding Neolithic period by the manufacture of bronze, writing, the domestication of the horse, class stratification, and a stable politico-religious hierarchy administering territory from a cult centre.

Bronze figure of a man on a high base, from Sanxingdui (below). The discovery of two sacrificial pits at Sanxingdui with one complete figure and many masks in bronze as well as elephant tusks, jades and gold, was the single most remarkable archaeological find of the 1980s in China.

The Shang period is unified to some extent by language, material culture and religious practice. Their material culture centred above all on bronze, but jade, ivory, lacquer and silk were also employed in temples, palaces and tombs. Early texts dealing with the Shang, especially the history written by Sima Qian in the second century BC, the *Shi Ji*, (*The Records of the Historian*), have been corroborated by finds of oracle bones containing king lists.

Although the Shang no doubt worshipped many spirits and deities, their predominant concern was reverence or respect for their ancestors. The wealth and attention paid to these rites is evident from the very fine cast-bronze vessels used for the offerings. Because the ancient Chinese seem to have believed that the dead themselves would continue to make such offerings, these bronze vessels were also buried in tombs.

The high quality bronze casting and jade carving of the period and the large numbers of surviving items suggest that the Shang had highly developed methods of production and a very organized society. Massed, organized labour would also have been needed to dig the tombs and to construct the massive rammed-earth city walls which survive in part to this day.

Early bronze age sites include those of the pre-Shang period of Yanshi Erlitou (c.1700–1600 BC), and a later large Shang site, at modern Zhengzhou. This city had a massive city wall, specialized workshops and buildings of differing standing. The influence of the Shang Dynasty in the Erligang period, c. 1600–1400 BC, was obviously considerable as vessels of this date in metropolitan style are found at widely separate sites in Shaanxi, Anhui, Hubei and Henan provinces.

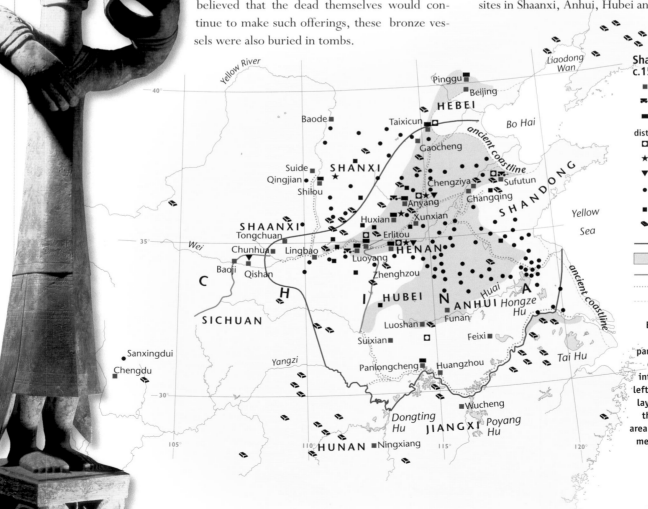

Shang China, c.1500–1050 BC

- ■ Shang sites
- ⚞ horse/wagon burial
- ▪ other rich burials

distribution of:
- ◻ lacquerwork
- ★ goldwork
- ▼ oracle bones
- • places mentioned in oracle bones
- ■ tin sources
- ⬱ copper sources

— Shang cultural area
▨ fertile area
— routeway
······ waterway
····· ancient river course

By c. 1800 BC prosperous farming communities in parts of northern and eastern China had developed into the Shang state (map left). The Shang heartlands lay at the western edge of the north China plain, an area both fertile and rich in metal deposits. Successive Shang capitals were at Erlitou, Zhengzhou and (from the 14th to 11th centuries) at Anyang.

The Shang had several capitals during their dynastic rule as their control over territory gradually waned. Their last major centre was at Anyang, also known as Yinxu. The Anyang site, excavated last century, revealed large palace buildings, workshops, burials both of kings and of nobles, and deposits, such as large finds of inscribed oracle bones. Among the most significant discoveries is the tomb of Fu Hao, consort of the Shang king Wu Ding (d. c.1200 BC), the only royal Shang tomb to have been found intact. When excavated, it held an extraordinary number of treasures including over 250 ceremonial bronzes and more than 750 jades.

NON-SHANG CULTURES IN CHINA

A number of quite separate peoples with their own distinctive cultures occupied Anhui, Hubei, Jiangxi, Hunan, Sichuan and areas of Hebei and Shanxi provinces. These peoples used Shang techniques in bronze casting but also developed their own religious practices, evident from the types of bronzes and jades employed and in their decoration. Contact with the Shang brought exotic motifs into bronze decoration and stimulated the use of new objects such as mirrors and animal-headed knives.

One of these peoples was only discovered in 1986 at Sanxingdui in Sichuan, where two large pits contained bronzes in the shapes of human heads, unknown in metropolitan Shang China, fragments of gold, jades and a large number of elephant tusks. Many of the bronzes were of a quality indicating great technical skill and that their makers worked within a complex society. Yet nothing is known about these peoples who lived around the latter part of the second millennium BC. The surviving Shang records make no mention of Sanxingdui and the peoples of Sanxingdui left no writing behind them, but they were obviously only one of several flourishing centres of power at that time. It was another of these outlying neighbours who overcame the Shang kings at Anyang and established a new dynasty called Zhou (see page 96).

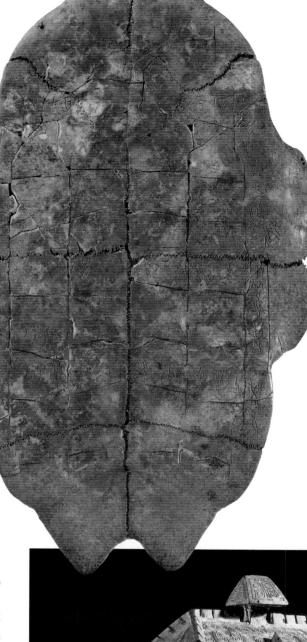

An inscribed oracle bone (left). Divination was one of the primary functions of the Shang ruling house and its nobles, officials and servants. Such texts were written in an early form of Chinese characters and record communications with the ancestors and spirits. The divinations were made by first applying hot brands to depressions in the bones or plastrons and interpreting the cracks. These inscriptions refer to various sacrifices to the ancestors and date to the period of the king Wu Ding c. 1200 BC.

This bronze ritual wine vessel (below) is called a *fangyi*. This shape occurs in the late Shang period and is stylistically similar to the vessels found in the tomb of Fu Hao. Such covered containers are rectangular versions of ceramic-covered jars. Most of the bronze ritual vessel shapes were ultimately based on ceramic forms, but by making some bronzes with flat sides, the casters created immediately visible distinctions between the two. The features of *taotie* faces in the four panels are separated by a background of spirals known as *leiwen*.

Age of Ideas
c. 1000–300 BC

The world that emerged from the end of the Bronze Age in Eurasia was very different from what had gone before. A series of imperial powers, Assyria, Babylon and Achaemenid Persia, dominated Mesopotamia and the surrounding areas, but further west and east the city-state was the dominant political form. Communities of Italians, Etruscans, Phoenicians and Greeks grew up around the Mediterranean Sea, while in India urban centres appeared along the eastern Ganges. In China the Bronze Age lasted longer, but the single central power there was eventually replaced by a large number of warring statelets.

The cities of this new age were no longer the ceremonial centres which had characterized Bronze Age civilization, but political centres, ruled not by an all-powerful king, but by aristocracies, oligarchies and democracies. The new social conditions made possible the development of new ideas, and this period saw the appearance of philosophers and religious thinkers whose influence continues until today: in China Confucius and Laozi, the founder of Daoism, in India Mahavira and Gautama Siddharta, the founders of Jainism and Buddhism, and in Greece Socrates, Plato and Aristotle. At the same time, at the edges of the Babylonian and Persian Empires, many of the texts were composed that make up the Hebrew Bible.

Spread of City-States in the Mediterranean, c. 800–500 BC

The centuries following the end of the Bronze Age systems in the Aegean and Anatolia saw the re-emergence of cities in the eastern Mediterranean, and the appearance of many new settlements around the coasts of the western Mediterranean and the Black Sea. The driving forces behind these developments were the Phoenicians and the Greeks.

There is evidence of Phoenician presence through much of the eastern Mediterranean from the tenth century BC, and a Phoenician community was established at Citium in Cyprus by the end of the ninth century. Not long after that, Phoenician presence in the west increased markedly. Settlements were set up to facilitate trade, with Phoenicia noted for its production of worked metal, fabrics and dyes. These early settlements were often on offshore islands and promontories, but by the end of the eighth century BC some of these settlements had been transformed into more substantial city-states, farming the territory around them. In southern Spain and in Sardinia Phoenician settlements were set up from the start as agricultural communities. The largest and most important Phoenician city after Tyre itself was Carthage, which came to dominate the other settlements in the western Mediterranean, and remained powerful long after the cities of Phoenicia had come under the domination of larger empires.

THE GREEKS OVERSEAS

The earliest Greek descriptions of the wider world, such as those in Homer's *Odyssey*, composed soon after 700 BC, depict a Mediterranean peopled by Phoenicians, but indicate that Greeks, too, were travelling overseas. The earliest Greek settlers in the west were from the island of Euboea, and they occupied the island of Pithecusae off the coast of Italy, a site they shared with Phoenicians, presumably engaged in trading activities with Etruscans or others on the Italian mainland. Although the search for goods may have been the initial stimulus for the Greek exploration of the Mediterranean, from quite early on expeditions went out looking for land to settle on and farm. Later such expeditions might be dispatched by mother cities needing to export surplus population, but often they were less formally organized, and indeed would have been indistinguishable from pirates, as parties of young men looked for land or goods to seize.

The growing networks of communication and exchange that developed across the Mediterranean

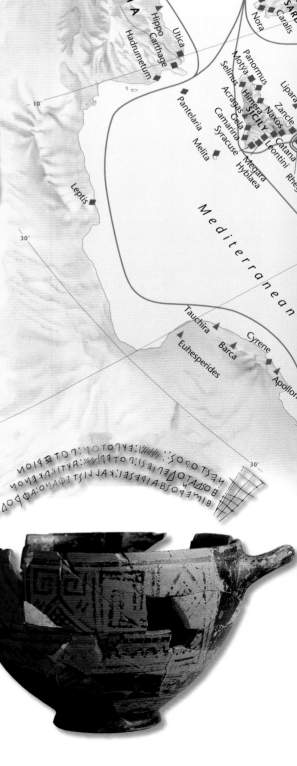

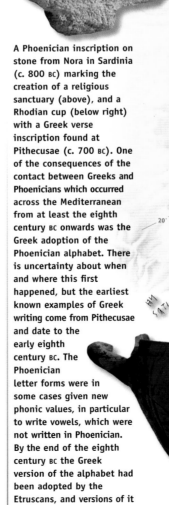

A Phoenician inscription on stone from Nora in Sardinia (c. 800 BC) marking the creation of a religious sanctuary (above), and a Rhodian cup (below right) with a Greek verse inscription found at Pithecusae (c. 700 BC). One of the consequences of the contact between Greeks and Phoenicians which occurred across the Mediterranean from at least the eighth century BC onwards was the Greek adoption of the Phoenician alphabet. There is uncertainty about when and where this first happened, but the earliest known examples of Greek writing come from Pithecusae and date to the early eighth century BC. The Phoenician letter forms were in some cases given new phonic values, in particular to write vowels, which were not written in Phoenician. By the end of the eighth century BC the Greek version of the alphabet had been adopted by the Etruscans, and versions of it spread through Italy and the Greek world.

world had an effect on those who remained at home. Access to prestige goods and to new ideas stimulated social and political developments in the Greek heartland, while in central Italy urbanization in Etruria and at Rome was related to increasing access to Greek and Phoenician goods.

While there was much cultural interchange between the new settlers and the indigenous populations, including intermarriage and shared recognition of some religious sites, nevertheless new settlements around the Mediterranean were not made without difficulty. There is evidence that Greeks settling in North Africa in particular faced prolonged resistance from the Libyans already settled there. In Egypt Greeks and Carians were employed as mercenaries by the 26th Dynasty pharaohs, and then settled in border garrison communities, while a trading centre was established at Naucratis, which became the sole point of access for Greeks coming to Egypt. Ultimately it was the large numbers of people who moved around the Mediterranean during this period, as much as any geographical unity, that laid the foundation for the Mediterranean-wide territorial domination that the Romans were able eventually to establish.

MEDITERRANEAN SETTLEMENTS IN C. 500 BC

Increasing communication through the Mediterranean world from the tenth century BC onwards was a stimulus for the development of city-states in Greece and Italy, and the spread of Greek and Phoenician settlements as far west as the Pillars of Heracles (the Strait of Gibraltar). Navigation across the Mediterranean was managed without charts or instruments, and sailors relied on astronomy, and on detailed knowledge of the coastlines around ports. Many of the city-states that grew up around the Mediterranean may have started as temporary settlements established to aid exchange, or on land gifted to mercenaries. Over time Greek cities would come to prefer more glorious versions of their own pasts, and so romanticized foundation-legends developed.

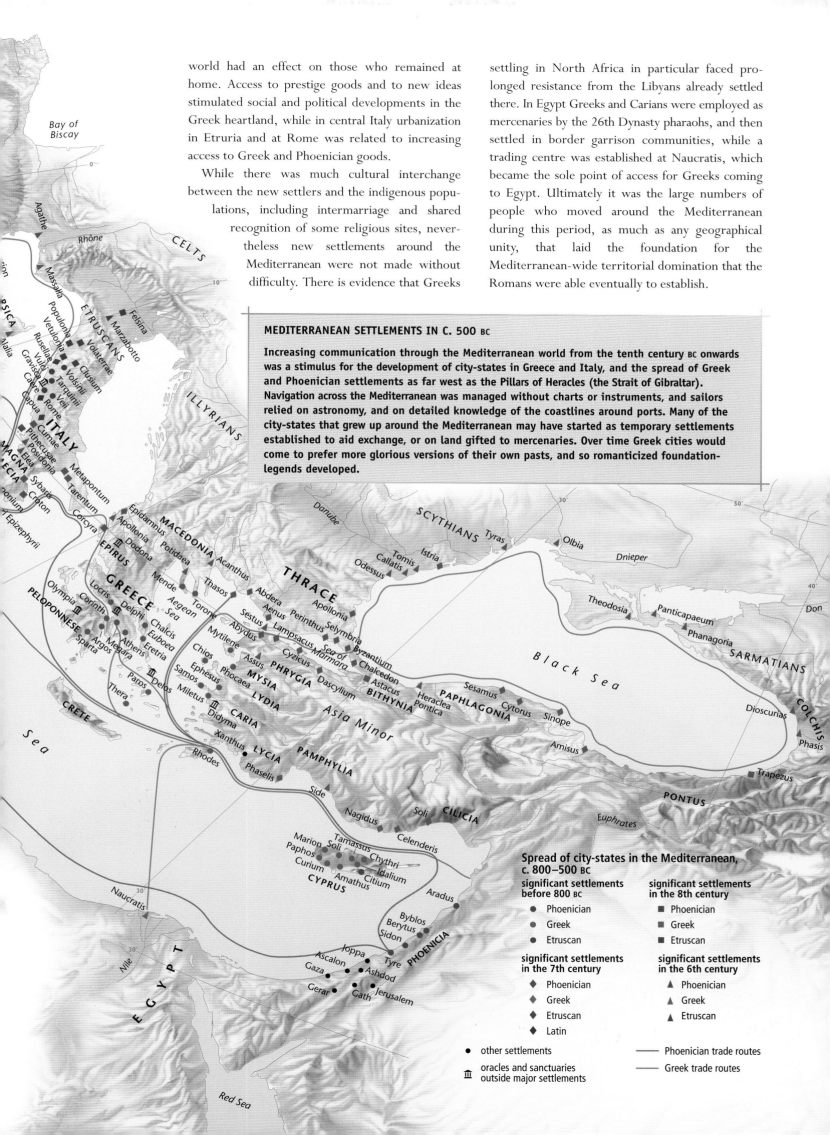

Spread of city-states in the Mediterranean, c. 800–500 BC

significant settlements before 800 BC	significant settlements in the 8th century
● Phoenician	■ Phoenician
● Greek	■ Greek
● Etruscan	■ Etruscan

significant settlements in the 7th century	significant settlements in the 6th century
◆ Phoenician	▲ Phoenician
◆ Greek	▲ Greek
◆ Etruscan	▲ Etruscan
◆ Latin	

● other settlements

🏛 oracles and sanctuaries outside major settlements

— Phoenician trade routes
— Greek trade routes

The **Etruscans**
c. **900–400** BC

The Etruscans inhabited the area of central Italy between the valleys of the Tiber and the Arno. Etruscan city-states emerged in the eighth century BC and, until the rise of Rome in the fourth century, were the most important communities in the Italian peninsula. No Etruscan literature has survived, and the Etruscan language is only partially understood. Roman writers produced distorted accounts of the Etruscan past and the result is that the Etruscans have remained mysterious and misunderstood.

Although there were probably village settlements in Etruria in the Late Bronze Age, led by local chieftains and possibly grouped together under paramount chiefs, it was the period after c. 900 BC that saw the emergence of the communities that were to become the Etruscan cities. Etruria contained twelve or more independent city-states and in the eighth to the sixth centuries BC groups of Etruscans settled further afield, in the Po valley to the north, Campania to the southeast and even Corsica in the west. In the seventh and sixth centuries BC the populations of the larger towns rose to around 35,000, and they were linked together by a developed road system.

Contact with Greeks and Phoenicians had a profound effect on Etruscan culture and society in this period. Greek traders and settlers, drawn in part by the rich deposits of metal ores in Northern Etruria, brought with them ideas which were rapidly absorbed into Etruscan culture: a form of the Greek alphabet was adopted for writing Etruscan, Etruscan craftsmen were influenced by Greek style, and images and stories from Greek myth became part of Etruscan tradition. This cultural contact is most apparent in the religious sanctuaries at the chief ports of southern Etruria such as Pyrgi, where there was a temple of the goddess Uni, who was identified with the Phoenician Astarte and the Greek Hera.

THE ETRUSCANS AND THE GREEKS

The Greeks called the Etruscans 'Tyrrhenian', and it seems clear that, at least until the fifth century BC, Etruscan control of the Tyrrhenian Sea was a cause of friction between them, in particular in the period after c. 550 BC when large numbers of Greek settlers, who had been driven from the East Aegean

A bronze model of a sheep's liver from Piacenza (below). The liver, the largest organ in the body, and the one containing the most blood, was seen to be the most important for divination throughout the ancient Mediterranean and the Near East. Domestic animals, and in particular sheep, were sacrificed, and their entrails examined, before any major undertaking. Models like this were probably used either as teaching aids or as practical guides for diviners who would 'read' the livers of the victims in order to learn the wishes of the gods. The model's surface is divided into 42 areas, which contain the names of Etruscan deities, and represents the heavens in microcosm.

by the growth of Persian power, came west in search of new land. The Greek historian Herodotus describes a battle between Greeks from Phocaea in Asia Minor who had attempted to settle in Alalia in Corsica and combined Etruscan and Carthaginian fleets, who drove them away. However, 70 years later, in 474 BC, the Etruscans were defeated in their turn by the combined navies of the Greek cities of Cumae in Campania and Syracuse in Sicily.

Powerful Etruscan 'warlords' left their mark on the city of Rome, just across the Tiber. Roman traditions held that in the sixth century BC two of its kings had been Etruscans, and Etruscan inscriptions have been found in the city, although there is no evidence to support the idea of an Etruscan conquest of Rome. Early in the fourth century BC, a little more than a century after the supposed expulsion of the Etruscan kings from Rome, Roman armies moved north across the Tiber and captured the southern Etruscan city of Veii, and soon after they settled colonists on the captured territory. It marked the beginning of the decline of Etruscan Italy, and of the rise of Rome.

Wall painting from the Tomb of the Leopards at Tarquinia (above). The most impressive monuments left by the Etruscans are the vast cemeteries built outside the cities. These were dominated by grand burials and groups of burials, at first somewhat haphazardly laid out, but increasingly organized into 'cities of the dead' (the Greek term is necropolis). Tombs were cut out of the soft tufo rock, either into the side of cliffs or like houses along streets. The interiors too were carved and painted to look like the interiors of houses or vast tents, open at the sides to the country around. Richer families would be buried and it later became common for tombs to house even larger groups. The dead were placed in sarcophagi and lined up on long benches, rather as if sharing a meal. Banquets, games, hunting and dancing were common subjects for tomb paintings.

An Etruscan vase with alphabet and syllabary (left). The Etruscan language, like modern Finnish and Basque, is not Indo-European, and is unrelated to other Mediterranean languages. The Etruscans adopted a version of the Greek alphabet, which they normally wrote from right to left, not long after the Greeks themselves had started to use it, in the eighth century BC. Many thousands of Etruscan texts survive, nearly all of them only a few words long, and mostly consisting of names. Outside Etruria they have been found in Rome and Pompeii, and even on the island of Lemnos in the northeast Aegean. The longest surviving text, a ritual calendar, was written on linen which was later used to bind up an Egyptian mummy. The existence of bilingual inscriptions in Etruscan and Latin or Phoenician has made it possible to establish the general meaning of most Etruscan texts, but since no substantial examples of continuous prose survive, not all aspects of the language are fully understood.

Rome and Italy
c. 800–264 BC

Roman traditions dated the foundation of Rome to somewhere between 754 and 728 BC. They also told of the reigns of seven kings, beginning with Romulus, the founder of the city, and ending with the Etruscan Tarquinius Superbus, who was expelled and a republic created. There is little truth in these stories, but the evidence of archaeology can reveal something of the earliest history of Rome. The accounts of later historians tell how the Romans dominated first Italy, and then the whole Mediterranean world.

Although Rome was still only a village at the time when the major urban centres of South Etruria developed in the eighth and seventh centuries BC, its location at the lowest crossing point of the River Tiber on the edge of Etruria brought the community into contact with the wider Mediterranean world. Greek pottery has been found in Rome from the eighth century BC, and Phoenician from the seventh. Signs of urbanization, with the building of stone houses in place of huts, and the erection of a temple in the Greek style in the Forum Boarium, are visible from around 600 BC, and are clearly influenced by developments in Etruria. The population of other settlements in Latium, such as Fidenae, increased at this time, and the prosperity that this suggests appears to have continued into the fifth century BC. By the end of the fifth century Rome was a significant city, and in c. 396 BC the Romans sacked the southern Etruscan city of Veii, redistributing much of its territory to Roman citizens. Soon after this Rome itself was sacked by Celts from northern Italy, but this does not appear to have had a long-term effect on the growth of Roman power.

The century and a half before 366 BC was known in later traditions as the time of 'the Conflict of the Orders', and characterized as a period of struggle between rich and poor or between patricians and plebeians over issues of debt and of access to political office. Identifying any reliable elements in these stories is difficult, but the outlines of the development of the Roman 'constitution' can be perceived. Before the middle of the fifth century BC Rome, like some other Italian communities, appears to have been ruled by warlords, not necessarily Romans themselves, whose power was based largely on their personal authority, and their ability to defend the community against hostile neighbours. Their position was perhaps similar to that of the Greek tyrants (see page 68). The

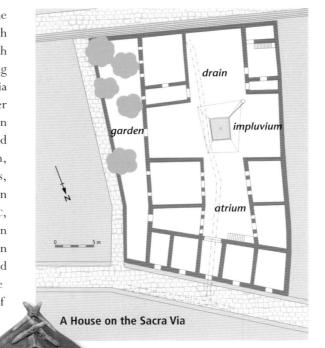

A House on the Sacra Via

publication of a law code known as the Twelve Tables (c. 450 BC) marked a shift towards more formal political institutions in Rome, and by this time Rome was governed by elected magistrates. From 366 BC the chief magistrates and military leaders of Rome were the two consuls, elected annually.

The second half of the fourth century BC saw Roman power spreading through Italy. The main opposition to Roman expansion came from the Samnites, who occupied territory on either side of the Apennines to the southeast of Rome and Latium. However, there were communities which supported the Romans in the wars, most notably many of the Greek cities of southern Italy. When the Romans were victorious over other Italian communities they continued the practice first employed at Veii of taking land from the defeated enemy and redistributing it to Roman citizens, either by setting up semi-autonomous colonies, or as individual allotments. Smaller garrison colonies were also set

A burial urn in the form of a hut (c. 800 BC), from the Forum at Rome (below left). Hut urns like this held the ashes of the dead, and were buried with other grave goods. They are models of the kind of building in which the dead person had lived, which would have been made from wood or reeds, covered with mud or clay. On the Palatine Hill in Rome foundations have been found of this kind of oval hut, measuring up to 4.9 x 3.6 metres. These would have been the typical form of housing in Rome and other Latin settlements until near the end of the seventh century BC, when much larger atrium-houses started to appear, such as the sixth-century houses on the Sacra Via in Rome (plan left). The appearance of these grand houses, presumably the homes of leading families in Rome, marks the increasing urbanization of the community.

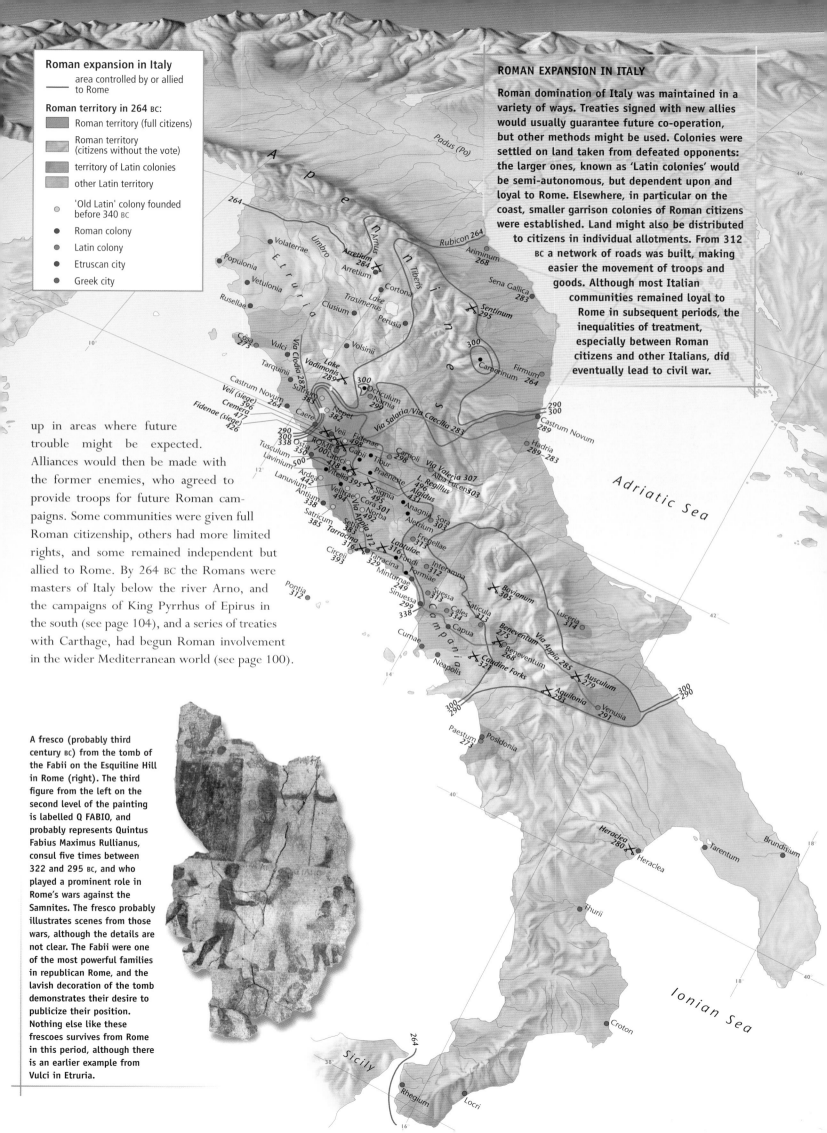

Roman expansion in Italy

— area controlled by or allied to Rome

Roman territory in 264 BC:

- Roman territory (full citizens)
- Roman territory (citizens without the vote)
- territory of Latin colonies
- other Latin territory

- ○ 'Old Latin' colony founded before 340 BC
- ● Roman colony
- ● Latin colony
- ● Etruscan city
- ● Greek city

ROMAN EXPANSION IN ITALY

Roman domination of Italy was maintained in a variety of ways. Treaties signed with new allies would usually guarantee future co-operation, but other methods might be used. Colonies were settled on land taken from defeated opponents: the larger ones, known as 'Latin colonies' would be semi-autonomous, but dependent upon and loyal to Rome. Elsewhere, in particular on the coast, smaller garrison colonies of Roman citizens were established. Land might also be distributed to citizens in individual allotments. From 312 BC a network of roads was built, making easier the movement of troops and goods. Although most Italian communities remained loyal to Rome in subsequent periods, the inequalities of treatment, especially between Roman citizens and other Italians, did eventually lead to civil war.

up in areas where future trouble might be expected. Alliances would then be made with the former enemies, who agreed to provide troops for future Roman campaigns. Some communities were given full Roman citizenship, others had more limited rights, and some remained independent but allied to Rome. By 264 BC the Romans were masters of Italy below the river Arno, and the campaigns of King Pyrrhus of Epirus in the south (see page 104), and a series of treaties with Carthage, had begun Roman involvement in the wider Mediterranean world (see page 100).

A fresco (probably third century BC) from the tomb of the Fabii on the Esquiline Hill in Rome (right). The third figure from the left on the second level of the painting is labelled Q FABIO, and probably represents Quintus Fabius Maximus Rullianus, consul five times between 322 and 295 BC, and who played a prominent role in Rome's wars against the Samnites. The fresco probably illustrates scenes from those wars, although the details are not clear. The Fabii were one of the most powerful families in republican Rome, and the lavish decoration of the tomb demonstrates their desire to publicize their position. Nothing else like these frescoes survives from Rome in this period, although there is an earlier example from Vulci in Etruria.

Sicily

C. 750–330 BC

Sicily, lying between Italy and North Africa, and between the eastern and western ends of the Mediterranean, was always a place of contact and of conflict between different cultures. Greeks began to settle on the east coast of Sicily during the last third of the eighth century BC, and Phoenician settlement in the west began soon after. Relations between these immigrants and the existing population were not always easy.

S yracuse, one of the earliest Greek settlements, was founded after the previous inhabitants had either been driven away or enslaved, but Megara, founded not long afterwards, appears to have been built on land given by a native ruler. Relations between Greek cities were also far from easy, and in the four centuries that followed the first settlements, Greek communities frequently found themselves allied with native Sicilians and Phoenicians against other Greeks.

Syracuse was always the most powerful of the Greek cities and much of the history of Sicily in this period is taken up with the attempts of Syracusan leaders to create larger empires. Little is known of events in the island before 500 BC, but in the early fifth century BC Gelon became tyrant, first of Gela, and then of Syracuse, allying himself with Theron, tyrant of Acragas, and making his brother Hieron tyrant of Gela. Gelon conquered Camarina, Megara and Euboea, transferring large parts of their populations to Syracuse. Gelon's success provoked Carthage into sending an army to Sicily in support of the Phoenician cities there. Gelon's victory over the Carthaginians at Himera in 480 BC left Syracuse the dominant power in the island, a position it retained under Hieron, who succeeded Gelon in 478 BC.

SICILY, ATHENS AND CARTHAGE

Neither the tyrants nor the unity of the Greek cities lasted long, and the second half of the fifth century BC saw two expeditions sent from Athens to support its allies, in particular Segesta and Leontini, against Syracuse. Soon after the second Athenian expedition was wiped out by the Syracusans, war broke out again with Carthage. Dionysius I (406–366 BC) was appointed sole commander of Syracuse in this crisis and soon made himself tyrant. In a reign of 40 years, despite setbacks, he defeated the Carthaginians and brought most of Sicily under his control, styling himself Archon (ruler) of Sicily, and even campaigned in North Africa and southern Italy. His son, Dionysius II, reigned for 12 years after his death before retiring in favour of the Corinthian, Timoleon. The

other Greek cities in Sicily were supported by Carthage against Timoleon, but by a combination of military and diplomatic skills he was able to maintain Syracusan dominance until his retirement in the 330s BC.

The frequent conflict between Carthage and Syracuse was not the result of a clash of cultures. There was much cultural interchange between the

Motya (plan above and picture left) was a Phoenician settlement created on an island within a bay and connected by a causeway to the mainland. It was occupied from the eighth century BC; in the sixth century BC a fortification wall was built around the whole island. The choice of an off-shore location, defensible but close to a populated area, is typical of Phoenician settlements in this period. The settlement at Motya included a tophet, a shrine to the goddess Tanit. A tophet has also been excavated at Carthage (see page 83) and in both there have been found urns containing the burnt remains of babies and young children.

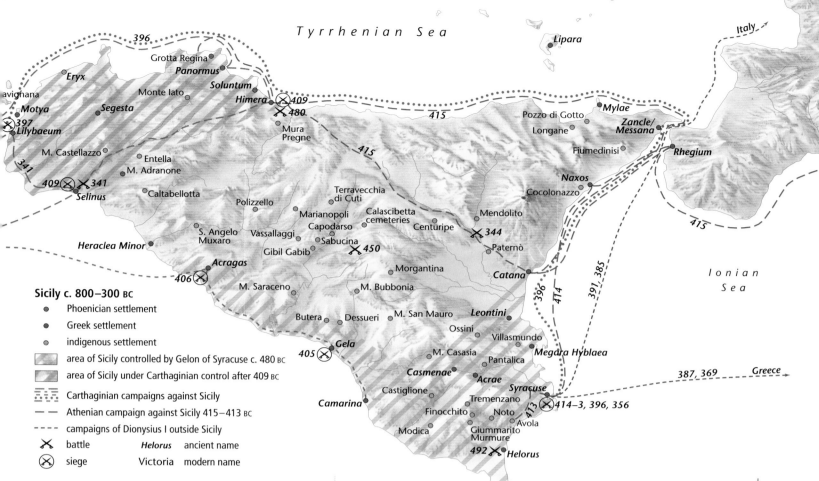

Tyrrhenian Sea

Italy

Lipara

396
Grotta Regina
Panormus
Eryx
Soluntum
avighana
Monte Iato
Himera ⊗ 409
Motya
Segesta
× 480
397
Lilybaeum
Mura Pregne
M. Castellazzo
Entella
M. Adranone
409 ⊗ × 341
Selinus
Caltabellotta
Polizzello
Terravecchia di Cuti
Marianopoli
Capodarso
Calascibetta cemeteries
Centuripe
341
S. Angelo Muxaro
Vassallaggi
Sabucina
× 344
Heraclea Minor
Gibil Gabib
× 450
Paternò
Acragas
406 ⊗
M. Saraceno
Morgantina
Catana
M. Bubbonia
Butera
Dessueri
M. San Mauro
Leontini
Ossini
Villasmundo
Gela
M. Casasia
Megara Hyblaea
405 ⊗
Pantalica
Casmenae
Acrae
387, 369 — Greece
Camarina
Castiglione
Syracuse
Tremenzano
414-3, 396, 356
Finocchito
Noto
Avola
413
Modica
Giummarito Murmure
492 × Helorus

Pozzo di Gotto
Mylae
Longane
Zancle/ Messana
Fiumedinisi
Rhegium
415
Naxos
Cocolonazzo
Mendolito
396
414
391, 385
415

Ionian Sea

Sicily c. 800–300 BC
- Phoenician settlement
- Greek settlement
- indigenous settlement
- area of Sicily controlled by Gelon of Syracuse c. 480 BC
- area of Sicily under Carthaginian control after 409 BC
- Carthaginian campaigns against Sicily
- Athenian campaign against Sicily 415–413 BC
- campaigns of Dionysius I outside Sicily
- × battle   *Helorus* ancient name
- ⊗ siege   Victoria modern name

Greek and Phoenician settlements in Sicily and the indigenous communities of the island were also influenced by them. The Greek cities in Sicily developed in different ways from those of the Greek homeland, sharing common features despite their mutual suspicion. Mercenary soldiers were used on a wider scale than in 'old' Greece and the greater frequency of tyranny in Sicilian cities may be linked to this, as citizens were more prepared to entrust the defence of their cities to powerful individuals, able to rely on mercenary support to sustain their position. However, the Sicilian cities were not isolated from the rest of the Greek world. Syracusan triremes supported the Spartans in the Aegean Sea on a number of occasions at the end of the fifth century BC and the beginning of the fourth. And although the actions of Alexander the Great and his successors had no direct impact on Sicilian affairs, their influence on Sicily in the Hellenistic period could not be ignored.

Gozo
Victoria

Malta
Melita

The earliest Greek settlement at Syracuse in the second half of the eighth century BC probably consisted of a number of separate hamlets on the mainland and on the island of Ortygia. By c. 700 BC, the hamlets had grown together and were reorganized with a grid-pattern of streets. On Ortygia the original grid formed the basis of the medieval street-plan, and as a result is visible today, as shown by the photograph (right). The island was the ancient heart of the city, with the principal temples built there. From the fifth century onwards, Syracuse became the most powerful city in Sicily and its rulers were great patrons of Greek poetry and art, in particular the tyrants Hieron (478–466 BC), who invited the tragedian Aeschylus to come to Sicily.

SICILY: PHOENICIANS AND GREEKS

The Athenian historian Thucydides asserts that even before the arrival of Greek settlers Sicily had experienced a long history of conflict between its inhabitants. While there must have been local conflicts between Greek and Phoenician settlers and the existing inhabitants of the island, and conflicts between Greek cities for dominance in the seventh and sixth centuries BC, it was the fifth century BC that saw the first large-scale conflicts, with wars between Syracuse and Carthage near the beginning and end of the centuries, and two campaigns led by Athens against Syracuse, in defence of other Greek cities in Sicily in the 420s and the following decade. For most of the time Phoenician control was limited to the western end of the island. The power of Syracuse was at its greatest under Gelon (c. 491–477 BC) and Dionysius I. Dionysius campaigned outside Sicily, in North Africa and southern Italy, and he also became involved in the military affairs of the cities of old Greece in the 360s.

Archaic Greece
The Age of the Tyrants c. **700–500** BC

The period between c. 700 and c. 500 BC was one of great changes in the Greek world. It saw the rise of urbanism, as monumental centres were created in many city-states and populations gathered around them. It was also a time of increasing contact with the wider world for both traders and the ruling elite, and a time when powerful individuals, known as 'tyrants', came to power in a number of cities.

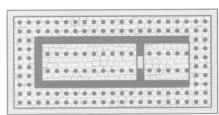

Third Temple of Hera, Samos c. 570 BC

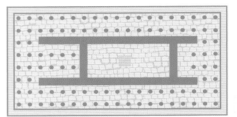

Temple of Artemis, Ephesus c. 560 BC

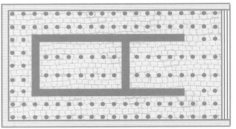

Fourth Temple of Hera, Samos c. 540 BC

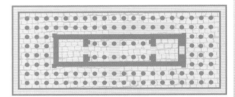

Temple of Olympian Zeus, Athens c. 520 BC

0   100 m

The Athenian historian Thucydides, writing in c. 400 BC, linked together a number of features in his description of the growth of the Greek city-states: increasing interest in sea-power, increasing wealth from revenues such as harbour tolls and taxes on traders and the emergence of tyrants. These were powerful individuals who were recognized as rulers of their cities, although they seldom had formal positions of authority, probably relying on their popularity with the majority of the populace.

There were clearly connections between the emergence of tyrants and the other factors mentioned by Thucydides: Corinth was an important city for traders, and was one of the first to develop an urban centre, and it was also home to one of the earliest tyrannies. Athens in contrast, with a larger territory under its control, was slower to get involved in trade, later in developing an urban centre, and was only ruled by tyrants from the middle of the sixth century BC. Sparta, which never experienced tyranny, never developed a proper urban centre, but remained a group of villages. There was probably also a close connection between the construction of triremes and the growth of an urban population prepared to row in them.

Developments in warfare on land were as significant as the growth of navies. In the early seventh century armies of heavily armed infantry, 'hoplites', engaged with their neighbours to establish the boundaries of their territories. The soldiers were peasant farmers, who fought to protect or to win the land they worked. In all Greek states, whether or not there was a tyrant in charge, political legitimacy required the support of these citizen-soldiers.

TYRANNY AND ART

The age of the tyrants was one which saw an increase in the wealth of the Greek cities, and this is reflected in artistic developments. Large public buildings were constructed to demonstrate the wealth and importance of the Greek states, and in the sixth century vast temples began to be constructed in Samos, Ephesus, Miletus and Athens. Statues, in bronze or marble, and of all sizes, increasingly became the most common form of offering at the temples in the archaic period. Other arts also flourished at the upper end of society, above all lyric poetry: the courts of Polycrates in Samos and Pisistratus in Athens were patrons of a number of important poets, while Alcaeus and Sappho, the greatest of all the lyric poets, lived in exile from the tyranny of Pittacus of Mytilene.

Tradition presented the Spartans as bringing an end to tyranny in Greece: this is an oversimplified view, although the Spartan king Cleomenes was involved in overthrowing the Pisistratids in Athens. From the mid sixth century Sparta's military reputation grew stronger, as its society became increasingly austere. Sparta dominated Greek history until its decline after 371 BC, but it had little to offer artistically after the archaic period.

The Major Tyrants

City	Tyrant	Date
Argos	Pheidon	early 7th century BC
Corinth	Cypselus	c. 655–625 BC
	Periander	c. 625–585 BC
Sikyon	Orthagoras	c. 650–600 BC
	Cleisthenes	c. 600–570 BC
Megara	Theagenes	c. 640–620 BC
Miletus	Thrasybulus	c. 625–600 BC
Mytilene	Pittacus	c. 620–570 BC
Athens	Pisistratus	c.560–559, c. 558–557 c. 546–527 BC
	Hippias	c. 527–510 BC
Naxos	Lygdamis	c. 540–525 BC
Samos	Polycrates	c. 545–522 BC

Building temples was a way for Greek cities to demonstrate their wealth and power to their neighbours. The third temple of Hera on Samos was the first colossal temple in Greece, and was swiftly followed by an even larger temple of Artemis near Ephesus. The collapse of their earlier temple allowed the Samians to construct a yet larger replacement, although it was never completed. The temple of Olympian Zeus at Athens, designed to rival those of the eastern Aegean, was started soon after this, but was only completed by the Roman emperor Hadrian over 600 years later.

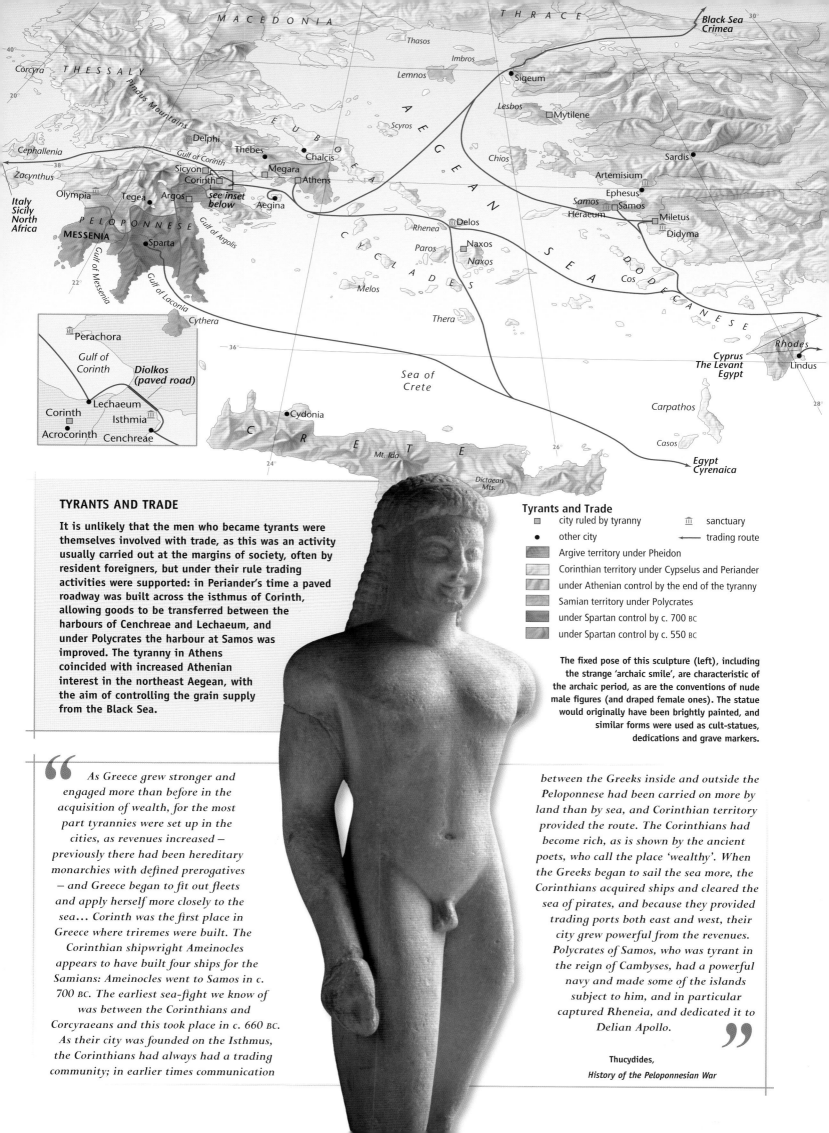

MACEDONIA   THRACE

Black Sea
Crimea

Thasos

THESSALY

Corcyra

Imbros

Lemnos

Sigeum

Scyros

Lesbos

Mytilene

Cephallenia

Pindus Mountains

Delphi

Gulf of Corinth

Thebes

Chalcis

Sicyon

Corinth

Megara

Athens

see inset below

Aegina

Zacynthus

Olympia

Tegea

Argos

PELOPONNESE

MESSENIA

Sparta

Gulf of Argolis

Gulf of Messenia

Gulf of Laconia

Cythera

Italy
Sicily
North
Africa

AEGEAN SEA

Chios

Sardis

Artemisium

Ephesus

Samos

Samos

Heraeum

Miletus

Didyma

Rhenea

Delos

CYCLADES

Paros

Naxos

Naxos

Cos

DODECANESE

Melos

Thera

Rhodes

Lindus

Sea of
Crete

Carpathos

Cyprus
The Levant
Egypt

Casos

CRETE

Cydonia

Mt. Ida

Dictaean
Mts.

Egypt
Cyrenaica

Inset:

Perachora

Gulf of
Corinth

Diolkos
(paved road)

Corinth

Lechaeum

Isthmia

Acrocorinth

Cenchreae

TYRANTS AND TRADE

It is unlikely that the men who became tyrants were themselves involved with trade, as this was an activity usually carried out at the margins of society, often by resident foreigners, but under their rule trading activities were supported: in Periander's time a paved roadway was built across the isthmus of Corinth, allowing goods to be transferred between the harbours of Cenchreae and Lechaeum, and under Polycrates the harbour at Samos was improved. The tyranny in Athens coincided with increased Athenian interest in the northeast Aegean, with the aim of controlling the grain supply from the Black Sea.

Tyrants and Trade

- ▫ city ruled by tyranny
- ● other city
- 🏛 sanctuary
- ← trading route

Argive territory under Pheidon

Corinthian territory under Cypselus and Periander

under Athenian control by the end of the tyranny

Samian territory under Polycrates

under Spartan control by c. 700 BC

under Spartan control by c. 550 BC

The fixed pose of this sculpture (left), including the strange 'archaic smile', are characteristic of the archaic period, as are the conventions of nude male figures (and draped female ones). The statue would originally have been brightly painted, and similar forms were used as cult-statues, dedications and grave markers.

As Greece grew stronger and engaged more than before in the acquisition of wealth, for the most part tyrannies were set up in the cities, as revenues increased – previously there had been hereditary monarchies with defined prerogatives – and Greece began to fit out fleets and apply herself more closely to the sea... Corinth was the first place in Greece where triremes were built. The Corinthian shipwright Ameinocles appears to have built four ships for the Samians: Ameinocles went to Samos in c. 700 BC. The earliest sea-fight we know of was between the Corinthians and Corcyraeans and this took place in c. 660 BC. As their city was founded on the Isthmus, the Corinthians had always had a trading community; in earlier times communication

between the Greeks inside and outside the Peloponnese had been carried on more by land than by sea, and Corinthian territory provided the route. The Corinthians had become rich, as is shown by the ancient poets, who call the place 'wealthy'. When the Greeks began to sail the sea more, the Corinthians acquired ships and cleared the sea of pirates, and because they provided trading ports both east and west, their city grew powerful from the revenues. Polycrates of Samos, who was tyrant in the reign of Cambyses, had a powerful navy and made some of the islands subject to him, and in particular captured Rheneia, and dedicated it to Delian Apollo.

**Thucydides,
*History of the Peloponnesian War***

The Greek City States
C. 500–350 BC

The fifth and fourth centuries BC are often considered to represent the highpoint of Greek civilization. It was the period of the Athenian democracy, and of Athens's greatest literary and architectural achievements, but it was also a period of more or less constant conflict between Greek cities, and always present to the east, ready to intervene when its interests were threatened, was the power of Achaemenid Persia.

The first two decades of the fifth century BC saw open conflict between Greeks and Persians. The cities of Asia Minor, supported by Athens, revolted unsuccessfully against the Persian Empire (499–494 BC), which responded with two campaigns against mainland Greece launched in 490 and 480–479 BC. Many Greek cities submitted to Persia, but those which resisted, led by Athens and Sparta, were able to drive back the invaders, and to end Persian control of the Greek cities in Asia Minor for nearly a century.

The Greek cities were autonomous states, but most were very small and unable to maintain real independence, especially in military affairs. Although some were democracies and others oligarchies, all Greek cities were effectively governed by their richer citizens, who were usually engaged in bitter rivalries. Many cities were thus under constant threat from the activities of exiled would-be leaders, who sought support from other powers, including the Persians, while those in power in the cities made alliances with stronger neighbours to secure their own positions.

WARFARE IN THE GREEK WORLD

At the same time the large cities sought to extend their own influence, making warfare a constant element of Greek life. To the northwest of Athens, Thebes was constantly engaged in trying to control the other Boeotian cities around it. In the Peloponnese Sparta attempted domination, and was not slow to use military force against its allies if ever they came under the control of leaders which were unsympathetic to the Spartans.

> *Remember that Athens has the greatest name in all the world because she has never given in to adversity, but has lavished more life and labour on war than any other city, and thus has won the greatest power that has ever existed – a power that, even if now a time may come when we have to yield (since all things are born to decay), will leave this memorial for posterity for ever after: that of all the Greek powers we ruled over the greatest number of Greeks; that we stood firm in the greatest wars against all and against each; and that we lived in the greatest and richest city there has been.*
>
> **Pericles in Thucydides's *Peloponnesian War***

The most powerful city of all however was Athens. The role of the Athenian fleet, above all in the victory over the Persians at Salamis (480 BC), gave Athens a position of dominance in the Aegean which it maintained for most of the period. In the immediate aftermath of the victory over the Persians, the Athenians built up an alliance of Greek cities to defend themselves against the very real threat of future Persian attacks. Some of the allies had fought with the Athenians against the Persians, while those which had fought on the Persian side had their discredited leaders replaced by men who owed their position to Athens. Some allies contributed ships to the allied fleet, but many instead paid an annual tribute, which was used to pay for crews, largely of Athenians. Relations between Athens and its allies remained good, except when anti-Athenian exiles were able to seize

Corcyra

Dodona ⅲ

Cephallenia

Classical Greek city states, c. 500–350 BC
- allies of Athens
- communities known to have paid tribute to Athens in the period 453–420 BC
- allies of Sparta in the Peloponnese
- Boeotian cities
- Neutral cities
- ⅲ major sanctuaries

A vase from the late sixth century BC showing a penteconter, a warship with two banks of oars (below far left), and a reconstructed Greek trireme (below left). Naval battles in Greece date back at least to the seventh century, and the trireme became the usual form of fighting ship by the beginning of the fifth century. The sail was used where possible on voyages, but in battles the trireme was powered by 180 oarsmen, who were free men rather than slaves. At the height of its power Athens had a fleet of over 100 triremes on active service, providing employment for large numbers of poorer citizens and resident aliens. The ships were commanded by richer citizens, who paid the crews from their own wealth, as a recognized service to the city. Ship's captains competed to have the best-turned-out vessel at the start of a campaign. Triremes were highly manoeuvrable, and their main weapon was a bronze ram at water-level at the prow of the ship.

Map labels: Selymbria, Abdera, Dicaea, Maronea, Bisanthe, Perinthus, Byzantium, Chalcedon, Berge, Thasos, Aenus, Propontis, Astacus, Argilus, Proconnesus, Cius, Stagira, Methone, Olynthus, Acanthus, Samothrace, Sestos, Cyzicus, Dascylium, Pydna, Potidaea, Imbros, Lampsacus, Abydus, Mende, Torone, Lemnos, Tenedos, Scione, Aegean Sea, Larisa, Astyra, Assos, Pherae, Methymna, Lesbos, Mytilene, Pharsalus, Sciathos, Icos, Peparethos, Histiaea, Cyme, Phocaea, Halae, Orchomenus, Hyettos, Anthedon, Chalcis, Chios, Clazomenae, Erythrae, Delphi, Coronea, Lake Copais, Eretria, Oenophyta, Colophon, Naupactus, Aegium, Thisbe, Thebes, Plataea, Ephesus, Ephesus, Patrae, Pellene, Sicyon, Megara, Athens, Carystus, Samos, Dyme, Corinth, Isthmia, Andros, Priene, Miletus, Elis, Phlius, Nemea, Ceos, Tenos, Myconos, Orchomenus, Argos, Epidaurus, Syros, Delos, Iasus, mpia, Mantinea, Epidaurus, Cythnos, Rhenea, Tegea, Seriphos, Paros, Naxos, Halicarnassus, Caunus, Sparta, Siphnos, Amorgos, Cos, Cnidus, Syme, Telmessus, Ios, Astypalaea, Camirus, Ialysus, Melos, Phaselis, Perge, Sillyon, Rhodes, Aspendus, Lindus, Celenderis, Sea of Crete, Carpathos, Tylissus, Knossos, Dreros, Itanus, Crete, Lyttos, Praesus, Gortyn, Hierapytna

power, and turned to Sparta or Persia for support. Such coups were seldom successful for long, however. Even after the alliance was forcibly broken up in 404 BC many of its members were willing to ally themselves to Athens again when the opportunity arose in 378 BC.

There was constant friction between the most powerful Greek states, and this often developed into armed conflict. The period of conflict described by the Athenian historian Thucydides and known as the Peloponnesian War (431–404 BC) was only part of a much longer war between the allies of Athens and Sparta, in which other powers, including Syracuse to the west and the Persians to the east, were involved. Indeed it was Persian financial intervention that was responsible for the Athenian surrender in 404 BC, and later the Persian King who oversaw attempts to make peace in the fourth century BC. Although a shared hostility to Athens had kept Thebes and Sparta allied in the fifth century, conflict between them grew in the fourth century, leading to the defeat of Sparta at Leuctra in 371 BC and the end of Spartan dominance of the Peloponnese. Thebes then became involved in a war with Phocis over control of the sanctuary of Apollo at Delphi. These events coincided with the accession of Philip II to power in Macedon; his subsequent involvement in the affairs of central Greece were to change the balance of power there for good.

A white-ground *lekythos* from Eretria (above), showing a hoplite fighter with his helmet and large round shield. The 'hoplite phalanx' was the standard fighting formation of the Greek city-states, developed in the seventh century BC, at a time when they were attempting to extend their control over the flat fertile lands of the plains. As well as shield and helmet, the hoplite would have a breastplate and greaves, and was armed with a thrusting spear and sword. Hoplites lined up in close formation, usually eight ranks deep, and aimed to drive their opponents from the battlefield by weight of numbers. They were in part protected by their neighbour's shield, and were thus vulnerable if their formation broke: under those circumstances careful retreat was considered wiser than standing alone, although for a hoplite to throw away his heavy shield to aid his flight was considered a sign of weakness.

Athenian Democracy
C. 500–300 BC

For almost two hundred years Athens was governed by a political system that involved most of its citizens in the administration of their own affairs. Although it had its critics, and was twice briefly replaced by narrower forms of government, the Athenian democracy was able successfully to control the largest city in Greece, and only ended when the Greek world came to be dominated by the monarchies of the Hellenistic period.

The reforms of Cleisthenes, agreed in 508/7 BC and put in place by 501 BC with frequent improvements being made thereafter, aimed to allow as many Athenians as possible to participate in the government of the city. Even so, only the richest citizens, who had the time and the wealth for training and education, and to support themselves while serving the city, would hold the major magistracies in Athens. The poorest citizens, especially those living in the countryside, would probably have little to do with the political life of the city, although they would attend meetings of their local deme assemblies (see map right). Nonetheless, the widespread use of the lot in appointments to posts, usually held annually, and the introduction of payment for office, meant that many citizens did take part in the running of the city: at least half the citizens must have taken their turn as members of the Council of 500, the body which oversaw the day-to-day business of Athens.

All decisions on public affairs in Athens had to be approved by the people in the Assembly, which met about forty times a year. Those who attended were probably the richer citizens, and those who lived in or near the city itself, who would include men who regularly rowed in the Athenian fleet. Meetings were better attended in the fifth century BC, when naval activity was a regular topic for discussion, than in the fourth, when Athens's power was more limited. The other powerful element of the democracy was the courts, manned by juries of up to several thousand citizens over the age of thirty. An important function of the courts was to hear charges of maladministration brought against public officials. Such cases often grew out of the competition between rival politicians, and the decisions of the jurors, standing for the people of Athens, were important in determining the course of Athenian politics.

ECONOMY AND CULTURE

With the opportunities for power available to the richest citizens came extra obligations. Most Athenian citizens paid no direct taxes, and emergency taxes were levied only on the richest five per cent. However, the very richest citizens, those who competed for political prominence, were required to spend large amounts of money funding activities at religious festivals, and equipping and crewing triremes. These obligations were called liturgies, and while they might involve considerable expense, they also gave the liturgists an opportunity to show themselves off in the best light.

Athens in this period produced some of the great literary figures of antiquity. As well as the dramatists, there were the historians Thucydides (c. 460–400 BC) and Xenophon (c. 430–350 BC) and the philosopher Plato (c. 429–347 BC). Both Plato and Xenophon were

This inscription (below far left) was erected in 337/6 BC, sometime after Athens had been defeated by Philip II of Macedon. The subject of the law, which aims to prevent an overthrow of the democracy, and the relief at the top, depicting the goddess Democratia (democracy) crowning Demos (the people), shows how much the idea of democracy still meant to Athenians, even after the city had become subordinate to Macedon. The inscription, written with equally spaced letters and no gaps between words (a style called *stoichedon*), is typical of the period. Even though the majority of citizens could not read, the publication of the decisions of the people of Athens was considered a vital aspect of administration.

The theatre of Dionysus (below left) on the side of the Acropolis was the setting for the two major dramatic festivals of Athens, the Lenaea and the City Dionysia. Each year playwrights would be chosen to compete at the festivals, with their plays performed by actors paid for by the city, and choruses sponsored through liturgies. Victory in the competition would bring great prestige to both the playwright and the sponsor. The festivals provided the occasions for the performance of the works of the great Athenian dramatists, including the tragedians Aeschylus, Sophocles and Euripides, and the comic poet Aristophanes. The theatre was rebuilt in the form it has now near the end of the fourth century BC, and in this form had a capacity of 15,000, making it the largest meeting place for citizens in Athens.

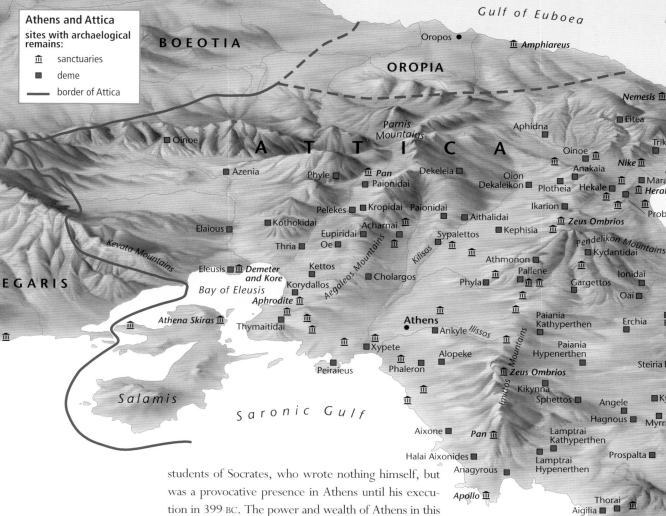

EUBOEA

Gulf of Euboea

BOEOTIA

Oropos ●

🏛 *Amphiareus*

OROPIA

Nemesis 🏛 ▪ Rhamnous

▪ Eitea

Oinoe ▪

Parnis Mountains

Aphidna ▪

Trikorynthos ▪

A T T I C A

Oinoe ▪ 🏛

Anakaia ▪

Nike 🏛

Plain of Marathon

Azenia ▪

Phyle ▪ 🏛

🏛 *Pan*

▪ Paionidai

Dekeleia ▪

Oion Dekaleikon ▪

Plotheia ▪

Hekale ▪ 🏛

Marathon ▪

Gulf of Petalion

Herakles 🏛

Peleke ▪

Kropidai ▪

Paionidai ▪

Ikarion ▪ 🏛

Probalinthos ▪

Elaious ▪

Kothokidai ▪

Eupiridai ▪

Acharnai ▪ 🏛

Aithalidai ▪

🏛 *Zeus Ombrios*

Thria ▪

Oe ▪

Sypalettos ▪

Kephisia ▪

Pendelikon Mountains

Kydantidai ▪

Kettos ▪

Cholargos ▪

Athmonon ▪

Araphen ▪

Eleusis ▪ 🏛 *Demeter and Kore*

Bay of Eleusis

Korydallos ▪

Phyla ▪

Pallene ▪ 🏛

Ionidai ▪

Oai ▪

Gargettos ▪

Aphrodite 🏛

Athena Skiras 🏛

Thymaitidai ▪

🏛

🏛

Athens ●

Ankyle ▪ 🏛

Ilissos

Paiania Kathyperthen ▪

Erchia ▪

Halai Araphenides ▪ 🏛

MEGARIS

🏛

🏛

Xypete ▪

Alopeke ▪

Phaleron ▪

Paiania Hypenerthen ▪

Steiria ▪

Philaidai ▪

🏛 *Artemis Brauronia*

Peiraieus ▪

Kifisos

Aegaleos Mountains

Imittos Mountains

🏛 *Zeus Ombrios*

Salamis

S a r o n i c   G u l f

Kikynna ▪

Sphettos ▪

Angele ▪

Kytherros ▪

Aixone ▪

Pan 🏛

Hagnous ▪

Myrrinous ▪ 🏛

Halai Aixonides ▪

Lamptrai Kathyperthen ▪

Prasiai ▪

Anagyrous ▪

Deiradiotai ▪

Apollo 🏛

Lamptrai Hypenerthen ▪

Prospalta ▪

Kephale ▪ 🏛

Fleves

Thorai ▪

Potamos Deiradiotes ▪

Aigilia ▪

Zeus 🏛 Phrearroi ▪

Arsidha

Besa ▪ 🏛

Thorikos ▪ 🏛

Anaphlystos ▪

Amphitrope ▪

Atene ▪

Sounion ▪

Poseidon 🏛

students of Socrates, who wrote nothing himself, but was a provocative presence in Athens until his execution in 399 BC. The power and wealth of Athens in this period also attracted important non-Athenians, some of whom settled permanently in the city, while others visited for shorter periods. These included the first historian Herodotus, from Halicarnassus, (c. 484–425 BC) and the speech-writer Lysias (c. 450–380 BC). Plato's most famous student Aristotle (384–322 BC), from Stageira in Chalcidice, spent much time in Athens, as did many of the group of rhetoricians and philosophers known as the sophists.

In 411 BC, when Athens was faring badly in the war with Sparta, and in 404 BC, after the Athenians had surrendered to Sparta, the democracy was briefly suspended. On both occasions it was rapidly restored. In the last quarter of the fourth century BC it was suppressed and restored several times by rival Hellenistic generals, but by this time Athens, like other Greek cities, was no longer in control of its own destiny.

> Now when we meet in the Assembly, then if the state is faced with some building project, I observe that the architects are sent for and consulted about the proposed structures, and when it is a matter of shipbuilding, the naval designers, and so on with everything which the Assembly regards as a subject for learning and teaching. If anyone else tries to give advice, whom they do not consider an expert, however handsome or nobly born or wealthy he may be, it makes no difference: the members reject him noisily and with contempt, until either he is shouted down and desists, or else he is dragged off or ejected by the police on the orders of the presiding magistrates. That is how they behave over subjects they consider technical. But when it is something to do with the government of the country that is to be debated, the man who gets up to advise them may be a builder or equally well a blacksmith or a shoemaker, rich or poor, of good family or none.

Socrates in Plato's *Protagoras*

Classical Greek Religion c. 500–300 BC

The main concerns of the inhabitants of the Greek cities were agriculture, warfare and religion, and these areas of life were closely linked. As well as providing food for the people, agriculture also provided the materials required for religious rituals, and in particular animal sacrifice. Religious rituals were an important part of military campaigns, and animals were regularly sacrificed so that their entrails could be studied to indicate the will of the gods.

Religious cults were organized at many levels, from families and groups of families up to the city as a whole. Each city was its own religious authority, and would have its own religious calendar, so that the various festivals and public sacrifices would be celebrated at the correct time and in the correct way. There was no idea of a separate priestly class, and priests were usually chosen in the same way as magistrates. In Sparta the two kings held the most important religious posts; in democratic Athens, although some priesthoods were held for life by members of particular groups of aristocratic families, others were appointed annually by lot.

THE ROLE OF SANCTUARIES

Sanctuaries developed particular functions which made them important to all Greeks. There were several prestigious oracles, where it was possible to consult the god (most commonly Apollo) about

The Stadium at Olympia (below) was about 200 metres long and sited on the edge of the sanctuary of Zeus; stone seats were provided for the officials. Olympic victors in particular gained enormous prestige, and would usually be given high honours by their own cities. In the archaic period athletes would normally be aristocrats, but the fifth and fourth centuries BC saw the emergence of professional athletes, and the practice of individuals representing cities other than those where they were born. Chariot-racing was one of the most important events at the Olympic games: the prize was awarded to the owner of the team rather than the charioteer, giving ambitious rich men an opportunity to show off their wealth. The Athenian Alcibiades entered seven chariot teams in the games of 416 BC, coming first, second and fourth.

public or private concerns. The most famous of these were Delphi, Dodona and, until it was destroyed by the Persians in 494 BC, Didyma near Miletus, but there were many other oracles which served their local areas. At Delphi, Apollo's words were spoken by a priestess who was understood to be inspired by the god. The circulation of versions of her responses put into verse helped to maintain the prestige of the oracle. Some oracles also functioned through the interpretation of dreams. There were other ways of consulting the gods, and skilled soothsayers were expected to be able to interpret the flight of birds and the livers of sacrificial victims, or omens such as earthquakes and thunder. The idea that the gods would reveal their will to mortals who paid due respect to them was a universal aspect of Greek religious understanding.

Some sanctuaries attracted people from beyond the immediate area, and the most famous of these were the 'panhellenic' athletic festivals, attended by Greeks from all over the Mediterranean and beyond. The most prestigious were the Olympic

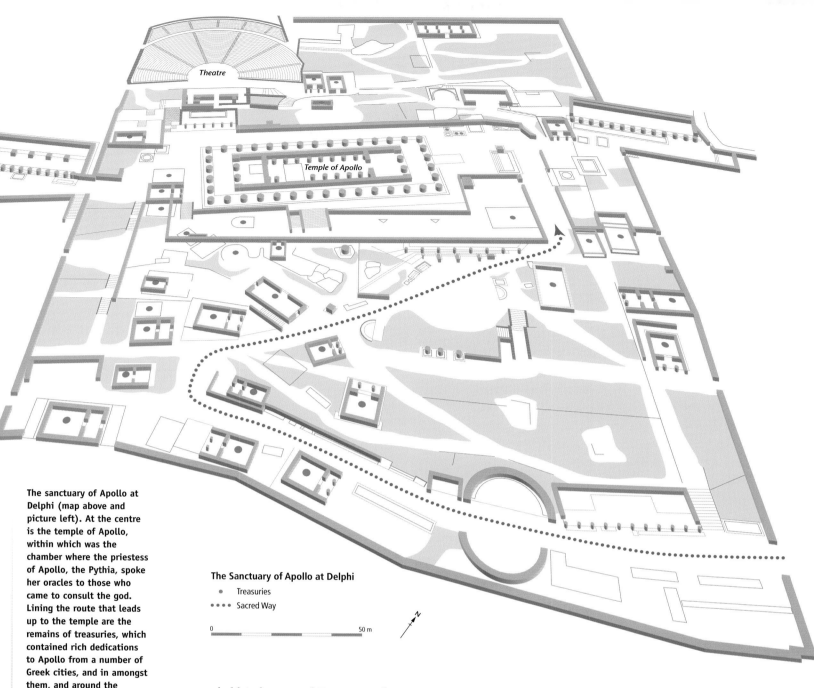

Theatre

Temple of Apollo

The Sanctuary of Apollo at Delphi

● Treasuries

●●●● Sacred Way

0   50 m

The sanctuary of Apollo at Delphi (map above and picture left). At the centre is the temple of Apollo, within which was the chamber where the priestess of Apollo, the Pythia, spoke her oracles to those who came to consult the god. Lining the route that leads up to the temple are the remains of treasuries, which contained rich dedications to Apollo from a number of Greek cities, and in amongst them, and around the temple, are bases on which statues dedicated to the god once stood. The theatre was a meeting place for the citizens of Delphi, and also used during the four-yearly Pythian Games. Above the sanctuary lies the stadium where races in the games also took place. In its period of greatest prestige, in the fifth and the first half of the fourth centuries BC, the sanctuary was enormously wealthy, with rich dedications from the sixth-century kings of Lydia, and monuments celebrating the Greek victories over the Persians. Much of this wealth was used up by the Phocians to pay for mercenary soldiers, after they took control of the sanctuary in 356 BC and fought a ten-year war against the Thebans, and later by Philip II of Macedon, in a vain attempt to hold on to it.

games, held in honour of Zeus every four years at Olympia in the Peloponnese, followed by the Pythian games held two years apart from the Olympics, in honour of Apollo at Delphi. In the intervening years were held the two-yearly Isthmian games, which were held near Corinth in honour of Poseidon, and the Nemean games, near Argos, in honour of Zeus.

WOMEN AND GREEK RELIGION

The religious activities of Greek cities were usually restricted to citizens alone, but they were one area of life where women could have an important role. Major city cults, for example that of Hera at Argos and of Athena in Athens, had priestesses. Women also played an important role in funerals and there were some festivals restricted to women. Some cults, known as mystery cults, were open only to initiates and the most famous of these, the Eleusinian Mysteries at Eleusis near Athens, were open to women and even slaves, so long as they were Greek.

An ox being led to sacrifice from the Parthenon frieze (below). Animal sacrifice was a central element of Greek religious ritual. The animals were always domestic, and the ritual also required the use of wine and barley, emphasizing the link between sacrifice and agriculture. At major festivals the usual victims were oxen, and while parts of the animal were burned on the altar, the rest of the meat would be distributed to the people attending the festival. Smaller-scale sacrifices might involve sheep or goats, or piglets and chickens. Military commanders would usually consult the livers of sacrificed sheep before taking major decisions in the field.

The Last Egyptian Kings
c. 1069–332 BC

The collapse of the New Kingdom was followed by an extremely complex and not well understood period of some 400 years, when Egypt, though nominally ruled by a single king or several co-rulers, was for much of the time effectively divided into several small states. In the face of pressure from Assyrians, Babylonians and then Persians, Egypt retained its independence until its conquest by the Persian king Cambyses in 525 BC.

At the end of the 20th Dynasty (1069 BC), Upper Egypt (the south) was ruled by the high priests of Amun at Thebes, whilst pharaohs of the 21st Dynasty (c. 1069–945 BC) governed from their capital of Tanis, in the delta. This situation lasted for about 120 years, during which time there were incursions from Libya and, increasingly, some groups were integrated into the Egyptian state. The 22nd and 23rd Dynasties were from related Libyan tribes and the 24th Dynasty (727–c. 715 BC) was also Libyan. The detailed history of this period is not well understood, but the fortunate survival of burials of some pharaohs of the 21st and 22nd dynasties show that Egypt was still a rich land.

Nubia in this period was independent and the 25th Dynasty (c.780–656 BC) emerged at the Nubian city of Napata. Under their ruler Piye (747–716 BC), the Nubians took control of the whole of Egypt (see page 78).

Egypt was relatively peaceful under its new rulers, until their involvement in the affairs of Palestine led to an attack on Memphis by the Assyrian Esarhaddon in 671 BC. The pharaoh Taharqa was forced to flee the city, but as no army of occupation was left, he returned. Four years later, however, under their new king, Ashurbanipal, the Assyrians attacked not only Memphis, but also Thebes, which they plundered. Assyria now appointed loyal vassals to rule over Egypt.

THE SAITE PHARAOHS

Amongst these client-kings was Necho I, ruler of Saïs in the delta. Although he never ruled independently of Assyria, Necho's son, Psammetichus I (664–610 BC), achieved independence and united Egypt under his own rule. By 656 BC, Psammetichus had extended control to Upper Egypt and sent his daughter to Thebes for adoption as the future 'God's wife of Amun' by the incumbent, who was sister of the late king Taharqa. Although exactly how Psammetichus achieved independence is not known, he obtained access to soldiers from Lydia, Caria, Greek cities and Syria-Palestine, and this must have helped him gain supremacy over his rival dynasts. As other rulers also had foreign soldiers in their armies, the reason for the greater success of the Saïtes is not yet understood. Many of these soldiers were given land in exchange for service and Egypt became increasingly cosmopolitan. This trend was helped also by the presence of Greek and Phoenician traders, to whom Psammetichus opened the country, and by the establishment of Naucratis and other trading stations. Customs-dues and taxes were charged on imports and exports to these emporia and, as a result, Egypt became immensely rich. Work began on a canal

Gold pectoral of Sheshonq II, 22nd Dynasty, c. 890 BC (below). Sheshonq II was briefly co-ruler with his father Orsokon I (924–889 BC), but died after a few months and was buried at Tanis. His coffin, made of silver and with a falcon's face instead of the king's, a unique feature of 22nd Dynasty burials, was found in the tomb of the 21st Dynasty ruler Psusennes I (see above right). The pectoral shows the sun-god Khepri, represented as a scarab beetle, flanked by the sister goddesses Isis and Nephthys. A pectoral with the same image was buried with Psusennes I.

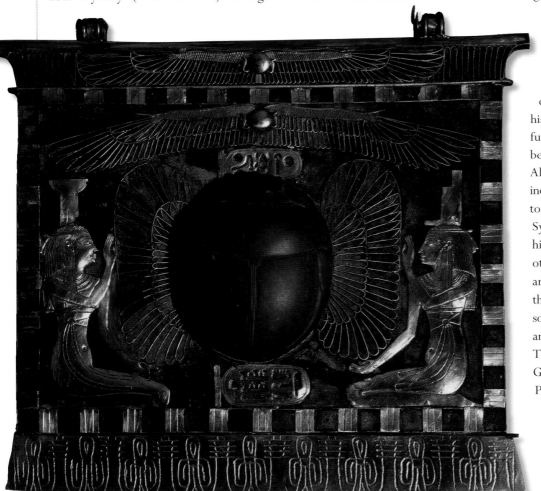

to link the Red Sea with the Mediterranean and Psammetichus and his successors built a navy and merchant fleet with Phoenician help. According to Herodotus, Necho II (610–595 BC) sent an expedition under Phoenicians that circumnavigated Africa. New-found wealth helped foster an artistic renaissance and the kings encouraged a revival of earlier art forms. As a result, particularly in the field of sculpture, there are many beautiful surviving examples of Saïte craftsmanship. It was possibly the Egypt of the early 26th Dynasty which was depicted in Homer's *Odyssey*. The later rulers of the dynasty, in the period after the fall of Assyria, had more contact with the Mediterranean world. Apries (589–570 BC) attacked the Phoenician cities of Tyre and Sidon, then under Babylonian control, in 588–7 BC, and later supported Libyan forces against Greek settlers in Cyrenaica. His successor Amasis, (570–526 BC), brought Cyprus under Egyptian control, and gave rich gifts to a number of Greek temples.

Gold mask of Psusennes I, 21st Dynasty, 1039–991 BC (left). The tomb of Psusennes I was discovered intact in the excavations at Tanis. His mummy, wearing the mask, was enclosed in a silver coffin, within a black granite sarcophagus, with a further outer sarcophagus of pink granite. The tomb also contained several other burials including those of his successor Amenemope (see above) and of the 22nd Dynasty pharaoh Sheshonq II (see far left), which had at some point been moved there from nearby tombs.

Gold bracelet from the tomb of Amenemope, 21st Dynasty, 993–984 BC (above). Amenemope's coffin was found in the tomb of his predecessor, Psusennes I (see left), and the bracelet is decorated with cartouches bearing the royal name of Psusennes.

THE PERSIAN CONQUEST

The 26th Dynasty pharaohs had established control over the Two Lands, but their aspirations to become a great power again were resisted by the Babylonians. Eventually, Egypt and Babylonia grew closer in the face of the rising power of Persia. In 525 BC, 14 years after their capture of Babylon, the Persians under Cambyses conquered Egypt, which now became a Persian province.

The last period of pharaonic splendour had ended. Nearly a century later, the Persians were driven out of the country, but returned in 343 BC; in the interim native Egyptian dynasties, supported by Greek mercenaries, fought with each other and rendered their country increasingly unstable and poor. In 332 BC, nine years after the return of the Persians, Alexander the Great was welcomed in Egypt as a liberator.

Napata

C. 850–310 BC

Contacts between Egypt and the lands lying south of the first cataract of the Nile already had a long history by the mid-ninth century BC, when the kingdom of Napata rose to power. There is evidence of a large town at Kerma, just south of the third cataract, which seems to have been the capital of an independent Nubian state. With the renewal of Egyptian control in the region during the New Kingdom (1550–1069 BC), Kerma disappeared.

N apata, the successor to Kerma, emerged at a time of Egyptian withdrawal following the end of the New Kingdom. The centre of this Nubian state, known as Kush, was at Napata, lying near the fourth cataract, where the cemeteries of El Kurru and Nuri and the temple and cemetery of Jebel Barkal are situated. Archaeological excavation of these sites has yielded a considerable amount of information about the rulers of Kush but little is known about the people in general. Most were probably engaged in agriculture and cattle-breeding and lived in houses made of mud, brick or matting, which leave little trace in the archaeological record. Horse-breeding was also important and horses were particularly valued by the Kushite kings. Because the tombs and temples show strong Egyptian influence, there has been a tendency to see Napata as little more than an imitation of Ancient

The ruinous condition of the El Kurru cemetery makes it difficult to imagine how the site would once have looked. Piye (747–716 BC) was the first ruler whose tomb was marked by a true pyramid (left). The burial chamber lies below in a rock-cut, vaulted chamber that was reached by a descending stairway. Despite obvious Egyptian influences, El Kurru preserves the ancient Kushite tradition of burial under mounds, although here the mound has been elevated into a pyramid.

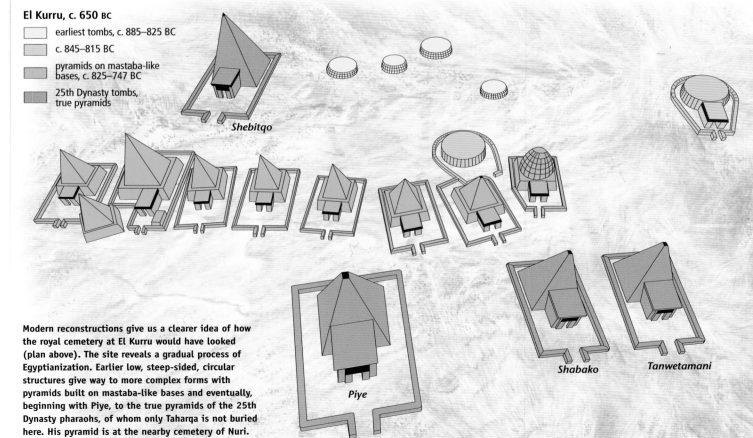

El Kurru, c. 650 BC

- ☐ earliest tombs, c. 885–825 BC
- ☐ c. 845–815 BC
- ☐ pyramids on mastaba-like bases, c. 825–747 BC
- ☐ 25th Dynasty tombs, true pyramids

Shebitqo

Piye

Shabako

Tanwetamani

Modern reconstructions give us a clearer idea of how the royal cemetery at El Kurru would have looked (plan above). The site reveals a gradual process of Egyptianization. Earlier low, steep-sided, circular structures give way to more complex forms with pyramids built on mastaba-like bases and eventually, beginning with Piye, to the true pyramids of the 25th Dynasty pharaohs, of whom only Taharqa is not buried here. His pyramid is at the nearby cemetery of Nuri.

Egypt, but at Sanam, the site not only of a cemetery and temple but also a large town, ceramic finds of a non-Egyptian type indicate the existence of an indigenous culture stretching back to Kerma and beyond.

THE KUSHITE PHARAOHS

During the reign of Piye (747–716 BC), the Kushites conquered Egypt and ruled there as the 25th Dynasty, thereby becoming the upholders of the pharaonic tradition which had once held their predecessors under its sway. It proved to be a time of economic and cultural revival for Egypt. The Napatan pharaohs promoted Egyptian religion and the arts both in Egypt and their native Kush, embarking on programmes of temple restoration and reviving the use of many archaic artistic and literary elements. Yet, despite this process of Egyptianization, Kushite culture never entirely lost its distinctive character and, in turn, had an invigorating impact on Egyptian art of the period. However, by the reign of Taharqa (690–664 BC), the Assyrians were posing an increasing threat to Kushite rule and with the support of the Saïte leader, Psammetichus I (664–610 BC), the Kushites were decisively defeated in 656 BC, bringing the 25th Dynasty to an end.

Nevertheless, the Napatan kingdom survived and its rulers persisted in using the titles of the Egyptian pharaohs, although the political focus of the state gradually shifted southwards to Meroë, situated about 200 kilometres downstream of Khartoum. Exactly when Meroë superseded Napata as the centre of the Kushite kingdom is unclear. The site dates back to the eighth century BC and as early as 591 BC, following the possible sacking of the Napatan site by Psammetichus II of Egypt, the royal residence may have been moved there. Even if this was so, Napata continued to be the ritual and ceremonial centre of the kingdom. The last king to be buried there seems to have been Nastasen (335–310 BC). Thereafter, royal burials took place at Meroë, indicating that by this time, if not earlier, Meroë had become the centre of the Kushite state.

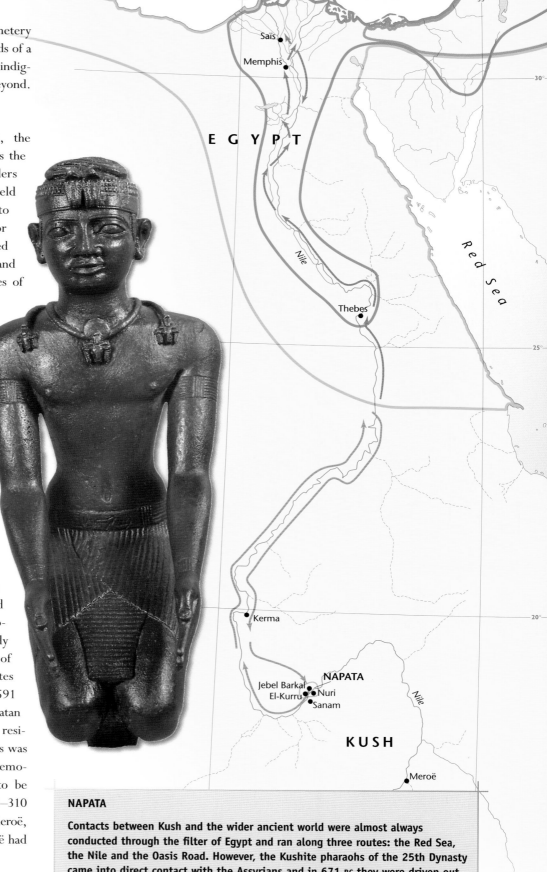

This bronze statuette (above right) shows the Kushite pharaoh Shabako in an attitude of offering. It combines Kushite and Egyptian elements in a highly distinctive way. The formal, rather stiff pose is typically Egyptian but the king's features, especially the accentuation over the cheeks, is characteristically Kushite. The king wears a skull cap, a Nubian symbol of sovereignty, which has been Egyptianized by the two uraei. The double, rather than single, uraeus is nevertheless uniquely Kushite.

NAPATA

Contacts between Kush and the wider ancient world were almost always conducted through the filter of Egypt and ran along three routes: the Red Sea, the Nile and the Oasis Road. However, the Kushite pharaohs of the 25th Dynasty came into direct contact with the Assyrians and in 671 BC they were driven out of Lower and Middle Egypt by Assyrian forces. Despite a brief recovery of power, the 25th Dynasty collapsed when the rulers of the western delta, based at Saïs, gave their support to the Assyrians. Retreating to the comparative isolation of Napata, the kingdom of Kush remained relatively untroubled by foreign invaders, apart from during a war with Egypt (593–591 BC) and an abortive campaign by the Persians, who conquered Egypt in 525 BC.

— approximate extent of the Neo-Assyrian Empire, 700–650 BC

— approximate extent of the Babylonian Empire, c. 625–c. 539 BC

— approximate extent of the Persian Empire in the late 6th/early 5th centuries BC

→ advance of Piy into Egypt c. 728 BC

→ route of Psammetichus II's army c. 591 BC

The **Near East:** Cities and Kings
c. **1000–600** BC

As they recovered from the upheavals of the late Bronze Age, the Mesopotamian powers reasserted their control over the Near East. Meanwhile, new kingdoms had emerged in Anatolia, and the Levant became an area of competing city-states. This situation, resulting from the relaxation of pressure from the major powers, did not last long. With the expansion of Assyria (see page 86) most lost their independence, becoming vassal states and ultimately provinces of the new empire.

The relations between these states and between them and Assyria, prior to their incorporation into the Neo-Assyrian Empire, the growth of that empire and the various stages of its attempt at control until it dominated most of the region, are the main themes of the history of these centuries. The impact of Assyria was widespread and was felt from Elam to Egypt.

The southwest coastal plain of the Levant had been settled by the Peleset, one of the Sea Peoples, employed as mercenaries by the Egyptians and placed here as garrison troops. Following Egypt's departure, these people, now known as the Philistines, controlled major cities, including Gaza and Ashkelon. Their conflict with the emerging Israelite state is described in the Bible. To the east,

Relief depicting Barrakkab, king of Sam'al, addressing his scribe, c. 730 BC (below). Inscriptions from Sam'al cast light on the position of small Levantine states in this period. In c. 840-830 BC Sam'al had been attacked by its more powerful neighbour Adana, and had turned to Assyria for help. Later, Barrakkab's grandfather was killed in a political coup and his son Panammu appealed to the Assyrian king Tiglath-pileser III (744–727 BC) for help in regaining his throne. In return Sam'al under Panammu and Barrakkab became a loyal subject-state of Assyria.

the neighbouring countries of Moab, Ammon and Edom were also now developing.

THE ARAMAEANS

Further to the north, most of Syria and Upper Mesopotamia were under Aramaean control by the mid-tenth century and Babylonia was being subject to their raids. These semi-nomadic pastoralists settled in tribal groups which developed into several small kingdoms, though in some cases domination was gradually imposed over an existing state. In southern Syria, Aram-Zomah, centred on Damascus, became the leading Aramaean state and was frequently in conflict with Israel. Although they joined alliances, most notably against Assyria in 853 BC, the Aramaeans never united, but competed with each other for hegemony, which ultimately assisted Assyria. By the end of the eighth century BC, they had become yet another group in the increasingly heterogeneous populations of Assyria and Babylonia. They adopted local culture but gave to the region their language, which became the lingua franca, and their script, a modified form of Phoenician alphabetic, which ultimately displaced cuneiform.

Not all of the Bronze Age city-system had vanished and some centres, such as the Phoenician cities (see page 82), having survived the changes, retained much of their earlier culture and political features. Similarly, the Neo-Hittite principalities of south-central Anatolia, Cilicia and north Syria had developed from administrative centres of the Hittite Empire that continued to survive as petty kingdoms, following the collapse of the central government. Their rulers' names were often Hittite or Hurrian and other recognizable Hittite features included the style of sculpture and a script directly developed from

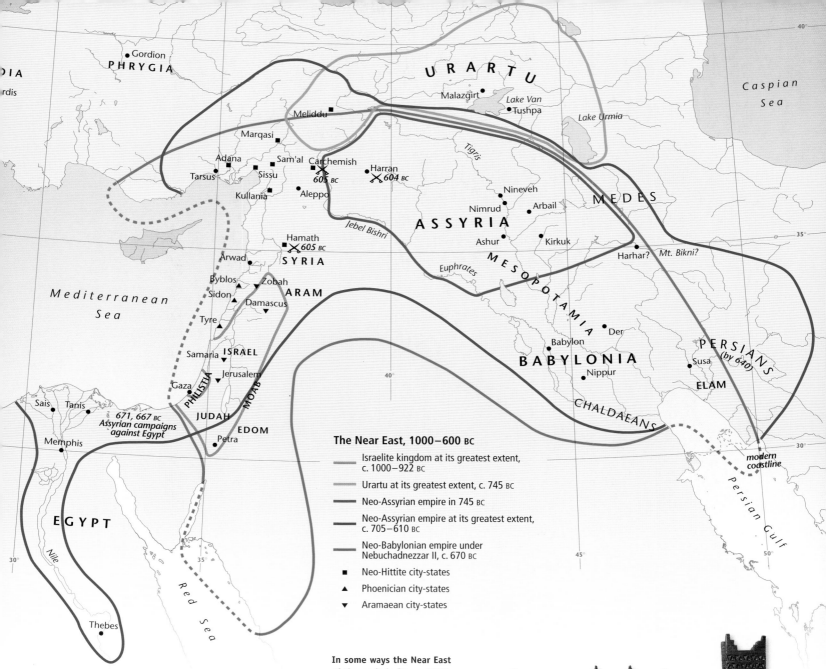

The Near East, 1000–600 BC

— Israelite kingdom at its greatest extent, c. 1000–922 BC

— Urartu at its greatest extent, c. 745 BC

— Neo-Assyrian empire in 745 BC

— Neo-Assyrian empire at its greatest extent, c. 705–610 BC

— Neo-Babylonian empire under Nebuchadnezzar II, c. 670 BC

■ Neo-Hittite city-states

▲ Phoenician city-states

▼ Aramaean city-states

Hittite hieroglyphs, rendering Luwian, one of the languages of the empire. Their population was probably a variegated ethnic mix. The most prominent of these wealthy states was Carchemish, controlling the Euphrates crossing, but all lay along major routes and were an important link between Assyria and the new kingdoms of Anatolia. Elements of neo-Hittite art were adopted by their neighbours and also influenced the 'orientalizing' phase of archaic Greek art. These states were conquered by Assyria in the eighth century BC.

The new Anatolian states are not well understood. The chief royal centre of Urartu was at Tushpa, and there is evidence of considerable material wealth. Sitting on Assyria's northern border it must have been a power to be reckoned with.

Archaeological remains, including rock-carvings and large tumuli used as burial mounds indicate something of the wealth of Phrygia, as do Greek legends about its most powerful ruler, the late 8th century king Midas. Midas maintained good rela-

In some ways the Near East of the period after c. 1000 BC (map above) resembled the same area in the period c. 1600–1200 BC (see page 48). The cities of the Levant were once again fought over by the great powers of the region, but now the weakness of Egypt and the absence of a powerful Anatolian empire allowed the Mesopotamian empires of Assyria and then Babylon to extend their power to the shores of the Mediterranean.

Fragment of a model fortress from the Urartian city of Toprakkale near Lake Van (above right). The area around Lake Van was the heartland of Urartu, which flourished from the ninth to the seventh centuries BC. Massive fortifications are a feature of many Urartian sites, but the history of the kingdom remains little known.

tions with Assyria, and eastern goods flowed into his capital at Gordion. The Greek historian Herodotus wrote a detailed, if unreliable, history of Lydia. In the 7th century BC the Lydians conquered the Greek cities on the Aegean seaboard, and the last king, the fabulously wealthy Croesus (c. 560–540 BC) gave lavish gifts to several Greek temples.

In the 7th century BC all the Anatolian kingdoms suffered raids from the Cimmerians to the north. They recovered, but like the rest of the region were conquered in the 6th century by the Achaemenid Persian king Cyrus (see page 88).

The Phoenicians

C. **1000–500** BC

The Phoenicians inhabited the narrow coastal strip between the Lebanon Mountains and the Mediterranean Sea, from southern Syria to northern Palestine. They were known to the Greeks as Phoinikes, signifying the colour purple, possibly a reference to their production of highly prized purple dye. In the Old Testament they are referred to as people of particular cities, for instance, Tyrians or Sidonians, though it is probable that they called themselves Kinahu, meaning Canaanites.

It seems most likely that the Phoenician city-states represent a development of the Late Bronze Age Canaanite coastal cities. Uncertainty over their origins derives from the fact that much knowledge about the Phoenicians comes from the records of people with whom they were in contact rather than from their own sources. Their scattered inscriptions provide little more than a few names, a scant legacy from the people famous for transmitting the alphabet.

The Phoenicians were famous also as mariners, explorers and craftsmen, especially in metalworking and weaving. The people of the Levantine coastal

The sarcophagus of King Ahiram of Byblos (below right). This masterpiece of Phoenician art combines Egyptian motifs such as sphinxes and the lotus flower in the king's hand, with Syrian or Hittite elements (such as the lions supporting the coffin). It also contains one of the earliest long inscriptions in the Phoenician alphabet, cursing any ruler or general who uncovers or defaces the sarcophagus (see detail below left).

cities had always traded their cedar wood and precious oils, particularly with Egypt, but it was the resurgence of Assyria (see page 84), which relied on Phoenicians to supply craft goods and raw materials, that led them to become great seafaring traders. It is thought also that at about this time the keel came into use, making possible longer voyages on the open sea.

PHOENICIAN COLONIES

From the tenth century the Phoenicians went in search of metals; they founded a settlement at Kition on Cyprus, the 'copper island', and later at Gades (Cadiz) in Spain to extract silver from rich deposits; and they perhaps obtained tin from Cornwall. Carthage, foundßed from Tyre, was originally a staging post on the long journey to Spain, but it grew to be a great city, eclipsing even Tyre itself.

The legendary Tyrian purple cloth, coloured with dye made from the murex sea snail, was one of the best known Phoenician products. The Phoenicians

A detail from the Ahiram sarcophagus (above) showing the Phoenician alphabet. The script and phonetic equivalents are shown in the table (right). Although the idea of an equivalency between a single sign and a single sound was not originally Phoenician – it originated in Sinai in the early second millennium BC – and other alphabetic systems arose in West Asia at about the same time – it was the Phoenician alphabet which ultimately spread most widely.

aleph	beth	gimel	daleth	he	waw		zayin	heth	teth
'	b	g	d	h	w		z	h	t

yod	kaph		lamed		mem			nun	samekh
y	k		l		m			n	s

ayin	pe	sade	qoph	resh	shin		taw	
'	p	s	q	r	sh/s		t	

also produced ivory carvings, glassware, luxury jewellery and metal goods as well as mass-produced trinkets, all of which have been found widely spread, from Mesopotamia to Spain. Their ivory carvings decorated the palace built by Omri, king of Israel, at Samaria and Phoenician ivories have been found at the Assyrian capital, Nimrud, where they had been taken as tribute or booty. Carved ivory frequently decorated expensive furniture and was often gilded.

The most ancient of the coastal cities was Byblos, at one point a major entrepôt for papyrus from Egypt, but Tyre was to become the wealthiest and greatest. Whenever possible, Phoenician cities were built on land jutting out into the sea, with harbours on either side, or for security on offshore islands. High stone walls and towers protected the inhabitants, who lived in two-storey houses with balconies. The Phoenicians were in fact famous for their skills as builders and were, for instance, employed to build King Solomon's temple at Jerusalem in the tenth century BC.

The Phoenician cities were the major entrepôts of the Near East between c. 1000 and 500 BC. During this time they retained their commercial pre-eminence, whatever the prevailing political situation. Certainly, they were well placed to exploit the wealth of almost any state in the area. It seems that they were able to take advantage of whatever conditions existed, and by adapting themselves to the political requirements of the time, continued their commercial activities without serious interruption. However, given their role as middle men and manufacturers of primarily luxury goods, they were dependent on the existence of strong states around them, both to buy their goods and to protect their trade routes.

The cemetery or *tophet* at the Carthaginian port of Salammbo (above). Excavations in many Phoenician cities have revealed large cemeteries containing terracotta urns with the ashes and bones of small children. Classical sources spoke of Phoenician child sacrifice and it is possible, but by no means certain, that the excavated tophets are an indication of this practice, and they do also contain votive offerings and inscriptions.

A glass pendant of the head of a bearded man (above). The Phoenicians were skilled glass-makers and such pendants have been found in nearly all the towns of the eastern Phoenician world, and most particularly in Cyprus. They probably had a religious significance and may represent deities. Some have survived strung together to form necklaces.

Assyria and Palestine
c. 1000–609 BC

Though weakened, Assyria had survived the disruptions of the late second millennium and despite Aramaean incursions, the ancient Assyrian heartland had remained intact and the line of kings unbroken. Now, under a series of strong kings, the first phase of the Neo-Assyrian Empire developed. Territory lost to the Aramaeans was regained and by the mid-ninth century BC, the western boundary reached the Euphrates. Tribute and booty flowed in and the kingdoms of north Syria became Assyrian vassals.

Although the reconstruction of Near Eastern history in this period is largely based on Assyrian evidence, Assyria's impact on other peoples in the region can be glimpsed through the Hebrew Bible, written down from the eighth century BC, which preserved Israelite laws and history.

Following the conquest and settlement of Canaan by the Israelites, the Kingdom of Israel was formed around 1000 BC, with Saul and David as the first kings. Solomon, David's son and successor, built the temple at Jerusalem with Phoenician craftsmen. On his death, the kingdom divided into the northern and southern states of Israel and Judah. Some 50 years later, Omri became king of Israel and moved the capital to Samaria. His son Ahab joined an alliance of rulers fighting the Assyrians in 853 BC (see below), with whom the history of Israel and Judah now became interwoven.

THE ASSYRIAN EMPIRE

The numerous inscriptions of the Assyrian king Ashurnasirpal II (883–859 BC) illustrate the political and military importance of his reign, during which the first stage of Assyria's renewed expansion took place. A visible expression of imperial might, Nimrud was expanded and rebuilt as the new capital and in the great palace reliefs of the king in his role as conqueror were erected.

Shalmaneser III (858–824 BC) fought an alliance of western states led by Hadadezer of Damascus and including Ahab of Israel, which attempted to stem Assyrian expansion. Although Shalmaneser claimed a great victory at the Battle of Qarqar on the Orontes in 853 BC, it was not complete, as he fought them again. Ultimately, however, most of the states paid tribute to Assyria to stop further attacks, amongst them King Jehu of Israel. In spite of subsequent revolt in Assyria, a period of weak rulers and loss of some Syrian states, the empire now remained virtually intact.

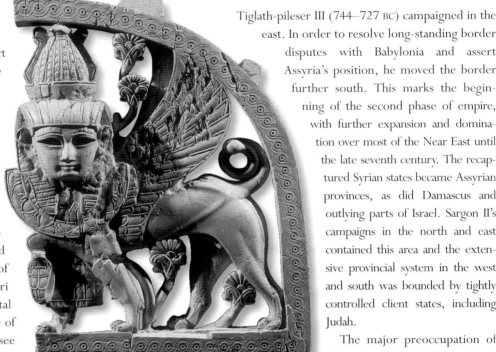

A winged sphinx in ivory, late eighth century BC, found in the arsenal at Nimrud (above). Nimrud, also known as Kalhu, became the second capital of the Assyrian Empire under Ashurnasirpal II. The ivory for the thousands of carvings which have been found on the site was imported from Phoenicia.

Relief from the palace of Sennacherib at Nineveh depicting the siege of the Jewish town of Lachish in 701 BC (far right). Although Sennacherib failed to capture Jerusalem during this campaign, the ability of Israel to obstruct Assyrian thrusts into Egypt was removed. Sennacherib sacked Babylon in 689 BC after his son was handed over to the Elamites by Babylonian rebels. The destruction of Babylon was seen as a sacrilegious act by many Assyrians and his assassination a few years later may have been the result.

Tiglath-pileser III (744–727 BC) campaigned in the east. In order to resolve long-standing border disputes with Babylonia and assert Assyria's position, he moved the border further south. This marks the beginning of the second phase of empire, with further expansion and domination over most of the Near East until the late seventh century. The recaptured Syrian states became Assyrian provinces, as did Damascus and outlying parts of Israel. Sargon II's campaigns in the north and east contained this area and the extensive provincial system in the west and south was bounded by tightly controlled client states, including Judah.

The major preoccupation of Sennacherib (704–681 BC) was Babylon, recently conquered after 12 years of independence. However, there were also frontier campaigns in Anatolia, Syria and the Levant, where a now-hostile Egypt supported rebellion; in 701 BC the armies met and Sennacherib's annals claimed a victory. The Assyrians then besieged Lachish and attacked Jerusalem, seat of Hezekiah of Judah, which was forced to buy off the aggressor with tribute. According to the Bible and Herodotus, however, the Egyptians defeated the Assyrians. Egypt's repeated meddling in Palestine provoked Assyrian activity in Egypt itself, by Esarhaddon (680–669 BC) and by Ashurbanipal (668–627 BC), who sacked Thebes.

With the conquest of Elam by Ashurbanipal, the empire reached its greatest extent. Despite the almost inevitable problems of control in frontier areas, Assyrian kings exercized power over a huge territory, with considerable success for some 70 years until c. 630 BC. Imperial administration was highly organized; provincial governors collected taxes and tribute, raised conscripts and provided supplies for the armies, as well as providing forced labour for road building and maintenance of the road system.

Caspian Sea

ANATOLIA

Sevan Ψ
Arinberd
Karmir-Blur
Armavir-Blur
Erebuni
Doğubayazit
Altintepe
Aznavur
Kancikli
Körzüt Kalesi
Bastam
Hirsiz Kale
Malazgirt
Rusahinili
Ψ Palu
Kayalidere
Adilcevaz
later royal capital
Toprakkale
Ψ Komurhan
Birkalein (tunnel)
Lake Van
Lake Rusa
Haftavan Tepe
Meliddu
Eğil
Tushpa
earlier royal capital
Çavuştepe
Lake Urmia
Amida
Kurkh
Gudi Dağ
Maraş
Kummukh
Anaz
Guzana
Babil
Mila Mergi
Qalatgar
Hasanli
Ferhatli
Kenk
Harran
Nisibis
Maltai
Topzawa
Kel-a Shin
Zencirli
Carchemish
Arslantaş
Fayda
Bandwai
Shibaniba
Najafehabad
Sakacogözü
Arpad
Til Barsib
Tell el Rimah
Khorsabad
Bastura Chai (tunnel)
Al Mina
Tell Tayinat
Karabur
(tunnel and canal head)
Negub
Nineveh
Arbil
Qasr Shamamok
Salamis
Cyprus
Aradus (Ruad)
✕ Qarqar 853 BC
Hamath
Sinjar
Tell 'Abta
Ashur
Arrapkha
Citium
Marathus
Nimrud
Uramanat
Byblos
Sheikh Hammad
Mediterranean Sea
Dog River
Berytus
Sidon
Damascus
Saba'a
MESOPOTAMIA
Sarepta
Tyre
Hazor
Hindana
Euphrates
Tigris
Shkaft-i Gulgul
Der
Megiddo
Beth Shan
Samaria
Shechem
Gezer
Jerusalem
Ashdod
Lachish
Gaza
Beth-zur

EGYPT

Nile

Red Sea

Babylon

Uruk
Ur

Susa

Persian Gulf

The Assyrian Empire

- • site location
- ------ ancient coastline

Assyria
- ▪ capital city
- ▪ provincial capital
- • important city
- ▼ rock relief
- ▮ stela

- —— Assyrian homeland
- ----- Assyrian Empire under Sargon II, 710–705 BC
- –·–· Assyrian expansion under Ashurbanipal 668–627 BC

Urartu
- ▪ fortress
- • town or city
- ▮ stela
- Ψ inscription

Levant
- ▪ Royal fortress of Israel
- • Phoenician city
- ▲ temple
- ▮ ivory

Assyria – the land around the city of Ashur on the River Tigris – had been an important state throughout most of the second millennium BC. However, by the tenth century BC Assyrian control had declined and was limited to a core area around Ashur and Nineveh. Assyrian kings began a new campaign of expansion in the ninth century BC (map above). Two powerful rulers, Ashurnasirpal II and Shalmaneser III, campaigned as far west as the Mediterranean coast and struck deep into southern Mesopotamia. During the reign of Tiglath-pileser III, the Assyrians seized lands as far as Israel and the Persian Gulf. Yet civil war weakened the empire and, within two years of an invasion by the Medes in 612 BC, Assyrian power had completely collapsed.

Principal Assyrian rulers

Tiglath-pileser II	966–935 BC
Tukulti-Ninurta II	890–884 BC
Ashurnasirpal II	883–859 BC
Shalmaneser III	858–824 BC
Tiglath-pileser III	744–727 BC
Sargon II	721–705 BC
Sennacherib	704–681 BC
Esarhaddon	680–669 BC
Ashurbanipal	668–627 BC
Ashur-uballit II	611–609 BC

The reasons for the sudden disappearance of the Assyrian empire are not well understood, as the sources reveal little about events in the final two decades. In 630 BC everything seemed secure, yet by 612 BC, Ashur, Nimrud and Nineveh had been destroyed by the armies of the Babylonians and Medes and after 608 BC, following a last stand at Harran, Assyria disappears from the record.

The **Neo-Babylonian Empire**

626–539 BC

Having been dominated by Assyria for most of the seventh century BC, Babylonia regained its independence under the leadership of Nabopolassar (626–605 BC), founder of the Neo-Babylonian dynasty. The Babylonians then defeated and destroyed the Assyrian Empire itself. Although its wealth and power enabled significant reconstruction in the city of Babylon, the new neo-Babylonian empire was relatively short-lived and within less than a century fell to the Persians.

After ten years of fighting, the Babylonians turned on the Assyrian heartland, capturing and destroying Nineveh, the capital, in 612 BC. Their victory and the sense of release it engendered are well described in an inscription of Nabopolassar's: 'I slaughtered the land of Subartu [Assyria], I turned the hostile land into heaps and ruins. The Assyrian who since distant days had ruled... and with his heavy yoke had brought injury to the people of the Land, his feet from Akkad I turned back, his yoke I threw off.'

The Babylonians had now effectively inherited the Assyrian Empire, but Egypt, Assyria's ally, tried to take advantage of its collapse by seizing control of the Levant. Having defeated and killed Josiah of Judah, an Egyptian force established itself at Carchemish, but soon afterwards, in 605 BC, was defeated at Hamath by the Babylonian crown prince, Nebuchadnezzar. Shortly after this double victory Nebuchadnezzar (604–562 BC) succeeded his father to the throne, returned to Syria and continued to establish Babylonian control in this region.

ADMINISTRATION AND RECONSTRUCTION

In March 597 BC Jerusalem was taken. Its king, Jehoiachin, was deported to Babylon and Nebuchadnezzar's nominee installed in his place; the Babylonian Chronicle records: '... the king of Akkad mustered his army and marched to Hattu [Syria]. He encamped against the city of Judah and on the second day of the month Adar [16 March 597] he captured the city [and] seized [its] king. A king of his own choice he appointed in the city [and] taking the vast tribute he brought it to Babylon.' Ten years later he attacked Jerusalem again after Zedekiah, his appointee, rebelled; he was blinded and deported.

The policy of deportation kept the leaders of defeated people under direct control and was a common practice in the ancient Near East. Babylonian governors ruled the conquered provinces, although some remained under loyal and trusted local rulers. Local taxes covered the costs of provincial administration. As in Assyria, officials swore a personal oath of loyalty to the king.

In Babylonia itself the new wealth of the empire permitted the rebuilding of the great ancient cities and, above all, the enormous city of Babylon itself, which was surrounded by huge double walls and a moat. As far as is known, the other cities were laid out in a plan similar to that of Babylon, walled, with a central sanctuary and major streets leading to it from the various city quarters. Although the king was the ultimate ruler of the empire, the chief cities had their own assemblies, probably limited to the richest citizens, and led by the city governor, which were responsible for administering their own affairs, and in particular the affairs of the city temples. Even after the end of Babylonian independence, the cities remained important and wealthy centres for many centuries.

Little is known of the last years of Nebuchadnezzar, but in the seven years following his death there were three kings before Nabonidus (555–539 BC) came to the throne in a palace coup. A devotee of the moon god Sin, whose shrines at Harran and Ur he restored, he neglected Babylon's cults, including that of Marduk, the city deity. His absence for several years at the oasis of Taima prevented the rituals of

A tablet with part of the Babylonian Chronicle (above), inscribed in 500/499 BC. The Chronicle, written in Akkadian on a series of clay tablets, records events year by year from 744 BC until the third century BC. This tablet covers the period 605–594 BC, including the start of Nebuchadnezzar's reign and his capture of Jerusalem.

A polychrome glazed brick relief of a *mushussu* dragon from the Ishtar Gate. The *mushussu* was sacred to the god Marduk, and reliefs like this lined the walls of the gate and the Processional Way that led to his sanctuary.

the New Year festivities, which renewed the land's fertility and which only the king could perform. He had also made reforms that gave control of the temple finances to the Crown.

Dissatisfaction among the Babylonians, particularly the temple functionaries, probably contributed to the support given to the Persian ruler Cyrus, whose accounts claim that Babylon fell to him without a struggle in October 539 BC. However, there seems to have been a fierce battle at Opis earlier that month, when it is possible that Belshazzar, the crown prince, died. The fall of Babylon to the Persians marked the beginning of the end of the old order, in which the region had for more than two millennia been dominated culturally or politically by Mesopotamia.

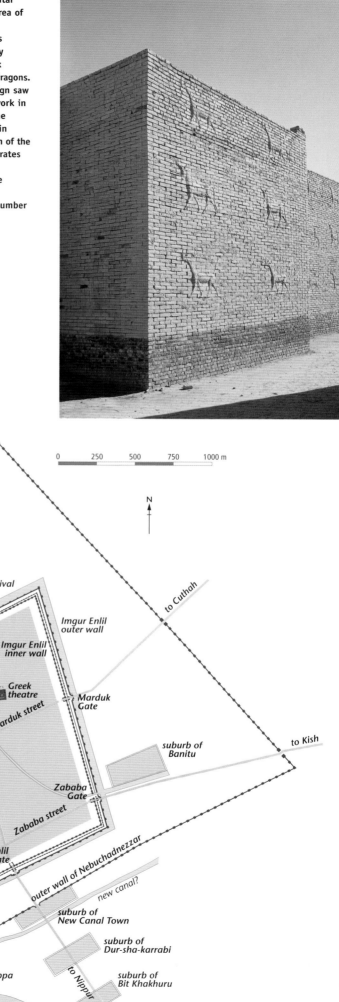

South Wall of the Ishtar Gate (right), in an area of the city rebuilt by Nebuchadnezzar. It is adorned with brightly coloured glazed brick depicting lions and dragons. Nebuchadnezzar's reign saw major construction work in the city, including the rebuilding of the main canals, the completion of the bridge over the Euphrates begun by his father Nabopolassar and the embellishment and reconstruction of a number of temples.

Babylon under Nebuchadnezzar (plan right). The site was excavated early in the 20th century, and Babylonian texts make it possible to identify the gates and some of the principal buildings of the city. At its centre was the great sanctuary of Marduk (Esagila) and the ziggurat Etemanaki ('The House of the Frontier between Heaven and Earth'), a vast temple-tower that gave rise to the legend of the Tower of Babel.

0   250   500   750   1000 m

N

Summer Palace

to Bit Habban

Euphrates

Akitu (New Year) house

temple of the New Year festival

?

to Cuthah

Imgur Enlil outer wall

Imgur Enlil inner wall

north citadel

museum

Ishtar Gate

Sin Gate

Sin street

south citadel

temple of Ninmakh

suburb of Lugalgirra Gate

Hanging Gardens City Castle
Libilkhegalla

Greek theatre

Marduk Gate

castle moat

Processional Way

temple of Ishtar

Marduk street

to Kish

inner town

Lugalgirra Gate

Enlil street

suburb of Banitu

temple of Belit Nina

?

Ziggurat (House of the frontier of Heaven and Earth)

Esagila

the Holy Gate

Zababa Gate

suburb of Nukhar

temple of Adad

?

the Holy House

new town canal?

Shamash street

temple of Marduk

Zababa street

Adad street

the new districts

Adad Gate

to Akus

temple of Gula

Enlil Gate

temple of Ninurta

outer wall of Nebuchadnezzar

new canal?

burial place of Babylon

?

temple of Shamash

Urash Gate

suburb of Litamu

suburb of New Canal Town

mausoleum

Shamash Gate

Euphrates (Arakhtu Canal)

suburb of Dur-sha-karrabi

?

to Larsa

suburb of Tuba

Borsippa Canal

to Borsippa

to Nippur

suburb of Bit Khakhuru

Nabu street

The **Achaemenid Empire**
c. **550–330** BC

The empire of the Persian Achaemenid dynasty, which at its most extensive
reached from the Indus valley to Egypt, was the largest the world had yet seen.
The founder of this empire, Cyrus the Great (559–530 BC), unified the Iranian
plateau for the first time, and this became the new power centre of the Near East.
This period also saw the beginnings of closer contact between the Near Eastern
and Greek worlds, when the Greeks of Ionia came under Persian control.

The Medes and Persians were descended from
Indo-European Aryans who had earlier settled the
Iranian plateau. By the seventh century the Medes
controlled a large area around Ecbatana (Hamadan)
and in 612 BC, allied with the Babylonians, helped
to defeat Assyria. As part of the spoils, they
received territory reaching to Central Anatolia. The
Persians, who had settled in Fars (in southwestern
Iran), were subjects of the Medes.

Astyages (585–550 BC), the last Median king,
was overthrown by Cyrus II (the Great), then king
of Anshan in Fars, a descendant of the Persian
dynastic founder Achaemenes. Now ruler of the
Medes and Persians, Cyrus defeated Lydia in 547 BC
and, after campaigning in central Asia, conquered
Babylonia in 539 BC. Within little more than a
decade, his domains reached from the Ionian coast
to Central Asia, where he was killed on campaign in
530 BC. The consolidation of this empire was helped
by his policy of moderation; tribute was not exces-
sive and local customs and institutions were left
intact. His son Cambyses added Egypt and Libya to
the empire, but died whilst returning to Persia to
put down a revolt, possibly led by his brother.

THE REIGN OF DARIUS

His successor, Darius I (521–486 BC), an
Achaemenid of a cadet branch of the family, spent
almost two years putting down this widespread
rebellion and restoring peace. His version of the
rebels' defeat is recorded on a large inscription at
Behistun (see page 90). Darius campaigned in
northwest India and under him the empire reached
its greatest extent, although he was unsuccessful in
an attack on the Scythians north of the Black Sea.

A brilliant administrator, Darius divided the
empire into provinces or 'satrapies', the governors
of which were usually loyal Persian nobles or members of the royal family. Each satrapy had a separate
official in charge of the army and for collecting the
annual tribute, paid in kind or precious metals. The
reliefs of the tribute-bearers at Persepolis (see page
90) illustrate the wide range of products offered

Archers from a frieze at Susa
(right). At the core of the
Persian army were 'The
Immortals', the king's personal guard of 10,000 infantry.
Foot soldiers expanded the
empire to the east, but the
effectiveness of the Lydian
cavalry in opposing the
Persian army during the
campaign of 546 BC led to
an increase in the numbers of
Persian cavalry. The infantry
henceforth were normally
mercenaries or levies from
allied nations. One such
group, employed by the
crown prince Cyrus to overthrow his brother in 401 BC,
was immortalized by the
Greek historian Xenophon,
who recounted their epic
march through Persia.

Achaemenid Persia,
550–330 BC

■ approximate extent of
Achaemenid heartland

■ added by Cyrus the Great by 550 BC

■ added by Cyrus the Great by 530 BC

□ added by Cambyses by 525 BC

▨ added by Darius I by c. 500 BC

— approximate maximum extent of
Achaemenid Empire, c. 500 BC

and include incense, textiles, ivory and animals such as camels and even giraffes.

Darius reorganized the army, built a fleet and had a canal cut from the Red Sea to the Nile. He also built a great system of roads, facilitating and speeding up travel – a royal courier using staging posts and fresh horses along the way could ride the 2,700 km from Susa to Sardis in a week. There was also a postal system and coinage (invented by the Lydians). A new royal capital was built at Persepolis, replacing Cyrus's capital, Pasargadae, and Susa, the ancient Elamite capital, now became the main administrative centre with Ecbatana as the royal summer residence.

The conflict between the Greeks and Persians that began in 494 BC with the revolt of the Ionian cities is not mentioned in Persian sources. Four years after the Persian defeat at Marathon Darius was succeeded by his son Xerxes (486–465 BC), who had then to crush a revolt in Egypt and three years later, put down a rebellion in Babylon. In 480 BC Greece was invaded, but the Persians suffered defeat at Salamis and Plataea. In addition to these conflicts and subsequent Persian involvement in the affairs of its Greek neighbour, there were more fruitful contacts, as politicians, scholars, merchants and even mercenaries travelled from one region to another and several Greek authors wrote about the Persians.

After the long reign of Artaxerxes II (405–359 BC) his sons disputed the succession and thereafter Achaemenid reigns all began or ended with murders and harem conspiracies. With the defeat of Darius III (336–330 BC), the last Achaemenid, by Alexander of Macedon, the territories embraced by this vast empire became part of the Hellenistic world. The Persian Empire was not in a state of decay; apart from Egypt and some of the Ionian cities, most subject people fought steadfastly on the side of the Persians. Why Alexander was able so easily to defeat the Persians remains a mystery.

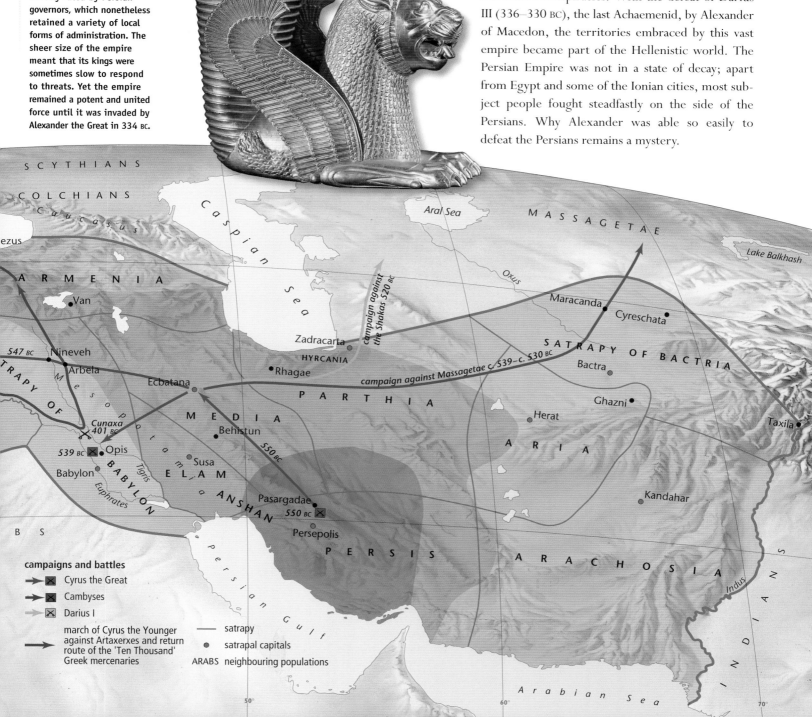

campaigns and battles
Cyrus the Great
Cambyses
Darius I
march of Cyrus the Younger against Artaxerxes and return route of the 'Ten Thousand' Greek mercenaries

satrapy
satrapal capitals
ARABS neighbouring populations

Behistun and Persepolis 521–330 BC

The Achaemenid kings left many important monuments, but amongst the most enduring has been Persepolis, which acted as a ceremonial capital and whose partial destruction in 330 BC by the conquering troops of Alexander the Great caused its remaining exquisite carvings to be preserved beneath the rubble. Equally important for the understanding of Achaemenid rule was Behistun, where an inscription in three languages, including Old Persian, allowed the decipherment of Achaemenid documents.

The Persians of this period spoke an early form of modern Persian, 'Old Persian'; texts in this Indo-European language were written in a cuneiform script, very different from Akkadian cuneiform. The trilingual Behistun inscription is not only the longest text in Old Persian language, but seems to have been the first; the script was probably an artificial royal creation, designed to make a visual impression and provide a script unique to the Persians.

Decipherment began in the early 19th century and was greatly advanced by Henry Rawlinson. Although other scholars, notably the German, Georg Grotefend, had worked on copies of Old Persian cuneiform inscriptions from Persepolis, these consisted mainly of royal names and titles and were too short for a full decipherment of the language. Rawlinson, a Persian-speaking officer in the British East India Company, was sent as a military adviser to Persia and was, in AD 1835 and 1844, able to copy and then translate this long Old Persian text, which provided the key to understanding in turn Akkadian and Elamite.

PERSEPOLIS

Persepolis, called Parsa in Old Persian, lies on the eastern edge of the Marv Dasht plain in Fars, 40 kilometres southwest of Pasargdae, which it

A carving from the Apadana staircase at Persepolis depicting Babylonian tribute-bearers (above). There are 23 such reliefs in all, showing delegations from all the lands ruled by the Achaemenids. The extent of the empire is graphically revealed in the number and diversity of the subject peoples depicted – from the Medes and Persians themselves, at the heart of the empire, to Indians from Sind, Babylonians, Bactrians from Central Asia, Scythians from the Black Sea with pointed caps and Ethiopians from the land of Kush, south of Egypt, bringing a giraffe and elephant tusks.

The Behistun inscription (left), a long cuneiform trilingual in Old Persian, Akkadian and Elamite, was carved in 520/519 BC on a smoothed rock face rising high above the plain of Behistun, near Kermanshah, dominating the ancient road from Persepolis to Ecbatana (Hamadan). Placed here by Darius I, it records his successful struggles for the kingship and justifies his claim to hold office. The accompanying relief depicts Darius, holding a bow and with his foot on the body of the usurper, Gaumata, and two attendants, facing nine captive rebel kings.

replaced as a new royal capital during the reign of Darius I. The high citadel or stone terrace, 300 by 400 metres, on which was erected a series of monumental royal buildings, was part of a vast complex commissioned by Darius. The new centre included the fortified hill to the east, the buildings at the foot of the citadel, the Achaemenid royal tombs in the cliffs of Naqsh-I Rustam and a city, which has not yet been located. Building was started about 500 BC and was continued by Xerxes I (485–465 BC) and Artaxerxes I (464–425 BC); some further work was also done later, under Artaxerxes III (358–338 BC).

Sacked and burned by the army of Alexander the Great, shaken by earthquakes and eroded by two millennia of harsh weather, Persepolis is nevertheless one of the best preserved of all the ancient Near Eastern sites. Most of the citadel was excavated by the Oriental Institute of Chicago in the 1930s; more recent studies have considerably enhanced understanding of the site.

THE STRUCTURE OF THE SITE

The citadel buildings include the *apadana*, probably the main reception hall of the king, two monumental gates, a series of palaces and the so-called treasury. They were approached by a large, sculpted, double stairway with reliefs of tribute-bearers from all corners of the Persian Empire; beyond this was a great gate built by Xerxes. The buildings had tall, slender columns, with stone capitals, surmounted by animal capitals. Walls were of mud-brick and flat roofs were supported by massive timber beams. The

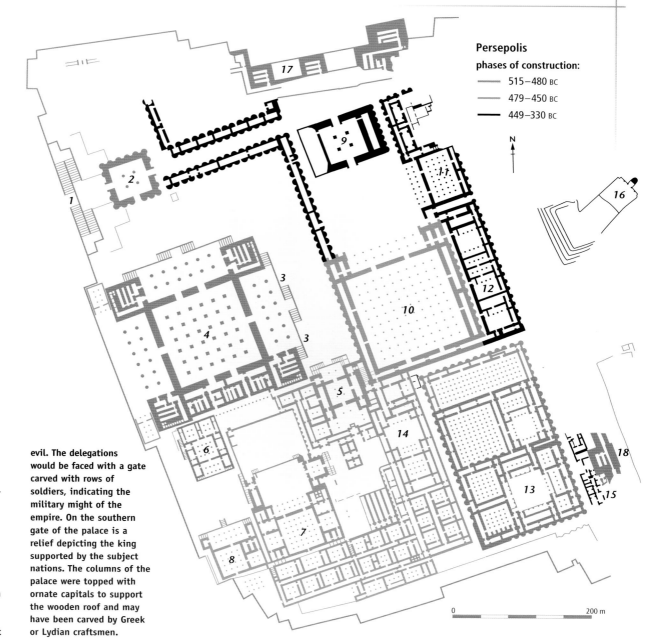

Persepolis (plan right) was the principal residence of the Achaemenid kings, its architecture and monumental scale clearly reflecting their grandiose aspirations.

1 Principal stairway
2 Gate Tower
3 Eastern stairway to Apadana
4 Apadana or principal audience hall of Darius I
5 Tripylon palace
6 Tachara or 'winter palace'
7 Hadish or Palace of Xerxes I
8 Palace of Artaxerxes I
9 Unfinished gate tower
10 Hall of 100 Columns or 'throne hall'
11 Hall of 32 Columns
12 Royal stables
13 Offices and storerooms
14 Additional treasury warehouse
15 Garrison quarters
16 Rock-cut royal tomb, attributed to Artaxerxes III
17 and 18 Remains of mud-brick fortification wall

The Hall of 100 Columns (below), with the Apadana behind it. This part of the palace was probably used for the reception of the subject peoples. The Persian king would enter through a side door where a carving depicts him battling against evil. The delegations would be faced with a gate carved with rows of soldiers, indicating the military might of the empire. On the southern gate of the palace is a relief depicting the king supported by the subject nations. The columns of the palace were topped with ornate capitals to support the wooden roof and may have been carved by Greek or Lydian craftsmen.

Persepolis

phases of construction:

— 515–480 BC
— 479–450 BC
— 449–330 BC

0   200 m

largest building, the Apadana, had 20-metre-high slender limestone columns surmounted by bull or lion-shaped capitals. At the edge of the western portico, the king's throne overlooked the plain; the wide colonnades of the porticoes permitted light to enter the dim interior of the great building. Monumental staircases, to the north and the east, rose about 3 metres to the porticos, their façades covered with reliefs depicting tribute-bearers and animals in combat.

The architecture and decoration contained elements from many traditions – Mesopotamian, Egyptian, Lydian and Greek. The concept of the complex itself and the subject matter of the reliefs seem to reflect an idealized conception of the empire, rather than a representation of the New Year festival. The whole scheme appears to reflect secular power, as no shrine or temple has been recognized. However, although the king himself is the focus of the decorations, he is often shown beneath the winged figure of the god Ahuramazda.

The **Rise** of **Macedon** and **Alexander the Great** c. **500–323** BC

Macedon, on the northern edge of the Aegean world, was always at the margin of Greek culture. While the southern parts of Macedonia were Hellenized, Greek-speaking and urbanized, the northern part of the kingdom, Upper Macedonia, was less influenced by Greece, and when the Macedonian throne was weak it often broke away from the kings' control. In the mid-fourth century BC Macedon's place in Mediterranean affairs changed dramatically under two kings, Philip II and Alexander the Great.

In 500 BC the Macedonian king Alexander I had been acknowledged as a Greek and permitted to compete in the Olympic games. When Xerxes invaded Greece in 480 BC, Alexander came to terms with him, and subsequently managed to hold on to his kingdom after the invasion failed. In the years that followed there were periods of stability, when Macedonian rulers such as Perdiccas II (c. 450–413 BC), his son Archelaus II (413–399 BC) and Amyntas (c. 393–370 BC) were able to unite their territory, and to play a role in the affairs of the cities to the south, but at other times struggles over the succession and internal feuds limited Macedonian influence.

MACEDON UNDER PHILIP II

When Amyntas's son Philip II (359–336 BC) came to the throne, matters changed. His military abilities enabled him to begin a process of expansion. Philip's capture of the gold and silver mining areas north of the Aegean gave him enormous financial reserves, which could be used to employ mercenary soldiers. He also created what was virtually a standing army of Macedonians. He developed new tactics, arming his men with long pikes called

sarrissas, which made them more than a match for the hoplite armies of the Greek cities, and reorganized the cavalry, creating an elite force of 'companions' made up of the leading Macedonian nobles.

Taking advantage of disputes in the regions to the south of Macedon Philip intervened first in Thessaly, then in the war between Thebes and Phocis, finally defeating the Thebans and Athenians at Chaeronea in Boeotia in 338 BC. This victory was followed by the creation of a the League of Corinth, an alliance of Greek states led by Macedon intended to maintain peace between the Greek cities and to pave the way for an invasion of the Persian Empire. The assassination of Philip two

Three portraits of Alexander the Great. The coin (above right) was made by Ptolemy I in Alexandria. The marble head (above) is also from Egypt. The mosaic (bottom) is from Pompeii, and based on a fourth-century BC original. Alexander's reign marked a turning point in portraiture, as the visual projection of the power of the ruler became a central element in Greek rulership.

THE CAMPAIGNS OF ALEXANDER THE GREAT

Alexander spent virtually the whole of his reign on campaign. After putting down rebellions in Greece he launched his attack on the Persian Empire. He defeated the Persian King Darius at Issus before taking control of the Levant and Egypt, and then defeated him again at Gaugamela, after which he proclaimed himself King of Persia. Alexander pursued Darius eastwards, until his assassination by a Persian noble, Bessus. The next years were spent settling the northeastern parts of his territory, and then invading India. When his troops refused to go any further, Alexander returned to Mesopotamia; he died from a fever in Babylon in 323 BC. Alexander did not make great changes to the administration of the empire, generally maintaining the existing system of regional government, and he also founded a number of cities, occupied usually by veteran soldiers.

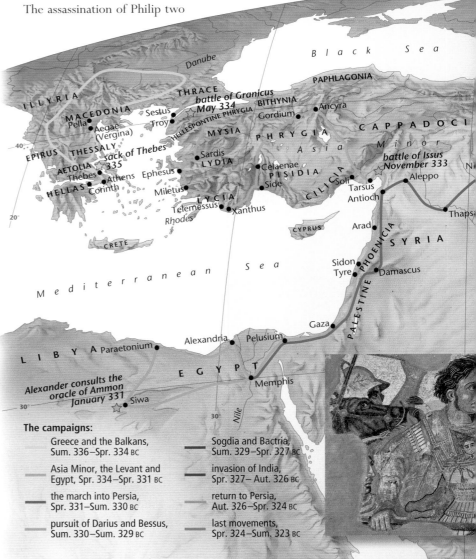

The campaigns:

- Greece and the Balkans, Sum. 336–Spr. 334 BC
- Asia Minor, the Levant and Egypt, Spr. 334–Spr. 331 BC
- the march into Persia, Spr. 331–Sum. 330 BC
- pursuit of Darius and Bessus, Sum. 330–Sum. 329 BC
- Sogdia and Bactria, Sum. 329–Spr. 327 BC
- invasion of India, Spr. 327–Aut. 326 BC
- return to Persia, Aut. 326–Spr. 324 BC
- last movements, Spr. 324–Sum. 323 BC

years later meant that task had to carried forward by his son Alexander.

THE REIGN OF ALEXANDER THE GREAT

Alexander, too, had some difficulty in securing his position, but he dealt rapidly with opposition in Macedon and in Greece, and in 334 BC he led his forces into Asia. In the next decade he brought the whole of the Persian empire under his control. This achievement is difficult to explain, since the Empire was not particularly weaker in the time of Alexander than it had been earlier: Alexander's own skill as a military leader must have been an important factor in his success. His death in 323 BC at the age of 32 prevented him from consolidating his rule, and the following decades saw his former generals fighting each other for possession of the territory he had conquered.

Relations between the Macedonian kings and the Greek cities were always uneasy. The factional nature of Greek politics meant that Philip and Alexander inevitably had supporters in all the cities, and it is far from clear that Philip wanted to fight against his southern neighbours, especially given that the lands to the east offered much richer

The ram's horns and diadem depicted on this coin (above) are thought to symbolize Alexander's relationship with the Libyan god Ammon.

One of the royal tombs of Macedon (right) at Aegae (modern Vergina). Aegae was the ancient capital of the Macedonians, and the palace became a focus for Greek culture in the fifth and fourth centuries BC. The royal court attracted Greek writers and artists, including the poets Pindar (c. 518–446 BC) and Euripides (c. 485–406 BC); Philip II invited the philosopher Aristotle (384–322 BC) there to act as tutor to Alexander the Great.

rewards. However, they had enemies too. There were attempts to rebel against Macedonian control when news was brought that Philip and later Alexander had died: on both occasions the Greek cities were soon brought under control again. The influential Athenian orator Demosthenes (384–322 BC) depicted the Macedonians as barbarians who were implacably hostile to Athens and the other Greek cities, and it was his advocacy that led Athens to disaster at Chaeronea. It is clear, however, that the rulers of Macedon, who spoke Greek and whose courts were noted for the Greek culture to be found there, had been fully part of the Greek world since at least the end of the sixth century BC. Alexander's conquests helped to spread the language and culture of Greece more widely over the Near East.

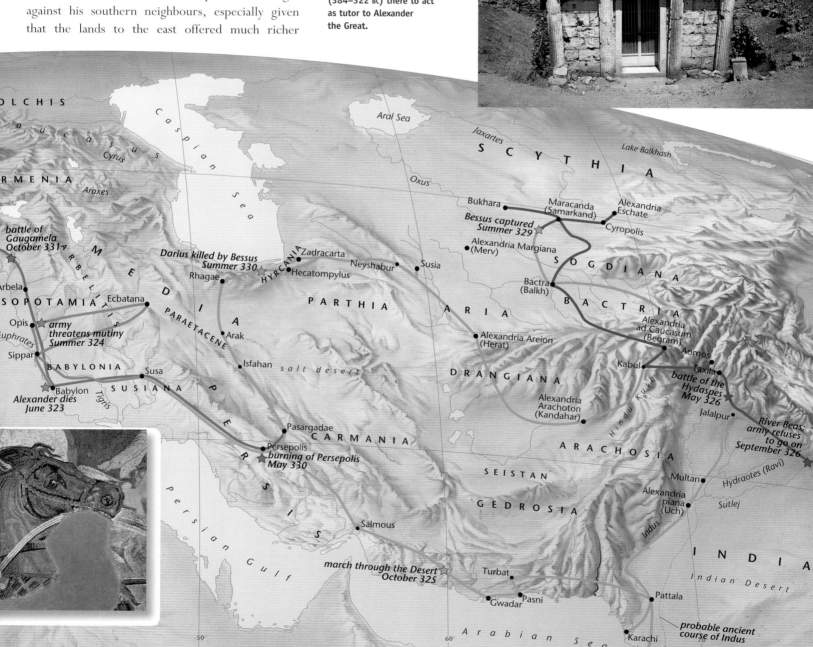

Early Historic India
C. **1000–300** BC

The period between 1000 and 300 BC witnessed the reappearance of urbanism and stable political structures following the disintegration of the Harappan urban civilization. By around 1000 BC, the centre of power had shifted towards the east in the Gangetic valley, where the beginnings of a settlement hierarchy can be traced. These processes culminate in the emergence of a centralized bureaucracy and the formation of the first pan-Indian state at the beginning of the fourth century BC.

The warring tribal territories described in the late Vedic texts culminated in the rise of a stratified society which was based around monarchical states governed by hereditary rulers. The development of extensive trading networks, coupled with the expansionist tendencies of the competing states, and a growing agricultural base formed the backdrop to the rise of urbanism in c. 600 BC.

THE RISE OF URBANIZATION

The *Anguttara Nikaya*, an early Buddhist text, gives the names of 16 major states (Mahajanapadas) and their capital cities, extending from Afghanistan in the north to the Deccan in the south. Over half of these state capitals have been identified in the archaeological record as fortified settlements associated with Northern Black Polished Ware (NBPW), a form of pottery dateable to c. 550 BC which marks the earliest phase of urbanization in the Indo-Gangetic divide and the upper Gangetic valley. For example, Rajgir, described in the Buddhist texts as the capital of Magadha, Rajghat, capital of Kasi, and Champa, capital of Anga, all appear to have reached a level of 'incipient urbanism' by this time. Other

The construction of massive fortification walls such as those at Rajgir (below), the ancient capital of Magadha, set the earliest towns apart from their rural landscape. The outer cyclopean wall runs for over 30 km along the crests of the surrounding hills, and is constructed from a rubble core strengthened by stone revetting and studded with circular towers. It is probably contemporary with a second inner wall circuit of 6 km, whose earthen core has been dated to c.550 BC on the basis of associated Northern Black Polished Ware. By c. 300 BC, fortifications had become a regular feature of early historic cities such as Vidisha in central India, whilst the ramparts at Pataliputra are described in Classical sources as having 570 bastions.

urban centres lying beyond the Gangetic region include Ujjain in central India, the capital of ancient Avanti, and Taxila and Charsada in the northwest, both of which were associated with the annexation of Gandhara and the Indus valley by the Achaemenid empire.

In the following years, increasing inter-state warfare and expansionism led to the consolidation of the 16 Mahajanapadas into four larger states: Avanti, Vatsa, Kosala and Magadha. By 400 BC, the focus of power had become concentrated upon Magadha, whose territory under the Nanda Dynasty extended as far as Orissa in the east, and Karnataka in the south. It is during this period that punchmarked and uninscribed coins first appear in the archaeological record, and texts attest to a professional bureaucracy and a rising class of merchants and traders. As sites towards the upper end of the settlement hierarchy grew in scale, there was a corresponding increase in the number of villages in the 'interior' areas. Meanwhile, much of the Achaemenid territory to the north came under Hellenistic rule following the invasion of Alexander the Great in 326 BC (see page 92).

URBANIZATION UNDER THE MAURYAS

By c. 321 BC, the whole of Magadha and the Hellenistic colonies in the north-west had become incorporated into the Mauryan empire under its first ruler, Chandragupta Maurya (c. 310–286 BC). The Magadhan capital was subsequently shifted to Pataliputra (modern Patna), which is described in early fourth-century Classical sources as a well-planned city with enormous fortifications. This marked increase in scale and grandeur is also attested archaelogically: excavations at Pataliputra revealed a pillared hall and a wooden palisaded rampart dateable to this period. This represents the beginning of the second major stage of urbanization which culminated in the third century BC under Chandragupta's grandson, Emperor Ashoka (see page 122). The older fortified capitals became fully-fledged cities, whilst urban culture spread into

previously undeveloped areas. Vaisali in the middle Gangetic valley, Vidisha, Eran and Tripuri in central India, and the earliest cities in south India all belong to this category.

THE IRON AGE

Iron objects, largely in the form of hunting weapons and craft tools, first appear in limited numbers at sites such as Atranjikhera and Hastinapura in the Gangetic valley in c.1000 BC, in association with Painted Grey Ware. However, it is only with the rise of urbanism in c.550 BC that iron becomes widely distributed, with the addition of tools of production such as axes and ploughshares. As such, the Iron Age often lies at the heart of explanations for the emergence of urban culture. Some argue that towns grew up as a result of the agricultural surplus generated by the introduction of the iron ploughshare, and population shifts into previously forested areas which had been cleared through the use of new iron tools. Archaeological and literary evidence, however, suggest that the use of iron weapons in inter-regional warfare might have had a greater impact on the formation of states and cities than agricultural surplus, which had already reached significant levels during the period preceding the Iron Age. Equally important was the consolidation of a stable political infrastructure and a growing trading network through which the exploitation of resources could be effectively channelled. The spread of Buddhism, whose close links with merchants and traders as instruments of lay patronage is well attested, may also have been an important agent of social change during this formative period.

Northern Black Polished Ware (NBPW), often in the form of shallow dishes and bowls, was the deluxe pottery used by the earliest town-dwellers (above left). First appearing at sites such as Champa, Rajgir, Rajghat and Ujjain, it coincides with the earliest stages of urbanization in the middle of the sixth century BC. Its distinctive 'metallic' shine was achieved through the application of an alkaline slip followed by high-temperature firing. The quality and distribution of NBPW reaches its peak in c. 400–300 BC with the rise of a fully developed urban culture.

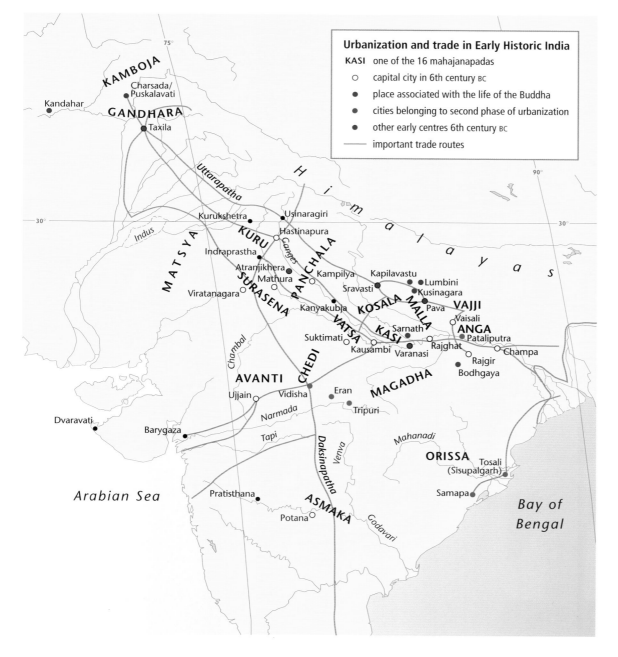

Urbanization and trade in Early Historic India

KASI   one of the 16 mahajanapadas
○   capital city in 6th century BC
●   place associated with the life of the Buddha
●   cities belonging to second phase of urbanization
●   other early centres 6th century BC
—   important trade routes

Sixteen major states and their capitals are described in early Buddhist texts (map left). The two major centres of urbanism during this period reflect the socio-economic currents of the time: the Achaemenid territories to the north, and a number of powerful states in the Gangetic valley, where many of the early historic cities are closely associated with heterodox religions such as Jainism and Buddhism. The economic and political strength of what would later grow into cities was due in part to the wealth generated by nearby trade routes: the Uttarapatha (literally the 'northern route') linked the Gangetic valley with north-west India, whilst the Daksinapatha (the 'southern route') led to the south via central India. Many of the later cities which came up during the Mauryan expansion were closely connected with these routes.

Zhou China
1050–221 BC

The Zhou Dynasty was the longest-reigning dynasty in Chinese history. They claimed to have inherited the mandate of Heaven from the Shang, granted them through their success in battle in 1050 BC against the Shang because the latter had by their behaviour proved themselves unworthy of trust. This theory of rulership, by which a claim to legitimate power was seen to be supported by the will of Heaven, manifested by success in war and prosperity in peacetime, endured until the 20th century.

The Zhou were at first vigorous rulers, setting up a capital at (present-day) Xi'an. Control over central and northern China was maintained by assigning large territories to relatives of the kings, who ruled them as fiefs. These many vassal states in the Western Zhou realm soon established their own governing systems, as well as individual economies and cultures, and progressively became independent kingdoms. Over the next few centuries the authority of the Zhou Dynasty gradually declined. In 771 BC the Quanrong nomads invaded and overran the Wei valley and the Zhou moved its capital to Luoyang in the east; historians have therefore traditionally divided the dynasty into the earlier Western Zhou (1050–771 BC) and the later Eastern Zhou periods.

During the Eastern Zhou period (771–221 BC) royal prestige was based on reverence for the king's sacred function as 'The Son of Heaven' rather than political power. The names of the kings and an outline of their exploits are known from early chronicles and the *Shujing*, from the *Shiji* (*Records of the Historian*) by Sima Qian (completed c. 90 BC), as well as from inscriptions on bronze ritual vessels. The material remains of the Zhou comprise large numbers of richly equipped tombs and traces of substantial cities. Many bronzes have been found in hoards, rather than tombs, and many of those were probably buried in 771 BC, when the Zhou fled eastwards from the nomadic invasions.

Political instability during the 'Spring and Autumn Period' (770–476 BC) was compounded during the Warring States period (476–221 BC), when China was divided into several hundreds of warring states, each competing with one another for hegemony within China. The various courts also vied with each other in splendour and luxury. The tomb of the Marquis of Zeng, buried in 433 BC, was discovered in 1978. He was not a particularly powerful or rich ruler but his tomb contained not only ten tons of bronzes, at a time when bronze was obviously much used for weaponry, but also solid-gold vessels, lacquers and jades, bamboo, leather armour and lacquered wooden objects.

The Zhou people's homeland lay west of the Shang kings in the valley of the Wei River (map below), a tributary of the Yellow River in Shaanxi province, and their first capital was at Xi'an. After the invasion by the Quanrong nomads and the Zhou Dynasty's move to a new capital in the east at Luoyang in 771 BC, the central power declined and there was a proliferation of quasi-independent states, amongst which Chu came to dominate southern China, producing distinctive specialized crafts such as lacquered, wooden objects and silks and an emphasis on Daoist and shamanic thought. However, it was the Qin state, with its legalistic base, which unified the country in 221 BC, creating the Chinese Empire.

This Eastern Zhou lampbearer (Zhongshan state, fourth century BC) is an outstanding example of the art of Chinese bronze casters and silversmiths (below). The head is made of silver and then inserted into the body which is cast in bronze. The details of the hair, garment, and of the animals climbing into the stem of the lamp are all very clearly delineated. Lamps were a very popular item for inclusion in tombs of this period and many elaborate ones are known.

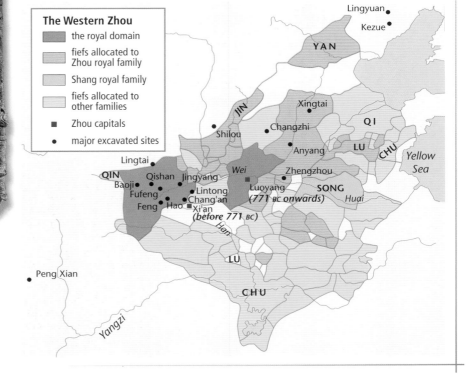

The Western Zhou
- the royal domain
- fiefs allocated to Zhou royal family
- Shang royal family
- fiefs allocated to other families
- ■ Zhou capitals
- • major excavated sites

Lingyuan
Kezue
YAN
Xingtai
JIN
QI
Shilou
Changzhi
LU
CHU
Anyang
Lingtai
Yellow
Sea
QIN
Qishan
Jingyang
Wei
Zhengzhou
Baoji
Fufeng
Lintong
Luoyang
SONG
Huai
Feng
Hao
Chang'an
(771 BC onwards)
Xi'an
(before 771 BC)
Han
LU
Peng Xian
CHU
Yangzi

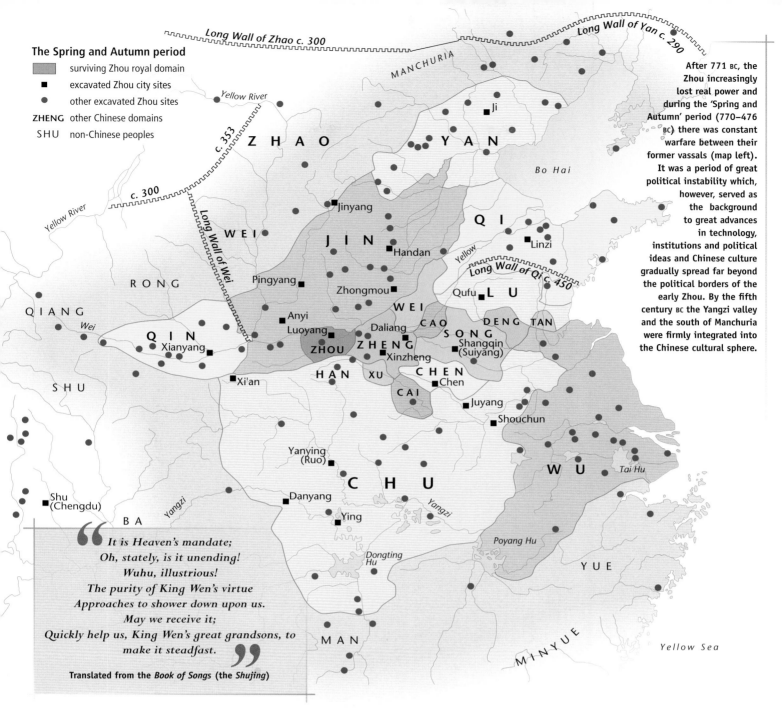

Long Wall of Zhao c. 300

Long Wall of Yan c. 290

MANCHURIA

Ji

Yellow River

c. 353

Yellow River

ZHAO

YAN

Bo Hai

c. 300

Long Wall of Wei

Jinyang

QI

WEI

JIN

Handan

Linzi

Pingyang

Zhongmou

Yellow

Long Wall of Qi c. 450

RONG

WEI

Qufu

LU

QIANG

Wei

Anyi

Daliang

DENG TAN

QIN

Luoyang

CAO

SONG

Xianyang

ZHOU

ZHENG

Shangqin
(Suiyang)

Xinzheng

Xi'an

HAN

XU

CHEN

SHU

CAI

Chen

Juyang

Shouchun

WU

Tai Hu

Yanying
(Ruo)

CHU

Shu
(Chengdu)

BA

Yangzi

Danyang

Ying

Yangzi

Poyang Hu

YUE

*Dongting
Hu*

MAN

MINYUE

Yellow Sea

> *It is Heaven's mandate;*
> *Oh, stately, is it unending!*
> *Wuhu, illustrious!*
> *The purity of King Wen's virtue*
> *Approaches to shower down upon us.*
> *May we receive it;*
> *Quickly help us, King Wen's great grandsons, to*
> *make it steadfast.*
>
> **Translated from the *Book of Songs* (the *Shujing*)**

The hedonistic lifestyle of this period was emphasized by the burial of 22 musicians specially slain to accompany him to the afterlife so that they could play the 125 musical instruments he had in his tomb, which included a set of 65 bells together with lacquered wooden stands.

The Eastern Zhou witnessed major advances in culture and technology. Cast-iron technology meant that both weapons and tools could be more cheaply made, canal and irrigation systems were constructed, the first money came into use, cities and trade flourished and technical improvements such as efficient ploughs and horse harnesses made labour more productive. It was also a time when philosophical thoughts and ideas flourished. The most influential Chinese thinker, Confucius (c. 551–c. 479 BC), lived during this period. He was followed by many other philosophers who disputed his view of duty and piety as the foundation of the good state and by the Daoist religion which promoted a more spontaneous, individualistic attitude towards the world.

Gradually the Warring States were reduced in number, one conquering the other, until the final unification of China by the Qin in 221 BC which brought to an end the period of co-existent kingdoms (see p. 124).

Kang Hou gui (Early Western Zhou period). This vessel (below left) is famous for its inscription which describes an attack on the Shang by the Zhou king and the establishment of the Kang Hou or Marquis of Kang in Wei, near present-day Huixian in Henan province. It was cast by Mei Situ Yi, possibly in conjunction with Kang Hou. It therefore provides important historical documentation, as well as being in itself an imposing vessel.

Age of Empires
c. 300 BC–AD 250

Terracotta warrior from Xian, buried in the grave of the Emperor Qin Shi Huangdi

In the first two centuries AD the whole of Eurasia, from the Atlantic to the Pacific, was straddled by four imperial powers, the Romans, the Parthians, the Kushans and the Han Chinese. These were empires built on earlier powers. The successors of Alexander the Great had carved out large kingdoms for themselves in the territory from Greece to the Indus, and in India the Mauryas had created an empire that covered most of the sub-continent.

Stability is a feature of this period. Emperors were expected to defend and increase their domains, and as long as they were successful they could rely on the support of their richest subjects, from whom the administrators of their empires were drawn. This stability made possible increased exchange of goods and ideas not only within the empires but also between them. Roman senators wore Chinese silk, while Syrian jugglers entertained the Chinese court. The great variety of goods being carried around Eurasia is well illustrated by a hoard buried in Begram in Afghanistan around AD 100, which contained bronzes and glassware from the Mediterranean, ivory from India and lacquer from China.

Carthage and Rome in the western Mediterranean 264–44 BC

The third century BC saw the transformation of the western Mediterranean world, with Rome twice defeating the Carthaginians and taking their European territories from them. In the next 150 years Carthage itself was destroyed and rebuilt as a Roman colony. After a long series of wars, Rome's other great enemies, the Gauls, were conquered and incorporated into the expanding Roman Empire. The Romans were left the undisputed masters of the western Mediterranean.

B efore 264 BC, no Roman army had campaigned outside Italy, but in that year the Romans were invited to intervene in the affairs of the city of Messana in Sicily. Their action led to conflict with the Greek city of Syracuse under its king Hieron II and with the Carthaginians led by their general Hamilcar. Hieron soon changed sides, but the war with Carthage, later called by the Romans the First Punic War, dragged on for over twenty years (264–241 BC). Roman land forces were superior to those of the Carthaginians, but for as long as they lacked an effective navy, they could do little with this advantage. The creation of a Roman navy at this point, and with it new tactics in naval warfare, laid the basis for much of Rome's subsequent imperial power. The Romans were ultimately victorious, and took control of Sicily; soon afterwards they seized Sardinia and Corsica as well. These provinces were not treated in the way that Rome's defeated neighbours in Italy had been. Instead they were administered by magistrates sent out annually by the Roman Senate, and paid tribute to Rome.

The good relations between Rome and the Greek cities of Italy extended to alliances with Greek

> *If we Greeks were familiar with the two states which disputed the rule of the world, there would perhaps have been no need for me to explain for what purpose or with what resources they were impelled to undertake a task of such a kind and such a size. But since the former power and earlier history of the Roman and Carthaginian states is something unfamiliar to most Greeks, I wanted no-one to find himself at a loss and to have to ask with what intentions, what powers and what resources the Romans had set out on that enterprise by which they became masters by land and by sea of our part of the world. Rather I shall show my readers that the Romans had from the outset sufficient reason to entertain the design of creating a world empire and sufficient resources to achieve their purpose.*
>
> **Polybius (c. 200–118 BC), *The Histories***

settlements in Spain and southern France, most importantly Massilia. Carthage meanwhile had relations with the Phoenician settlements in southern Spain, and increasing Carthaginian military activity in Spain led to a new conflict with Rome. The Second Punic War (218–201 BC) saw Hannibal invade Italy from the north, supported by the Gallic communities between the Alps and the Po valley. The great reserves of manpower available to the Romans meant that despite a series of disastrous defeats they were able to prevent Hannibal from achieving much in Italy, and when a Roman army invaded Carthaginian territory in north Africa, Hannibal had to withdraw. Carthage was defeated in 201 BC, and ceased to be a significant power. In 146 BC the Romans declared war for a third time, and sacked the city.

THE CONQUEST OF GAUL

Although the wars between Rome and Carthage are the most well known of Rome's military activities in this period, the long-running conflict with the Gauls was a greater threat to Roman security. Gallic settlement in northern Italy had begun in the sixth century BC, and thereafter there had been attempts to advance south of the Apennines until 225 BC, when the Romans and their allies defeated a Gallic army and began the conquest of the area known as Cisalpine Gaul. Although the Romans rapidly

The harbours at Carthage, built in the third or second century BC (left). According to the historian Appian, 'The harbours were interconnected and there was one entrance from the sea, 70 feet wide, which could be closed with iron chains. The first harbour was for merchant ships and much and various tackle was collected here. Within the inner harbour was an island, and the island and the harbour edge were built over with ship sheds. The area contained berths to hold 220 vessels, and in addition to these there were stores for the equipment for the triremes.'

Numantia

Numantia
133

• Salamantica

H I S P A N I A

ULTERIOR

Toletum

40°

• Felicitas Julia

197

CI

• Corduba

Baetis
208 ✕

✕ Baecul
208

• Malaca

During the third century BC Rome gained control of much of the western Mediterranean as a result of its two wars with Carthage. Sicily was the first territory that the Romans took over and administered as a province, at the end of the First Punic War (264–241 BC), and it was soon followed by Sardinia and Corsica. Victory in the Second Punic War (218–201 BC) gave Rome mastery over eastern Spain, and over the next century nearly all of the Iberian peninsula was brought under Roman rule. Hannibal's invasion of Italy demonstrated the danger Rome might face from the north, and the Romans responded by taking control of Cisalpine Gaul, subsequently creating the province of Narbonensis in what is now southern France, and later conquering the rest of Gaul. Meanwhile the sack of Carthage in 146 BC, and the creation of the province of Africa, completed the Roman encirclement of the western Mediterranean.

Carthage, Rome and the Western Mediterranean

— extent of Carthaginian control before the first Punic War c. 264 BC

-- extent of Carthaginian control before the second Punic War c. 220 BC

···· extent of Carthaginian control before the third Punic War c. 149 BC

area under Roman control before the first Punic War c. 264 BC

area under Roman control before the second Punic War c. 220 BC

area under Roman control before the third Punic War c. 149 BC

area under Roman control before the consulship of Julius Caesar 59 BC

area under Roman control at the death of Julius Caesar 44 BC

GALLIA 49 Roman province with date of creation

✗ principal battle with date

⊗ principal siege with date

Roman soldiers of the second century BC from the Altar of Domitius Ahenobarbus in Rome (left). There was no standing army in the period of the Roman republic. Instead troops, drawn from the peasant farmers of Rome and its allies, were called up for each new campaign. They were expected to provide their own armour, and to return to their farms once the campaign was over. This system worked reasonably well when fighting was limited to Italy, but it was less appropriate for long campaigns overseas. By the first century BC, the Roman army was made up largely of poor men equipped at the state's expense. These troops were often provided with grants of land upon retirement, paid for by their commanders. The number of veterans who owed their security to individual generals rather than the city of Rome was one of the factors that led to civil war and the end of the Roman republic.

gained control of the area, Hannibal's invasion interrupted their actions, and it was only in 191 BC that war with the Gauls ended. In the next few years virtually all of the land south of the river Po was seized and settled by Roman colonists. Later, the Romans tightened their control of Gaul west of the Alps, creating the province of Gallia Narbonensis in 121 BC. Finally, the ten-year campaign of Gaius Julius Caesar (58–49 BC) ended with Rome in control of Gallic territory as far as the Rhine and the English Channel.

Republican Rome
509–27 BC

During the period of its rise to empire the city of Rome was governed by a close-knit oligarchy of powerful families. These families filled the priesthoods, the magistracies and the Senate of Rome. Although elections and the passing of legislation were the responsibility of popular assemblies, these were dominated by the richer citizens.

A Roman political career involved winning election to a series of offices, each held for a single year (see the table on the next page). The system (known as the *Cursus Honorum*) meant that for most of his career a Roman politician was not holding office. However, ex-magistrates became members of the Senate, and this body of 300 men was extremely influential.

Rome's wars of conquest outside Italy in the second century BC had a profound effect on the life of the city itself. Small farmers found themselves conscripted for long campaigns overseas, and were unable to maintain their farms, especially when the booty from wars promised a better return. The wars also enriched Roman commanders, and provided a supply of prisoners of war who might be employed in agriculture, replacing the citizen-farmers. The population of the city of Rome grew dramatically in the first century BC, as veterans and landless Romans moved there from the countryside. The growth of slave-run farms and the threat of slave revolts became a topic of political debate.

The wars in the east also saw an influx of Greek culture into Rome. First Greek ideas, and later Greek works of art looted from conquered cities, found their way to Italy. Although there were complaints about moral corruption, Greek influences could be seen in political practices, with an increasing emphasis on the power of rhetoric, in the development of Roman philosophy, and in Roman art and architecture.

Rome's Italian allies bore a disproportionate share of the burden in these wars, providing most of the soldiers, but receiving much less reward, and with their leaders excluded from the world of Roman politics. The resentment that resulted led eventually to a civil war in Italy (the Social War, 91–89 BC), in which the Italians were defeated. However, in the increasing political competition at Rome itself, the Italian communities were recognized as areas of

> ❝ *The truth is that the present regime is the most infamous, disgraceful and uniformly odious to all sorts and classes and ages of men that ever was, more so upon my words than I could have wished, let alone expected. These 'popular' politicians have taught even quiet folk to hiss. Bibulus is sky-watching, I don't know why but they laud him as though he were the man who 'singly by delaying saved our all'. My beloved Pompey, to my great sorrow, has been the author of his own downfall. They hold nobody by goodwill; that they may find it necessary to use terror is what I am afraid of. For my part I do not fight what they are doing on account of my friendship with him, and I do not endorse it, for that would be to condemn all that I did in days gone by. I take a middle way.* ❞

Cicero, *Letter to Atticus*, July 59 BC

A bust of Marcus Tullius Cicero (left). Much of our understanding of how the Roman Republic worked, especially in its last decades, comes from the works of Cicero (106–43 BC). He was an active politician, consul in 63 BC, who played an important part in events, despite his lack of experience as a military commander. His influence came from his ability as an orator, and a number of his speeches survive, delivered in law courts and in the Senate. He also wrote philosophical works which were influential for later thinkers. However, it is his letters which are most valuable to historians. Over 900 letters survive, not written for publication but published by his freedman Tiro after his death. Cicero corresponded with the most powerful men in Rome, but most of all with his friend Titus Pomponius Atticus, who was not politically active. In over 400 letters to Atticus Cicero provides an inside view of political life in one of the most important periods in Roman history.

The so-called temple of Fortuna Virilis in the Forum Boarium at Rome (left). The identity of the god or goddess worshipped at this temple is not certain. It was probably built some time after 150 BC, but possibly earlier. Roman buildings in this period, and especially temples, were often heavily influenced by Greek models, as in this case. Although Rome had always been indirectly influenced by Greek culture through its contacts with the Etruscans, increasing contact with the Greek communities of southern Italy and Sicily had a profound effect on Roman culture. Although there was a tradition of hostility to what were considered the demoralizing effects of Greek influence, it grew as Roman involvement with the Greek world increased (see page 104).

The Cursus Honorum

Office	Minimum Age	Number after 81 BC
Quaestor	30	20
Aedile	none	4
Tribune of the Plebs	none	10
Praetor	39	10
Consul	42	2

The sequence of offices which might be held by a Roman politician (The *Cursus Honorum*) was formalized in the second century BC, and again by Sulla in 81 BC. Each office was normally held only once, except the consulship, which could be held again after a ten-year interval. The number of praetors and quaestors was gradually raised as Roman territory increased in size. The number of consuls, however, had been fixed at two since at least the fourth century BC. After the reforms of Sulla all magistrates were supposed to serve their year of office in Rome, and then be given a provincial posting. In earlier periods the consuls would be sent directly to deal with the most important issues facing the city, whether at home or abroad, with other magistrates looking after less serious matters.

potential support, and legislation by various politicians meant that within a few years the Italians had been granted everything they had previously fought for.

THE END OF THE REPUBLIC

Rome's rise to power had always depended on the activities of individual leaders, and in times of crisis such men were given sweeping powers. In peacetime however, the collective power of the Senate tended to dominate. Nevertheless, the more or less continuous wars of the first century BC increased the opportunities for ambitious men: the wealth gained from conquests abroad and the large numbers of veterans ready to fight again made possible a series of civil wars, between Marius and Sulla (88–82 BC), between Pompey and Julius Caesar (49–45 BC), and finally between Mark Antony and the future emperor Augustus (33–30 BC). Stability came only with the recognition that Roman armies would always be on campaign, and with the creation of the position of emperor as permanent commander of Rome's legions.

- —— Servian wall
- —— roads
- ----- aqueducts
- ▭ marshland

REPUBLICAN ROME

Relatively few monuments survive from the period of the Roman Republic. The building programmes of the emperors have obliterated most of what was built before. The greatest period of building was the last two centuries BC, and in particular the last 50 years of the republic (c. 80–30 BC) when powerful individuals like Sulla (138–78 BC), Pompey (106–48 BC) and Julius Caesar (100–44 BC) paid for the construction of major public works. Pompey's theatre was the first stone theatre in Rome. The splendour of these buildings contrasts with the squalor which must have characterized much of the city. By the end of the period the city of Rome had a population of about a million, three times larger than any other city at the time.

Largo Argentina
Campus Martius
Temple of Bellona
Porticoes of Pompey
Portico of Minucius
Theatre of Pompey
Temple of Fortuna
Temple of Juno
Circus Flaminius
Porticoes of Metellus
Capitoline Hill
Forum Romanum
Basilica Aemilia
Temple of Apollo
Temple of Jupiter
Temple of Castor
Temple of Vesta
Oppian Hill
Temple of Aesculapius
Temple of Fortuna and Mater Matuta
Cloaca Maxima
Forum Boarium
Temple of Magna Mater
Palatine Hill
Temple of Portunus
Temple of Hercules Victor
Tiber
Temple of Luna
Circus Maximus
Temple of Juno Regina
Aventine Hill
Esquiline Hill

The **Hellenistic World**
323–30 BC

When Alexander the Great died the Greek world stretched from Sicily to the Indus. This vast area was dotted with city-states, some of which emerged in the eighth century BC, while others were new foundations, and new cities continued to be created. Like the archaic Greek world it was a world full of movement: there were many exiled or rootless men willing to serve as mercenaries, and there were powerful individuals anxious to carve out kingdoms for themselves from the remains of Alexander's empire.

A Roman silver denarius: the city of Rome, as a republic with annually elected magistrates, did not issue portrait coins until Julius Caesar started the practice after 48 BC.

In the years immediately following Alexander's death his generals and close companions fought between themselves, first for control over the whole empire, and then to establish their own personal kingdoms. By early in the third century BC, three dynasties had established themselves, the Antigonids, whose power was based in Macedonia and Greece, the Seleucids, who controlled the Asian parts of Alexander's empire, and the Ptolemies, who ruled Egypt. In the course of the third century BC, as Seleucid power waned, a fourth dynasty, the Attalids, rulers of Pergamum in Asia Minor, expanded their domain eastwards. It would be wrong to imagine that these kingdoms had stable or recognized boundaries: each ruler had to maintain his position by fighting his neighbours. The Aegean islands and the Levant were scenes of frequent conflict.

The developments in the east had their effect further west. Soon after Alexander's successors had started to style themselves as kings, the practice spread. Agathocles of Syracuse called himself king, and created a personal kingdom covering most of Sicily, and even including parts of Italy.

Throughout this vast area power was held by a tiny group of Greeks and Macedonians. The ruling dynasties were linked to each other by marriage, and intermarriage continued to be a feature of political manoeuvring. Not that this in any way lessened the rivalries between and within the dynasties, and historians recounted in some detail the murders of parents by children, brothers by sisters, and so on. Meanwhile, the cities they ruled administered themselves, and were thus able to continue to flourish regardless of the power struggles that carried on between their masters.

DECLINE OF THE HELLENISTIC KINGDOMS

The power of the Hellenistic rulers ultimately declined. In the east the Parthians took over most of the territory of the Seleucids, while in the west the Romans came increasingly to dominate the Mediterranean. The Greek cities of southern Italy were quick to make alliances with Rome, as was

Hieron II of Syracuse. Several Hellenistic kings made wills leaving their kingdoms to Rome, in part as 'insurance' against the threat of assassination by their rivals, and in this way when Attalus III of Pergamum died in 133 BC his kingdom passed to the Roman people. Earlier in the second century the Antigonid Philip V had taken on the Romans and been defeated: Macedon eventually became a Roman province in 146 BC. The areas of Seleucid territory not absorbed by the Parthians went through a period of upheaval before being brought under Roman control, and, in 30 BC after the suicide of Cleopatra VII, Egypt also was taken over by Rome.

For most of the inhabitants of the Greek cities, it made little difference whether their overlord was a Greek king or the Roman Senate. Greek continued to be the language of administration and of culture in the eastern Mediterranean, and even under the Parthians Greek culture remained influential. Although the Hellenistic period is often seen as one of decadence after the glories of the Classical period, it produced much of lasting value (see page 106).

Titus Quinctius Flamininus (consul 198 BC) campaigned against Philip V, defeating him at Cynoscephelae in 197 BC and declaring 'the freedom of the Greeks' at the Isthmian Games in the following year. He involved himself in affairs in the East a number of times after this. The coin, minted in Greece, is a result of his practice of establishing personal relations with Greek communities, as well as allying them with Rome.

Hieron II of Syracuse (c. 271–216 BC) seized control of Syracuse in a coup. When the Romans invaded Italy, he first allied himself with the Carthaginians, but then came to terms with the Romans. His continuing loyalty to Rome secured the prosperity of Syracuse.

HELLENISTIC KINGDOMS AND ROME

The power of the Hellenistic rulers was based on their ability to compel obedience either by diplomacy or by military force. The boundaries of their rule were never fixed, and conflict between different rulers was almost constant. One of the ways in which kings could advertise their power and their achievements was through the issue of coinage. Gold and silver coins were rarely used in everyday transactions, but were necessary for taxation and the payment of public officials and soldiers. It was these groups, and the richer inhabitants of the Hellenistic world, for whom the images on the coins would have had some significance.

Demetrius Poliorcetes (306–283 BC) was son of Antigonus I, one of Alexander's generals. With his father he spent much of his life fighting against rival generals. He was briefly king of Macedon (294–287 BC) but spent his last years in captivity after an unsuccessful attempt to regain territory his father had held in Asia.

Philip V (221–179 BC) attempted to extend his influence throughout Greece and further afield. He made an alliance with Hannibal during his war with Rome, and fought the Romans when they invaded Macedonia. He was defeated, and subsequently attempted to co-operate with the Romans against Antiochus III

Eumenes II of Pergamum (197–158 BC) allied himself with Rome against Antiochus III. Pergamum benefited from Antiochus's defeat, and under Eumenes the city became a great cultural centre. However, his influence waned after the end of the Macedonian monarchy in 168 BC, and Pergamum declined in importance.

Mithradates VI of Pontus (120–63 BC) added the Crimea to his kingdom on the south coast of the Black Sea. He later seized Bithynia and Cappadocia, and came into conflict with the Romans. He was able to resist them successfully until Pompey forced him from Asia Minor to the Crimea, where he committed suicide after a palace coup.

Antiochus I of Commagene (69–36 BC) ruled Commagene, mostly with support from Rome. He claimed descent from the royal families of Persia and Macedonia

Ptolemy I (323–283 BC) with his wife Berenice. Ptolemy was one of Alexander the Great's generals, and the author of a history of his campaigns. He took control of Egypt after Alexander's death and also seized Alexander's body, which he brought with him to Alexandria when he made it his capital. Outside Egypt he established good relations with the Aegean islanders and controlled Cyprus.

Ptolemy II (283–246 BC) with his wife Arsinoe. He brought Syria and parts of Asia Minor under his control and also established control over Cyrene. He was responsible for many of the public buildings in Alexandria and also for expanding Egyptian interest in the Black Sea Ports.

Cleopatra VII (51–30 BC) maintained her position as ruler of Egypt with support from the Romans, first Julius Caesar and later Mark Antony. The defeat of her and Antony's forces at Actium in 31 BC led to her suicide. The last Ptolemaic ruler of Egypt, she was reputedly the first to know Egyptian.

Antiochus III (223–187 BC) regained territories lost in the previous decades, and took over Syria and Judaea from Ptolemaic control. Campaigns in Western Anatolia and Thrace brought him into conflict with Rome, leading to military defeat and the loss of much of Asia Minor.

Antiochus I (281–261 BC) was the son of Alexander's general, Seleucus. He founded a number of cities throughout his territories, and established a royal centre at Sardis, to add to Antioch and Seleucia on the Euphrates. He used the practices of Babylonian kingship and respect for Babylonian traditions to maintain control of the Mesopotamian heartland of his empire.

Hellenistic Culture
and **Power 323–30** BC

The world that the Hellenistic kings ruled over was a world of Greek cities. In Sicily and southern Italy, the Aegean and western and southern Asia Minor, the cities were long established, while in the lands that had made up the Achaemenid Empire there were new colonies created by Alexander, a practice continued by his successors. In Egypt the non-Greek inhabitants continued to live for the most part in villages, and the pharaonic division of the country into nomes was retained.

U nder the Seleucids many new cities were created, but much of the Achaemenid system was maintained, and Aramaic remained the language of administration. While there was friendly contact between Greeks (including Macedonians) and non-Greeks, this did not lead to the integration or Hellenization of these territories at any but a very superficial level.

The relationship between cities and kings in this period is visible in a number of ways. Cities were required to pay to support the military activity of their rulers, but they also paid another sort of tribute, honouring kings with titles and privileges, and often with religious rites, acknowledging the power of the rulers to do good or harm to the cities. In return, the cities might expect to receive benefactions, including the erection of new public buildings. The second century BC in particular saw dramatic changes in the shape of towns, with formal monumental

Although it was founded by Alexander the Great, Alexandria (plan below) owed its form to the first two Ptolemies, who ruled their territories from the city. Its citizens were drawn from all over the Greek world, and it was nominally an independent city. As its full name of Alexandria-next-to-Egypt shows, it was not considered formally part of Egypt, and Alexandrian citizenship was not open to Egyptians; the city had a large Jewish population that was also not given citizenship. The city was noted for its broad and regular streets and for its monuments, including the Lighthouse on the island of Pharos, the library, known as the Museum, and the tomb of Alexander the Great.

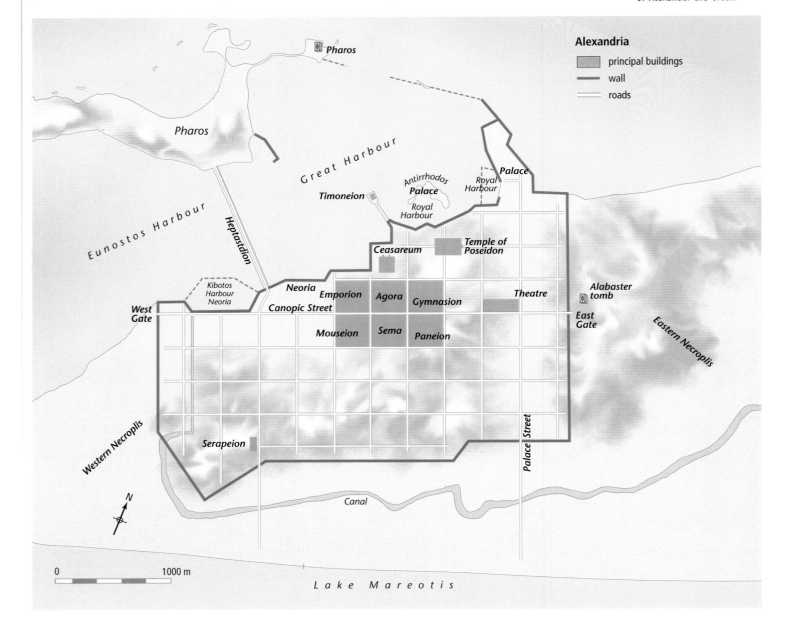

centres being created, and gymnasia, stoas (porticoes) and temples being built or rebuilt. In many cities new street plans were created, with neat grid patterns replacing the earlier haphazard arrangements. Some cities, like Priene in Asia Minor, were completely rebuilt on a new site.

HELLENISTIC LITERATURE AND SCIENCE

The larger Greek cities, and in particular the cities where the royal courts were established, saw a flourishing of literary culture throughout this period, although the vast majority of what was written has not survived. In older cities like Athens literary production was an activity of the social elite, as it had been for centuries, in which works of poetry and prose were written for an audience or readership of like-minded people; in Alexandria, Pergamum and the other centres of power the possibilities of royal patronage also encouraged the creation of new works of literature. One of the ways in which the Hellenistic rulers emphasized their Greek heritage was in their reverence for the past, and the creation of the great libraries at Alexandria and Pergamum are the most monumental results of this concern. Alexandria became a great centre for scholarship but also, stimulated in part at least by the grandeur of the Ptolemaic court and its lavish ceremonials, for poetry: some of the greatest of all Greek poetry, by poets including Theocritus, Callimachus and Apollonius of Rhodes, was written in Alexandria in the third century BC.

The relationship between literary and scientific writing in this period can be illustrated by the work of one of Callimachus's pupils, Eratosthenes of Cyrene (c. 285–194 BC), who succeeded Apollonius as head of the Library at Alexandria. As well as writing poetry, philosophy and literary criticism, Eratosthenes devised a theoretically sound method

of calculating the circumference of the earth. The work of the two most renowned ancient mathematicians, Euclid, who was working in Alexandria sometime around 300 BC, and Archimedes of Syracuse (c. 287–211 BC), who was a friend of Hieron II, also indicates that Hellenistic thought was concerned with both the theoretical and the practical. Archimedes, who was famous for developing machines to protect Syracuse from besiegers, also calculated the value of pi and the ratio between the volumes of a sphere and the cylinder that encloses it. Euclid, who systematized and developed understanding of arithmetic and geometry, was also concerned with optics and harmonics, which had practical applications.

Such intellectual endeavour should not be seen simply as 'progress' achieved by disinterested scholars and scientists. The measuring out of the earth (the literal meaning of 'geometry'), and the gathering and organization of knowledge about its inhabitants, whether humans, animals or plants, represented the intellectual counterpart to the kings' control and administration of their territories. Both were concerned with creating an ordered, Hellenized world: one from which the non-Greeks were largely excluded.

A rare surviving example of Hellenistic technology, recovered from an ancient shipwreck in 1901, the Antikythera mechanism (left and below) was made in Rhodes in the first half of the first century BC. It was a device for determining the movements of the sun and moon over long periods, intended for use in navigation. The mechanism was originally housed in a wooden box, and was operated by turning a shaft that protruded from the casing. It illustrates the kind of practical concern that underlay approaches to science, in this case astronomy, in this period.

A fragment from a third century BC copy of an unidentified tragedy on papyrus, and a papyrus grove (below left). Papyrus, made from the pith of the Papyrus plant, was used for writing on in Egypt from 3000 BC. The plant grew widely in wet areas of lower Egypt, but virtually nowhere else. The Hellenistic period saw a great increase in the production of books, in the form of papyrus rolls, with the establishment of great libraries in particular in Alexandria (which had up to 500,000 rolls) and Pergamum (at least 200,000). Ptolemy V (203–181 BC) is said to have confiscated all books brought into Egypt, returning copies of the works to the owners. He also restricted access to papyrus, as a result of which Eumenes II of Pergamum (197–159 BC) encouraged the development of parchment, a particularly fine form of vellum (stretched and cleaned animal skin), as a substitute. While many Hellenistic rulers encouraged writers at their courts, the great libraries also developed into centres of research, where books might be written about books about books.

Meroë

c. 500 BC–c. AD 350

By the fourth century BC, if not earlier, the capital of the kingdom of Kush had been moved southwards from Napata to Meroë. Archaeological work at Meroë has revealed an extensive urban site with palaces, temples, iron-smelting and pottery kilns, cemeteries and the sun-dried brick houses of the commoners. Although the Meroitic civilization is comparatively well known through sites of this sort, much of its history eludes us because the indigenous language is still not understood.

Precisely why the Kushite capital was moved to Meroë is unclear. Economic and environmental factors may have played a part. Meroë's location on a navigable stretch of the Nile between the fifth and sixth cataracts and at the terminus of various caravan routes running eastwards to the Red Sea was convenient for trade. The region offered good grazing and agricultural land capable of supporting a large urban population and was rich in iron ore and wood, both essential for iron-working, of which Meroë was an important centre from at least the fifth century BC. The move possibly stemmed from a power struggle between the Kushite rulers and the priests of Amun at Jebel Barkal, which undermined the prestige of the Napatan site.

DEVELOPMENT OF KUSHITE STYLE

Relations between Meroë and Ptolemaic Egypt (323–30 BC) were generally friendly and Egyptian culture continued to exert considerable influence on its southern neighbour. This is particularly obvious in the enduring worship of Egyptian gods, such as Amun and Isis, in the construction of pyramids for royal burials and in the use of the Egyptian language and hieroglyphs. However, the development of a distinctive Kushite style, more marked than during the Napatan phase, is seen, for example, in the worship of indigenous deities such as Apedemek, the lion god, and in the official use of the Meroitic language and script from about the second century BC onwards.

Meroë is well-known for its stone pyramids (right), marking the tombs of Meroitic rulers and royal family. They are much smaller and steeper-sided than Egyptian pyramids and have truncated tops over which a capstone would have been placed. They also do not enclose the burial chambers, which are located underground. A chapel and an enclosure wall would have completed the superstructure.

Queen Amanitare is shown at the Apedemek temple at Naqa (far right), grasping her defeated enemies by their hair. The relief combines Meroitic and Egyptian elements. The theme of the victorious ruler is typically Egyptian but the depiction of a woman in this role is not. In particular, her full figure, emphasizing the hips, is characteristically Meroitic and conveys the importance of women as powerful rulers and as the mothers of future kings.

In Meroitic times the kingdom of Kush extended from Sennar in the south to Maharraqa in the north (map right). Ties with Egypt continued to be strong and brought the Kushites into contact with the great empires of the day: Persian, Hellenistic and Roman. Relations with the rulers of Egypt, which were occasionally hostile, provide us with much-needed information about Kush through the accounts of classical writers. Meroitic Kush also had trading links with the African interior and exported items such as gold and slaves to Egypt and beyond. Nevertheless, the influence of Meroitic culture does not seem to have extended southwards to any appreciable extent. Even the once commonly held view that iron technology spread from there to other parts of Africa is now doubted.

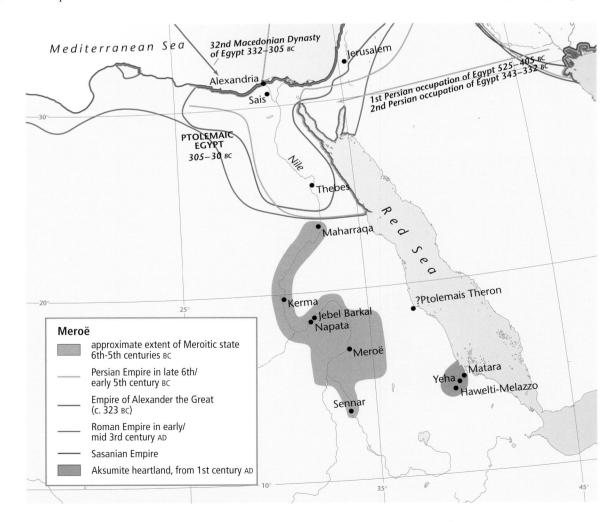

Mediterranean Sea

32nd Macedonian Dynasty of Egypt 332–305 BC

Jerusalem

Alexandria

1st Persian occupation of Egypt 525–405 BC
2nd Persian occupation of Egypt 343–332 BC

Sais

PTOLEMAIC EGYPT 305–30 BC

Nile

Thebes

Maharraqa

Red Sea

Kerma

?Ptolemais Theron

Jebel Barkal
Napata

Meroë

Matara
Yeha
Hawelti-Melazzo

Sennar

Meroë

▨ approximate extent of Meroitic state 6th-5th centuries BC

── Persian Empire in late 6th/ early 5th century BC

── Empire of Alexander the Great (c. 323 BC)

── Roman Empire in early/ mid 3rd century AD

── Sasanian Empire

▨ Aksumite heartland, from 1st century AD

During the first centuries BC and AD Meroë was at the peak of its power. This was a period during which several women bearing the titles Kandake and Qere seem to have ruled in their own right. Contact with the Romans, who conquered Egypt in 30 BC, was initially hostile. In 23 BC the Romans attacked Kush, probably in retaliation for an earlier Kushite attack on Upper Egypt, and were victorious, although not decisively so since the terms of the ensuing peace treaty were not unfavourable to the Kushites. Thereafter relations were generally peaceful and Meroë enjoyed a period of prosperity, characterized by the building and restoration of temples, monuments and pyramids.

THE DECLINE OF MEROË

Meroë's decline began during the second century AD and it is thought that an Aksumite military expedition of c. AD 350 could have dealt the final blow. But it may be that the Aksumite expedition was in fact a result, rather than a cause, of this decline. The appearance of new types of mound burial and pottery indicates a change of material culture in the Meroitic region and classical writers refer to two previously unknown peoples, the Nobatae and Blemmyes, who may possibly be associated with these changes. Other possible factors include deforestation and a consequent decline in the iron industry, soil impoverishment and changing patterns of trade leading to Meroë's economic isolation. Whatever the precise reasons, by the end of the fourth century AD the Meroitic state had ceased to exist.

The Meroites developed two types of script: a form based on Egyptian hieroglyphs and a cursive form based on Egyptian demotic (right and above right). However, the Meroitic script, consisting of 23 characters, is fundamentally different in that it includes vowel notations.

Although the script has been deciphered, we do not know what the writing means because the Meroitic language is not understood. Possibly belonging to a group of languages known as Nilo-Saharan, its linguistic classification essentially remains uncertain.

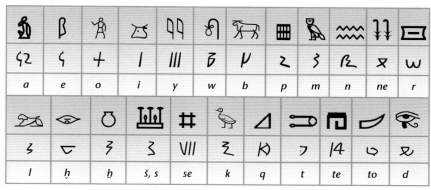

The **Roman Empire**
31 BC–AD **235**

The civil wars which characterized the late Roman Republic ended with the defeats of Antony and Cleopatra at Actium and outside Alexandria in 31 BC. The victor, Octavian, who was awarded the title Augustus in 27 BC, reconciled the conflict between the existing state institutions of the Republic and his own monarchic power through a series of constitutional and political negotiations and thereby established himself as the first recognizable Roman emperor and the founder of an imperial dynasty, the Julio-Claudians.

Although first-century emperors frequently clashed with senators, and this gave rise to a predominantly hostile historical tradition, the Augustan system proved remarkably stable and was to survive without notable change into the third century AD.

This political stability was reflected in the empire as a whole. Augustus himself was a great military leader and presided over a significant extension of Roman imperial power, especially in Germany, Spain and the Danubian lands. Following a series of military crises late in his reign and the accession of his adopted son Tiberius in AD 14, the pace of military expansion slowed markedly. Over the next three centuries Roman military ambition was limited to expansion in North Africa, the conquest of Britain from AD 43 and, under Trajan, the conquest of the Dacians. Although there were occasional revolts and the Romans sparred with Parthia in the East, most of the empire escaped significant conflict.

THE EMPEROR AND THE PROVINCES

For the provincials, the imperial system clarified political arrangements and, instead of attempting to negotiate the complex factions within the senatorial aristocracy, they merely had to manage their relationship with a single (if sometimes unpredictable) individual. One consequence was the development of a 'symbolic economy' whereby provincials demonstrated their loyalty to Rome and the emperor by granting the emperor honours. Octavian's victory at Actium was followed by the first request to establish a divine cult to him. Although some had qualms about worshipping a living emperor, the granting of divine honours to a dead emperor became common and temples to the emperors were erected across the empire.

Another way of showing loyalty to Rome, and by so doing making a claim for imperial support, was to adopt elements of Roman culture. Since by the first

This Egyptian statue (above) represents the Egyptian god Anubis dressed as a Roman legionary. It neatly exemplifies the cultural fusions of the Roman Empire.

century AD Rome had incorporated many elements of Hellenic culture, imperial power in the East came to be associated with 'Hellenization' while in the West, Romanization altered the face of many traditional societies. Latin and Greek spread from Britain to Egypt and from Spain to Syria. The emperor and his representatives encouraged the development of Roman-style cities so that many cities came to enjoy similar civic facilities and display common architectural elements. Roman influence was also felt in clothing, in pottery, in the decor and architectural style of houses, in foods and in most aspects of community life. The city came to represent these imperial values. The Roman city, with its magistrates and administrative structure, its regular grid plan, its forum, baths and basilica, was exported to every province of the empire.

Although the Roman Empire brought some form of cultural unity to the Mediterranean, the interaction of imperial and provincial cultures produced a variety of local forms so that archaeologists talk of Gallo-Roman or Romano-Egyptian cultures. This cultural interchange also in turn affected Rome so that elements of provincial cultures permeated the imperial centre from where it then spread throughout the empire: the cults of the Egyptian god Sarapis and the Persian god Mithras spread as far as Britain. The empire became a multi-cultural environment.

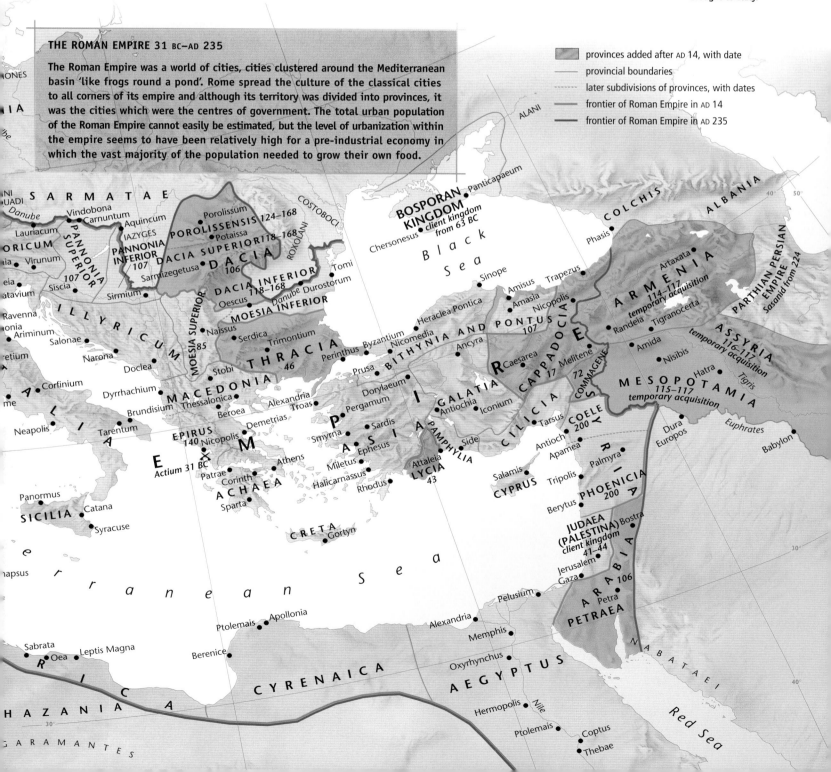

The Gemma Augustea (left): Augustus, seated looking left, is depicted in divine semi-nudity, being crowned with a symbol of his victory by a goddess. In his left hand he holds a staff or spear with point turned down to symbolize victory. In his right hand he holds the *lituus*, symbol of priestly office. At his feet sits an imperial eagle. To the left a general, perhaps Tiberius (his successor), dismounts from a chariot having paraded through Rome in triumph. To the right, at the feet of an unidentified god, sits a goddess whose children and cornucopia signify the prosperity Augustan rule has brought to Italy.

THE ROMAN EMPIRE 31 BC–AD 235

The Roman Empire was a world of cities, cities clustered around the Mediterranean basin 'like frogs round a pond'. Rome spread the culture of the classical cities to all corners of its empire and although its territory was divided into provinces, it was the cities which were the centres of government. The total urban population of the Roman Empire cannot easily be estimated, but the level of urbanization within the empire seems to have been relatively high for a pre-industrial economy in which the vast majority of the population needed to grow their own food.

provinces added after AD 14, with date
provincial boundaries
later subdivisions of provinces, with dates
frontier of Roman Empire in AD 14
frontier of Roman Empire in AD 235

The **Roman Army** under the Empire 27 BC–AD C. **250**

The Roman army was the largest single institution in the Roman Empire. In its lower ranks the army was professional, with the soldiers serving normally for 25 years. Senior officers were drawn from the imperial elite and served for shorter terms. The army was divided into three basic groups: the legionaries, the auxiliaries and the praetorians. The legionaries were normally Roman citizens and in the early first century AD most were recruited from Rome and Italy.

Progressively, however, more troops were recruited from the provinces until, by the reign of Trajan (AD 98–117), provincials outnumbered Italians. While the legions consisted of about 5,000 men, the auxiliaries were organized into smaller units of about 500 or 1,000. These units often carried an ethnic designation (eg. II Thracian cohort) and this probably reflects the ethnic origins of the first soldiers of the unit. Gradually, as with the legions, the ethnic character of these units was lost. After 25 years of service, the auxiliaries were discharged from the army with a grant of citizenship.

The praetorians were citizen-soldiers stationed in Italy and Rome. Under Sejanus, the notorious Prefect of the Guard under Tiberius (AD 14–37), the praetorians became a major political force, arresting political dissidents and enforcing imperial commands. At times of political crisis, the praetorians could make emperors (Claudius, Otho, Didius Julianus), or break them (Galba, Nero, Nerva).

MILITARY OPERATIONS

The army relied greatly on the heavily armed legionary infantry, though the auxiliaries eventually became more numerous. The auxiliaries provided a greater element of tactical flexibility with cavalry of various types, light and heavy infantry and various specialist units. The army had engineering expertise which gave the Romans considerable advantages in siege warfare. It was, however, slow and could experience difficulties bringing more mobile opponents to battle. Most of its notable military defeats occurred when legions were forced to retreat through difficult territory when being harassed by more mobile enemy troops, such as at the Teutoburger

Wald in AD 9 where three legions were wiped out by the Germans as they retreated through a heavily forested area. In the East, the Romans were unable to inflict a decisive defeat on the Parthians since the Parthian cavalry normally preferred to skirmish with the Roman infantry and then outrun them if the Roman infantry started to enjoy success.

The tactical efficiency of the army meant that it was normally able to reach strategic targets and crush rebellions. The Romans often treated conquered peoples with notable savagery, laying waste whole regions and enslaving or massacring populations. Occasional brutality allowed Rome to exercise political control without continually having to deploy military force and, gradually, much of the

A Roman centurion of the first century AD, with a standard and portrait of Caesar (above).

This late first-century fort in Scotland (below) was never completed. The fort was laid out to a predefined order. The two main roads through the fort intersect at the headquarters building. The barrack blocks are grouped in sixes, each block containing a century and each group a cohort (c. 480 men), though the first cohort (near the East Gate, may be double strength.

Tay

temporary camp for tr[o]
constructing fortres[s]

gate-tower

officers' temporary compound

cohort
cohort
cohort
cohort
officers' houses

cohor[t]

gate-tower

stores compound

cohort

principia (headquarters)

court

fabrica (work shop)

court

valetudinarium (hospital)

coho[rt]

cohort

cohort

gate-t[o]

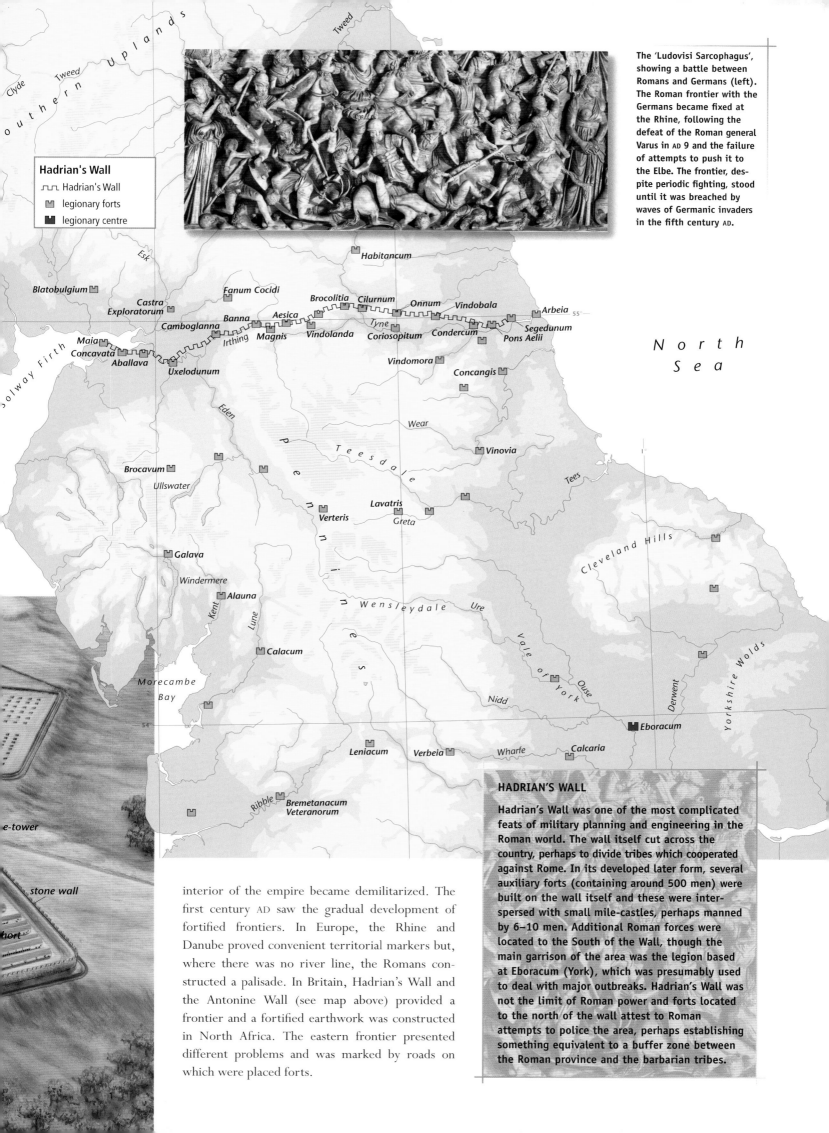

Hadrian's Wall
- ⌐ Hadrian's Wall
- 🏛 legionary forts
- 🏰 legionary centre

The 'Ludovisi Sarcophagus', showing a battle between Romans and Germans (left). The Roman frontier with the Germans became fixed at the Rhine, following the defeat of the Roman general Varus in AD 9 and the failure of attempts to push it to the Elbe. The frontier, despite periodic fighting, stood until it was breached by waves of Germanic invaders in the fifth century AD.

Clyde

Tweed

Southern Uplands

Tweed

Esk

Habitancum

Blatobulgium

Fanum Cocidi

Castra Exploratorum

Brocolitia *Cilurnum* *Onnum* *Vindobala* *Arbeia* 55

Camboglanna *Banna* *Aesica* *Tyne* *Segedunum*

Maia *Irthing* *Magnis* *Vindolanda* *Coriosopitum* *Condercum* *Pons Aelii*

Concavata *Aballava* *Uxelodunum* *Vindomora*

Solway Firth

Eden

Vindomora

Concangis

North Sea

Wear

Brocavum

Ullswater

Teesdale

Vinovia

Tees

Lavatris

Verteris

Greta

Cleveland Hills

Galava

Windermere

P e n n i n e s

Wensleydale

Ure

Alauna

Vale of York

Kent

Lune

Calacum

Morecambe Bay

Nidd

Ouse

Derwent

Yorkshire Wolds

54

Eboracum

Leniacum

Verbeia

Wharfe

Calcaria

Ribble

Bremetanacum Veteranorum

e-tower

stone wall

hort

interior of the empire became demilitarized. The first century AD saw the gradual development of fortified frontiers. In Europe, the Rhine and Danube proved convenient territorial markers but, where there was no river line, the Romans constructed a palisade. In Britain, Hadrian's Wall and the Antonine Wall (see map above) provided a frontier and a fortified earthwork was constructed in North Africa. The eastern frontier presented different problems and was marked by roads on which were placed forts.

HADRIAN'S WALL

Hadrian's Wall was one of the most complicated feats of military planning and engineering in the Roman world. The wall itself cut across the country, perhaps to divide tribes which cooperated against Rome. In its developed later form, several auxiliary forts (containing around 500 men) were built on the wall itself and these were interspersed with small mile-castles, perhaps manned by 6–10 men. Additional Roman forces were located to the South of the Wall, though the main garrison of the area was the legion based at Eboracum (York), which was presumably used to deal with major outbreaks. Hadrian's Wall was not the limit of Roman power and forts located to the north of the wall attest to Roman attempts to police the area, perhaps establishing something equivalent to a buffer zone between the Roman province and the barbarian tribes.

Rome and Pompeii
c. 31 BC–AD 250

By the end of the first century BC, Rome was the political centre of a huge empire. The conquest of that empire and its subsequent economic exploitation enriched Rome and encouraged many to seek fame, fortune, or merely a living in the imperial metropolis. By the Augustan period, Rome was a huge, cosmopolitan city with many different ethnic groups, worshipping many different deities located in the city. The best estimates put the population of the city at about one million.

The Casa del Fauno at Pompeii (right). The typical Pompeiian town-house was focused around the atrium (a hall with a central roof-opening and a catchwater basin in the floor) and the peristyle (a colonnaded garden situated at the rear).

Living conditions within Rome may have been difficult, as there was no proper urban planning until the reign of Nero (AD 54–68). Much of the population lived in blocks of flats, known as *insulae*, many of which had either very primitive water and sanitary facilities or none at all. Without a fire brigade, and with the extensive use of wood in constructions, fire was an ever-present danger. The city needed a continuous flow of food from its hinterland, and the possibility that the food supply might be cut was a constant worry. In the second century BC land resettlement programmes exported some of the population to rural areas. Later, corn doles were introduced and in times of crisis Roman politicians were given vast powers to organize the provisioning of the city. The emperor Augustus maintained popular support through his provision of a corn dole to at least 200,000 men. In addition, with his close associate Agrippa, he built three new aqueducts and enlarged the existing four, probably doubling the supply of fresh water to the city.

Rome was also a centre for political display. The pinnacle of a military career was to process in a triumph through the streets of Rome, an honour that came to be monopolized by the imperial family. The city was adorned with monuments attesting to the triumphs or just the generosity of the politicians of Rome. The emperors used buildings to reinforce their status. Julius Caesar, Augustus, Vespasian, Nerva and Trajan all built new forums in which the buildings, statues and inscriptions made references to their military triumphs and often legendary forebears. Shows held in theatres and circuses also provided emperors with opportunities to display their wealth and power and to entertain the urban masses.

This fresco (right) from the Casa dei Vettii, Pompeii, shows a Roman engaged in making an offering, accompanied by two attendants. The snake, normally a symbol of Apollo, may here represent the gods of the household, the *lares*. Household cults were an important aspect of Roman life and shrines were located across Roman houses. We should envisage regular and perhaps daily offerings at such shrines.

The Pompeiian Forum (below left) was a largely open, rectangular area, surrounded by the city offices, the assembly room (comitium), a basilica (for various kinds of official business), at least one market (macellum), a temple to the gods of Rome (capitolium) and temples to the emperors. The Eumachia building appears to have been a meeting room. In addition, the forum was filled with statues and monuments of prominent local politicians or members of the imperial family. The main northern entrances to the temples were marked by arches.

THE CITY OF POMPEII

Pompeii, destroyed in the eruption of Vesuvius in AD 79, provides a typical example of an Italian city of the period. Less densely occupied than Rome, the majority of the population lived in one- or two-storey houses. At the centre of the Pompeiian house was the atrium, in which much of the private business of the householder would be transacted. In the houses of the rich, there were frequently quite extensive garden-areas, often lined with columns, and adorned with works of art. The walls of the houses were normally decorated with elaborate frescoes. Pompeii also provides examples of bars, brothels and shops of many different kinds. Much of the political business of the city was probably located in the forum (see plan).

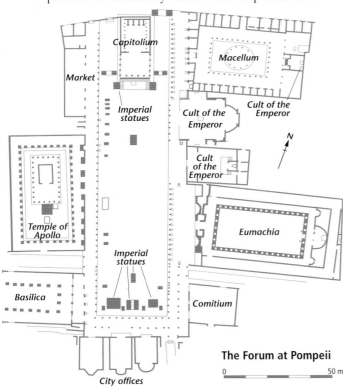

The Forum at Pompeii

Capitolium

Macellum

Market

Imperial statues

Cult of the Emperor

Cult of the Emperor

Cult of the Emperor

Temple of Apollo

Eumachia

Imperial statues

Basilica

Comitium

0   50 m

City offices

N

THE CITY OF ROME

1 Forum Romanum: the political centre of ancient Rome, first laid out in 6th century BC. 2 Forum of Trajan: AD 102–117, with the markets of Trajan. 3 Circus Maximus: used for racing events and athletic contests, first laid out in 4th century BC. 4 Flavian amphitheatre (Colosseum): opened AD 80, holding 70,000 spectators. 5 Stadium of Domitian: late 1st century AD. 6 Imperial palace: 1st–3rd century AD. 7 Temple of Divine Claudius: mid-late 1st century AD. 8 Temple of Capitoline Jupiter: built in the Etruscan style in the 6th century BC. 9 The Pantheon of Hadrian: AD 117–138. 10 Mausoleum of Hadrian: AD 130–139. 11 Mausoleum of Augustus: 28 BC. 12 Baths of Caracalla: 3rd century AD. 13 Baths of Trajan: early 2nd century AD. 14 Baths of Diocletian: early 4th century AD. 15 Porticus Aemilia: a large market hall. 16 Horrea Galbea: warehouses restored mid-1st century AD. 17 Camp of the Praetorian Guard: 1st century AD. 18 Aurelian Wall: late 3rd century AD.

Religious Developments in the Roman Empire c. **31** BC—AD **395**

At the start of the first century AD the religion of the Roman Empire was little different in kind from that of the city-states from which the empire had grown. By the fourth century AD, the Roman Empire and the Christian church were inextricably linked. This transformation is closely related to the social and administrative changes that took place over the same period, and both the empire and Christianity itself appeared very different in the fourth century from how they had been in the first.

The vast majority of religious activity in the Roman Empire was focused on local cults in individual cities, where priesthoods would be held by leading members of the aristocracy. In the city of Rome the Senate oversaw all religious matters, and all the most important priests were senators. As well as the traditional cults of the city, the Romans had over the centuries adopted some gods from their allies or their subjects, often by bringing a cult-statue to Rome. From the time of Augustus, the imperial cult, worship of the living emperor, spread rapidly through the empire. Although emperors had an interest in the way it developed, much of the impulse for the growth of the imperial cult came from the cities of the empire, and it was locally organized.

THE SPREAD OF CHRISTIANITY

Christianity began to be spread by the followers of Jesus (c. 4 BC–c. AD 33) soon after his execution by the Romans. Although they were Jews, they very soon gathered non-Jewish adherents, and there were certainly Christian groups in Rome by the middle of the first century AD. It is difficult to be certain how fast or how firmly Christianity established itself. The younger Pliny, who was governor of Bithynia and Pontus in c. AD 110–112, claims that it was widespread in his province, and also that his actions were successful in entirely suppressing it. Both claims are likely to be exaggerations, but the evidence suggests that supporters of Christianity may not always have seen their support as requiring the rejection of other religious practices. Although Christian writers in the fourth century AD in particular had much to say about the role of martyrs, it is clear that persecution of Christians was not common. Only in the early fourth century do there appear to have been widespread attempts, led by the emperors, to suppress the religion, and even this was not pursued whole-heartedly throughout the empire. Although at first Christianity was a religion of the poorer urban communities, it

gradually gained the patronage of members of the elite in the towns of the empire, and it was this literate section of society which made Christianity increasingly respectable.

The third century AD saw a number of religious developments throughout the empire. The increasing concentration of power in the hands of the emperor was reflected in the growing popularity of cults which recognized a single god with power of the whole empire, such as Sol Invictus (the Unconquered Sun), Mithraism and Christianity. There were similarities in the imagery of these cults, and the first Christian emperor, Constantine (AD 312–337), appears at first to have drawn little

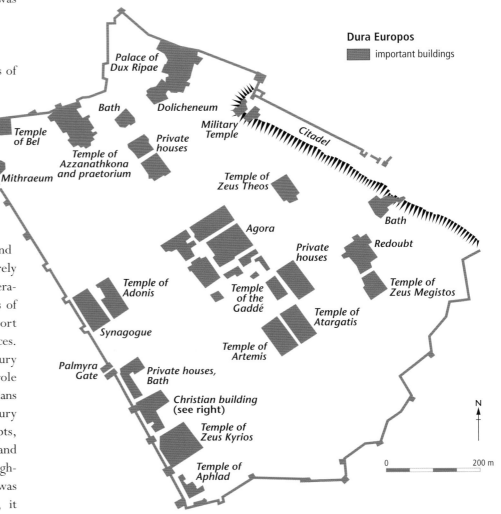

Dura Europos
■ important buildings

Palace of Dux Ripae

Bath
Dolicheneum

Temple of Bel
Military Temple
Citadel

Temple of Azzanathkona and praetorium
Private houses

Mithraeum
Temple of Zeus Theos

Temple of Zeus Theos

Agora
Bath

Private houses
Redoubt

Temple of Adonis
Temple of the Gaddé
Temple of Zeus Megistos

Synagogue
Temple of Atargatis

Palmyra Gate
Temple of Artemis

Private houses, Bath

Christian building (see right)

Temple of Zeus Kyrios

Temple of Aphlad

N

0   200 m

distinction between the God of the Christians, the Sun and Apollo.

It was the favouring of the Christian religion by Constantine and his successors, with the exception of the short-lived Julian (AD 361–3), which led to its becoming the official religion of the Roman Empire. Not only did the emperors bestow their patronage on bishops and grant financial favours to churches, but in a series of Ecumenical councils they attempted to enforce a unity of doctrine onto what had previously been a rather disparate and disputatious set of communities. What had started as a radical movement within Judaism had become the religion of emperors, and was made to fit its new role.

Frescoes from the synagogue at Dura Europos (left). There had been Jewish communities in the eastern parts of the empire outside Judaea since Hellenistic times; these diaspora communities were generally hellenized, speaking Greek and playing a full part in civic life, but they also maintained links with the Temple in Jerusalem until its destruction in AD 70, with the payment of temple tax, and kept practices such as male circumcision and observance of the sabbath. Under the Romans diaspora communities continued to grow, and they were given official exemption from some activities that conflicted with their religious requirements. The existence of these communities was one of the factors that helped Christianity to establish itself in the first century AD. The continuous movement of people throughout the empire for commercial and military reasons also helped spread religious practices.

The Roman garrison town of Dura Europos in eastern Syria (left) provides an opportunity to examine the range of religious cults which were practised in the third century AD. The town was never reoccupied after it was sacked by the Sasanians in AD 256. Fourteen religious buildings have been identified in this small community, each drawing different groups of worshippers. Some of the cults, such as those of Artemis and Zeus Megistos (Zeus the Greatest), probably date back to the foundation of the town under the Seleucids, while others, such as that of Azzanathkona and Zeus Kyrios (Zeus the Lord, or Baalshamin), belong to the period of Parthian control. Other examples, such as the Christian building and the temple of Mithras, belong to cults spread widely through the empire. The architecture of the temples varied over time, with the Greek-speaking elite happy to create oriental temple-buildings for Greek gods who would be addressed in Aramaic by the majority of their worshippers.

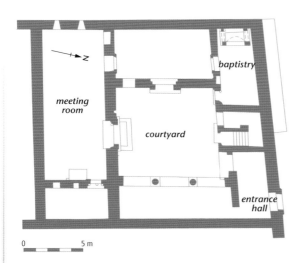

The Christian building at Dura Europos (above). This is the only surviving example of a building used for Christian ritual activity before the fourth century AD. It was probably constructed in AD 232, and destroyed when the town was sacked in AD 256. From the outside the building would have looked no different from the houses around it, and the room most clearly used for Christian ritual, the baptistry, would not have been visible to those passing in the street. The baptistry contained a font, looking like a large bath, at its western end, and was decorated with scenes from the Hebrew Bible and the Gospels. The large room on the south side of the building had no decorations at all, but its size, and the raised platform at the east end, suggest that it was used for meetings, and perhaps for celebrations of the eucharist. Elsewhere in the Roman Empire, fourth-century churches were built over the remains of substantial houses, and this suggests that before Christianity received the support of the emperors, houses, in particular those of rich patrons, were the usual meeting places for Christian congregations.

The 'Fresco of Conon' from Dura Europos (above). The fresco appears in the Temple of Bel, founded in the first century AD. The cult was introduced to Dura from Palmyra in Syria, and most of those who worshipped there were probably Palmyrenes. The fresco depicts a sacrifice being made on behalf of a leading family by two priests. The chief priest Conon bears a Greek name, but wears the conical white hat of a Persian magus. This blending of elements from different parts of the world is a feature of several of the cults found at Dura Europos, of which Mithraism is the best known. Although there was a Persian god called Mithras, Mithraism was a western creation which made use of some Persian imagery. It was most popular in Rome and Ostia, and also with the soldiers and officials in northern Britain and on the Rhine-Danube frontier. The cult was open only to initiates, and its rituals were celebrated by small groups of men in caves, or in chambers built to represent caves. As Christianity became dominant within the empire by the end of the fourth century, so, along with local city-based cults, Mithraism disappeared.

The **Parthian State**

c. **247**BC–AD **224**

The Parthians were originally Central Asian nomads referred to as the Parni by later Classical writers, who describe how they migrated into the former Achaemenid province of Parthia in the 3rd century BC. Owing to the scarcity of surviving Parthian documents other than potsherds from Nisa, Classical sources and Parthian coins provide the framework for reconstructing Parthian political history and the approximate dates of Parthian kings.

D uring the third and early second centuries BC the Parthians were Seleucid subjects, but their fortunes changed with the accession of Mithradates I (171–138 BC). Mithradates constructed a royal citadel named after himself ('Mithradatokert') at Nisa and rapidly over-ran the eastern Seleucid provinces, before invading Iran. He founded a second capital at Hecatompylos and later seized the Seleucid capital at Seleucia-on-the-Tigris, where he was crowned king in 141 BC. Mithradates founded a new capital nearby, known as Ctesiphon, 'the crowning ornament of Persia'. His coins depict him with a Greek beard and diadem, accompanied by the Greek legend 'the great king Arsaces, the philhellene'.

The latter part of the reign of his successor, Phraates II (c. 138–128 BC), was characterized by a Saka (Scythian) threat on the eastern frontier, Seleucid counter-attacks into Babylonia and Media, and a local revolt when Hyspaosines (c. 140–122 BC) founded the independent kingdom of Characene at the head of the Persian Gulf.

GROWTH OF PARTHIAN POWER

Mithradates II (123–87 BC) re-established Parthian central authority. Characene was reduced to vassal kingdom status, Parthia and Aria were recovered, Adiabene, Osrhoene and Gordyene seized, Armenia attacked, and a more secure western frontier established on the Euphrates. However, after his death the Parthian Empire again fell victim to internal struggles. Rome also attempted to meddle in Parthian politics until the crushing of its own army at Carrhae in 53 BC. Later years witnessed frequent changes in Parthian royal succession. The reign of Vologases I (AD 51–80) saw the emergence of a more distinctively Parthian culture, including the replacement of

Glazed ceramic coffins (right) are one of the most remarkable Parthian products. The coffins were made by adding slabs of clay to form a shoe-like form which was decorated by impressing the surfaces with carved stamps and covering the outside with a blue or green glaze. The lid was added after the body was placed inside. Grave-goods found with these first–second century AD coffins included gold, jewellery, glass bottles and glazed pottery.

The Parthian state was rarely centralized and should not be regarded as an empire (map below). The disunited political situation is reflected in the material record as there is archaeological evidence for local styles of pottery and everyday material culture. The Parthian state was periodically troubled by internal revolts and had complex political economic relationships with small autonomous neighbouring kingdoms such as Elymais, Characene, Hatra and Palmyra upon whose art and architecture it exerted a strong influence.

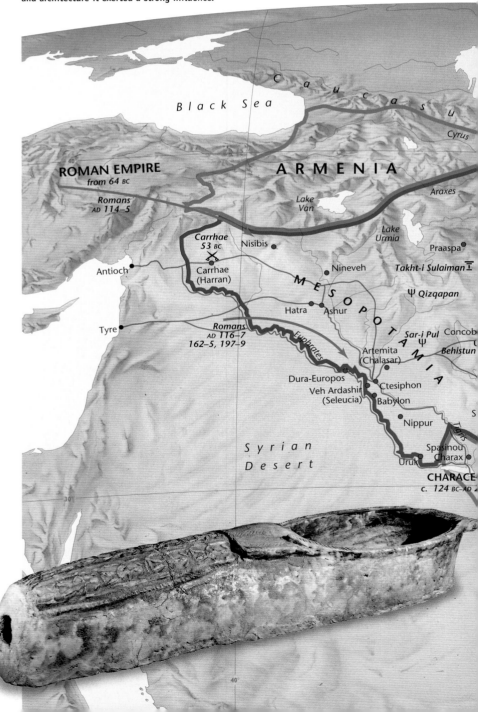

Aramaic for Greek and a fire-altar for the figure of an archer on coins. A rival city to Seleucia, Vologesias, was deliberately founded nearby.

In AD 115, Trajan crossed the Euphrates to sack Ctesiphon before reaching Charax, although his successor, Hadrian, dropped claims to this territory. Seleucia-Ctesiphon was again captured by Roman armies under Cassius (AD 165) and Septimius Severus (AD 197) although excavators report few signs of destruction. Artabanus V (AD 213–224), the last Parthian king, drove the Roman forces back but

Painted gypsum-plaster or stucco was widely used during the Parthian and later periods in Mesopotamia, Iran and Central Asia as a cheaper means of reproducing carved stone statuary, architectural elements and wall panels. The plaster was poured into moulds and allowed to set before being painted with bright colours. This small column capital (below left) belongs to a popular type showing a face framed by acanthus leaves, and dates to the second century AD.

Customary Parthian male dress was well suited to horse-riding and consisted of trousers and a belted tunic. This is shown in contemporary art and, in miniature, on some of the belt-buckles themselves. This example (below right) also shows the rider wearing a lobed sword on his left thigh and dates to the second century AD.

was later killed at the battle of Hormizdagan fighting a coalition of nobles led by the future Sasanian king Ardashir I (AD 224–240).

The adoption of a new style of vaulted reception hall marks one of the most distinctive Parthian influences on architecture in Iran and Mesopotamia. Rock reliefs illustrate scenes of investiture, worship and combat which were designed to illustrate the legitimacy of rule by local individuals. These typically show male figures dressed in belted tunics and baggy trousers, features which recur in contemporary sculptures in the independent desert states of Palmyra and Hatra and eastwards into the art of Gandhara. Comparison of these sculptures show similar styles of belts and jewellery, and offer a useful means of dating. Other forms of Parthian material culture, such as figurines and pottery, clearly developed from Seleucid traditions although highland Iran appears to have been more conservative in its fashions.

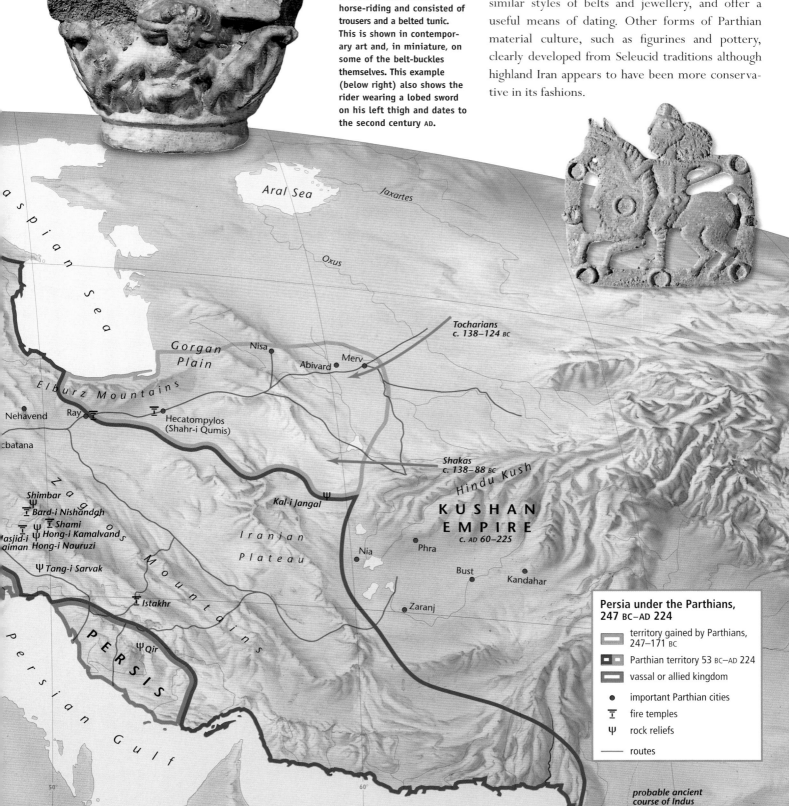

Persia under the Parthians, 247 BC–AD 224

- territory gained by Parthians, 247–171 BC
- Parthian territory 53 BC–AD 224
- vassal or allied kingdom
- ● important Parthian cities
- ⊤ fire temples
- Ψ rock reliefs
- — routes

probable ancient course of Indus

India: The Kushan Empire
C. AD **30–350**

The Kushan kings, who dominated northern India and Central Asia for three centuries, have remained largely forgotten, but they were powerful contemporaries of the Roman Empire and the Han Empire of China, dominating the trade routes of the so-called 'Silk Road' between those two powers. Their memory was revived in the 19th century by travellers, numismatists and historians, looking for the remains of Alexander the Great's successors in Afghanistan.

Along with the coins of Greek kings travellers along the Silk Road found thousands of coins inscribed in Greek, but inscribed with the names of previously unheard of non-Greek kings. Brief allusions to the same rulers were found in Chinese, Tibetan and Kashmiri texts, identifying the kings as Kushans and referring to them as patrons of Buddhism, ruling a vast empire several centuries after the Buddha. Over the last century and a half, painstaking research has pieced together an outline of Kushan history from their coins, inscriptions and archaeological remains. They were descendants of a nomadic people, the Yuezhi ('moon tribe'), thought to have been of Iranian origin, who entered history in the second century BC as rivals of the Xiongnu (Huns) in northwestern China. During the reign of the Yuezhi king Jizhu, (c. 174–160 BC), the Yuezhi began their migration into Central Asia, arriving in northern Afghanistan by about 130 BC.

THE KUSHANS IN INDIA

By the beginning of the first century AD, the Kushans had taken over the Greek kingdoms in Afghanistan, establishing a tribal confederacy reaching from north of the Oxus to the Kabul valley. The Kushans, under their clan chief Kujula Kadphises (c. AD 30–80), became leaders of the confederacy. Kujula, 'king of kings, son of the gods, the Kushan', defeated local Scythian and Iranian (Parthian) rulers to take Kashmir and northern Pakistan. His son, Vima Takto (c. AD 80–115) and grandson Vima Kadphises (c. AD 115–127) extended Kushan rule into India. By the reign of his great-grandson Kanishka I (c. AD 127–151), the Kushan Empire was established across the north of India, reaching deep into Central Asia and briefly including the eastern part of Xinjiang.

The Kushan Empire held this territory during the next two reigns, under Huvishka and Vasudeva I, but then gradually lost its northern territories to the growing power of the Sasanian Empire and the incursions of Hun tribes, while its Indian territories were eroded by the re-emergence of local states, culminating in the Gupta

This bronze pot (bottom), containing copper coins of the Kushan kings Vima Kadphises, Kanishka I and Huvishka, was used as a reliquary to bury a relic of the Buddha in a stupa at Kuhwat, Wardak district, Afghanistan. The inscription on it records the deposit of the relic in the reign of Huvishka in the 51st year of the era of Kanishka I (c. AD 177). It was found in 1836 by the British adventurer and numismatist Charles Masson.

This gold stater issued in the last year of the reign of Kanishka I (c. AD 151), has his portrait on the front and an image of the Buddha on the back. Kanishka's portrait, showing him dressed in the traditional nomad dress of the Yuezhi tribe, is remarkably similar to his portrait sculpture found in the Kushan shrine at Mathura. The Buddha image is based on a stone sculpture of the Gandharan region.

Empire. The last Kushan kings held on in the northern Punjab until the mid-fourth century AD, when they were crushed between the imperial ambitions of the Sasanian king Shapur II (AD 307–379), the Hun leader Kidara (c. AD 350–380) and the Gupta king Samudragupta (AD 335–380).

BUDDHISM IN THE KUSHAN EMPIRE

The Kashmir chronicle *Rajatarangini* preserves an account of the Kushan kings ruling in Kashmir as patrons of Buddhism. This is echoed in Chinese and Tibetan Buddhist sources, which name Kanishka I as a convert to Buddhism who summoned an assembly of the Buddhist community in Kashmir to reaffirm its unity and to re-establish its scriptural traditions. Coins issued by Kanishka I with Buddhist images provide contemporary testimony. Under Kushan rule many Buddhist monuments and monasteries were erected, some named after Kushan kings (inscriptions preserve the memory of a Kanishka monastery at Peshawar and a Huvishka monastery at Mathura). The Kushan period also saw the flourishing of Buddhist art in northern India, particularly in Gandhara and Mathura.

Buddhism was not, however, the official religion of the Kushan Empire. An inscription found at Rabatak in northern Afghanistan in 1993, erected on the orders of Kanishka I in memory of his three predecessors, records the dedication of a shrine to the Bactrian goddess Nana, and to various Iranian gods, including Ahuramazda and Mithra. Similar shrines have been excavated at Khalchayan, erected for Kujula in Uzbekistan, at Surkh Kotal, erected for Kanishka I in Afghanistan, and at Mathura, erected for Vima Takto in India. The gods appearing on Kushan coins also confirm the dynasty's close association with the goddess Nana and a range of Iranian gods.

The Kushans appear to have had an inclusive attitude towards religions. Hindu Jain art flourished alongside Buddhist art, yet apart from on their coins there is little evidence of images of the deities worshipped by the Kushans.

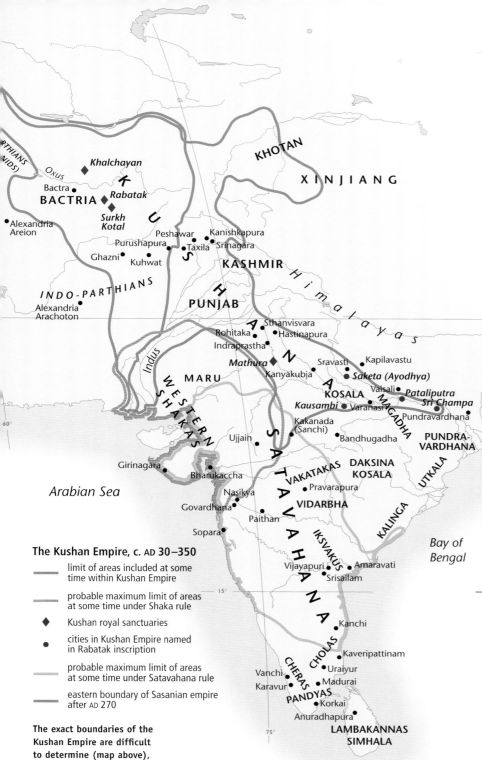

The Kushan Empire, c. AD 30–350

— limit of areas included at some time within Kushan Empire

— probable maximum limit of areas at some time under Shaka rule

◆ Kushan royal sanctuaries

• cities in Kushan Empire named in Rabatak inscription

— probable maximum limit of areas at some time under Satavahana rule

— eastern boundary of Sasanian empire after AD 270

Arabian Sea

Bay of Bengal

Indian Ocean

The exact boundaries of the Kushan Empire are difficult to determine (map above), but are thought to reflect the distribution of its dynastic shrines, inscriptions and copper coinage. The inscription found at Rabatak names five Indian cities which had submitted to Kanishka I, representing the extent of Kushan rule in India at the start of his reign. Only four of the names can be read with certainty: Saketa, Kausambi, Pataliputra and Sri Champa. During the third century AD the Kushan Empire lost its heartland in Afghanistan and Central Asia to the Sasanian Empire, which established its own 'Kushan kingdom' to rule former Kushan territory. In the fourth century AD Kidarite Huns also established a 'Kushan kingdom' on former Kushan territory in the Punjab.

> " ... of the great salvation, Kanishka the Kushan, the righteous, the just, the autocrat worthy of divine worship, who had obtained the kingship from Nana and from all the gods, who has inaugurated the year one as the gods pleased. And he issued a Greek edict and he put it into Aryan. In the year one it has been proclaimed unto India, unto the whole of the realm of the ksatriyas, that (as for) them – both Wasp(?), and Saketa, and Kausambi, and Pataliputra, as far as Sri-Campa – whatever rulers and other powers (they might have), he had submitted (them) to (his) will, and he submitted all India to (his) will. Then King Kanishka gave orders to Shafar the karalrang at this... to make the sanctuary which is called B... , in the plain of the (royal) house, for these gods, whose service here the... glorious Umma leads, (namely) the above-mentioned Nana and the above mentioned Umma, Aurmazd [Ahuramazda], Mazdooan [the Gracious One], Sroshard, Narasa, (and) Mihr [Mithra]. He gave orders to make images of the same, (namely) of these gods who are written herein, and he gave orders to make (them) for these kings: for King Kujula Kadphises (his) great grandfather, and for King Vima Takto (his) grandfather, and for King Vima Kadphises (his) father, and for himself, King Kanishka... "

Inscription from the Rabatak stone

Kushan Kings

Kujula Kadphises	c. AD 30–80
Vima Takto	c. AD 80–115
Vima Kadphises	c. AD 115–127
Kanishka I	c. AD 127–151
Huvishka	c. AD 151–190
Vasudeva	c. AD 190–227
Kanishka II	c. AD 227–247
Vasishka	c. AD 247–266
Kanishka III	c. AD 266–280
Vasudeva II	c. AD 280–320
Shaka	c. AD 320–350
Kipunadha	mid-4th century AD

The Kushan inscription found at Rabatak in Afghanistan (left) is the most important document of Kushan history so far discovered. It lists the names of the first four Kushan kings and the gods whom they worshipped. The inscription was written in Greek letters, but in the Bactrian language. Bactrian is an Iranian language and in the inscription it is recorded that Kanishka had the inscription translated from Greek into Aryan (i.e. Bactrian).

Ancient India:
the Mauryan Empire c. **310–185** BC

India's first approach towards becoming a unified state occurred under the first three kings of the Mauryan Empire. The founder of the dynasty, Chandragupta Maurya (c. 310–286 BC), king of Magadha in eastern India, unified under his control the other kingdoms of the Gangetic Plain. His grandson, Ashoka (c. 270–234 BC), consolidated Mauryan imperial rule, extending it into eastern and southern India. After Ashoka, the dynasty declined, and was succeeded by smaller regional powers in 185 BC.

Chandragupta and Ashoka are remembered today because of their roles in the religious history of India. Jain tradition identifies Chandragupta as a convert who abdicated to become a Jain ascetic, and starved himself to death in accordance with Jain beliefs. Ashoka is considered an important participant in the development of Buddhism. Converting after repenting the brutality of his military campaigns in eastern India (Kalinga), he gave Buddhism official recognition. He sent missionaries abroad and summoned a meeting of the Buddhist community to re-establish its unity. The political doctrines and practices of the Mauryans have been reconstructed from inscriptions erected on the orders of Ashoka throughout India, and from a manual of statecraft, the *Arthashastra*, attributed to Chandragupta's chief minister, Kautilya.

THE ASHOKAN INSCRIPTIONS

The inscriptions of Ashoka, carved on rocks or pillars in many parts of the subcontinent, represent India's earliest readable records. They were written in Brahmi script, the ancestor of modern India's writing systems, except in the northwestern part of the subcontinent where they were written in Greek, Aramaic or Kharoshthi (a local script). It is possible that both Brahmi and Kharoshthi were invented for use in these inscriptions. The inscriptions describe Ashoka's repentance and his adoption of the *Dharma* (also spelt Dhamma, literally 'law', but implying a spiritual sense of justice and piety) as the guiding light of his rule. Some inscriptions refer specifically to his participation in the Buddhist faith and its promulgation. In one inscription, datable to the thirteenth or fourteenth year of his reign (c. 283/4 BC), he proclaimed the rule of the *Dharma* as far as Syria, Egypt, Cyrenaica in North Africa, and Macedonia and Epirus in Greece. (The identification of the rulers of these foreign kingdoms provides the firmest external evidence for the dating of ancient Indian history.)

Mauryan punch-marked silver coins (above right) are characterized by the five separate symbols punched on their upper face. Two symbols, a solar emblem and a six-pointed disc, are to be seen on all issues. The other three symbols are often simple pictorial devices representing animals, weapons, tools or religious emblems. Their functions on the coins are not understood, but they point to a carefully controlled administration of issue.

The stone pillars bearing inscriptions erected by Ashoka provide the clearest evidence of artistic developments during the early Mauryan period. Each was originally surmounted by a carved stone capital (below), representing a symbol of Buddhist belief, mostly in the form of an animal, carefully carved and polished in a fine naturalistic style.

> *When he was consecrated eight years the Beloved of the Gods, the king Piyadassi [Ashoka], conquered Kalinga. A hundred and fifty thousand people were deported, a hundred thousand were killed and many times that number perished. Afterwards, now that Kalinga was annexed, the Beloved of the Gods very earnestly practised Dhamma, desired Dhamma, and taught Dhamma. On conquering Kalinga the Beloved of the Gods felt remorse, for, when an independent country is conquered, the slaughter, death, and deportation of the people is extremely grievous to the Beloved of the Gods, and weighs heavily on his mind.*
>
> *...For the Beloved of the Gods wishes that all beings should be unharmed, self-controlled, calm in mind, and gentle.*
>
> *This inscription of Dhamma has been engraved so that any sons or grandsons that I may have should not think of gaining new conquests, and whatever victories they may gain should be satisfied with patience and light punishment. They should only consider conquest by Dhamma to be a true conquest, and delight in Dhamma should be their whole delight, for this is of value in both this world and the next.*
>
> **13th Rock Edict of Ashoka**

As well as the development of a writing system for India, the Mauryan Empire also saw the establishment of India's first national monetary system. Chandragupta and his successors turned the local punch-marked silver coinages in use in many cities in northern India into a unified imperial currency, adding to it small change in the form of cast copper coins. The silver coinage was so successful that it spread throughout the subcontinent, beyond the boundaries of the empire into the far south and east and to Sri Lanka.

An account of India in the time of Chandragupta was recorded by a Greek emissary from the Seleucid court, Megasthenes. His description only survives

The Mauryan Empire, c. 310–185 BC

—— Mauryan Empire under Chandragupta, c. 297 BC

—— Mauryan Empire under Ashoka, c. 260 BC

▓ ancestral home of the Mauryas

Sanci site of Ashokan inscriptions

• site of Mauryan-age Buddhist stupa

• site of punch-marked coin find

ANGA regions (place names in brackets are Prakrit forms)

The inscriptions carved on rocks and pillars in many parts of the subcontinent are our most informative sources for understanding the Mauryan Empire (map right). Their locations provide a guide to the extent of its power, while their contents describe the political and spiritual aims of Ashoka, its most powerful emperor. The inscriptions include fourteen imperial edicts on rocks and seven on pillars, three local edicts, four inscriptions addressed to the Buddhist community and various shorter inscriptions. Some of the edicts are repeated in several locations. The distribution of Mauryan coins reaches beyond the boundaries of the empire suggested by the edicts. In most areas the production and circulation of silver punch-marked coins declined after the end of Mauryan rule. A few local issues were made by the small states which emerged after the fall of the Mauryan Dynasty, and in southern India and Sri Lanka local copies of Mauryan coinage continued to be made and used into the first century AD.

in second-hand versions, but provides many details about the Mauryan state. He described the capital Pataliputra (modern Patna) as encircled by wooden walls. He also referred to aspects of the administration of the city and the state, and gave a confused interpretation of the Hindu caste system.

Many details of the political, economic and social structures of the Mauryan Empire can also be found in the *Arthashastra*. It is, however, a manual of statecraft and it describes how these structures should be, rather than how they actually were. The *Arthashastra* as it survives today is a later compilation, so it is not always possible to distinguish the original Mauryan elements of the text.

Qin and Han China
221 BC–AD 220

The state of Qin did not become politically significant before about the seventh century BC, but by 221 BC it had conquered all the remaining Warring States and Qin Shi Huangdi proclaimed himself the August First Emperor of China. Although the Qin Dynasty was short-lived it was crucial to the formation of China as a unified and homogenous state. It also gave China its name in European languages, Qin being pronounced 'chin'.

Q in Shi Huangdi consolidated his power by centralizing the administration as had already been done within Qin's own state boundaries. He standardized scripts, weights, measures and coins throughout the empire. Road networks were established and a number of walls unified, thus forming the first Great Wall which served to keep out the marauding nomads. Garrison stations and signal towers were also built. The emperor conscripted hundreds of thousands of workers to work on building projects in his capital, including replicas of the palaces of the states which he had conquered. He was buried in a tomb complex that included the pits where the impressive underground pottery army was discovered.

The Han Dynasty which succeeded the fall of Qin after a short period of civil wars was one of the most notable dynasties in all Chinese imperial history, lasting over four hundred years (206 BC–AD 220) and building on the foundation inherited from Qin. Its rule was contemporaneous with the Roman

The Qin emperor, leaning on his sword,
While the vassal lords galloped to the west
to submit;
He pared down their land and pacified
the empire,
Unified the script, standardized wheel gauges.
Mount Hua served as his ramparts,
Purple Gulf was his moat.
His breast was filled with ambitious plans,
And he never used his martial might to the full.
He built a bridge of turtles and alligators,
And toured the area right of the sea to escort
the sun westwards.

From *Rhapsody* by Jiang Yan (AD 444–505)

A general of the Qin dynasty, 221–206 BC (left). This imposing figure represents a general of Qin Shi Huangdi's army and is larger than life-size to indicate his importance. His rank is indicated by decorative tassels on his upper chest. The armour would originally have been painted but this has now faded. However, the lamellate form of the armour is well indicated and would originally have been made of lacquered leather plates, sewn together.

Qin became a serious contender for supremacy after expanding in 328 BC. The other states were eliminated until in 221 BC Qin controlled all China (map below). The Qin then expanded its territories to the south and north-east. The first Qin emperor united and improved existing earthworks to create the 'Great Wall'.

to Sogdiana
(Kangzhu)

to Ferghana

Issyk Q

Kashgar
(Shule Shache)
Yarkand
(Sha-ch'e)

to Bactria
(Daxia)

Guma
(Pishan)

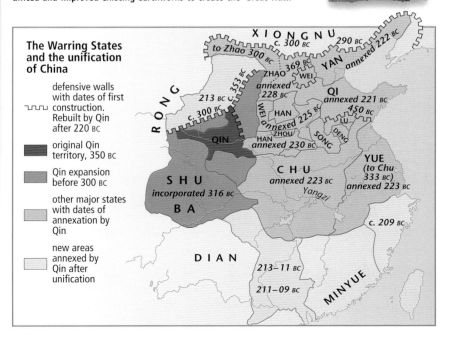

The Warring States and the unification of China

- defensive walls with dates of first construction. Rebuilt by Qin after 220 BC
- original Qin territory, 350 BC
- Qin expansion before 300 BC
- other major states with dates of annexation by Qin
- new areas annexed by Qin after unification

XIONGNU
c. 300 BC
to Zhao 300 BC
290 BC
annexed 222 BC
RONG
369 BC
YAN
ZHAO
353 BC
annexed 228 BC
WEI
QI
annexed 221 BC
213 BC
c. 300 BC
HAN
WEI
annexed 225 BC
450 BC
LU
ZHOU
HAN annexed 230 BC
SONG
DENG
QIN
YUE
(to Chu 333 BC)
annexed 223 BC
SHU
incorporated 316 BC
CHU
annexed 223 BC
Yangzi
BA
c. 209 BC
DIAN
213–11 BC
211–09 BC
MINYUE

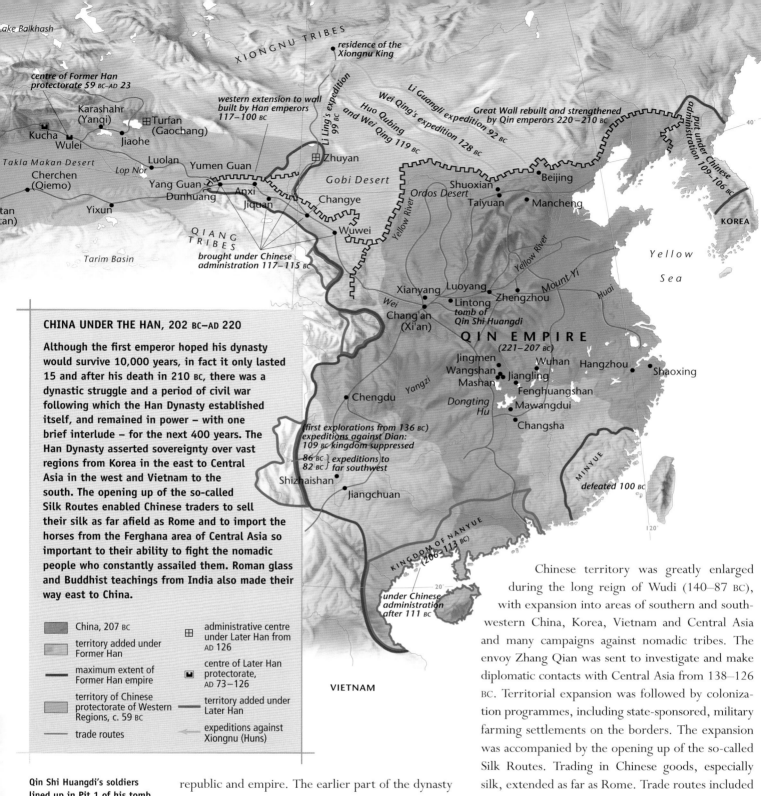

Map labels:
- ake Balkhash
- XIONGNU TRIBES
- residence of the Xiongnu King
- centre of Former Han protectorate 59 BC–AD 23
- Karashahr (Yangi)
- Kucha
- Wulei
- Turfan (Gaochang)
- Jiaohe
- Luolan
- Lop Nor
- Takla Makan Desert
- Cherchen (Qiemo)
- Yumen Guan
- Yang Guan
- Dunhuang
- Anxi
- Jiquan
- Yixun
- QIANG TRIBES
- brought under Chinese administration 117–115 BC
- Tarim Basin
- western extension to wall built by Han emperors 117–100 BC
- Li Ling's expedition 99 BC
- Wei Qing's expedition 99 BC
- Huo Qubing and Wei Qing 119 BC
- Li Guangli expedition 92 BC
- Huo Qubing and Wei Qing 128 BC
- Great Wall rebuilt and strengthened by Qin emperors 220–210 BC
- put under Chinese administration 109–106 BC
- Zhuyan
- Gobi Desert
- Ordos Desert
- Shuoxian
- Beijing
- Changye
- Taiyuan
- Mancheng
- Wuwei
- Yellow River
- Yellow River
- KOREA
- Yellow Sea
- Xianyang
- Luoyang
- Zhengzhou
- Mount Yi
- Huai
- Wei
- Chang'an (Xi'an)
- Lintong tomb of Qin Shi Huangdi
- QIN EMPIRE (221–207 BC)
- Jingmen
- Wuhan
- Hangzhou
- Shaoxing
- Wangshan
- Jiangling
- Mashan
- Fenghuangshan
- Chengdu
- Yangzi
- Dongting Hu
- Mawangdui
- Changsha
- first explorations from 136 BC; expeditions against Dian: 109 BC kingdom suppressed
- 86 BC, 82 BC expeditions to far southwest
- Shizhaishan
- Jiangchuan
- MINYUE
- defeated 100 BC
- KINGDOM OF NANYUE (206–113 BC)
- under Chinese administration after 111 BC
- VIETNAM

CHINA UNDER THE HAN, 202 BC–AD 220

Although the first emperor hoped his dynasty would survive 10,000 years, in fact it only lasted 15 and after his death in 210 BC, there was a dynastic struggle and a period of civil war following which the Han Dynasty established itself, and remained in power – with one brief interlude – for the next 400 years. The Han Dynasty asserted sovereignty over vast regions from Korea in the east to Central Asia in the west and Vietnam to the south. The opening up of the so-called Silk Routes enabled Chinese traders to sell their silk as far afield as Rome and to import the horses from the Ferghana area of Central Asia so important to their ability to fight the nomadic people who constantly assailed them. Roman glass and Buddhist teachings from India also made their way east to China.

Legend:
- China, 207 BC
- territory added under Former Han
- maximum extent of Former Han empire
- territory of Chinese protectorate of Western Regions, c. 59 BC
- trade routes
- administrative centre under Later Han from AD 126
- centre of Later Han protectorate, AD 73–126
- territory added under Later Han
- expeditions against Xiongnu (Huns)

Qin Shi Huangdi's soldiers lined up in Pit 1 of his tomb complex (left). There were three pits filled out of the four dug by the emperor (he probably died before the fourth could be filled). Pit 1 is the largest and probably held 6,000 figures of soldiers, aligned in battle array, together with archers and chariots, in eleven parallel corridors. Pit 2 held over 1,400 cavalrymen and chariots and Pit 3 had about 70 soldiers and one chariot and was supposedly a command post.

republic and empire. The earlier part of the dynasty is referred to as the Western Han, as the capital was in the West of China at Chang'an (now Xi'an). The dynasty began with a period of political consolidation, followed by expansion and finally retrenchment and a weakening of political and social cohesion.

ADMINISTRATION UNDER THE HAN

The Han Dynasty retained the centralized administrative system bequeathed by the Qin as well as many of their laws; one of their main contributions to imperial China was their gradual development of the civil service and the structure of central and provincial government. It was during the Han that Confucianism was accepted as the state ideology and the idea of a meritocracy created by an examination system began in embryonic form.

Chinese territory was greatly enlarged during the long reign of Wudi (140–87 BC), with expansion into areas of southern and south-western China, Korea, Vietnam and Central Asia and many campaigns against nomadic tribes. The envoy Zhang Qian was sent to investigate and make diplomatic contacts with Central Asia from 138–126 BC. Territorial expansion was followed by colonization programmes, including state-sponsored, military farming settlements on the borders. The expansion was accompanied by the opening up of the so-called Silk Routes. Trading in Chinese goods, especially silk, extended as far as Rome. Trade routes included the Silk Routes through Central Asia as well as sea routes to Burma and India and thus at least indirect contact was made with Iranian, Hellenistic and Roman cultures.

The Western Han period ended when a powerful consort family gained power and established a new dynasty, the Xin, for a brief interlude from AD 9–25. After this the second period of the Han Dynasty, the Eastern Han, began in AD 25, so-called because its capital was located in the east at Luoyang. Many later Han emperors were weak and under the influence of eunuchs and powerful families. The rivalry between eunuchs, bureaucrats and consort families, and the growth of popular revolts by messianic groups, finally led to the downfall of the dynasty. Civil war followed and the country finally split in AD 220.

Han Culture
221 BC–AD 220

The Han Dynasty endured for 400 years and built on many of the foundations laid by Qin Shi Huangdi. It went on to form one of the largest and greatest empires of its day, consolidating the process of unification begun by the Qin, and to some extent homogenized the various regional cultural influences which had flourished during the Warring States period. A revival of learning and an opening up of China to outside influences also characterized the Han period.

There was a general revival of learning after the burning of the books by the Qin emperor. Orders were given to search for lost classics, and various Confucian and other texts became necessary learning tools for officials and candidates for the civil service, presaging the more formal examination system which would begin in the Tang Dynasty. Sima Qian and Ban Gu wrote histories, rather than mere chronicles, of China and their formats were followed by all Chinese dynastic historians until the end of the imperial period. The first Chinese dictionary, *Shuo wen*, was compiled c. AD 100 and the records of titles in the imperial library have been preserved and constitute China's first bibliographic list.

Cultural exchange and assimilation, facilitated by diplomacy and trade, opened up China to the outside world. Buddhism penetrated China in the first century AD, although it did not take root until the fall of the Han Dynasty. The influences from Western Asia brought along the silk roads are embodied in burial artefacts found in Han Dynasty tombs. The Han explorer Zhang Qian discovered that the West wanted to trade with China, primarily for silk, though also for other items such as lacquerware. Chinese lacquers, silk, ivory and jade were of astonishing quality, produced by highly organized manufacturing processes involving the subdivision of labour. China imported items such as horses, fruit, aromatics and jewels.

RELIGIOUS BELIEF UNDER THE HAN

The Han Dynasty ruled at a time when changes were taking place in the way the afterlife was viewed. Tombs were built to represent the universe in which the dead were expected to live, with rooms for different functions, decorated with paintings and carvings of scenes from everyday life. Ideas about a paradise in the western mountains or eastern seas were also being formulated. Other aspects of the burial, such as jade suits and mirrors, focused on the search for immortality and illustrated

Model of a manor, Western Han, second century BC (below). This exceptionally large and complete model is typical of the period. It represents a strongly fortified building, which has its own fields and vegetable garden enclosed within its boundaries. The interior of the courtyard-style manor has a hall for feasting and banqueting. The owner would have been an important, rich landlord, who expected to enjoy such surroundings in the afterlife.

Lacquer cup. Han Dynasty, dated AD 4 (right). The long 67-character inscription gives the names of the workers and the product inspectors involved in each stage of its manufacture. It is one of a number of similarly inscribed lacquer pieces made in the same period, which document the widespread and early use of division of labour in manufacturing in China.

a concern with deities who could bestow eternal life. Liu Sheng, a brother of the famous emperor Wudi, and his consort Dou Wan, who died around 113 BC, were buried in jade suits, a garment restricted to royalty and believed to preserve the body for the afterlife. The side chambers of the tombs were filled with provisions as well as chariots and horses for use in the afterlife. The range of goods buried in tombs changed also, with ceramic replicas gradually taking the place of more precious items.

Archaeological discoveries of the Han have included funeral banners on silk, such as at Mawangdui (186–168 BC), possibly depicting the afterlife. In the same tomb were found the remains of many foods which tell us a lot about the eating habits of rich Chinese of the time. Colourful lacquered items were now prevalent and more expensive and popular than bronzes. Sculpture survives as stone guardian animals lining the routes to important tombs, and in the so-called *mingqi*, ceramic funerary sculptures. These are models, generally of pottery with a lead glaze of paint in the form of figures (though considerably smaller than the Qin terracotta army figures), animals, buildings, boats and vehicles. Many were individually modelled or mass produced in moulds.

The unification of China which the Han Dynasty consolidated resulted in a synthesis both cultural and artistic. So Liu Sheng at Mancheng in northern Hebei and the King of Nanyue in southern Guangdong were both buried in similar jade suits as well as many luxuries such as the extraordinary jade rhyton in the latter tomb revealing Central and Western Asian influences.

> *The prime duty of all ministers is to formulate policies, unify the people, universalize our culture and cultivate good customs. The Five Emperors [the legendary Sages] brought peace and prosperity to the country because they emphasized love and righteousness as the moral foundation of the nation. I never cease to hope that I can attain this goal.*
>
> **Decree of Han Wudi, 128 BC**

A silk banner from the tomb of Lady Dai, Han Dynasty 186–168 BC, at Mawangdui (left). Lady Dai herself can be seen in the centre leaning on a stick, with the sun and moon depicted at the top of the banner.

Jade horse with immortal rider, Western Han Dynasty (below). The figure is some kind of immortal, with peculiar facial features, long ears, flowing hair and wings protruding from his shoulders. In his right hand he holds a magic fungus or *lingzhi*. The celestial horse is also winged, and perhaps represents one of the imported Ferghana horses so valued by the Chinese. This carving may well be a representation of the desire to be spirited away to the lands of the immortals. It was found near an imperial tomb complex.

PART V

Age of Transformation
C. AD 250–750

Bahram V (AD 420–38) King of Persia, hunting lions.

After the splendour of the preceding centuries, the period from the third century AD is often depicted as an age of decline and decay. Such a picture is far from accurate. After a period of upheaval, new regimes emerged which built on the foundations laid by their predecessors. The power of the Byzantines, Sasanians, Guptas and the Tang was as great as that of the empires which had gone before them, and their cultural achievements were no less.

A common feature of these new regimes was the prominence of religion. In Europe and north Africa Christianity, in Persia Zoroastrianism, in India Hinduism and in China Buddhism were important elements both in the way in which rulers represented themselves and in the administration of their realms.

The seventh century AD saw the appearance of a new religion and a new power. From its beginning in AD 622 Islam spread rapidly, and Arab armies came up against, and held their own against, all the powers of the Old World. The Abbasid Caliphate, which took control in AD 750, inherited a dominion which reached from the Atlantic to Afghanistan.

It was the dawn of a new age.

The Roman Empire
AD 235–395

The relative political stability of the first two centuries AD ended with the death of Severus Alexander in AD 235. The Roman Empire then entered a period of political flux in which various contenders for the throne struggled to establish themselves and maintain their authority. The emperors of the third century were mostly military figures who struggled to respond to an upsurge in barbarian threats to the frontier and to concentrate military authority in their own hands.

This porphyry relief (above), known as 'The Tetrarchs', and usually thought to represent Diocletian and his three colleagues, represents them as equals, sharing power. Each one is in military uniform and carries a sword, depicting their military values. Even their facial characteristics are similar. The emperors are depicted as a unit. They stand or fall together.

> *Thus the almighty sovereign himself accords an increase both of years and of children to our most pious emperor, and renders his sway over the nations of the world still fresh and flourishing, as though it were even now springing up its earliest vigour. Every enemy, whether visible or unseen, has been utterly removed: and henceforward peace, the happy nurse of youth, extends her reign throughout the world.*
>
> **Eusebius of Caesarea, Speech in Praise of Constantine, AD 336**

The price of failure was removal and death. Although the emperors had always depended upon the army to bolster their position, the third century saw this reliance become much more explicit and the civilian and constitutional qualities of the imperial position became much less significant. The emperor tended to locate his governmental activities away from Rome, nearer the crucial Danubian and German frontiers, and many emperors of the period never managed to visit the Eternal City at all. As a result, the traditional aristocracy of the empire became increasingly marginalized.

The political problems of the Roman Empire culminated in a disastrous sequence of events in the middle of the century which saw Gaul break away from the main body of the empire under its own emperor and much of the east come under the control of the city of Palmyra, first under Odenathus and then under his wife, Zenobia. Palmyra's revolt was only finally crushed in AD 272. The emperor Decius was killed campaigning against the Goths (AD 251) and the emperor Valerian was captured and later killed by the Persians (AD 260). The situation improved under Aurelian (AD 270–5) who reconquered the East but was only stabilized under Diocletian (AD 284–305) who associated his rule with three other generals to establish a tetrarchy.

Diocletian is associated with a thorough reorganization of Roman administration, though it remains unclear how much was his own work and how much should be associated with the emperors of the earlier third century or with Constantine. This reform entailed a notable reduction in the size of provinces and thus governors became more numerous, but had less power to threaten an emperor.

THE FOURTH AND FIFTH CENTURIES

The insecurities of the third century led to subsequent emperors taking extreme measures to reinforce their status. Both Decius and Diocletian appear to have made the worship of the emperor a symbol of political loyalty, which posed significant problems for groups such as the Christians. As a result, Christian writers depict the late third century as a period of crisis. After Constantine's defeat of Licinius in AD 324 all the emperors, apart from Julian (AD 361–3), were Christian and Christianity emerged as the religion of the empire.

The fourth century saw a return to relative stability. The family of Constantine provided emperors until

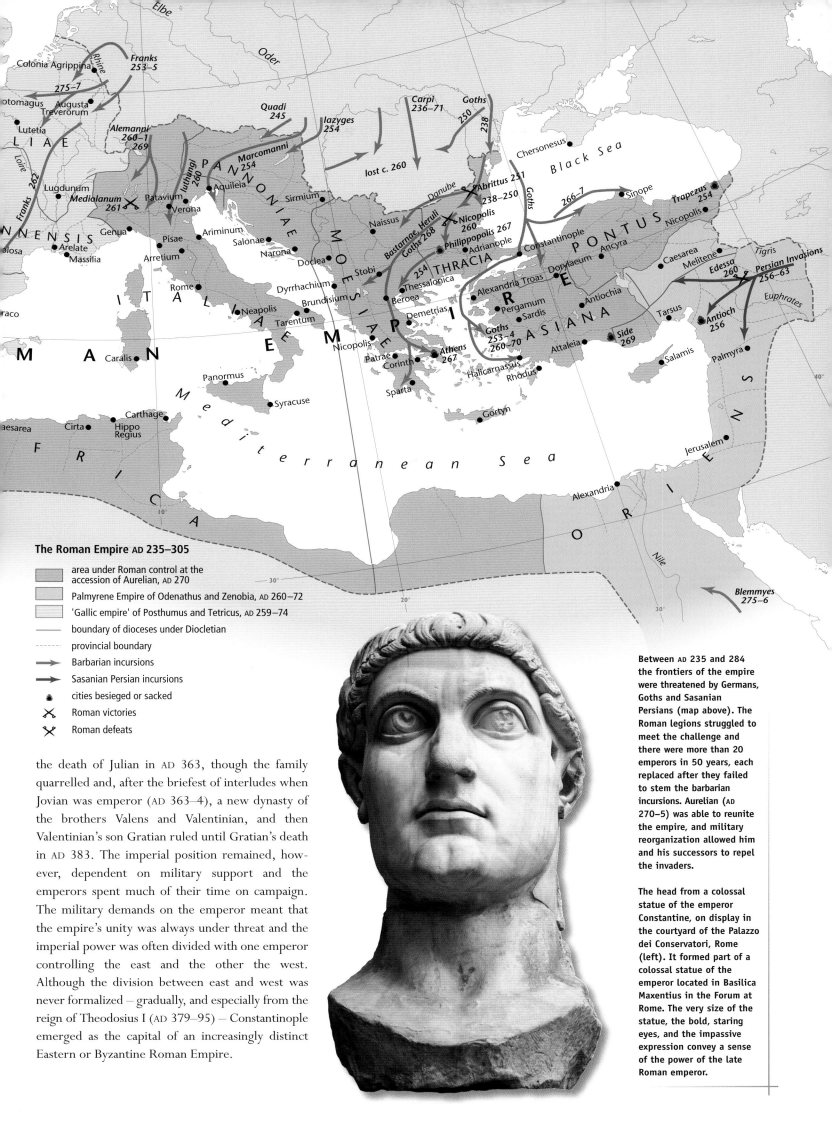

The Roman Empire AD 235–305

Franks 253–5
275–7
Colonia Agrippina
Rhine
Rotomagus
Augusta Treverorum
Lutetia
Loire 262
Lugdunum
Franks 257
Mediolanum 261
Patavium
Verona
Genua
Arelate
Massilia
Arretium
Pisae
Ariminum
Rome
Neapolis
Tarentum
Caralis
Panormus
Syracuse
Carthage
Cirta
Hippo Regius
Caesarea

Alemanni 260–1 269
Iuthungi 260
Quadi 245
Iazyges 254
Marcomanni 254
Aquileia
Sirmium
Salonae
Narona
Doclea
Stobi
Dyrrhachium
Brundisium
Nicopolis
Patrae
Corinth
Sparta
Athens 267
Gortyn

Carpi 236–71
Goths 250
Goths 238
lost c. 260
Naissus
Abrittus 251
238–250
Bastarnae, Heruli
Goths 268
Nicopolis 267
Philippopolis 267
Adrianople
Constantinople
Thessalonica
Beroea
Demetrias
254
254
THRACIA

Chersonesus
Black Sea
Goths 266–7
Sinope
Trapezus 254
Nicopolis
PONTUS
Ancyra
Caesarea
Melitene
Edessa 260
Persian Invasions 256–63
Dorylaeum
Alexandria Troas
Pergamum
Sardis
ASIANA
Antiochia
Tarsus
Antioch 256
Goths 253–4 260–70
Attaleia
Side 269
Halicarnassus
Rhodus
Salamis
Palmyra

Tigris
Euphrates
ORIENS
Jerusalem
Alexandria
Nile

Elbe
Oder
Mediterranean Sea

Blemmyes 275–6

Legend:
- area under Roman control at the accession of Aurelian, AD 270
- Palmyrene Empire of Odenathus and Zenobia, AD 260–72
- 'Gallic empire' of Posthumus and Tetricus, AD 259–74
- —— boundary of dioceses under Diocletian
- ----- provincial boundary
- → Barbarian incursions
- → Sasanian Persian incursions
- ⌖ cities besieged or sacked
- ✗ Roman victories
- ✗ Roman defeats

---

the death of Julian in AD 363, though the family quarrelled and, after the briefest of interludes when Jovian was emperor (AD 363–4), a new dynasty of the brothers Valens and Valentinian, and then Valentinian's son Gratian ruled until Gratian's death in AD 383. The imperial position remained, however, dependent on military support and the emperors spent much of their time on campaign. The military demands on the emperor meant that the empire's unity was always under threat and the imperial power was often divided with one emperor controlling the east and the other the west. Although the division between east and west was never formalized – gradually, and especially from the reign of Theodosius I (AD 379–95) – Constantinople emerged as the capital of an increasingly distinct Eastern or Byzantine Roman Empire.

Between AD 235 and 284 the frontiers of the empire were threatened by Germans, Goths and Sasanian Persians (map above). The Roman legions struggled to meet the challenge and there were more than 20 emperors in 50 years, each replaced after they failed to stem the barbarian incursions. Aurelian (AD 270–5) was able to reunite the empire, and military reorganization allowed him and his successors to repel the invaders.

The head from a colossal statue of the emperor Constantine, on display in the courtyard of the Palazzo dei Conservatori, Rome (left). It formed part of a colossal statue of the emperor located in Basilica Maxentius in the Forum at Rome. The very size of the statue, the bold, staring eyes, and the impassive expression convey a sense of the power of the late Roman emperor.

The **End** of the **Roman Empire** in the **West** AD **378–476**

In AD 378, at Adrianople, the emperor Valens faced a Gothic army. Valens had trapped the Goths while their cavalry was out foraging. He decided to attack without waiting for his nephew Gratian and the armies of the West. The Goths destroyed the Roman army and Valens was killed. The Roman Empire was plunged into crisis which, ultimately, was to lead to the total collapse of the Empire in the West.

Although the loss of so many troops and an emperor was a severe blow to Roman prestige, the Romans had suffered such losses before and recovered. The strategic situation in the late fourth century AD, however, seems to have been rather more difficult. Although Gratian was able to stabilize the empire with the help of the new emperor Theodosius I, the Goths were to become a quasi-independent element within the Roman Empire. As part of the settlement, the Romans provided the Goths with land and the Goths provided significant numbers of troops to the Roman army. These barbarian federates showed remarkable loyalty to their paymasters, but they remained a distinctive group within the army, capable of turning against their commanders.

In the early fifth century AD, the situation deteriorated. The German frontier collapsed and the Danube was threatened by the Huns. Barbarian tribes drove deep into the Western Empire. The Vandals crossed into Africa at the straits of Gibraltar and transformed Africa into an independent kingdom. Rome lost one of its most valuable provinces. The Roman emperors, now located in Ravenna, attempted to play off the various barbarian groups in complex alliances. Roman money kept soldiers in the field fighting for the empire. Yet the Roman armies remained dependent on barbarian soldiers and so generals would often rather come to an accommodation with a defeated enemy than inflict a decisive defeat. At the centre of such complex political wranglings stood individuals, often of barbarian origin, whom the emperor and the various barbarian groups trusted. The most notable of these was the general Stilicho: a man of Germanic origin but whose family had been largely assimilated into the Roman elite. Such men made enemies and the price of political failure was high. In AD 408 Stilicho was executed on the orders of the emperor Honorius. Soon after, the defences of Italy were breached. Alaric and his Visigoths stormed Rome in AD 410, an event which sent shockwaves across the Mediterranean. Rome, centre of the most powerful empire the world had seen, had fallen.

THE LAST YEARS OF THE WESTERN EMPIRE

The fall of Rome did not mark an end to Roman power in the West. The emperor remained safe behind the marshes in Ravenna and the Romans continued to put armies in the field in Gaul, the Northern Balkans and in Italy. The urban aristocracies of the West tended to show allegiance and loyalty to Rome, but gradually the imperial position disintegrated in the first decades of the fifth century. Britain was lost, Spain and Africa followed. The Franks, Burgundians, Romans and Ostrogoths disputed Gaul. The Huns under Attila, defeated in AD 451 by the Roman leader Aetius and his Visigothic allies, were driven out of Gaul but then campaigned in Italy and it was the Hunnic leader Odoacer who effectively brought an end to the Roman empire in the West when he deposed Romulus Augustulus in AD 476.

Sutton Hoo burial mask (above). This helmet with face mask was deposited as part of a seventh-century royal burial. The helmet follows late antique typology and is similar to the dress helmets in use in the fourth and fifth centuries. Its continued use for ceremonial purposes suggests the lasting prestige of Rome into the 7th century.

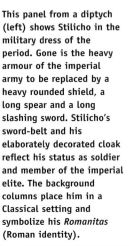

This panel from a diptych (left) shows Stilicho in the military dress of the period. Gone is the heavy armour of the imperial army to be replaced by a heavy rounded shield, a long spear and a long slashing sword. Stilicho's sword-belt and his elaborately decorated cloak reflect his status as soldier and member of the imperial elite. The background columns place him in a Classical setting and symbolize his *Romanitas* (Roman identity).

CALEDONIA

PICTS

SCOTS

Hadrian's Wall
c. 429

North Sea

JUTES

ANGLES

Baltic Sea

Vistula

Elbe

GERMANIC PEOPLES

451

Eburacum

CELTIC PEOPLES

ANGLES

Glevum

ANGLES

BRITONS

Londinium

SAXONS

JUTES

FRISIANS

420–450

SAXONS
FRANKS

TOXANDRIA

Meuse

BURGUNDIANS

Colonia Agrippina

VANDALS

Atlantic Ocean

FRANKS

by 420

406

Augusta Suessionum (Soissons)

Augusta Treverorum

ALEMANNI

Borbetomagus (Worms)

BAIOVARII

Castra Regina

Danube

RUGII

SLAVS
590

HUNS
(from 425)

Rotomagus

Lutetia

406

Somme

BURGUNDIANS
407–43

LOMBARDS

OSTROGOTHS
(from 454)

BRITONS

Civitas Aurelianorum

✕ Catalaunian Fields 451

ALEMANNI

Aventicum

568

SLOVENES

Singidunum

Portus Namnetum

VANDALS
ALANS
SUEVES
406–9

AQUITANIA

Lugdunum

BURGUNDIANS
443–534

Mediolanum

449

Verona

Po

Ravenna

451

408

CROATS

Salonae

(SERBS after 626)

Burdigala

✕ Vouillé 507

413

Augusta Taurinorum

Genua

Pisae

OSTROGOTHS
489–552

Falerio

KINGDOM OF THE VISIGOTHS

VISIGOTHS
418–507

Tolosa (Toulouse)

Rhône

412

Massilia

Corsica

VISIGOTHS
410

Goths sack Rome
410

Rome

Brundisium

Lucus Augusti

Pompaelo

WESTERN ROMAN EMPIRE

Neapolis

✕ Mons Lactarius 552

Tarentum

SUEVES (SUEBI)
411–585

Douro

KINGDOM OF THE SUEVES

ALANS

VISIGOTHS
507–711

Tarraco

Sardinia

450s

Toletum
overrun by Moors 711

Tagus

Valentia

Palma

Carales

Panormus

Alaric dies
410

Felicitas Julia

409

Corduba

Mediterranean Sea

Syracuse

VANDALS
ALANS
409–429

Carthago Nova

Gades

Caesarea

Carthage

429

Tingis

439

VANDALS, ALANS
SUEVES
439–534

✕ Ad Decimum 533

KINGDOM OF THE VANDALS

BERBERS

The Germanic settlements, AD 395–476

— frontiers, AD 395

☐ official Roman withdrawal, AD 410

▨ kingdoms established by Germanic federates and the Vandals in the Western Roman Empire by AD 443

☐ regions settled by other federates in the Western Roman Empire, AD 450

▨ given up by the Romans to the Huns by AD 446

▨ other western Roman territories occupied by Germanic peoples by AD 476

▨ Western Roman Empire, until AD 476

▨ Eastern Roman Empire, AD 476

movements of peoples

→ Huns and campaigns of Attila

→ Vandals, Alans, Sueves

→ Visigoths

→ Ostrogoths

→ Franks

→ other Germanic peoples

→ Scots, Picts and Britons

THE GERMANIC SETTLEMENTS

In the early fifth century the Roman frontier in Germany collapsed and barbarians poured into the empire. Similar problems on the Danube had already led to Goths settling within the empire. Some of these tribes, such as the ferocious Huns, were raiders. Others, although often raiding and pillaging, were looking to settle. Although the Romans were able initially to drive the barbarians from Italy and maintain a hold in Gaul, the emperors were forced to concede territory to the barbarian kingdoms and Roman Gaul dissolved. Spain and Africa, two wealthy provinces, fell to the Vandals and their allies and eventually the Goths returned to Italy to bring an end to the Roman Empire in the West.

The **Christian West**

AD **379–750**

The reign of Theodosius (AD 379–395) saw the triumph of Christianity in the West. Travellers from the East brought news of the monastic movements which had become important in Egypt and Syria and Athanasius's *Life of St Anthony* popularized asceticism in the West. After the fall of Rome a series of Germanic successor states emerged, in which the Christian Church acted as the principal agent of continuity with Roman traditions and learning.

C hristianity established itself firmly during the late Empire. In Rome itself, Jerome (c. AD 342–419) preached his particular brand of asceticism and encouraged the building of monastic communities. In Milan, Bishop Ambrose (c. AD 339–397) clashed spectacularly with emperors such as Gratian and Theodosius, publicizing these clashes through his letters. Emperors were forced to recognize the independence of bishops in matters religious and, to a certain extent, political. Contemporary to Ambrose and Jerome was one of the most important early Christian philosophers, Augustine of Hippo (AD 354–430), whose frank *Confessions* describe his personal struggle to attain a proper Christian lifestyle and whose *City of God* developed a political and personal theological system which laid the ground for much of the theological discussion of the Middle Ages.

These men combined a strong spiritual sense and Christian knowledge with a Classical education and deployed the conventional skills of rhetoric in defence of their causes. In general, although knowledge of Greek appears to have been in decline in the Latin West, Classical culture remained vibrant in Italy and Gaul and survived the political collapse of Rome.

Many early medieval churches in Rome were built on the sites of earlier, pagan temples. The 6th-century Santa Maria in Cosmedin (left) lies on the site of an earlier temple of Heracles.

THE SUCCESSOR STATES TO ROME

In Italy, the fall of Rome in AD 476 was followed by the emergence of a Gothic state under Theodoric (AD 493–526). The Goths maintained good relations with their Roman subjects, happily sponsoring new building and repairs, and allowing the Senate to continue functioning as more than a political relic. Much of the late Roman administrative structure was retained, with magistrates and officials appointed from the Roman elite by the Gothic king. The Goths were served by men of great learning such as Cassiodorus and Boethius, the first of whom produced a famous collection of letters following an epistolary tradition which went back at least to the second century AD, while the second produced *The Consolations of Philosophy*, a text which has some claim to be the last major work of philosophy within the Classical tradition. The modus vivendi established between the Gothic king and the Roman aristocracy collapsed with the sixth-century Byzantine invasion of Italy, led by Justinian's general Belisarius (see p. 136). After a series of long and difficult wars in which much of Italy was devastated, the Gothic army was finally destroyed. The price of victory was, however, very high and the archaeological evidence suggests widespread depopulation.

Although Rome had lost all political power and probably much of its population, it remained an important religious centre. Its fortunes were raised by the energetic Pope Gregory the Great (AD 590–604). Not only was Gregory responsible for a spate of church-building within the city itself, he also exerted papal authority through his letters throughout much of the former Western Roman Empire.

Outside Italy, the old Roman elite sought some reconciliation with the barbarian kings. At least some fifth-century Gallo-Romans looked to the Church to further their careers and secure their control of localities. Many sought to associate themselves, their towns and their bishoprics with saintly figures of the past with the result that the period saw a tremendous expansion in hagiography and in the cult of relics. Although there had been some religious scepticism about relics, in both Eastern and Western

Roman churches, 7th–8th century AD

- Aurelian walls
- Christian churches c. AD 500
- churches c. AD 500–600
- churches c. AD 600–750
- major Latin monasteries to AD 700
- major Eastern monasteries to AD 700

S Silvestro
St Peter's
S Maria in Adriano
St Peter's
Mausoleum of Hadrian
Sto Stefano Maggiore

S Maria in Trastevere

Christianity they became a source of religious power. The clothing of Caesarius of Arles, for instance, was washed and the dirtied water drunk to cure men of fever. Saints' days became opportunities for pilgrimage and festivities which raised the profile of both particular bishops and cities.

This divine power countered the loss of political power to the barbarian kings and their armies. The barbarians were not in general hostile towards Classical culture. The material wealth of Roman culture was recognized, as were the benefits of the Classical system which had provided such wealth. Rome remained a source of great prestige and barbarians were often anxious to maintain good relations with Byzantium in order to benefit from that prestige. The Church ensured the survival of Classical culture in Gaul and Italy, even if in diminished form, and passed that culture on to the Middle Ages.

This crown (right), presented by the Visigothic king, Recceswinth, combines the Classical, the Christian and the Byzantine. The cross, marked out with pearls, symbolizes Christianity. The script is Latin. The crown, with its heavy jewellery, follows Byzantine techniques and tastes, while the finely worked patterning owes something to Germanic metalworking. Thus, in this demonstration of devotion, wealth and power the cultural mix of the West is displayed.

Tiber

Baths of Diocletian

Quirinal Hill

S Lorenzo in Lucina

S Vitale

S Andrea Catabarbara

Stadium of Domitian

S Maria in Aquiro

S Agata de Caballis

Viminal Hill

S Maris Maggiore

Pantheon

S Marcello

S Pudeziana

Esquiline Hill

S Eustachio

S Maria inVia Lata

S Bibiana

S Marco

S Agata dei Goti

S Martino ai Monti

Capitoline Hill

S Adriano

S Lucia in Selcis

S Pietro in Vincoli

SS Sergio e Bacco

SS Cosma e Damiano

Oppian Hill

S Teodoro

S Maria Antiqua

Colosseum

S Crisogono

S Giorgio in Velabro

S Anastasia

Palatine Hill

S Clemente

S Croce in Gerusalemme

Imperial Forum

SS Giovanni e Paolo

S Maria in Cosmedin

Circus Maximus

S Erasmo

Caelian Hill

S Greforio in Clivo Scauro

Lateran Basilica

S Maria in Domnica

Sto Stefano Rotondo

S Sabina

Aventine Hill

Tiber

Little Aventine Hill

S Sisto Vecchio

S Saba

Baths of Caracalla

Constantine was responsible for the first churches in Rome, the major centres being the Lateran basilica and St Peter's on the out-skirts of the city. Gradually, Christianity penetrated the old Classical city (map left). The forum received its own church and the Pantheon, one of the finest achievements of Classical architecture, was converted into a church. A monastic tradition developed along-side the churches, mostly after AD 400. The Christ-ianization of Rome was piecemeal and slow, but the number of Christian institutions operating within the city by the eighth century AD shows the transformation of Rome into a Christian capital for the West.

The **Byzantine Empire**
AD **395–750**

By the early fifth century, Constantinople had emerged as the centre of Roman power in the East and effective capital of the Empire. Although the Eastern Empire faced many of the same problems as the Western, with barbarian threats to the Danubian frontier and significant military difficulties on the frontier with Persia in the East, it managed to retain its territorial integrity until the Avar raids of the late sixth century AD.

The fifth century was a period of relative stability which seems to have been one of prosperity and growth throughout the East. Constantinople itself was equipped with long walls and impressive aqueducts, far longer than those which had supplied the great cities of the early Roman Empire. In AD 532, the influential circus factions at Constantinople joined forces against the emperor Justinian (AD 527–65), probably with some tacit political support among the political elite, and threatened to drive the emperor from the city. Supposedly steadied by his wife Theodora, Justinian was able to mobilize sufficient military force under his general Belisarius to defeat the rioters and bring peace to the city. Perhaps in response to his domestic difficulties and taking the opportunity of relative peace on the Eastern frontier, Justinian sent Belisarius to Africa in AD 533, where he was soon able to overcome the Vandal kingdom and bring North Africa back into the imperial fold.

THE RECONQUEST OF ITALY

Buoyed by this success, Belisarius invaded Italy in AD 534, hoping to benefit from chronic political divisions within the Gothic royal house. Again, Belisarius met with instant success, marching through Italy and capturing Rome. The Goths, however, regrouped. Starved of resources, Belisarius was unable to retain his Italian territories. The resulting wars devastated Italy until the Byzantines finally triumphed under the general Narses in AD 552. Although victory had come at a significant cost, the Byzantines had won back some of the heartlands of the old Roman Empire.

The gains, however, were short-lived. Lombard invasions after AD 568 threatened the Byzantine hold on Italy while the Avars raided and devastated much of the Balkans. In the seventh AD century the emperor Phocas (AD 602–610) was overthrown by Heraclius (AD 610–641) after a long civil war. Heraclius was faced with a major Persian invasion which swept through Syria and Egypt and reached the gates of the imperial capital by AD 626. Heraclius, however, inflicted a series of defeats on the Persians and managed to regain all the lost territory. This triumph, too, was short-lived for although the power of the Persians was broken, the Arabs took advantage of the new situation and not only conquered many of the Persian lands but defeated the Byzantines at Yarmuk in AD 636 and were, for nearly a century, almost unstoppable. First Syria, then Egypt, then much of Eastern Asia Minor, followed by Africa by AD 700 and finally parts of Spain fell before the Arab invaders. Although the Byzantines staged a fightback in the eighth century AD, the East and Africa were lost forever.

This medal (below) commemorates the victories of the Byzantine general Belisarius in Italy. In AD 533 he was sent to reconquer the former western Roman territories. Belisarius retook North Africa from the Vandals, and from AD 535 began the reconquest of Italy, taking Rome by AD 536. Justinian, wary of his general's success, recalled him, and, despite permitting Belisarius to return in AD 544, never allowed him sufficient resources to complete the task.

KINGDOM OF THE SUEVES

CANTABRIANS

FRANKIS

BASQUES

SABARIA

KINGDOM OF THE VISIGOTHS

Visigoths 571

Corduba

OROSPEDA

Malaca

Carthago Nova

Balearics

B Y Z A N T I N E

B E R B E R S

Arabs

The Byzantine Empire to AD 732

- Byzantine Empire, AD 527
- added AD 533–5
- added by AD 554
- Byzantine Empire, AD 732
- frontiers, AD 565
- → invasions after the reign of Justinian

Mosaic of Theodora, from the Church of San Vitale, Ravenna (right). This is a companion piece to a depiction of Justinian and his court. Theodora is depicted at the centre of the scene making an offering. As this depiction was made after Theodora's death, it is likely that the darkened doorway to which she is progressing symbolizes her passage into another world and that the fountain within that doorway represents eternal life.

Sporadic attempts to restore Byzantine power in the West in the fifth century AD came to nothing. Under Justinian, the empire again expanded to the West (map below), with a brilliant campaign in Africa. The conquests of Italy and of parts of Spain were more drawn out though ultimately successful. Nevertheless, fresh waves of barbarian activity led to the loss of North Italy and tracts of Danubian land. In the seventh century AD, Arab invaders seized Syria, Egypt, coastal Asia Minor and Africa, so establishing the geo-political divisions of the Mediterranean which were to dominate the Middle Ages.

Constantinople and Byzantine Culture AD 327–750

The reigns of Theodosius I (AD 379–395) and Arcadius (AD 395–408) saw the triumph of Catholic Christianity in the Eastern Roman Empire. Imperial and episcopal hostility destroyed the institutions of paganism. Paganism appears to have continued in some rural communities and, perhaps more significantly, among the educated elite. Some of those who preserved an interest in philosophy also continued an interest in pagan religion but paganism never again challenged Christian predominance.

The fourth century saw a sudden resurgence in non-Greek literary traditions within the Eastern empire, particularly Coptic and Syriac literature in Egypt and Syria. Both languages appear to have been associated with monastic traditions and leading Egyptian monastic figures such as SS Antony and Pachomius and the slightly later Schenoudi made much of their village (non-Greek) origins and preference for Coptic. In Syria, Simeon Stylites, who advertised his particular devotion by spending his days standing on a pillar, probably communicated in Aramaic with the crowds attracted by his spectacular example and, allegedly,

converted whole tribes to Christianity. Although there were considerable tensions between urban and rural elements and between bishops and monks, some of which seem to have manifested themselves in a stated hostility to things 'Greek', these divisions do not appear to have been ethnic. Pachomius (AD 292–346), for instance, appears to have arranged for simultaneous translation between Egyptian and Greek for non-Egyptian speakers. At the monastery of Epiphanius at Thebes in Egypt, inscriptions on the walls recorded the wisdom of Egyptian religious thinkers in Greek and Coptic.

The continuities in Roman government are demonstrated by this fifth- or sixth-century portrait of Flavius Palmatus (right). Palmatus was the leading citizen of the city of Aphrodisias in Asia Minor, and is here shown in an elaborate toga, the formal dress of a Roman citizen, holding a cloth in his left hand (another symbol of office) and a sceptre in his right, symbolizing consular power.

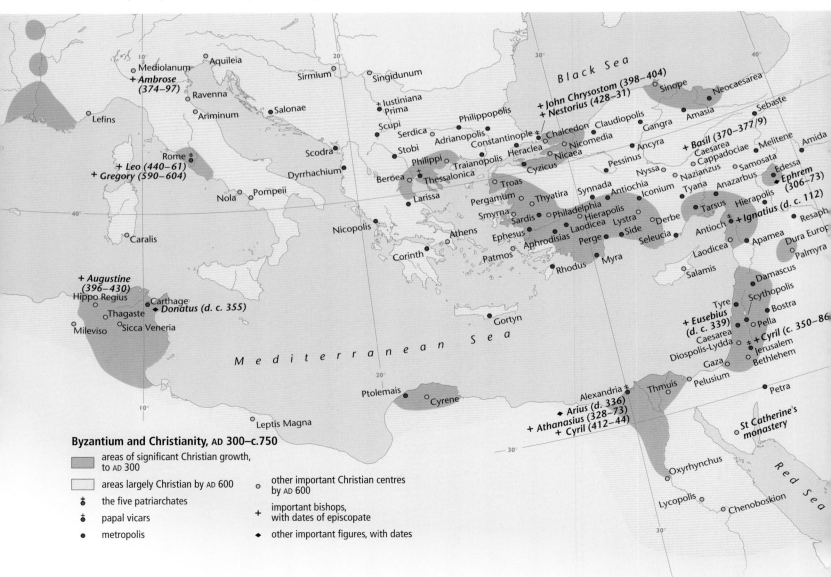

Byzantium and Christianity, AD 300–c.750

- areas of significant Christian growth, to AD 300
- areas largely Christian by AD 600
- ‡ the five patriarchates
- ⸸ papal vicars
- ● metropolis
- ○ other important Christian centres by AD 600
- + important bishops, with dates of episcopate
- ◆ other important figures, with dates

The monastic traditions of asceticism came to influence episcopal Christianity and bishops such Athanasius of Alexandria (c. AD 290–373) and John Chrysostom (AD 347–407) lived as ascetics while performing their episcopal duties. Monasteries and, especially, 'Houses for Virgins' were established within cities or sometimes in the suburbs so that solitary monks or communities of monks and virgins became common in urban communities. Monks also came to play an increasingly important part in the sometimes violent politics of the Church.

BYZANTINE URBAN CULTURE

Within the cities especially, although Christianity was extremely influential, other cultural institutions continued and flourished. The unbroken traditions of Greek literature were maintained with historians such as Procopius and Agathias and poets such as Christodoros of Coptos. Classical philosophy was taught in Aphrodisias in Asia Minor, Alexandria, and Athens while Beirut became a centre of legal training. Learning was not restricted to a small urban elite and a chance discovery of an archive of documents from the insignificant Egypt village of Aphrodito unearthed at least some of the work of the local poet and scribe, Dioscoros.

The traditions of urban civilization seem also to have been maintained. Public baths operated in many areas until the seventh century AD. The circus appears to have largely replaced the theatre as the major popular entertainment, though mime (comic theatre) was important. This vibrant urban culture may have come under pressure after the onset of plague pandemic in AD 542 and many traditional population centres were abandoned in the sixth, seventh and eighth centuries AD. Literary traditions were eroded and the use of Greek retreated to the Byzantine heartlands. The late seventh century witnessed the end of the cultural, political and religious unity of the Byzantine lands in the face of Arab expansionism.

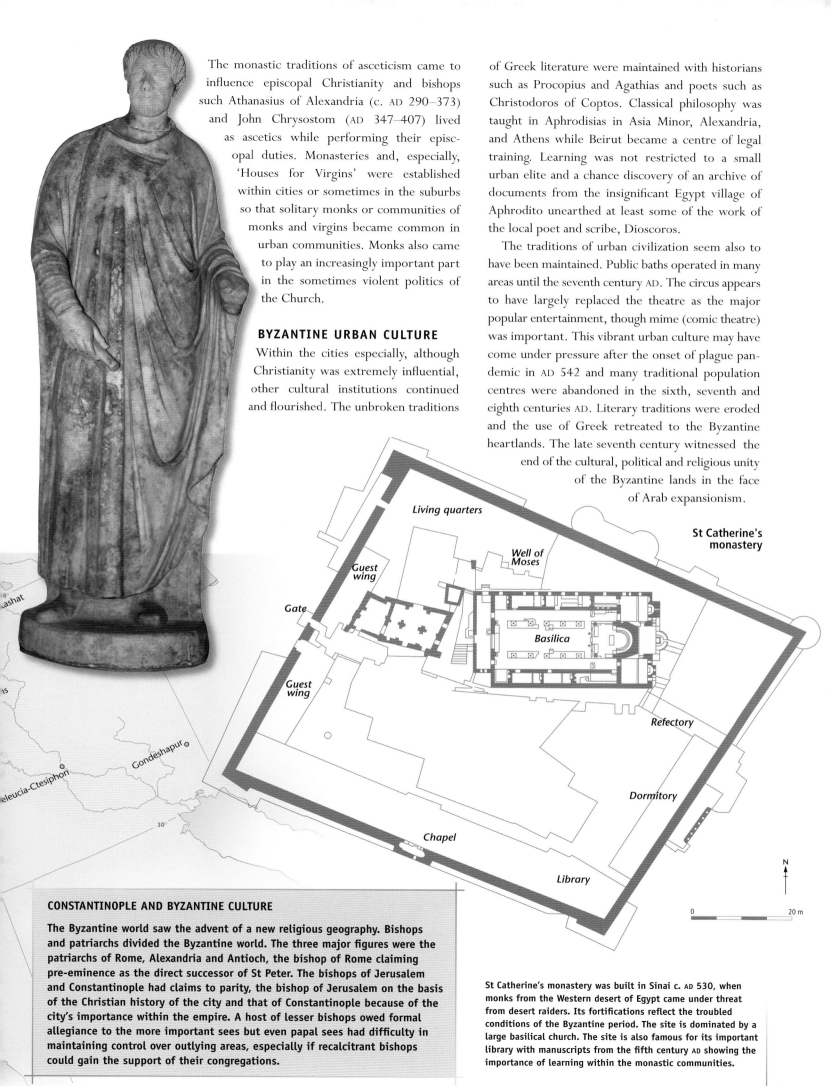

St Catherine's monastery

Living quarters

Well of Moses

Guest wing

Gate

Basilica

Guest wing

Refectory

Dormitory

Chapel

Library

0   20 m

N

CONSTANTINOPLE AND BYZANTINE CULTURE

The Byzantine world saw the advent of a new religious geography. Bishops and patriarchs divided the Byzantine world. The three major figures were the patriarchs of Rome, Alexandria and Antioch, the bishop of Rome claiming pre-eminence as the direct successor of St Peter. The bishops of Jerusalem and Constantinople had claims to parity, the bishop of Jerusalem on the basis of the Christian history of the city and that of Constantinople because of the city's importance within the empire. A host of lesser bishops owed formal allegiance to the more important sees but even papal sees had difficulty in maintaining control over outlying areas, especially if recalcitrant bishops could gain the support of their congregations.

St Catherine's monastery was built in Sinai c. AD 530, when monks from the Western desert of Egypt came under threat from desert raiders. Its fortifications reflect the troubled conditions of the Byzantine period. The site is dominated by a large basilical church. The site is also famous for its important library with manuscripts from the fifth century AD showing the importance of learning within the monastic communities.

The Sasanian Empire
C. AD 224–651

The Sasanian period marks a high point of Ancient Near Eastern history and culture. The Sasanian kings were titled 'shahanshah' ('king of kings') and traced descent from an ancestor called Sasan. Following his revolt and defeat of the last Parthian king, Artabanus V, the Persian nobleman Ardashir was crowned at Ctesiphon in c. AD 224. His accession marked the beginning of over four centuries of Sasanian rule.

Ardashir's reign was marked by rapid military advances which were continued and consolidated by his son Shapur I (AD 240–272). Neighbouring kingdoms such as Hatra were seized and political power was more effectively centralized. Sasanian advances in Mesopotamia and the Caucasus led them into direct conflict with Rome, often with one-sided results. The Roman emperor, Gordian III, was killed in battle on the Euphrates and his successor Philip 'the Arab' was obliged to pay a heavy tribute. This was

The Sasanian Empire stretched over 2,000 kilometres from the plains of northern Syria to the mountains of the Caucasus, the deserts of Central Asia and the headwaters of the River Indus (map below). The capital was at Ctesiphon in modern Iraq but the Sasanians also founded or rebuilt cities throughout the empire. The fertile lowland plains of Mesopotamia and south-west Iran were intensively cultivated following the construction of massive irrigation canal systems. These boosted agricultural production, sustaining an expanding population and providing a lucrative source of tax revenue. The borders of the empire were defended by permanent garrisons stationed in forts, sometimes positioned behind huge long walls which were constructed to block vulnerable routes.

Sasanian Persia, AD 224–651

- Sasanian heartland, before AD 224
- Lakhmid kingdom, c. AD 224–604
- territory governed by Persian 'kings of the Kushans'
- maximum extent of Sasanian Empire, 6th century AD
- ● important Sasanian cities
- ⊥ fire temples
- Ψ rock reliefs
- — routes

followed by Shapur's repeated invasions of Syria (AD 253–256, 258), when he sacked over 35 cities and took the Roman emperor Valerian as captive. Shapur II's reign (AD 309–379) was again marked by successful wars against Rome but fortunes changed in the fifth century with the capture and death of King Peroz (AD 459–484) at the hands of Hephthalite enemies in Central Asia. The reign of Kavad (AD 488–531) witnessed a serious social movement led by Mazdak, who believed that wealth and women should be shared equally: Kavad's initial acceptance of these teachings led to his overthrow by his own nobility and clergy.

THE LAST SASANIANS

The reign of Khusrau I (AD 531–579) marked an economic revival and cultural renaissance. He is credited with instituting widespread tax reforms and the development of a state army. During the reign of Khusrau II (AD 591–628), Sasanian armies over-ran

and ruled the eastern provinces of the Byzantine Empire for over a decade, capturing major cities such as Antioch and Jerusalem. He was succeeded by no fewer than seven rulers in twenty years. This political instability offered an opportunity for the Arab armies which gradually defeated Sasanian forces in Mesopotamia before sacking Ctesiphon and besieging cities across Iran. In AD 651 the last Sasanian king, Yazdgard III, was murdered close to the eastern edge of his empire, near the city of Merv, thus bringing this dynasty and period to an end.

Unfortunately there are few primary historical sources for the Sasanians, as parchments rarely survive and official inscriptions are rare. The exception is Shapur I's trilingual inscription in Greek, Parthian and Middle Persian (Pahlavi) on the Ka'bah-i Zardusht at Naqsh-i Rustam. This outlines the administrative organization of the empire. Additional evidence is provided by inscriptions on official seals and sealings as these refer to the names of provinces, districts and officials. Other historical sources include Roman historians, Syriac Church records, Armenian histories, the Babylonian Talmud, Islamic authors describing the Arab Conquest, and Persian literature.

The principal sources for Sasanian art are rock reliefs, stuccoes, coins, silver plates, seals and textiles while archaeological excavations add details about aspects of daily life. Pottery was mass produced but certain types of decorated glassware and silver plate served as luxury wares. These were also traded to neighbours to the north and east although the importance of the so-called 'Silk Route' has been over-emphasized. Another direction of foreign trade and contact was southwards through the Persian Gulf to India, southern Arabia and the Horn of Africa, from where the Sasanians obtained gems, ivory, incense and perfume.

SOGDIANA

indu Kush

GANDHARA

RIA

Indus

probable ancient course of Indus

Plain, moulded and cut glass vessels were manufactured within the Sasanian Empire (picture below left). Many of the shapes resemble contemporary Roman types but the styles of decoration are different. The luxury wares were decorated with elaborate cut facets with sparkle being the sought-after effect, rather than the colour of the glass. This bowl dates to the sixth century AD. Similar bowls were exported as far as China, Korea and Japan where they survived in imperial treasuries and high-status tombs.

Silver plates are among the most famous forms of Sasanian art (below). They typically show hunting, investiture or banqueting scenes. They were made by hammering single sheets of almost pure silver into the required shape, engraving the patterns and highlighting areas with gilding; separate bases were soldered onto the undersides. They were intended for display. Ironically, many have been found outside the limits of the Sasanian Empire, particularly in Siberia, where they were valued in shamanistic cults.

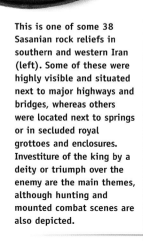

This is one of some 38 Sasanian rock reliefs in southern and western Iran (left). Some of these were highly visible and situated next to major highways and bridges, whereas others were located next to springs or in secluded royal grottoes and enclosures. Investiture of the king by a deity or triumph over the enemy are the main themes, although hunting and mounted combat scenes are also depicted.

Aksum

C. AD 100–700

The Aksumite state, with its heartland located in present-day northern Ethiopia and Eritrea, was well established by the first century AD. Aksum was once regarded as little more than a South Arabian offshoot, but its African origins are now more clearly understood. Archaeological evidence, for example, points to connections with the Nubian cultures of Kerma and Meroë while trade with the African interior, especially in luxury items such as gold, was undoubtedly an important factor in its growing wealth.

Stela 3 in the main stelae field at Aksum (below). Standing 21 metres high and weighing 160 tonnes, this fourth-century granite monolith is thought to mark the site of a royal tomb. It has been carved on three sides to represent a multi-storeyed building of characteristic Aksumite design. Rows of ornate windows, a door complete with a lock, recessed wooden beams and projecting beam-ends are all meticulously reproduced in stone. A metal plaque, held in place with pegs, would once have adorned the top.

S outh Arabia proved to be an enduring focus of Aksumite economic, political and military ambitions. During the second century AD, Aksum became increasingly involved in wresting control of Red Sea trade from the kingdom of Himyar, culminating in the capture of areas formerly under Himyarite rule. This marked the beginning of Aksum's long involvement in South Arabian affairs, which ended only with the Persian conquest of that region at the end of the 6th century AD. The growth of Aksumite power has also been linked to the decline of Meroë. It is thought that an Aksumite military expedition in the mid-fourth century may have dealt the final blow to the Meroitic state but it is equally possible that Aksum's expansion was a result, rather than cause, of this decline.

CHRISTIANITY IN AKSUM

From the reign of Endubis in the late third century coins, conforming to the Romano-Byzantine weight system, were minted in Aksum, a development that facilitated economic activity whilst proclaiming Aksum's wealth and imperial status. It is from the coinage that we also have evidence of one of the most significant events in Aksumite history; the conversion to Christianity. The cross appears for the first time on coins minted during the reign of the fourth-century king, Ezana, and is paralleled by the adoption of Christian terminology in his inscriptional invocations. At this stage, however, Christianity does not seem to have spread much beyond the capital and ruling elite, and probably had as much diplomatic as religious significance, not least the strengthening of ties with the Roman Empire following the conversion of Constantine the Great (AD 312–337). It seems that it was only in the late-fifth century, with the arrival of monophysite Christians fleeing persecution in the Eastern Roman empire, that Christianity began to spread throughout the region with the building of churches and founding of monasteries.

Early in the sixth century AD, at the request of the Byzantine emperor Justin I, the Aksumites launched a successful military campaign against the king of

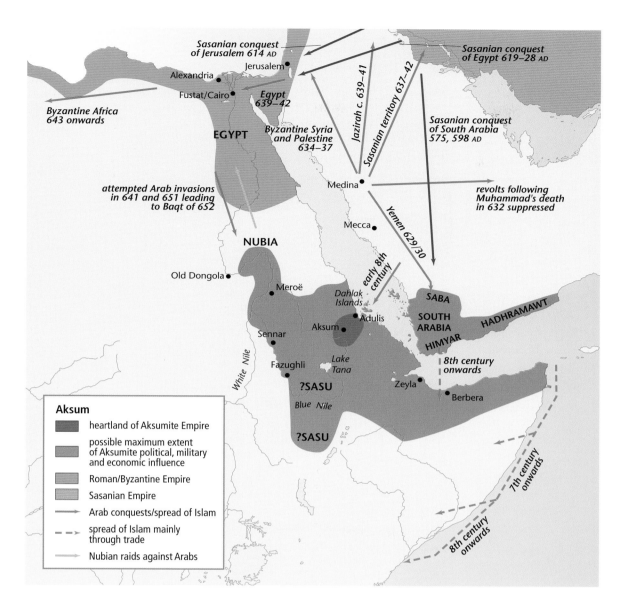

Sasanian conquest of Jerusalem 614 AD

Sasanian conquest of Egypt 619–28 AD

Jazirah c. 639–41

Sasanian territory 637–42

Sasanian conquest of South Arabia 575, 598 AD

Alexandria

Jerusalem

Fustat/Cairo

Byzantine Africa 643 onwards

Egypt 639–42

EGYPT

Byzantine Syria and Palestine 634–37

attempted Arab invasions in 641 and 651 leading to Baqt of 652

Medina

revolts following Muhammad's death in 632 suppressed

Yemen 629/30

Mecca

NUBIA

Old Dongola

Meroë

Dahlak Islands

early 8th century

SABA

SOUTH ARABIA

HADHRAMAWT

HIMYAR

Aksum

Adulis

Sennar

White Nile

Lake Tana

Fazughli

?SASU

Blue Nile

8th century onwards

Zeyla

Berbera

?SASU

7th century onwards

8th century onwards

Aksum
- heartland of Aksumite Empire
- possible maximum extent of Aksumite political, military and economic influence
- Roman/Byzantine Empire
- Sasanian Empire
- Arab conquests/spread of Islam
- spread of Islam mainly through trade
- Nubian raids against Arabs

The heartland of the Aksumite Empire comprised the region around the city of Aksum and the port of Adulis (map left). However, the precise extent of the empire remains unclear. This is partly because surviving geographical information is often obscure and because borders were never clearly delineated. Control of outlying regions was maintained through such means as vassal rulers, tribute collection and military reprisals. The map shows the largest notional area of political and economic control or influence at different times throughout the Aksumite era. Aksum lay at the centre of a trading network that linked the African interior with the Red Sea and Indian Ocean trading systems. It was the disruption of this network, especially after the rise of Islam, that contributed to Aksum's eventual collapse.

Himyar to avenge his persecution of Christians. This victory greatly enhanced Aksum's prestige and for a brief time it ranked as one of the world powers of late antiquity. However, it also marked the beginning of Aksum's decline. The precise reasons for this decline are uncertain but by the early seventh century the city of Aksum had apparently ceased to be the state capital, although it continued to function as a religious centre. The Persian conquests, the rise of Islam and Arab control of the Red Sea must have been significant contributory factors since they cut Aksum off from most of its former trading links. But whatever the causes, by about the end of the seventh century the Aksumite Empire had ceased to exist.

Examples of Aksumite coins from the pre-Christian, early Christian and later Christian Phases. The gold coin of Ousanas (early fourth century), shows the king crowned, with spear in hand, and framed by two ears of wheat (1, above right). Above his head appears the pre-Christian disc-and-crescent symbol. The gold coin of Ezana (mid-fourth century) employs the same design elements but the cross appears above, below and on either side of the bust (2, above right). Both legends are in Greek. The obverse side of the bronze coin of Armah (early seventh century) shows the king crowned, enthroned and holding a staff topped with a cross (3, right). On the reverse side the royal bust has been replaced by the cross, although the two ears of wheat remain (4, right). The legends are in Ge`ez, the language of Aksum.

West Africa

C. AD **300–800**

The development of civilization in West Africa south of the Sahara is not yet well understood. By the time Islamic traders made contact with the area in the ninth and tenth centuries AD there were already a number of urban communities along the inland delta of the Upper Niger and on the edges of the rainforest in what is now eastern Nigeria. Some are known from archaeology, others only from later written sources.

Around 1000 BC the drying up of lakes in the savannah at the southern edge of the Sahara had forced populations which had previously relied mainly on hunting and fishing to turn to agriculture, cultivating millet. At Tichitt in Mauretania there was a small settlement by the third century BC, and the important site of Jenne-jeno was settled at about the same time. There is evidence of copper-working in Mauretania in the period before 500 BC, and it is possible that the techniques had been spread from Phoenician communities on the Atlantic coast of Africa. By c. 400 BC iron-working was established in the area of the Nok culture in northern Nigeria, and it is likely that this technology had been introduced from the Mediterranean by way of a route across the Sahara which had been used since the second millennium BC. The first millennium AD saw the growth of the powerful states of Meroë and Aksum to the east. Although it is possible that there was communication between this area and West Africa, there is insufficient evidence to demonstrate this.

JENNE-JENO

The best evidence for urban development in West Africa comes from Jenne-jeno, a substantial settlement built on an island in the Upper Niger delta, in what is now Mali. In the major phase of occupation, c. AD 300–800, the site covered an area of around 33 hectares, and the population of the centre and its satellite communities may have exceeded 25,000. Excavation has revealed mud-built houses. There are also a number of walls, which are evidence of some kind of social organization. However, there are no signs of monumental public or religious buildings, and little or no evidence of any social stratification. This suggests that urban development in this area did not follow the pattern of many other parts of the world. Although the land around the settlement has similarities to that exploited by earlier civilizations in other parts of the world, the inhabitants of Jenne-jeno did not practice the same kind of intensive agriculture, and it appears to have functioned without a powerful ruling elite.

Other settlements probably appeared at about the same time as Jenno-jeno, although less is known about them. At Gao, further east on the Upper Niger, there appears to have been a significant settlement by c. AD 500, and the emergent state of Ghana to the west, mentioned in early Arabic writings, was probably established before AD 800, although no city-site of that period has been identified.

THE NOK CULTURE AND IFE

The Nok culture in modern Nigeria, noted for its iron-working and for the production of fine terracottas from the end of the first millennium BC, appears not to have produced any very large settlements, but the situation was different on the edge of the rain-forest. The site of Ife has substantial mud walls, and although large parts of them are only a few hundred years old, the site dates back to the first millennium AD, and may have been a substantial settlement by AD 800. The same may be true of other, sites such as Igbo Ukwu. The early history of civilization in this part of the world is still fully to be explored and understood.

West Africa before AD 800 (above). The emptiness of much of the map illustrates two important features of the history of the region. The Sahara desert created a considerable, but not totally impenetrable, barrier between tropical West Africa and the civilizations to the north and east. Although there was communication across the desert from time to time, the distances were too great for any general cultural influence to extend into the area. Other blank spaces on the map are indications of the limitation of current knowledge about the area. Further archaeological survey and excavation, and low-level aerial photography, may one day allow some of the blanks to be filled in.

Rock painting from the Sahara, c. 1200 BC (right). Rock painting in the Sahara desert is a practice that dates back many millennia. The appearance of chariots in these paintings at sites which stretch in a line from Tripoli in Libya to near Timbuctoo in Mali are seen as evidence for regular traffic across the desert in the second millennium BC, and probably later. This is the most likely route by which knowledge of iron-working technology was introduced to West Africa.

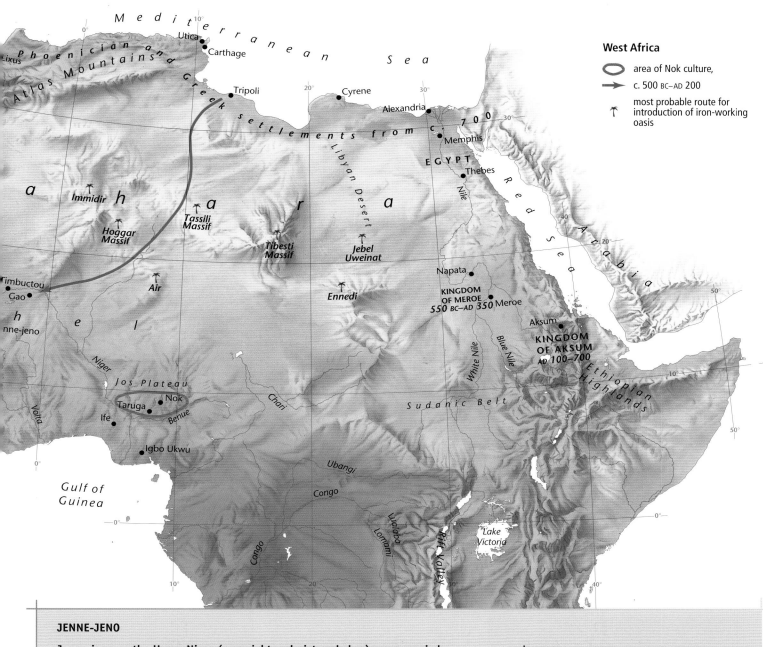

Mediterranean Sea

Phoenician and Greek settlements from c. 700

Atlas Mountains

Utica
Carthage
Lixus
Tripoli
Cyrene
Alexandria
Memphis
EGYPT
Thebes

Libyan Desert

Sahara

Immidir
Tassili Massif
Hoggar Massif
Tibesti Massif
Jebel Uweinat
Air
Ennedi

Timbuctou
Gao
nne-jeno

Sahel

Niger

Jos Plateau
Taruga   Nok
Ife
Benue
Igbo Ukwu

Volta
Chari

Gulf of Guinea

Ubangi
Congo
Congo
Lualaba
Lomami

Rift Valley

Lake Victoria

Sudanic Belt

Napata
KINGDOM OF MEROE
550 BC–AD 350   Meroe
Aksum
KINGDOM OF AKSUM
AD 100–700

White Nile
Blue Nile
Nile

Red Sea

Arabia

Ethiopian Highlands

West Africa

⬭ area of Nok culture,
➜ c. 500 BC–AD 200

⍗ most probable route for introduction of iron-working oasis

JENNE-JENO

Jenne-jeno on the Upper Niger (map right and picture below) was occupied from c. 250 BC until it was finally abandoned around AD 1100 when the remaining population moved to a new site at Jenne (also called Djenné), a few miles away: Jenne-jeno means 'Old Jenne'. Excavations have continued at the site since the 1970s, and the area around it has been surveyed so that the settlement can be understood in relation to its hinterland. The buildings identified on the plan belong to Phases III (c. AD 300–800) and IV (c. AD 800–1100). The absence of a substantial ruler's house or of burials with rich grave-goods points to a society without strong divisions between rich and poor.

houses:
● round
■ square
▼ indeterminate
▲ funerary urn
═ city wall

inhumation cemetery
residential area
residential area

0   200 m

N

Gupta India

C. AD **300–606**

Shortly after AD 300 the Sasanians made a violent foray into India and destroyed the last vestiges of the Kushan Empire (see p. 120). With the disappearance of Kushan rule, a host of local Indian rulers emerged, the final victor in the struggle for power being Samudragupta, founder of the Gupta Dynasty. For two centuries the Guptas held sway over large parts of northern India, until a Hun invasion shattered their power in the late 5th century AD.

Samudragupta's armies conquered all of the northern plains from Bihar and Bengal in the east to the frontier of Afghanistan in the northwest. He also undertook campaigns into the Himalayas and towards the south in order to bring petty rulers and forest people under his sway. Giving concrete shape to the ideals of Indian political theory, Samudragupta created a 'circle of kings', an imperial formation with himself at the centre. His exploits were celebrated in inscriptions and he established a new calendar, the first Gupta year corresponding to 319–20 AD. Samudragupta and his successors performed elaborate royal rituals, the most notable being the Horse Sacrifice, a year-long solemn rite used by ancient Indian kings to ratify their status as 'Chakravartins', or universal sovereigns. These sacrifices were commemorated in a series of exquisite gold coins.

THE REIGN OF CHANDRAGUPTA II

The oldest monumental remains of the Gupta Dynasty date to the reign of Chandragupta II (c. 385–413 AD). The greatest king after Samudragupta, Chandragupta is connected with the 'rustless wonder', an iron pillar in Delhi which has survived for 1,500 years with little sign of corrosion. An inscription incised on the pillar records that Chandragupta gained 'supreme sovereignty on earth', and then established this 'flag staff of Vishnu', probably a reference to the fact that the pillar originally stood near a temple of Vishnu, the god associated with the preservation of righteousness and universal order. The pillar was once surmounted with a figure of Vishnu's eagle-like mount Garuda, an iconographic form used by the Guptas as their royal emblem. This use of religious imagery as political allegory was especially encouraged by Chandragupta. The most important site where the practice was elaborated is Udayagiri in central India. There, carved directly into the mountain-side, is a monumental image of Vishnu in his form as the Cosmic Boar. This massive relief tells the story of how Vishnu incarnated himself as a boar so he could rescue the earth from the abyss. In the Gupta ideal of kingship, the ruler was meant to replicate Vishnu's merciful act by saving the world from social disorder and the rule of evil kings. This imagery was used by the Guptas to articulate their political control of India and legitimate their granting of vast estates to loyal subordinates. The Gupta aristocracy used

Udayagiri, a mountain in central India that was sacred from at least the second century AD, has a host of cave-shrines and images. The most impressive relief panel represents Varaha, the incarnation of Vishnu as the Cosmic Boar (left). This colossal images shows the Boar rescuing the earth, depicted as a female figure riding on the Boar's tusk.

The Gupta kings issued gold coins to celebrate their military and ritual achievements (see below). Some of the coins carry horses and were minted to commemorate the Horse Sacrifice, a solemn rite used in ancient India to ratify a King's status as a universal sovereign or 'Cakravartin'.

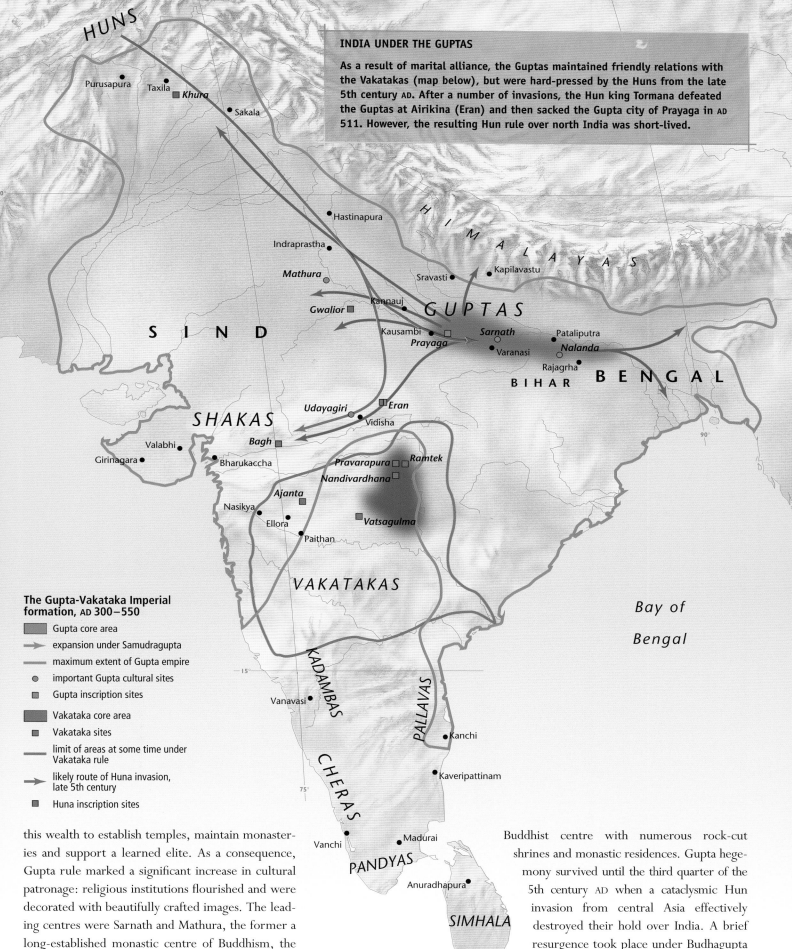

HUNS

Purusapura
Taxila
Khura
Sakala

HIMALAYAS

Hastinapura

Indraprastha

Mathura
Kannauj
Sravasti
Kapilavastu

SIND

GUPTAS

Gwalior
Kausambi
Sarnath
Pataliputra
Prayaga
Varanasi
Nalanda
Rajagrha

BIHAR   BENGAL

Udayagiri
Eran
Vidisha

SHAKAS

Valabhi
Bagh

Girinagara
Bharukaccha
Pravarapura *Ramtek*
Nandivardhana

Ajanta
Nasikya
Ellora
Vatsagulma
Paithan

VAKATAKAS

Bay of

Bengal

KADAMBAS

PALLAVAS

Vanavasi

Kanchi

Kaveripattinam

CHERAS

Vanchi
Madurai

PANDYAS

Anuradhapura

SIMHALA

INDIA UNDER THE GUPTAS

As a result of marital alliance, the Guptas maintained friendly relations with the Vakatakas (map below), but were hard-pressed by the Huns from the late 5th century AD. After a number of invasions, the Hun king Tormana defeated the Guptas at Airikina (Eran) and then sacked the Gupta city of Prayaga in AD 511. However, the resulting Hun rule over north India was short-lived.

The Gupta-Vakataka Imperial formation, AD 300–550

- Gupta core area
- → expansion under Samudragupta
- — maximum extent of Gupta empire
- ● important Gupta cultural sites
- ■ Gupta inscription sites
- Vakataka core area
- ■ Vakataka sites
- — limit of areas at some time under Vakataka rule
- → likely route of Huna invasion, late 5th century
- ■ Huna inscription sites

this wealth to establish temples, maintain monasteries and support a learned elite. As a consequence, Gupta rule marked a significant increase in cultural patronage: religious institutions flourished and were decorated with beautifully crafted images. The leading centres were Sarnath and Mathura, the former a long-established monastic centre of Buddhism, the latter a cosmopolitan city where all faiths prospered.

To the south in the Deccan plateau, the most powerful allies of the Guptas were the Vakatakas, with whom they intermarried in the course of the fifth century AD. The Vakataka seat was at Ramtek but the most famous site in their domain was Ajanta, a

Buddhist centre with numerous rock-cut shrines and monastic residences. Gupta hegemony survived until the third quarter of the 5th century AD when a cataclysmic Hun invasion from central Asia effectively destroyed their hold over India. A brief resurgence took place under Budhagupta (c. AD 477–500) but after his death the Guptas became a secondary power restricted to eastern India. The decline of the Guptas encouraged the development of new and more complex forms of political organization which characterized medieval India from the late sixth century AD.

India after the Guptas
AD 606–752

The two centuries after the fall of the Gupta Empire saw the crystallization of a pattern that was to characterize India until the 13th century AD. After the eclipse of the Sveta Huns in northern India in the first half of the sixth century, the balance of power shifted between newly independent royal houses, many of which had once been underlords of the imperial Guptas or Vakatakas. It was only in the seventh century AD that powerful new empires emerged.

During the seventh century, the Pusyabhuti Dynasty expanded its base from Sthanvisvara to the neighbouring kingdom of the Maukharis, with its prized city of the 'Hump-backed maiden', Kanyakubja (or Kanauj), which was to become the most important imperial centre in northern India until the establishment of the Delhi Sultanate. At the beginning of the seventh century AD, the Pusyabhuti king, Siladitya I, also known as Harsa (AD 606–47), established a powerful empire stretching across most of northern India. The Karkota Naga dynasty based in Parihasapura in Kashmir remained independent. In central peninsular India, or the Deccan, the Calukyas of Badami filled the power vacuum left by the declining Vakataka kingdom, and in the far south the Pallava kings of Kanchi triumphed over the older 'Sangam' dynasties.

POLITICAL ORGANIZATION

As these major regional powers fought amongst themselves to gain 'paramount overlordship' of the subcontinent, a pattern of regional conflict between three or four empires sharing a common political theory and culture was set. India was imagined as a hierarchically arranged *rajamandala*, or 'circle of kings', in alliance and contest with one another. Kings with imperial ambitions were assisted by 'underlords' or 'feudatories', called *samantas*. The courts of these dynasties were magnificent and most of the kings were great patrons of literature and religion. The splendour of Harsa's court was famous throughout Asia; it was visited by envoys from the imperial Tang court in China and by the famous Buddhist monk Hsuan-tsang.

The economic power of these kingdoms was based on agriculture. Land grants formed the basis of political linkage between king and servants, independently ruling underlords and religious institutions. Beyond the creation of a class of landed lords, which put new pressures on the existing peasantry, many grants of uncultivated land had the effect of expanding the agrarian order. For the indigenous communities living in these areas the shift to sedentary agricultural work was usually accompanied by incorporation into the lower orders of caste society and the adoption of Hindu religious beliefs. The importance of land as a source of power, however, did not signal a decline in urban development. New imperial cities like Kanyakubja and Kanchi emerged in the regional centres and numerous smaller settlements in the countryside functioned as points of economic and cultural integration.

RELIGIOUS DEVELOPMENTS

Religiously, India witnessed the gradual consolidation and triumph of the theistic orders of Saivism and Vaisnavism – which later came to be known as 'Hinduism'. Though Harsa was celebrated by the visiting monk Hsuan-tsang as a devout Buddhist, the Pallavas, Calukyas and Karkota Nagas all favoured theistic religions. The Pallavas and Calukyas built spectacular temples, and this period witnesses the first widespread construction of stone temples to house the images of the gods. Texts called the *Agamas* and *Samhitas* were composed by priests detailing the proper liturgy to be performed during worship.

The Papnatha Siva temple at Pattadakal (above), built by the Calukyas in the eighth century AD. Pattadakal was the setting for the coronation ceremonies of Calukyan kings, and contained seven major temples. In comparison to Gupta art (c. AD 350–550), the temples at Pattadakal show increasingly elaborate ornamentation and stylization, a trend which characterized not only art but literature and court ritual from the sixth century AD.

The 'Arjuna Ratha' at Mamallapuram (right). Of the many monuments at Mamallapuram built by the Pallavas during the reign of Narasimhavarman (AD 630–668), who sacked the Calukya capital in AD 642, the five 'rathas' or 'chariots' (a misnomer, as these temples were not conceived as chariots, but as houses or shrines) are the earliest surviving rock-cut monuments in India. These temples are carved entirely from a huge outcropping of rock rather than being assembled with separately carved pieces.

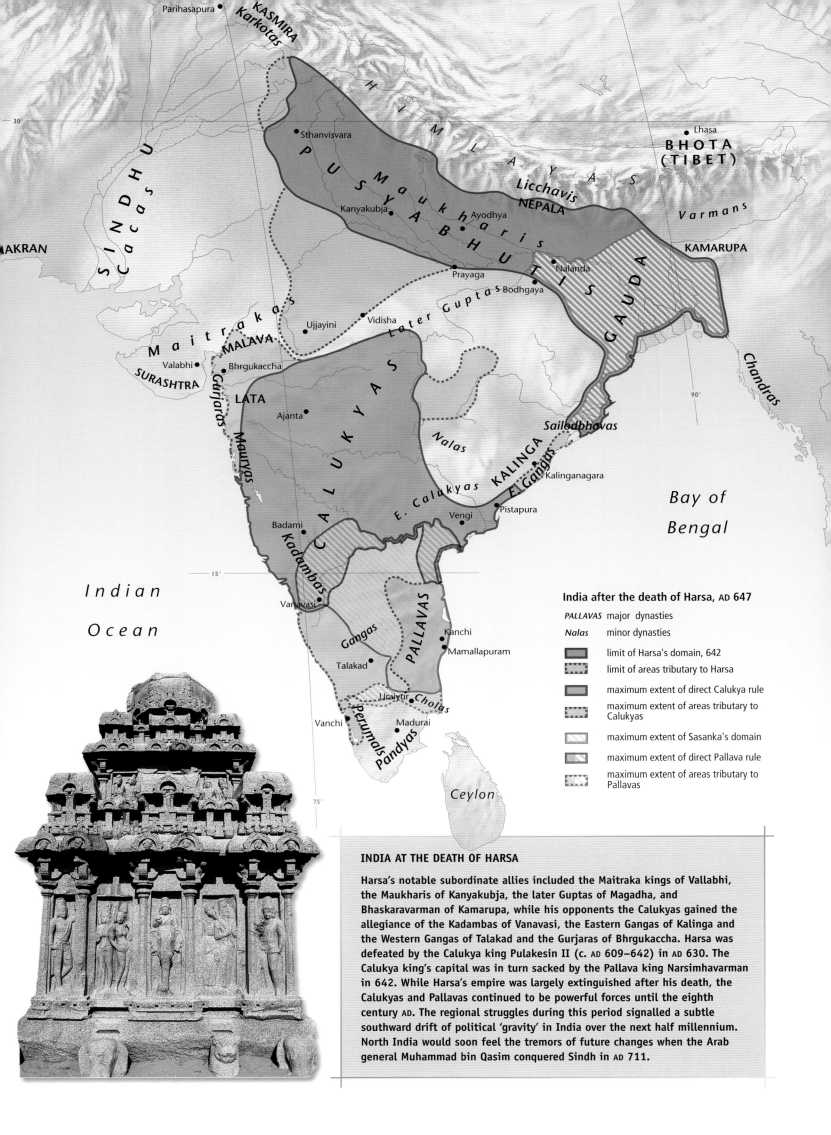

Parihasapura • KASMIRA
Karkotas

SINDHU
Cacas

MAKRAN

30°

H I M A L A Y A S

Sthanvisvara •

P U S Y A B H U T I S

Maukharis

Kanyakubja •
Ayodhya •

Licchavis
NEPALA

• Lhasa

B H O T A
(TIBET)

Varmans

Prayaga •
S Bodhgaya

Later Guptas

Nalanda •

KAMARUPA

M a i t r a k a s

MALAVA

Valabhi •
Bhrgukaccha •

SURASHTRA

LATA

Gurjaras

Mauryas

Ujjayini •
Vidisha •

C A L U K Y A S

Ajanta •

Badami •

Kadambas

Vanavasi •

G A U D A

Chandras

90°

Sailodbhavas

Nalas

E. Calukyas

KALINGA

E. Gangas

Kalinganagara •

Vengi •
Pistapura •

Bay of
Bengal

15°

Indian

Ocean

Gangas

PALLAVAS

• Kanchi

Talakad •

• Mamallapuram

Uraiyur •
Cholas

Vanchi •

Perumals
Pandyas

• Madurai

75°

Ceylon

India after the death of Harsa, AD 647

PALLAVAS major dynasties

Nalas minor dynasties

◾ limit of Harsa's domain, 642

⬚ limit of areas tributary to Harsa

◾ maximum extent of direct Calukya rule

⬚ maximum extent of areas tributary to Calukyas

◻ maximum extent of Sasanka's domain

◪ maximum extent of direct Pallava rule

⬚ maximum extent of areas tributary to Pallavas

INDIA AT THE DEATH OF HARSA

Harsa's notable subordinate allies included the Maitraka kings of Vallabhi, the Maukharis of Kanyakubja, the later Guptas of Magadha, and Bhaskaravarman of Kamarupa, while his opponents the Calukyas gained the allegiance of the Kadambas of Vanavasi, the Eastern Gangas of Kalinga and the Western Gangas of Talakad and the Gurjaras of Bhrgukaccha. Harsa was defeated by the Calukya king Pulakesin II (c. AD 609–642) in AD 630. The Calukya king's capital was in turn sacked by the Pallava king Narsimhavarman in 642. While Harsa's empire was largely extinguished after his death, the Calukyas and Pallavas continued to be powerful forces until the eighth century AD. The regional struggles during this period signalled a subtle southward drift of political 'gravity' in India over the next half millennium. North India would soon feel the tremors of future changes when the Arab general Muhammad bin Qasim conquered Sindh in AD 711.

China Divided and Reunified AD 220–755

With the collapse of the Han Dynasty in the third century AD, China was divided into three kingdoms and then subdivided again north and south in the following centuries. The country began a long period of political disunity, social change and intellectual ferment. Nanjing was the capital of a succession of dynasties which ruled in southern China (the Six Dynasties) and the north was ruled by a series of rulers, many of whom were not ethnically Chinese, though over time they became quite sinicized.

After the fall of the Han Dynasty in AD 220, China was fragmented for about three and a half centuries, during which period the country was divided and subdivided many times. China was finally reunited in the late sixth century under the Sui (map below).

Although this period was often disrupted by rebellion and civil strife and war was endemic, it certainly did not constitute a dark age. Agriculture when left in peace was remarkably productive, yielding a surplus to support a rich and leisured ruling class in the countryside and in the great cities, and, by the sixth century AD, many thousands of Buddhist monasteries and convents. At the Yue kilns in Zhejiang province an early form of porcelain was developed into the first mass-produced, high-quality stoneware serviceable for daily use, rather than just for burial, thus replacing both bronze vessels and lacquerware. Literature, philosophy, painting, calligraphy and art theory flourished simultaneously in many areas and particularly at the Nanjing courts where many of the cultural forms which were to dominate the whole of China for centuries were first developed. The troubled political background led to much philosophical speculation and writings.

Buddhism grew in importance rapidly during this period as many of the northern rulers were Buddhists, as was the emperor Liang Wudi (AD 502–49), the greatest southern patron of Buddhism. Many cave temples were built, notably at Yungang, near Datong in Shanxi province, and carved in cliffs at the Longmen temples near Luoyang. Many Buddhist texts were also translated into Chinese.

At the end of the period of division a Northern Zhou general reunited all of China under the Sui dynasty from AD 589–618. The dynasty reunified northern and southern China and laid political, educational and economic foundations on which the Tang and later dynasties were able to build. New laws were promulgated and a complex bureaucratic system established. A new census was undertaken and the tax system reformed. An extensive programme of public works was instituted including the construction of the Grand Canal system. However, the Sui's active foreign policy was costly and ultimately a failure, and the dynasty fell in AD 618 to be replaced by the Tang, ushering in a new so-called golden age of Chinese history.

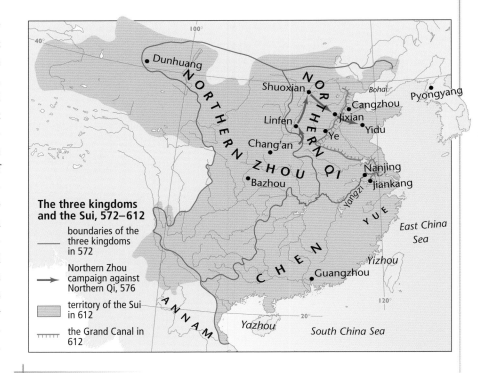

The three kingdoms and the Sui, 572–612

— boundaries of the three kingdoms in 572

→ Northern Zhou campaign against Northern Qi, 576

▨ territory of the Sui in 612

┄ the Grand Canal in 612

A bullock cart of the Six Dynasties period, sixth century AD (below). Such relatively rare ceramic examples anticipate the large tomb-figure industry which grew from the seventh century AD. The goods carried along the Silk Route were carried on the backs of camels and in vehicles such as these.

CHINA UNDER THE TANG

The Tang dynasty spanned three centuries of Chinese history (AD 618–906) and this was regarded by the Chinese as one of their most glorious periods and an affirmation of the integrity of China as a single, unified empire. It was an era of cultural brilliance, territorial expansion and great prosperity for much of the time, so that by the reign of Xuanzong, AD 712–56, China was the richest and most powerful political unit in the world. It was also a golden age for poetry and the arts generally.

As in the Han dynasty, the boundaries of the empire were greatly extended, further westwards than ever before, well into Central Asia, and eastwards as far as Korea, with the empire incorporating parts of Mongolia, Manchuria and Annam. Trade flourished, bringing exotic goods, textiles, animals and above all fine horses to the court at Chang'an. As well as the silk sent westwards along the Silk Route, the Chinese exported ceramics by sea to Southeast Asia, India and Western

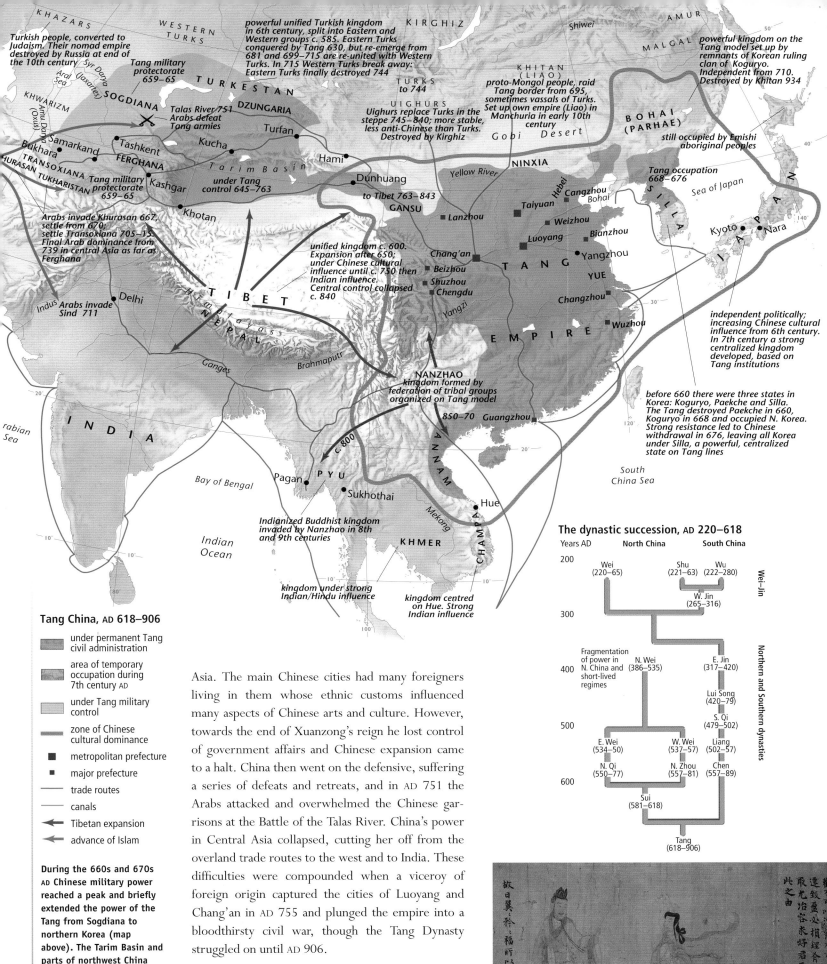

KHAZARS

Turkish people, converted to Judaism. Their nomad empire destroyed by Russia at end of the 10th century

WESTERN TURKS

powerful unified Turkish kingdom in 6th century, split into Eastern and Western groups c. 585. Eastern Turks conquered by Tang 630, but re-emerge from 681 and 699–715 are re-united with Western Turks. In 715 Western Turks break away: Eastern Turks finally destroyed 744

KIRGHIZ

TURKS to 744

UIGHURS Uighurs replace Turks in the steppe 745–840; more stable, less anti-Chinese than Turks. Destroyed by Kirghiz

Shiwei

AMUR

MALGAL

powerful kingdom on the Tang model set up by remnants of Korean ruling clan of Koguryo. Independent from 710. Destroyed by Khitan 934

KHITAN (LIAO) proto-Mongol people, raid Tang border from 695, sometimes vassals of Turks. Set up own empire (Liao) in Manchuria in early 10th century

Gobi Desert

BOHAI (PARHAE)

still occupied by Emishi aboriginal peoples

Tang military protectorate 659–65

TURKESTAN

SOGDIANA

DZUNGARIA

Talas River 751 Arabs defeat Tang armies

Turfan

Kucha

Hami

Aral Sea

Syr Darya (Jaxartes)

Samarkand

Tashkent

FERGHANA

Bukhara

TRANSOXIANA

KHWARIZM Amu Darya (Oxus)

KHURASAN

TUKHARISTAN Tang military protectorate 659–65

Kashgar

Tarim Basin under Tang control 645–763

Khotan

Dunhuang

to Tibet 763–843

GANSU

Yellow River

NINXIA

Taiyuan

Lanzhou

Cangzhou Bohai

Hebei

Weizhou

Tang occupation 668–676

SILLA

Sea of Japan

Arabs invade Khurasan 667, settle from 670; settle Transoxiana 705–15. Final Arab dominance from 739 in central Asia as far as Ferghana

Indus

Arabs invade Sind 711

Delhi

TIBET

NEPAL

Himalayas

unified kingdom c. 600. Expansion after 650; under Chinese cultural influence until c. 750 then Indian influence. Central control collapsed c. 840

Luoyang

Bianzhou

Chang'an

Beizhou

Shuzhou

Chengdu

TANG

Yangzhou

YUE

Changzhou

Yangzi

EMPIRE

Wuzhou

Kyoto Nara

JAPAN

independent politically; increasing Chinese cultural influence from 6th century. In 7th century a strong centralized kingdom developed, based on Tang institutions

Ganges

Brahmaputra

NANZHAO kingdom formed by federation of tribal groups organized on Tang model

c. 800

850–70

Guangzhou

ANNAM

before 660 there were three states in Korea: Koguryo, Paekche and Silla. The Tang destroyed Paekche in 660, Koguryo in 668 and occupied N. Korea. Strong resistance led to Chinese withdrawal in 676, leaving all Korea under Silla, a powerful, centralized state on Tang lines

INDIA

Arabian Sea

Bay of Bengal

Pagan

PYU

Sukhothai

Indian Ocean

Mekong

Hue

CHAMPA

South China Sea

Indianized Buddhist kingdom invaded by Nanzhao in 8th and 9th centuries

KHMER

kingdom under strong Indian/Hindu influence

kingdom centred on Hue. Strong Indian influence

The dynastic succession, AD 220–618

Years AD	North China	South China	
200	Wei (220–65)	Shu (221–63) / Wu (222–280)	Wei-Jin
		W. Jin (265–316)	
300			
400	Fragmentation of power in N. China and short-lived regimes / N. Wei (386–535)	E. Jin (317–420)	Northern and Southern dynasties
		Lui Song (420–79)	
500		S. Qi (479–502)	
	E. Wei (534–50) / W. Wei (537–57)	Liang (502–57)	
	N. Qi (550–77) / N. Zhou (557–81)	Chen (557–89)	
600	Sui (581–618)		
	Tang (618–906)		

Tang China, AD 618–906

- under permanent Tang civil administration
- area of temporary occupation during 7th century AD
- under Tang military control
- zone of Chinese cultural dominance
- ■ metropolitan prefecture
- ▪ major prefecture
- — trade routes
- — canals
- ← Tibetan expansion
- ← advance of Islam

During the 660s and 670s AD Chinese military power reached a peak and briefly extended the power of the Tang from Sogdiana to northern Korea (map above). The Tarim Basin and parts of northwest China fell to the Tibetans in AD 763–783 after Tang garrisons were withdrawn. Chinese institutions and literary culture extended over parts of the Far East, which although never ruled by China, still came under Chinese cultural hegemony.

Asia. The main Chinese cities had many foreigners living in them whose ethnic customs influenced many aspects of Chinese arts and culture. However, towards the end of Xuanzong's reign he lost control of government affairs and Chinese expansion came to a halt. China then went on the defensive, suffering a series of defeats and retreats, and in AD 751 the Arabs attacked and overwhelmed the Chinese garrisons at the Battle of the Talas River. China's power in Central Asia collapsed, cutting her off from the overland trade routes to the west and to India. These difficulties were compounded when a viceroy of foreign origin captured the cities of Luoyang and Chang'an in AD 755 and plunged the empire into a bloodthirsty civil war, though the Tang Dynasty struggled on until AD 906.

A detail from The Admonitions of the Court Instructress (right). This is the finest extant work attributed to Gu Kaizhi c. AD 344–406, the first Chinese painter known to us by name and probably the best-known Chinese painting in existence. However, the Chinese have always had a tradition of copying great works of art, and this is a copy probably made during the Tang Dynasty. The scroll illustrates quotations from a moralizing text discussing the correct behaviour of ladies of the imperial harem.

Religion in China
500 BC–C. AD 750

China's primary religions define man's relationship to his society, meaning first of all the family and secondly the state, whose structure was modelled on the family. This is a very different emphasis from the Western search for individual salvation. Gods and spirits were significant elements in Chinese beliefs, but a good relationship with the ancestors was considered essential as it was hoped that, if accorded proper respect, the dead would intercede with the spirits on behalf of the living.

Rituals that paid respect to ancestors were a constant element of religious practice from at least the Shang Dynasty and some such rites are still practised today. At the state level, rites were enacted in which the emperor sacrificed to his ancestors and interceded with the spirits on behalf of his subjects. The more abstract systems of Confucianism and Daoism existed alongside these fundamental beliefs about the world.

Confucianism is one of the three primary philosophical systems in China and its philosophy derives largely from transmissions of Confucius's teachings by his students, particularly as assembled in *The Analects*. Confucianism embraced China's most ancient religious beliefs and later popular cults as well as the moral teaching of Confucius (c. 551–479 BC). Central to his teaching was *li*, a

proper observance of ritual, which included the traditional rites for offering sacrifices to the ancestors and the worship of Heaven, Earth and other deities. In addition, Confucius cultivated *ren*, often translated as virtue, through which society and political life could be transformed. Confucianism thus provided a moral framework for the conduct of social and public life. The third strand of Confucianism comprised what are generally called known as folk beliefs.

Confucian rites were celebrated at all levels of society with the most august ceremonies presided over by emperors at altars dedicated to Heaven and Earth in the capital. The harmony of the natural

Glazed ceramic figure (below) of a *luohan*, Liao Dynasty (AD 907–1125). The figure belongs to a set of eight, of which seven survive. All the known examples are remarkable for the character of their faces and represent the aspirations of the educated man to attain spiritual enlightenment. Luohans (or *arhats* in Sanskrit) were followers of the Buddha and were believed to use magical powers to remain alive indefinitely and so preserve the Buddha's teaching.

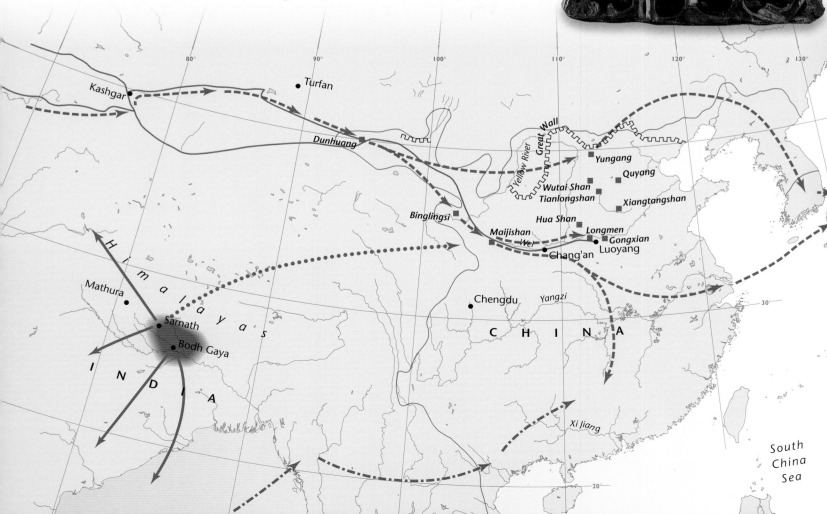

Massive figure of the Buddha in cave 20 at Yungang, near Datong in Shanxi province, Northern Wei period, late fifth century AD (far right). These rock-cut figures were meant to reinforce the permanence of the teaching of the Buddha.

Massive figure of the Buddha in cave 20 at Yungang, near Datong in Shanxi province, Northern Wei period, late fifth century AD (far right). These rock-cut figures were meant to reinforce the permanence of the teaching of the Buddha.

White marble figure of the Buddha Amitabha (below right). Dated fifth year of Kaihuang (585). The inscription on the base records its dedication in a village in Hebei province. The figure's solid form and drapery with flat folds are typical of the Sui period. The missing hands would have been fixed into the sockets of the arms with wooden dowels.

The Buddhist doctrine was modified by Chinese translators to accept a modicum of ancestor worship and Confucian precepts and the Northern Wei rulers made full use of the Chinese habit of using sculpture to spread official doctrines. The cliff shrines at Yungang and Longmen, carved near their capitals, were in part their answer to the imperial tombs of the south (map below left).

world was seen as responding to the moral conduct of the sovereign and his people, and the cosmos was thus drawn into the ritual practices of the state. Family altars were set up in homes.

Daoism was the converse of Confucianism, stressing non-action — *wuwei* — referring to the passive, empty and non-assertive aspects of nature, in contrast to the Confucianists' focus on man and the fulfilment of responsibility. Its fundamental aim was to achieve an understanding of nature, to live in accord with the *dao*, a natural, universal harmony that could only be understood intuitively. In common with Confucianism, Daoism exhibited several distinct strands, including philosophical and religious ones, which over time were wound together. The philosophical texts include the *Daodejing*, attributed to a figure known as Laozi, and the *Zhuangzi* by Zhuang Zhou c. 399–295 BC. These texts stressed the need to retire from the world and master the *dao* whereupon, away from the constraints of morality, ritual and politics, a free, happy and independent life could be achieved. References to health benefits gained from living in harmony with the *dao* promoted the association between Daoism and the quest for longevity and immortality. Under the Qin and Han emperors Daoism was thus espoused in attempts to control the body and achieve immortality through diet and respiratory exercises and through

The spread of Buddhism in China

——— Han Empire in AD 2

▨ area of origin of Buddhism

——▶ early spread of Buddhism

- - ▶ spread of Mahayana Buddhism

- - ▸ spread of Theravada Buddhism

••• ▶ spread of Tibetan Buddhism

■ Buddhist cave sites

——— the Silk Road

> *Do not exalt the worthy,*
> *and the people will not compete.*
> *Do not value the goods that are hard to come by,*
> *and the people will not steal.*
> *Do not display objects of desire,*
> *and the people's minds will not be disturbed...*
> *He does nothing (wuwei) and there is nothing*
> *that is not brought to order.*
>
> **Laozi, the *Daodejing***

elixirs. Many recluses practised alchemy, dietary and breathing exercises and sexual techniques and their practices influenced popular society also.

The third major religious force in Chinese history, Buddhism, was foreign, probably reaching China from the Indian subcontinent and Central Asia as early as the Han Dynasty but not becoming firmly established until patronized by the Northern Wei rulers AD 386–535 and other non-Chinese dynastic houses who ruled north China after the third century AD. At that time texts were introduced from India and translated, and images and temples constructed. The tenets of Buddhism follow the teaching of the Indian sage known to history as the Buddha who lived in what is now the state of Bihar in the fifth century BC. He taught that release from suffering came through subjugating the desires of the world. If desire could be extinguished, the cause of rebirth, *karma* (one's actions), would no longer be generated, karmic debt would be repaid and the endless cycle of rebirth would cease. The individual would then achieve supreme Enlightenment or Nirvana and his individuality would end. In the search for merit which would ensure rebirth in a better life, the faithful made lavish offerings and many monasteries were constructed. Large numbers of images were dedicated as their quantity reflected the merit of their donors and patrons. The success of Buddhism in China was largely due to its tolerance of other religious practices and its willingness to adopt and adapt to Daoism and Confucianism. It reached the peak of its popularity during the Tang Dynasty, when it was supported by all levels of society.

The **Rise** of **Islam**

AD **622–750**

Less than 80 years after its birth in Arabia in AD 622, the Islamic Empire stretched from the valley of the Indus to the shores of the Atlantic. It encompassed all of the old Sasanian Empire and much of the Byzantine Empire and was the largest power west of China. Traditionally seen as a historical break, the Islamic Empire actually formed a bridge between the classical and post-medieval world, by preserving and transmitting the scholarship and many of the cultural traditions of antiquity.

The Islamic religion originated in Arabia. Muhammad, its prophet, received the first of a series of revelations in AD 610 and soon had a large number of supporters. Hostility from the prosperous merchant community forced him and his followers to move to Medina in AD 622 (this migration, *hijra* in Arabic, marks the beginning of the Islamic era and the start of the Islamic calendar). After consolidating and increasing his support in Medina, Muhammad returned to take Mecca in AD 630 and by his death in AD 632, his control extended across Arabia and the Hijaz.

GROWTH OF THE ISLAMIC EMPIRE

The fledgling Islamic Empire was greatly expanded by Muhammad's immediate successors. Under the four Orthodox Caliphs (AD 632–61) Syria, Palestine, Egypt, Iraq and Iran were conquered. In AD 661, Mu`awiya, kinsman of the third Caliph `Uthman, won the Caliphate and established the Umayyad dynasty (AD 661–750). He had served as Governor of Syria for 20 years and so made Damascus the capital of the empire. From there the Umayyads pushed the borders of the empire west to include North Africa and Spain and expeditions in the east won Transoxania, Ferghana and Sind. Various (unsuccessful) sieges of the Byzantine capital Constantinople and two battles, at Poitiers in France in AD 732 and

the Talas River in western China in AD 751, mark the furthest advances of the Muslim armies.

The extraordinary speed with which the relatively inexperienced Arab troops conquered forces superior in number and training and captured this enormous area eludes simple explanation. Several factors played a part. The long war between the Sasanian and Byzantine Empires had weakened and demoralized both armies, whereas the Arab troops were fuelled by a potent combination of religious fervour and desire for power, land and booty. The speed and mobility of the relatively small groups of Arab soldiers were even turned to advantage against the larger, more ponderous armies of their oppo-

Arabic version of Dioscorides' *De Materia Medica* copied in northern Iraq in AD 1229 (below left). This treatise on natural remedies written by a Greek botanist in AD 77 was translated into Arabic in the first centuries of Islam and often copied. The works of many Greek philosophers and scientists were studied and translated into Arabic in the great libraries of the Islamic world, such as Baghdad and Córdoba, and copies were widely circulated amongst scholars.

The spread of Islam outside the Arabian peninsula began almost immediately after the Prophet's death in AD 632 (map below). By AD 711, Arab armies were simultaneously attacking Sind in northeast India and preparing for the conquest of the Iberian peninsula. By 750, when the Abbasids ousted the Umayyad dynasty, the empire to which they succeeded was the largest civilization west of China.

The rise of Islam

growth under Muhammad	expansion of Umayyad Caliphate, (661–750)
growth under Abu Bakr, (632–4)	routes of advance
growth under `Umar, (634–44)	*638* date of Muslim conquest
growth under `Uthman (644–56) and `Ali (656–61)	

nents. The local population often welcomed the Arabs as liberators; the Arab policy of religious tolerance appealed especially to those who had suffered persecution. Once under way, the expansion of the empire was effectively self-financing as slaves and valuables acquired in newly conquered territories paid for further campaigns and helped maintain momentum.

FRAGMENTATION

The Umayyads found it increasingly hard to maintain military or political control. In AD 750 they were overthrown by the Abbasids, and the capital of the empire moved from Damascus to Baghdad. Within a few years the empire had begun to fragment, undermined by its unwieldy size and religious disagreements, and by the ninth century many local rulers had absolute or virtual autonomy. But by then Islam was well established within local communities across the empire.

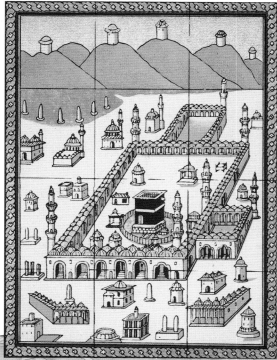

The Kaaba, the local shrine in Mecca (left), which became the focal point of the new religion, marking the direction of prayer. Muslims are exhorted to visit the Kaaba at least once in their lifetime and so it became and remains an important pilgrimage destination.

The revelations of Muhammad were later gathered and written down to form the Quran. Muslims believe that the Quran is a direct communication from Allah and so the Arabic script of the Quran (bottom) acquired a special significance. The need for a basic understanding of Arabic is a unifying force for Muslim communities across the world.

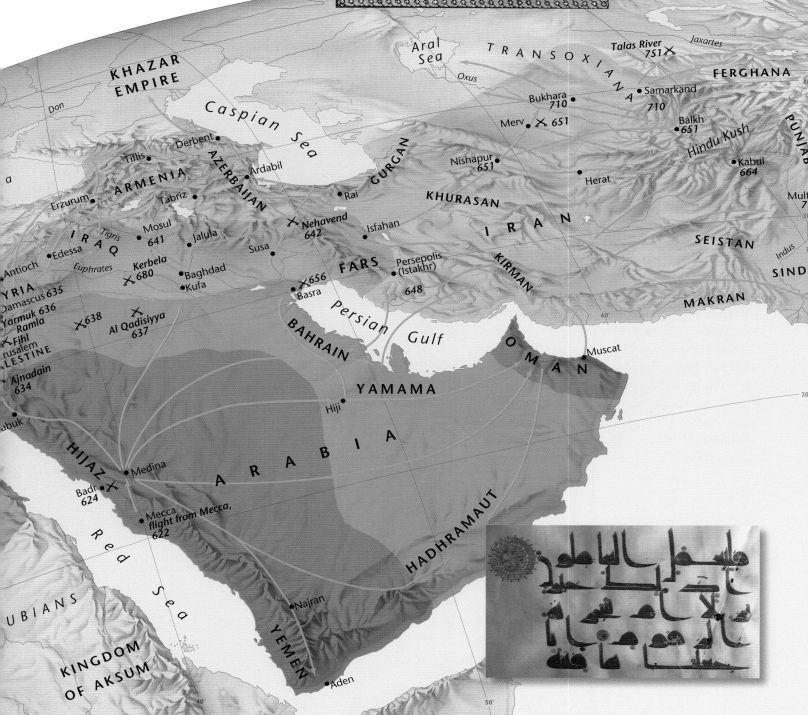

Islamic Culture and Government to C. AD 750

By spanning the continents of Asia, Africa and Europe, Islam facilitated a creative intercourse between east and west, both commercial and intellectual. The resulting fusion between local and imported traditions led to an enormous variety in culture across the Islamic Empire. Yet the shared religion of Islam encouraged the development of a common vocabulary understandable by Muslims everywhere which helped to create and maintain a level of cultural unity across changing political boundaries.

Inevitably the government and religion of the fast-expanding Islamic Empire began their development in the form of a thin veneer on the surface of local communities which retained their own cultural traditions. Islamization was a gradual process, encouraged by contact and intermarriage between local populations and Arab Muslim immigrants, a desire for personal advancement within the ruling class and the impact of the magnificent mosques and other buildings which were erected within the conquered lands. The stories of the gradual Islamization of the Central Asian city of Merv and the Spanish city of Córdoba, revealed by excavations and contemporary descriptions, are similar to those of many outposts of the new Islamic Empire.

MERV

The last Sasanian king, Yazdigird, was killed at Merv in AD 651 and the city negotiated a treaty with the Arab conquerors. This guaranteed the safety of its inhabitants in return for an annual tribute of money, wheat and barley and the provision of lodgings for soldiers manning the garrison. Only essential new buildings, such as a mosque and governor's house, were erected within the ancient city walls. But Merv was used as a military base for expeditions to the east as well as being the political and mercantile centre of Khurasan. The population was soon swollen by immigrants, including 50,000 Iraqi Arabs in AD 671, and another mosque was built at the market gate to the city. By the mid-eighth century AD, the population had completely outgrown the ancient city and a splendid new administrative centre was built adjacent to the old city, with a government house and markets and a large congregational mosque at its heart. This developed into a flourishing cultural centre under the Seljuq sultans, until its sack by the Mongols in the 13th century.

> *In the midst of Rusafa has appeared to us a palm-tree in a Western land far from the home of palm-trees. So I said, this resembles me, for I also live in distant exile and separated by a great distance from my children and my family. Thou hast grown up in a foreign land and we are both exiled from home*
>
> **Abd al-Rahman, Umayyad refugee from Syria who founded the Spanish Umayyad Dynasty in al-Andalus in 756, is said to have composed the above homesick verse about Rusafa, his palace outside Córdoba.**

The walls of Merv (below). Mud-brick is not an enduring material and little has survived above ground of this important early Islamic city. It was built within and around the Hellenistic city, with 2-km walls to keep out the drifting sands, and an impressive citadel. The citadel may have inspired the famous circular plan of Baghdad, the capital of the Abbasids, founded in AD 768 (plan bottom). The circular city, with a diameter of 2.64 km, was surrounded by a rampart with 360 towers. Very soon it became too small for the growing population and expanded south to the suburb of al-Karh. By the early ninth century it may have been the world's largest city.

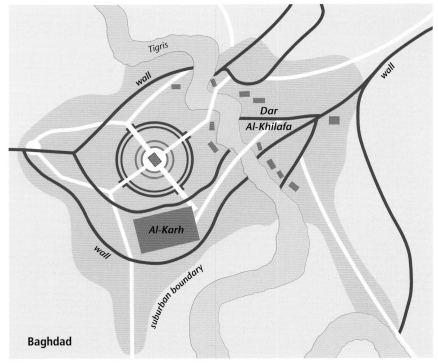

Baghdad

CÓRDOBA

Córdoba was captured in AD 711 with only a token struggle from the demoralized Visigothic army and with the active help of the local Jewish community. Religious tolerance was evident in Córdoba as elsewhere in the Islamic world. Christians and Jews paid an additional tax but were allowed to worship freely and to administrate their communities undisturbed. The Muslims are said to have 'agreed with the barbarians of Córdoba to take half of their largest church which was situated within the city; in this half they constructed the mosque, while leaving the other half to the Christians.' It was on the site of this church that the Great Mosque of Córdoba was built about 70 years later, after Córdoba had become the Umayyad capital of al-Andalus and the Muslim population had outgrown the earlier makeshift mosque. Successive additions to the building, which more than trebled in size over the next two hundred years, reflect Córdoba's increasing Muslim population, and its prosperity under the Umayyad caliphs. The building remained a mosque until after the Christian Castilian reconquest in 1236.

> *The land is fertile; its people are clean. Residences are tall and solid; market quarters are level and neat. Wherever wood is used it is carved and patterned, and plasterwork is painted with designs*
>
> **Merv described by Du Huan, a Chinese prisoner captured at the Battle of the Talas River in AD 751.**

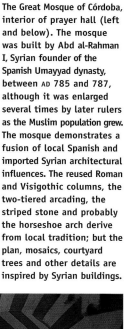

The Great Mosque of Córdoba, interior of prayer hall (left and below). The mosque was built by Abd al-Rahman I, Syrian founder of the Spanish Umayyad dynasty, between AD 785 and 787, although it was enlarged several times by later rulers as the Muslim population grew. The mosque demonstrates a fusion of local Spanish and imported Syrian architectural influences. The reused Roman and Visigothic columns, the two-tiered arcading, the striped stone and probably the horseshoe arch derive from local tradition; but the plan, mosaics, courtyard trees and other details are inspired by Syrian buildings.

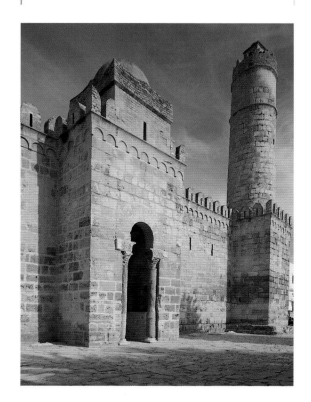

The Ribat at Sousse in modern Tunisia (left). Completed in around AD 820 by the Aghlabid ruler, Ziyedet Allah I, the Ribat formed part of a chain of fortifications to defend Muslim North Africa against Christian raiders. In common with many early Muslim buildings (such as the Umayyad Great Mosque at Damascus), the Ribat made use of materials from earlier sites, incorporating antique columns into its structure, on either side of the main door. The fortress is some 38 square metres, with four towers, the main one being the high watchtower which dominated the surrounding area.

PART VI

Ancient Civilizations of the New World

The European adventurers who arrived on the American mainland in the years after AD 1500 found themselves in lands that had been home to complex societies for thousands of years. The dominant powers had, however, been in control for less than a century and violent conflict was a major feature of American life.

Civilizations appeared more or less simultaneously in two areas of the New World, southern Mexico and the central Andes. In Mesoamerica complex societies developed on the Gulf Coast, in the Oaxaca valley and the Valley of Mexico, and in the Yucatan peninsula. Although there were differences between these civilizations, they shared many cultural features spread by peaceful contact, but also no doubt by war and conquest.

Topography played a significant role in the development of the civilizations of South America. The Andean highlands, with their moderate rainfall and climate, and the fertile river valleys of the west coast, became the cradles of a number of societies. Over more than two thousand years, as states and empires rose and fell, power swung back and forth between the highland and coastal zones.

The 15th century AD saw the appearance of the last empires of the New World, the Aztecs in Mexico and the Incas in the Andes. Each came rapidly to control a territory greater than any of their predecessors, but at the height of their power they were brought down by conquerors from the Old World.

Mesoamerican Civilizations 1200–500 BC

From around 1500 BC until the arrival of the Spaniards in AD 1519, most Mesoamerican societies depended primarily upon agriculture for subsistence and were based around a very simple village life. Between 1200 and 300 BC, these simple village societies were transformed into urban civilizations in parts of Central America around the Valley of Mexico, the Gulf Coast and the Valley of Oaxaca. By Old World standards technology in Mesoamerica was primitive, with metal being used only after AD 800.

Teotihuacán was built on a grid plan and the so-called Avenue of the Dead divided the north-south axis of the city (below). The northern end of the Avenue of the Dead was marked by the Pyramid of the Moon, and the wide avenue over five kilometres long was lined with more than 75 temples. The largest of these was the Pyramid of the Sun, which is over 70 metres high. It was constructed on a cave, which was symbolic of the origins or beginnings of the settlement.

B etween around 1200 and 150 BC, the fundamental features of Mesoamerican civilization appeared: stelae and monuments commemorating rulers, a hieroglyphic writing system, a complex notation of calendrical calculations, and the ritual ball game. From the earliest appearance of urban cultures in Mesoamerica, the need to glorify the gods and to provide appropriate spaces in which to carry out rituals was fundamental to architecture and city planning. The architectural focus of a Mesoamerican city or town such as Monte Albán, was a complex of plazas and temples. The main temples were unvaryingly raised on substantial platforms of pyramidal form. The temples themselves were small buildings, reached by steep stairways leading up the fronts of their platforms from the plazas onto which the temples faced. A large city might have a single enormous plaza with dozens of associated buildings or a series of more modest plazas leading one into another, each with its own set of temples. A small town might have just a single plaza with temples, or even only one temple, facing it. Ceremonial architecture was suited to rituals conducted inside and in front of the temples and on the stairways and stepped facades of the pyramidal structures – rituals watched by huge crowds gathered in the plazas. This tradition of organizing public space, which still continued at the time of the Spanish conquest, probably dates back to at least 1000 BC.

The elaborate palaces of rulers and members of the elite were built near temples, often opening onto the same plazas. These masonry structures contained spacious rooms arranged around one or more enclosed patios to which entrance was highly restricted. The proximity of the residences of these

A monumental head from the Olmec ceremonial centre at San Lorenzo (above), probably depicting an Olmec ruler. Eight such colossal heads were excavated at San Lorenzo, each up to 2.85 metres high, and each wearing a helmet-like headdress. San Lorenzo was abandoned, for reasons unknown, around 900 BC.

elites to the religious centres of Mesoamerican cities reinforced the extremely close links between the political and religious spheres in the region.

OLMEC CIVILIZATION

The most important culture of the Pre-Classic period was that of the Olmecs, who occupied the river valleys of the Gulf Coast of Mexico. By 1200 BC the small chiefdoms which had occupied the area for a millennium had become complex political units, with religious institutions and monumental architecture.

Archaeological investigations at the monumental sites of San Lorenzo – the oldest Olmec site, which flourished from c. 1200 BC–900 BC – and La Venta – which succeeded it as the principal Olmec centre – indicate a distinct cultural identity, with similar religious practices and symbols, and extensive trade networks which linked centres within and beyond Olmec heartland of the Gulf Coast .

The Olmecs were masters in the working of hard stone, and their monumental stone-works, including massive heads are amongst the masterpieces of the ancient world. The Olmecs also produced magnificent carvings in jade and greenstone. Greenstone functioned as a sign of status for the Olmec elite.

The main subjects of the Olmecs' art were their leaders, rulers and ancestors. Colossal heads seem to be ruler-portraits. The Olmecs also carved thrones – huge rectangular stone monuments showing the ruler and his divine ancestry. Other depictions of rulers include seated figures carved in the round, the most dynamic sculptures known in ancient America, and standing representations on stelae.

Around 400 BC the Olmecs developed the Long Count Calendar, known variously as the Epi-Olmec, Isthmian or Tuxtla script. It used hieroglyphs to express the calendar, but carvings depict the lives of rulers and important people.

Most scholars believe that Olmec influence spread throughout Mesoamerica through trade and diplomacy, rather than through physical conquest or occupation. Yet the question remains of whether the Olmecs were the 'Mother Culture' of Mesoamerica, with their intellectual and cultural achievements being passed onto the Maya and other civilizations that followed. Alternative theories hold that the Olmec may in fact have been no more than one of many regional cultures that contributed in varying degrees to later civilizations, or that their cultural traits were developed and shared by many distinct societies across the whole of Mesoamerica, rather than being exclusively Olmec.

Whatever the truth, by around 300 BC the great Olmec site at La Venta was, in its turn, abandoned, as San Lorenzo had been before it. Olmec influence gave way to that of towns in the highlands such as Monte Albán and Teotihuacán (see page 162).

An Olmec carving depicting a wrestler (right). Olmec sculpture-work was both very realistic and very intricate. This sculpture gives a very clear idea of the Olmec ethnic type.

The first millennium BC saw the emergence of a series of increasingly developed societies in Mesoamerica (map below). The Gulf of Mexico was the main area of settlement of the Olmecs, though there were major highland Olmec sites, too. By 500 BC, the Maya had appeared as a distinct group, while to the southwest the Zapotecs were also emerging as a separate culture.

Periods in Mesoamerican History

	Maya Region	Mexican Region
Early Pre-Classic	2000 BC–1000 BC	2000 BC–900 BC
Middle Pre-Classic	1000 BC–300 BC	900 BC–400 BC
Late Pre-Classic	300 BC–AD 250	400 BC–AD 100
Classic	AD 250–800	AD 100–900
Terminal Classic	AD 800–1000	
Early Post-Classic	AD 1000–1250	AD 900–1150
Late Post-Classic	AD 1250–1500	AD 1150–1500

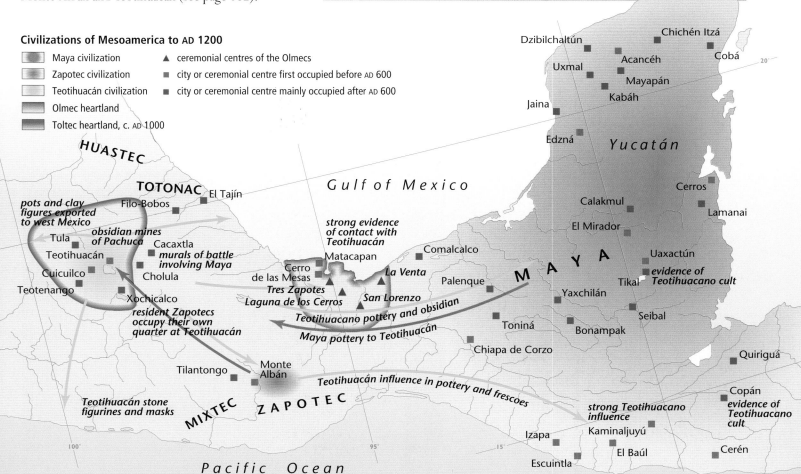

Civilizations of Mesoamerica to AD 1200

- Maya civilization
- Zapotec civilization
- Teotihuacán civilization
- Olmec heartland
- Toltec heartland, c. AD 1000
- ▲ ceremonial centres of the Olmecs
- ■ city or ceremonial centre first occupied before AD 600
- ■ city or ceremonial centre mainly occupied after AD 600

HUASTEC
TOTONAC   El Tajín
pots and clay figures exported to west Mexico
Filo-Bobos
obsidian mines of Pachuca
Tula
Cacaxtla
Teotihuacán   murals of battle involving Maya
Cuicuilco
Cholula
Teotenango
Xochicalco
resident Zapotecs occupy their own quarter at Teotihuacán
Tilantongo
Monte Albán
Teotihuacán stone figurines and masks
MIXTEC   ZAPOTEC

Gulf of Mexico
strong evidence of contact with Teotihuacán
Cerro de las Mesas
Matacapan
Comalcalco
La Venta
Tres Zapotes
Laguna de los Cerros   San Lorenzo
Teotihuacano pottery and obsidian
Maya pottery to Teotihuacán
Palenque
Yaxchilán
Toniná
Bonampak
Chiapa de Corzo
Teotihuacán influence in pottery and frescoes
strong Teotihuacano influence
Kaminaljuyú
Izapa
El Baúl
Escuintla

Dzibilchaltún
Chichén Itzá
Uxmal
Acancéh
Cobá
Mayapán
Kabáh
Jaina
Edzná
Yucatán
Cerros
Calakmul
Lamanai
El Mirador
Uaxactún
Tikal   evidence of Teotihuacano cult
M A Y A
Seibal
Quiriguá
Copán   evidence of Teotihuacano cult
Cerén

Pacific Ocean

Civilizations of the Mexican Highlands c. 500 BC–AD 750

In the period after c. 500 BC two major cities developed in the highland valleys of Mexico. In the Valley of Oaxaca in the south, the Zapotecs established a regional centre at Monte Albán, where they built a substantial ceremonial centre that survived until c. AD 750. In the Valley of Mexico, near the modern-day Mexico City, the city of Teotihuacán grew up in the first century BC, and rapidly became the largest city in the New World from c. AD 200 until its sudden collapse 500 years later.

Monte Albán, situated on a 400-metre high hill on the outskirts of present-day Oaxaca, was the greatest centre of Zapotec civilization. By 500 BC this early urban site had become the capital of a state that remained influential for more than 1,000 years. Monte Albán had a civic ceremonial centre with several stone temple platforms and a small resident population existed at the site. Early Monte Albán art, especially the distinctive *Danzante* carvings, which depict the corpses of captives slain or sacrificed by the rulers of Monte Albán, shows Olmec influence. Early Monte Albán glyphs contain the oldest evidence of the development of Mesoamerican writing yet discovered.

By 200 BC Monte Albán had become the most prominent centre in Zapotec territory, and by AD 200 it dominated the area surrounding the central valley of Oaxaca. The civic centre atop the ridge included temple-pyramids, palaces, richly furnished tombs and an astronomical observatory. The lower slopes were terraced for dwellings, which housed a population of 30,000 or more. Carved stelae containing one of the oldest hieroglyphic 'texts' from Monte Albán – though not yet fully deciphered – show that Zapotec culture had its initial centre in the central valleys of Oaxaca. A significant number of relief carvings appear to emphasize the themes of militarism and conquest. During the Classic period, the Zapotecs also erected stone stelae honouring their leaders.

Around AD 700, Monte Albán was abandoned; Zapotec and Mixtec nobles were still buried there, however, during the following centuries. One tomb

A detail of a carving from the temple of the Feathered Serpent (Quetzalcoatl) at Teotihuacán (left). Carvings of feathered serpents alternate on the walls of the pyramidal-shaped temple with fire serpents, as an expression of the opposition between fertility and the fiery, hot desert.

A wall painting, known as the Tlalocán, or Paradise of the god of Rain, Tlaloc, from Tepantitla, Teotihuacán (below). The painting dates from c. AD 350–600. Those who have suffered watery deaths (for example by drowning) frolic in an idyllic heaven filled with flowers, butterflies and trees.

Carvings on one of the earliest buildings at Monte Albán were originally thought to represent dancers, and they were called *Danzantes*. It has now been suggested that they depict the corpses of prisoners captured in war and executed. The glyphs inscribed next to the figures may be the names of individuals, or of communities conquered by Monte Albán. The *Danzantes* at Monte Albán date from 500–200 BC and earlier examples have been found at the Zapotec settlement at San José Mogote.

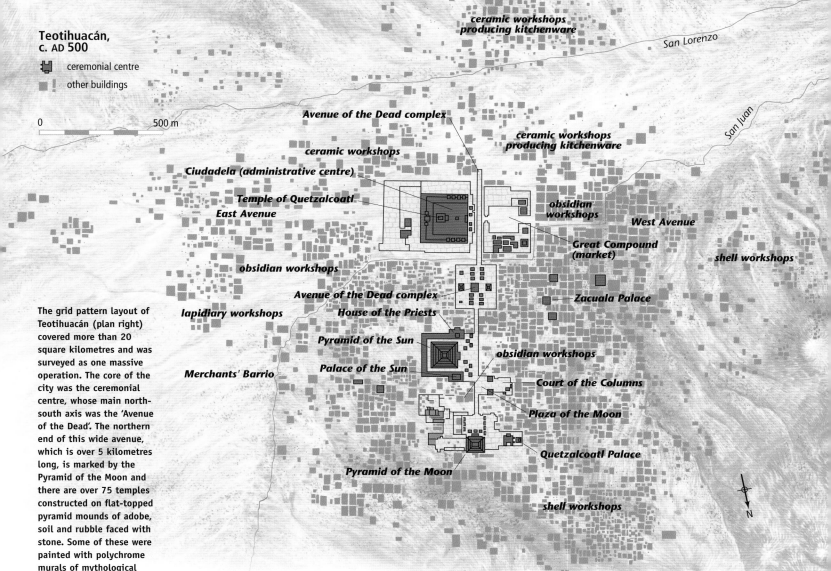

Teotihuacán,
c. AD 500

🏯 ceremonial centre

▪ other buildings

0 _____ 500 m

ceramic workshops
producing kitchenware

San Lorenzo

San Juan

Avenue of the Dead complex

ceramic workshops
producing kitchenware

ceramic workshops

Ciudadela (administrative centre)

Temple of Quetzalcoatl
East Avenue

obsidian
workshops

West Avenue

Great Compound
(market)

shell workshops

obsidian workshops

Avenue of the Dead complex

Zacuala Palace

lapidiary workshops

House of the Priests

Pyramid of the Sun

obsidian workshops

Palace of the Sun

Court of the Columns

Merchants' Barrio

Plaza of the Moon

Quetzalcoatl Palace

Pyramid of the Moon

shell workshops

N

The grid pattern layout of Teotihuacán (plan right) covered more than 20 square kilometres and was surveyed as one massive operation. The core of the city was the ceremonial centre, whose main north-south axis was the 'Avenue of the Dead'. The northern end of this wide avenue, which is over 5 kilometres long, is marked by the Pyramid of the Moon and there are over 75 temples constructed on flat-topped pyramid mounds of adobe, soil and rubble faced with stone. Some of these were painted with polychrome murals of mythological scenes. The Avenue of the Dead also contains the oldest and largest structure at Teotihuacán; the Pyramid of the Sun, which is 70 metres high. At the intersection of the Avenue of the Dead with an east-west axis are the Great Compound and the Ciudadela, a vast complex forming the political, religious and administrative centre of the city.

(Tomb 7) contained more than 300 Mixtec-style jewels and ornaments of gold, silver, jade and other precious materials. Finally, Monte Albán became simply a necropolis and a place of pilgrimage.

TEOTIHUACÁN

In the Late Pre-Classic period two dominant centres emerged in the Basin of Mexico: Cuicuilco and Teotihuacán. Little is known about Cuicuilco, but Teotihuacán grew considerably during the first few centuries AD, with a population of over 100,000 and possibly 200,000 by the middle of the Classic period. This made the city the largest in Mesoamerica and one of the largest in the world at the time. Teotihuacán's inhabitants lived in apartment compounds which were located in a rigid grid plan of streets at regular intervals. It was a very important religious, political and economic centre that drew a huge population not only from the Basin of Mexico but also from Veracruz and Oaxaca. Obsidian was one of the most important trade items and was available nearby.

Religious architecture dominated the city with magnificent mural paintings. The most important buildings were placed along the north-south avenue popularly known as the 'Avenue of the Dead'. The largest structures to be seen in the Americas are the so-called Pyramid of the Sun and Pyramid of the Moon.

Teotihuacán dominated the entire region politically as the capital of a vast empire created and maintained by military force. The nature of the contacts with the Maya lowlands, however, seem to have been peaceful. The influence of Teotihuacán was also felt in the southern Maya lowlands (near modern-day Guatemala City) mainly in the style of the architecture.

The Maya
C. 250 BC–AD 1519

Maya civilization had its origins before the Late Pre-Classic period (300 BC–AD 250) in the highlands and the Pacific coastal plain of Mesoamerica. It developed a brilliant urban culture with pyramid-studded ceremonial centres and extensive suburbs. Yet between AD 790 and the mid-ninth century many of its towns were abandoned. Even so, the Maya are far from a vanished civilization, as there are at least four million Maya-speaking peoples living in the region today.

The ancient Maya region is usually divided by archaeologists into two areas, the highlands and the lowlands. Up until the Classic period, the principal centres of Maya power were situated in the lowlands, such as the vast early Maya city at Kaminaljuyú near present-day Guatemala City, founded in the Early Pre-Classic period c.850 BC. During the Late Pre-Classic, more complex societies began to emerge in the Maya lowlands, exhibiting social stratification and monumental architecture. The site of El Mirador, situated in the lowlands of Guatemala, has a series of platforms topped by pyramids even larger than those constructed by the Maya during the later Classic period.

Building on this long development during the Pre-Classic period, around AD 250 a flowering of Maya civilization took place. This period, called the Classic, is characterized by highly organized civic and religious ceremonies, military organization and tactics, art, markets and the manufacturing of craft goods for local and long-distance trade. It is also typified by the development of agricultural practices to support a high population density, intellectual pursuits, and the control of most civic and religious

A reclining *chacmool* figure (below left), from the Maya city of Chichén Itzá. Reclining figures of this sort were first invented at the Toltec capital of Tula and may be connected with a cult of human sacrifice.

A carved figurine from the Maya site at Acancéh (below). The town, which was only excavated from 1996, probably reached its apogee during the Early Classic period before being eclipsed by nearby Mayapán. A unique feature of Acancéh is the three 'Masks' which were unearthed on the sides of the site's pyramid, a structure which measures 32 metres square at its base.

MAYA HIEROGLYPHS

The Maya hieroglyphic script was the most complete script system in the ancient Americas. Hundreds of inscriptions survive, on stelae, lintels and other stone monuments, although only four Post-Classic codices survive (the rest having been destroyed in the aftermath of the Spanish conquest). At the heart of the writing system lies the Long Count calendar, a complex of five different calendrical systems which could measure cycles of time as long as 4,000 years. The birth and accession dates of rulers were frequently marked on Classic monuments as well as the conquest of their foes. The glyphs for several major Maya cities are given below.

Tikal

Naranjo

Yaxchilán

Palenque

Copán

Quiriguá

concentration of power in the lowland Maya regions in the form of city-states. These sought to control and occupy all viable lands, and warfare between them to expand their territory and gain wealth became rife. In AD 562, for example, the defeat of Tikal, one of the largest cities in the southern lowlands, by the allied states of Caracol and Calakmul led to further warfare in the area by other Maya cities bent on expansion.

Cities such as Palenque, Toniná, Bonampak and Piedras Negras flourished in the western lowlands and along the Usumacinta River. Archaeological excavations and the study of written Maya texts from those sites provide a similar story of dynasties, warfare, ritual sacrifice, trade, intense agricultural practices and an eventual weakening of royal authority that had been centralized in the king.

THE LATER MAYA KINGDOMS

At the end of the Late Classic, after AD 800, the population of the southern lowlands — for reasons still not entirely clear — abandoned the area and moved to more prosperous areas such as Yucatán in the north of the peninsula. The cities of Uxmal, Labná, Sayil, Dzibilchaltún and Cobá, and later Chichén Itzá and Mayapán, gained dominance in northern Yucatán.

The political structure of the Post-Classic (AD 900–1521) is characterized by rule by elite councils and a social structure that reflected cultural influences from the highlands of Mexico. Outside influences such as *chacmools* (reclining personages), warrior columns and prowling jaguar motifs may have been brought to Chichén Itzá through intermediaries such as the Putun Maya of the Gulf Coast. The Late Post-Classic period was marked by the decline of Chichén Itzá and the rise of Mayapán, a walled city in the west. The control of Mayapán collapsed c. AD 1450 and the state was divided into smaller units under the control of the lesser elite. In 1524, the Spanish entered a politically divided Yucatán and gained control of a large portion of it with relative ease.

Early Classic Maya urban architecture is characterized by plazas surrounded by stone-built pyramids (above), crowned by temples and palaces. These large politico-religious centres evolved into full-scale cities by the beginning of the Classic period.

The Maya area was extraordinarily diverse, both geologically and in terms of ecological resources. Products such as obsidian, jade and shell were traded widely (map left). Two main trade routes – one lay overland, the other by sea along the Caribbean coast – were used between AD 300 and 900, when Maya civilization was at its height. Some sites have only recently been excavated, such as Acancéh, from 1996.

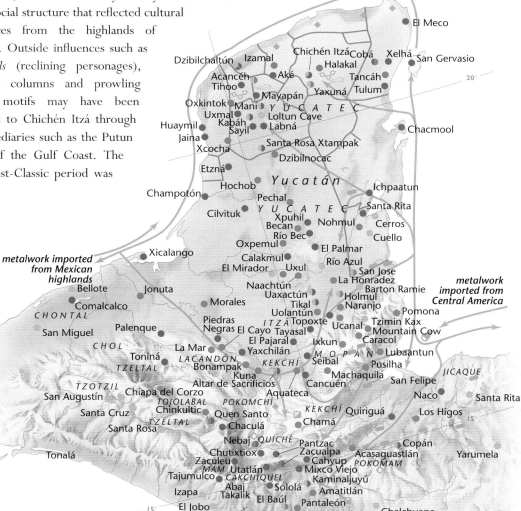

The realm of the Maya
settlements

- late formative and proto-Classic site (300 BC–AD 300)
- major Classic site (AD 300–900)
- other Classic site (AD 300–900)
- important post-Classic site (AD 900–1500)

trade and traded items

- → trade routes
- cacao
- ☑ obsidian
- ◇ jade
- ⇒ feathers
- ⚬ᴼ slaves
- ⚘ marine products and shells
- ◆ salt
- —— approximate border of Post-Classic Mayan state
- *ITZÁ* language group

The **Toltecs** and **Aztecs**
C. AD **900–1521**

The Valley of Mexico was dominated successively by the cultures of the Toltecs (AD 900–1200) and the Aztecs (mid-12th century–AD 1521). At its peak the Toltec state included much of central Mexico and adjacent areas to the north. The Aztecs, after a slow consolidation, expanded rapidly to dominate the whole of central Mexico, with their influence reaching as far as modern Guatemala, Belize and El Salvador. Their empire was abruptly ended by the Spanish conquest in 1521.

The name Toltecatl (or Toltec in English) refers to an inhabitant of the Toltec capital Tula. To the Aztecs, the term Toltec also described the skilled craftsmen and all legendary past glories were attributed to the Toltecs.

The Toltecs were a multi-ethnic group made up of people from north, northwest and central Mexico. The Toltec period (AD 900–1200) corresponds to the Early Post-Classic period. Tula exhibits in its archaeological remains many traits inherited from Teotihuacán and other earlier Mesoamerican civilizations, such as a city laid out along a grid plan, with a spacious central plaza, flanked by pyramids, ball-courts, and *tzompantli* or skull racks. But *chacmool* sculptures, Atlantean figures, extensive use of columns as roof supports and a *coatepantli*, or Serpent Wall, are thought to have been Toltec innovations which influenced both contemporary and later civilizations in Post-Classic Mesoamerica, especially the Mayan city of Chichén Itzá and the Aztecs.

Toltec influence can be particularly seen at Chichén Itzá, a major contemporary Mayan city in Yucatán, which not only shares similar architectural features and motifs with the Toltecs, but also a reverence for the same legendary hero called Quetzalcoatl in Nahuatl (Kukulcan in Maya), both meaning 'Feathered Serpent, who is said to have established the Toltec civilization.

Shortly before 1200 the Toltec state collapsed. Archaeology has shown that Tula was sacked and its buildings destroyed, probably by barbarian tribes from the north. The fall of Tula is thought to have been caused by internal problems as well, such as difficulties in feeding the populace and social dissension.

THE AZTECS

The Aztec empire was the last and most powerful in Mesoamerican history. The Aztecs were a Nahuatl-speaking people, who thrived from the mid-12th century to the time of the Spanish Conquest in 1519–21.

After the fall of Tula, the Chichimecs from the North invaded the Central Valley of Mexico, and the last Chichimec group was called the Aztecs or Mexicas. Aztec legend related their departure in 1168 from Aztlán, 'the Place of the Herons', a legendary homeland, thought to have been somewhere in northwest Mexico.

The Aztecs entered central Mexico from the north. They departed from a legendary homeland called Aztlán, 'the place of the herons', in 1168. In the course of the 15th century, they built a large, tribute-based empire (map right) controlled from Tenochtitlán, their capital, which was founded in the early 14th century. The appetite of the Aztec Empire for sacrificial victims for its gods and for wealth (in the form of jade and gold) for propaganda purposes and for offerings, was the source of both its strength and weakness. The need to acquire vast quantities of tribute explains its great reach and its unsustainable consumption.

Tenochtitlán (map below) was the heart of the Aztec empire. It was a stone-built city of up to 200,000 inhabitants, situated on an island and linked to the mainland by causeways. The Aztecs were skilled agricultural and hydraulic engineers and they drained marshes to create extremely productive agricultural land. The food surpluses fed both the Aztec army and the large urban population of the capital. Tenochtitlán remained impregnable until the arrival of the Spaniards under Cortés in 1519.

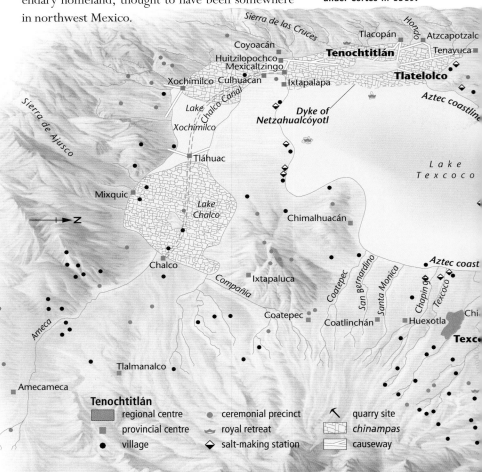

Tenochtitlán
- regional centre
- provincial centre
- village
- ceremonial precinct
- royal retreat
- salt-making station
- quarry site
- *chinampas*
- causeway

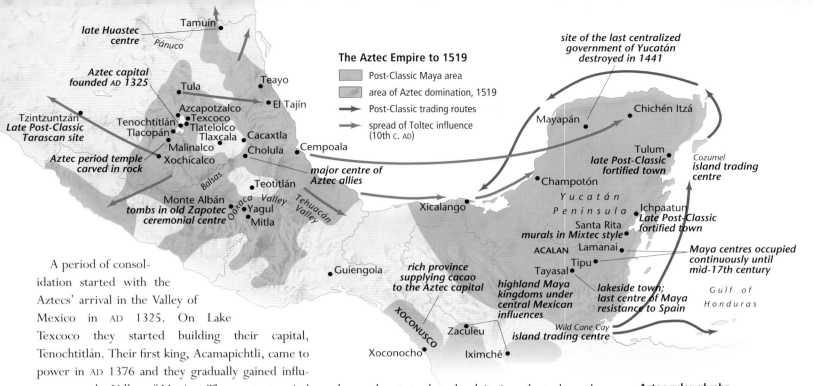

Tamuín

late Huastec centre

Pánuco

Aztec capital founded AD 1325

Tula

Teayo

El Tajín

Azcapotzalco

Tenochtitlán
Texcoco
Tlatelolco
Tlacopán
Tlaxcala

Malinalco
Cholula
Cacaxtla
Cempoala

Xochicalco

Tzintzuntzán Late Post-Classic Tarascan site

Aztec period temple carved in rock

Balsas

Teotitlán

Monte Albán
tombs in old Zapotec ceremonial centre

Oaxaca Valley
Yagul
Mitla

Tehuacán Valley

site of the last centralized government of Yucatán destroyed in 1441

Chichén Itzá

Mayapán

Tulum
late Post-Classic fortified town

Cozumel
island trading centre

Champotón

Yucatán Peninsula

Xicalango

Ichpaatun
Late Post-Classic fortified town

Santa Rita
murals in Mixtec style

ACALAN
Lamanai

Maya centres occupied continuously until mid-17th century

Tayasal
Tipu

Guiengola

rich province supplying cacao to the Aztec capital

major centre of Aztec allies

highland Maya kingdoms under central Mexican influences

lakeside town; last centre of Maya resistance to Spain

Gulf of Honduras

XOCONUSCO

Zaculeu

Wild Cane Cay
island trading centre

Xoconocho

Iximché

Post-Classic Maya area

area of Aztec domination, 1519

Post-Classic trading routes

spread of Toltec influence (10th C. AD)

A period of consolidation started with the Aztecs' arrival in the Valley of Mexico in AD 1325. On Lake Texcoco they started building their capital, Tenochtitlán. Their first king, Acamapichtli, came to power in AD 1376 and they gradually gained influence over the Valley of Mexico. The greatest period of Aztec expansion began in AD 1440, when the fifth ruler, Moctezuma Ilhuicamina (Moctezuma I), ascended to the throne. During this period the Aztec Empire continued to increase its territory and to gain political power by means of alliances, tribute and trade. At the time of the Spanish Conquest in 1519–21, Aztec influence reached as far as Guatemala, Belize and western parts of Honduras and El Salvador.

Aztec religion was based on the concept that the universe was maintained by the collaboration of gods and human beings. Human sacrifice was practiced as an important ritual for the purpose of offering human hearts to the solar deity in order to keep the sun in motion, and blood to the earth deity to nourish the soil. To the Aztecs, fighting in war meant not only gaining territory and tribute, but also obtaining captives for human sacrifice.

The most important religious and economic site was the Great Temple, a twin pyramid dedicated to the Aztecs' two principal deities: Huitzilopochtli, god of war, and Tlaloc, god of rain. This structure symbolizing a dual notion of the universe in which a balance of opposites, such as gods and humans, heaven and earth, life and death, was considered to be crucial for maintaining the stability of the world.

Aztec ruler glyphs

Acamapichtli
(1376–91?)

Huitzilihuitl
(1391–c. 1416)

Itzcoatl
(1428–40)

Moctezuma I Ilhuicamina
(1440–68)

Ahuitzotl
(1486–1502)

Moctezuma II Xocoyotzin
(1502–20)

Cuauhtemoc
(1520–1)

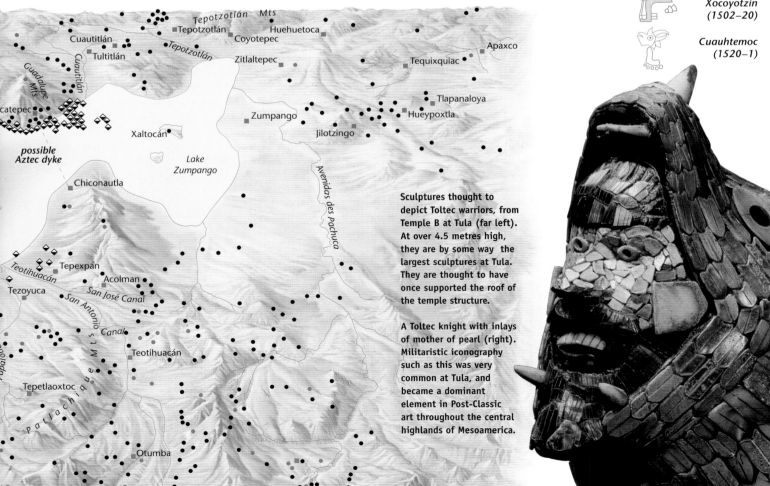

Tepotzotlán Mts

Cuautitlán
Tepotzotlán
Coyotepec
Huehuetoca

Apaxco

Tultitlán
Tepotzotlán
Zitlaltepec

Tequixquiac

Guadalupe Mts

Cuautitlán

Zumpango
Jilotzingo

Tlapanaloya

Hueypoxtla

Ecatepec

Xaltocán

Lake Zumpango

possible Aztec dyke

Chiconautla

Avenidas des Pachuca

Teotihuacán
Tepexpán

Acolman

Tezoyuca

San José Canal

San Antonio Canal

Teotihuacán

Patlachique Mts

Tepetlaoxtoc

Otumba

Sculptures thought to depict Toltec warriors, from Temple B at Tula (far left). At over 4.5 metres high, they are by some way the largest sculptures at Tula. They are thought to have once supported the roof of the temple structure.

A Toltec knight with inlays of mother of pearl (right). Militaristic iconography such as this was very common at Tula, and became a dominant element in Post-Classic art throughout the central highlands of Mesoamerica.

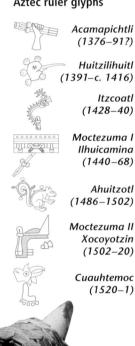

First Civilizations of the Andes
c. 2600–200 BC

The Inca Empire was the largest in pre-colonial South America. It rose to dominate an area stretching from present-day Ecuador to Chile in less than a century. But it was by no means the first developed civilization in the area. The blueprint for the Inca Empire was established in the civilizations that rose and fell over several thousand years of prehistory in South America, and particularly in the Andes. These cultures displayed features that appeared in all subsequent traditions.

The lowlands of South America have often been thought of as culturally barren, with small shifting populations. This is not the case, as evidence for the Amazon region suggests that it did support a large population and settlements are apparent. However, the scale and density of these settlements are different to the ancient cities that remain today in the Andean region. The Andes displayed the greatest variety and diversity in political strategies and artistic traditions. Archaeologists have devised a chronology for this area, named Periods and Horizons, that attempts to divide times of widespread uniformity and interactions between centres (Horizons), from times of regional diversity (Periods).

THE CHAVÍN CULTURE

The early years of this particular Horizon saw the spread of ceramic technology and the construction of ceremonial centres. By 200 BC, international art styles and religions, urban centres and economic and political systems were established and trade between distant regions had developed. A series of new, larger-scale societies, called Chavín, appeared to flourish between 1200 and 200 BC. These ceremonial centres were the focus of administration and religion for regional populations. The type-site, Chavín de Huántar, in the Peruvian highlands, peaked between 850 and 200 BC and has traditionally been described as the earliest Andean civilization, although recent information from the site of Caral on the coast challenges this.

The homogeneity and spread of the Chavín culture appeared to change after 200 BC, when regional differences appeared. The river valleys along the Peruvian coast saw the development of their own distinctive local cultures and an intensification of irrigation agriculture, (with less dependence upon shellfish), perhaps to satisfy larger populations.

In this period several groups stand out on the south coast, first Paracas and then Nasca, and on the north coast, Moche. The southern highlands and the Titicaca Basin already had their own religious traditions. Iconography at Paracas suggests a local reworking of Chavín mythology with the Smiling God and, later, the Staff God and Goddess both being adopted. Information comes from ceramics and textiles and the famous mummy bundles wrapped in decorative cloth and buried in multiple tombs. An image called the Oculate Being appears to have been a major deity, as the figure is repeated in many forms in many media. It is a creature with a human or feline body, round eyes and semi-circular smile. It is often shown holding knives and severed human heads, (trophy heads), perhaps an indication of the warfare and head-taking that characterized later centuries. Fortified sites with defensive walls also appear in the archaeological record throughout much of Peru.

Chavín sculpted Tenon head set into the wall of the Old Temple at Chavín de Huántar as architectural ornamentation (above). Its scale is more than twice the size of a human head. It has been suggested that these heads represent Shamans in the process of transformation into felines, (the snarling mouth is typical in Chavín imagery). Hallucinogens such as the San Pedro cactus (depicted elsewhere at Chavín) were used in this transformation.

MUMMIFICATION: (LIFE AFTER DEATH)

Burial practices differed throughout South America. The amount of time and care devoted to burying an individual also varied within a single site, denoting hierarchy and importance in life. Mummification of bodies occurred naturally, through desiccation or freezing, or artificially, where bodies were prepared in a special way. Very early examples from Chinchoros show an attempt to preserve the life-like form by skinning and disassembling the bodies, removing the internal organs and inserting cane or wood supports into the arms and legs. Cavities in the body were filled with feathers or fibres and the whole was coated in clay and painted, often with a mask added over the face (see picture below). At Paracas, mummies were buried in a seated position, wrapped in several layers of textiles and then buried underground in vaults alongside other mummies (possibly members of the same family).

One of the most elaborate pre-Columbian burials (though not a mummy) was that of the Moche 'Lord of Sipan' who was buried deep in the ground with

a vast array of gold-work and ceramics. In addition, animals and six humans were buried alongside his body. After death, Inca lords were regarded as being 'half-alive' and sometimes taken into council meetings or paraded about. There have been several finds of perfectly preserved Inca ice mummies in the Andean region. The bodies, often found on burial platforms on mountain peaks, are mostly those of children between the ages of 8 and 14. These children were sacrificed, perhaps by being drugged and then buried alive and freezing to death. Freezing enables hair, skin and internal organs to remain intact and the ice mummies provide good information on Inca diet and nutrition, as well as ritual practices.

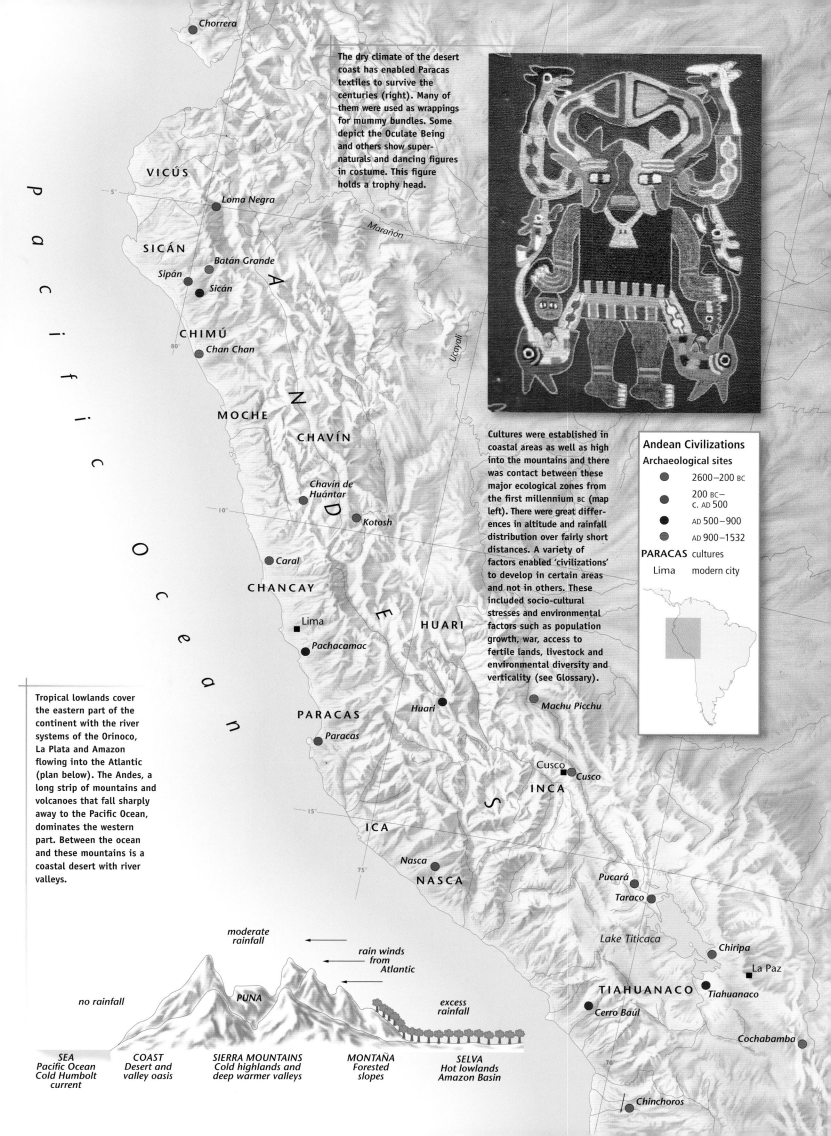

The dry climate of the desert coast has enabled Paracas textiles to survive the centuries (right). Many of them were used as wrappings for mummy bundles. Some depict the Oculate Being and others show supernaturals and dancing figures in costume. This figure holds a trophy head.

VICÚS

Chorrera

Loma Negra

SICÁN

Batán Grande

Sipán

Sicán

CHIMÚ

Chan Chan

Marañón

Ucayali

MOCHE

CHAVÍN

Chavín de Huántar

Kotosh

Caral

CHANCAY

Lima

Pachacamac

HUARI

Huari

PARACAS

Paracas

Machu Picchu

Cusco

Cusco

INCA

ICA

Nasca

NASCA

Pucará

Taraco

Lake Titicaca

Chiripa

La Paz

TIAHUANACO

Tiahuanaco

Cerro Baúl

Cochabamba

Chinchoros

Cultures were established in coastal areas as well as high into the mountains and there was contact between these major ecological zones from the first millennium BC (map left). There were great differences in altitude and rainfall distribution over fairly short distances. A variety of factors enabled 'civilizations' to develop in certain areas and not in others. These included socio-cultural stresses and environmental factors such as population growth, war, access to fertile lands, livestock and environmental diversity and verticality (see Glossary).

Andean Civilizations
Archaeological sites

● 2600–200 BC

● 200 BC– c. AD 500

● AD 500–900

● AD 900–1532

PARACAS cultures

Lima modern city

Tropical lowlands cover the eastern part of the continent with the river systems of the Orinoco, La Plata and Amazon flowing into the Atlantic (plan below). The Andes, a long strip of mountains and volcanoes that fall sharply away to the Pacific Ocean, dominates the western part. Between the ocean and these mountains is a coastal desert with river valleys.

Pacific Ocean

moderate rainfall

rain winds from Atlantic

no rainfall

PUNA

excess rainfall

SEA
Pacific Ocean
Cold Humbolt
current

COAST
Desert and
valley oasis

SIERRA MOUNTAINS
Cold highlands and
deep warmer valleys

MONTAÑA
Forested
slopes

SELVA
Hot lowlands
Amazon Basin

Ancient Civilizations of the New World

The **Andes** from the **Nasca** to the **Huari** c. **200** BC–AD **900**

From around AD 200 the Andes gave rise to cultures with a greater level of urbanization than in the preceding centuries. The Nasca produced the characteristic zoomorphic 'lines' which can be seen from the air. The Moche engaged in large-scale public works, while the Huari and Tiahuanaco had emerged by the ninth century AD as large-scale empires possessing complex social structures, with expansionist religious and political movements.

The Nasca culture, which followed directly on from Paracas, differed from its predecessor in its ceramic manufacturing techniques (slip painting) and its greater urbanization. Polychrome painted ceramics show local deities, agriculture, fishing and warfare. The other major artifacts of Nasca culture still visible today are the 'Nasca desert lines', which are best seen from the air.

From AD 100–600, the Moche inhabited the north coast of Peru. Much of what we know about them comes from burials and studies of their highly realistic art style. Ceramic vessels, known as stirrup-spout due to their shape, show incredibly diverse scenes of everyday life, rituals, sexuality, portraits, fauna and clothing. Moulds enabled these ceramics to be mass produced.

The major site in the Moche valley consists of two platforms, the Pyramids of the Sun and Moon, made entirely of around 50 million adobe 'bricks'. These bricks carry different makers' marks and possibly correspond to a labour tax levied on the surrounding villages.

Over the centuries, Moche seems to have consisted of several polities or states, perhaps gained through military conquest. Ice cores reveal that there was a long period of drought from AD 560 until around AD 594, which could have precipitated the break up of the Moche state. The Pyramids were abandoned for locations further inland where these regionalized groups came into conflict with the Huari.

The Nasca people created huge geoglyphs by clearing away dark surface stones to reveal the lighter underlying gravel, and so forming white lines. They show representations of animals (such as monkeys, birds and a killer whale) or geometric shapes. They were possibly ceremonial pathways that led to family or town shrines. This one (right) depicts a Hummingbird.

The stirrup-spout libation vessel (above) is a typical Moche ceramic. Many were created using multi-piece moulds. Some are decorated with naturalistic portraits of people and animals, others, like this one, have 'fine-line' drawings of human and supernatural figures. This vessel also shows a cactus, possibly a psychotropic one.

The 'Gateway of the Sun' (right) is a monolithic doorway at Tiahuanaco, carved from a single block of stone. Its elaborate frieze depicts a Staff God with 'weeping eyes' wearing a Sun ray headdress and holding two Condor-headed staffs. It is surrounded by rows of smaller winged figures. Tiahuanaco was the highest ancient city in the Andes, with two temple complexes, sunken courts and monumental architecture. A land reclamation scheme was developed to provide food for its population.

MILITARISTIC AND RELIGIOUS MOVEMENTS AD 500–900

Two inter-related polities dominated much of the central and southern Andes and parts of the coast from c. AD 500–900. Both had a tendency for state formation and expansionist religious and political movements. Close to Lake Titicaca, high up in the Bolivian altiplano, the site of Tiahuanaco had been occupied for at least 500 years before it became a major urban centre. Irrigation and canalization were used to reclaim land for intensive cultivation to support a large population.

Tiahuanaco conquered and administered the altiplano as the core of its large state. Its religious

and artistic influence is evident from Chile to the Moquegua valley on the Peruvian coast. It is in this mineral rich valley that the Tiahuanaco empire met the southern extent of Huari, perhaps competing for copper and semi-precious stones.

The militaristic Huari state expanded very rapidly, establishing regional political centres in the highlands and the coast. These religious, administrative and military sites were connected by a road system similar to the one created by the Incas several centuries later. The sites had living quarters and immense storage facilities, perhaps to contain tribute levied on conquered regions.

The site of Huari displayed increasing wealth in the numbers of stone buildings, multi-story residential and ceremonial structures. Agrarian technology probably aided the economy. Irrigation and terracing systems enabled maize and coca to be produced. Huari's religious and artistic style shares elements with that of Tiahuanaco. However, it is likely that they are both derived from the earlier Pucará religion. The Huari state was short-lived and its collapse around AD 900 saw a population decline and the abandonment of urban settlements.

METALLURGY IN SOUTH AMERICA

Metallurgy appears to have begun in the central Andes from where it spread northwards as far as modern-day Mexico. The earliest worked metal was hammered gold and at Waywaka a gold-worker's toolkit dating to c.1800 BC was found. By 200 BC, in addition to hammering, technological innovations meant that welding, soldering, alloying, gilding and copper smelting were possible. An intensive period of metal experimentation followed. On the north coast the Moche smelted oxide and sulphate ores into sheets and hammered these into ornaments, masks, ear-spools etc. Metal was also combined with shell and stone inlays (Spondylus shell and turquoise for example). It appeared to have special symbolism for the Moche and the dead were often buried with a piece of metal in their mouths. In later centuries the Inca valued gold very highly – it was for them the 'sweat of the Sun'.

By AD 800 metalworking had reached an 'industrial' scale. At Batán Grande an entire smelting workshop was revealed with furnaces, ceramic blowtorch tips, crushed slag and charcoal. Metal was also being used for more utilitarian objects such as chisels, ingots and 'axe money', (a possible 'currency' found at Sicán). The Quimbaya, Muisca and Sinú produced some of the most highly skilled and elaborate gold-work in areas now in present-day Colombia. This Sicán ceremonial knife or *tumi* (left), dating to c. AD 1200–1400, has a handle in the form of a richly dressed man wearing a headdress, tunic and ear-spools with turquoise inlays.

Empires in the Andes
AD 900–1532

After the collapse of the Huari, the highlands became politically fragmented, while a series of coastal states arose. From these emerged the two largest states in pre-Columbian South America. The first was the kingdom of Chimor which flourished on the north coast from AD 700 until around AD 1476, when the it was conquered by the Inca. At its height, the Chimor Empire encompassed some 1,500 kilometres of Pacific coastland. It also integrated the population of the Northern Andes under one nation.

I nformation on the Chimor dynasty is scant, but it is believed that there were around eleven pre-Inca rulers. These Chimú kings were based at the metropolis of Chan Chan, the main settlement of the Chimú. Chan Chan covers 15 square kilometres and is built entirely of sun-baked mud-brick. Ten compounds (ciudadelas) built over a 250-year period lie at the city's heart. It is probable that these were royal compounds and that upon the death of a king his compound was sealed and a new one constructed for his successor. The Chimú had a hierarchical social framework and a hereditary elite governed and saw to the administration of the Chimor Empire. The Chimú's efficient communications network and colonial policy were among several features adopted by the Inca after AD 1470.

The Inca were originally a small farming group that began conquering neighbouring groups in the highlands. By AD 1438, a strong centralized state had been established with Cusco as its capital and much territory annexed. In less than a century the Inca went on to build the greatest empire in pre-Columbian South America, whose development was prematurely cut short by the arrival of Francisco Pizarro in 1532.

INCA SOCIETY

The Inca did not have a formal writing system and they traded goods and built cities without the help of the wheel. State architects designed administrative and religious sites, roads and way-houses and enlarged the terracing system found over much of the Andes. Inca ceramics were standardized and they assimilated the more developed Chimú techniques of mass production, metalworking and textile weaving.

Inca social organization developed from basic principals instigated by their Andean predecessors and is still seen amongst certain communities today. In order to exploit resources in an unusual and extreme environment, Andean communities needed to execute different tasks (herding and farming) at the same time. Groups of related and married individuals cooperated with each other to manage land, irrigation and

Machu Picchu (above) was a small Inca settlement about 70 kilometres west of Cusco. A sequence of small plazas are positioned on the flat crest, with terraces running along the steep flanking slopes. The site covers 18 square kilometres and, at an altitude of 2,700 metres, was fairly inaccessible. Its function is not clear, but it possibly served as a military barracks.

An audencia, or U-shaped structure at Chan Chan, the coastal state which was eventually conquered by the Inca. This building (above) has two large niches in the interior walls and may originally have been roofed. Its adobe frieze depicts sea birds, an indication that maritime resources were a vital part of Chimor subsistence. This is just one of a vast number of mud-brick structures that comprise Chan Chan (plan right).

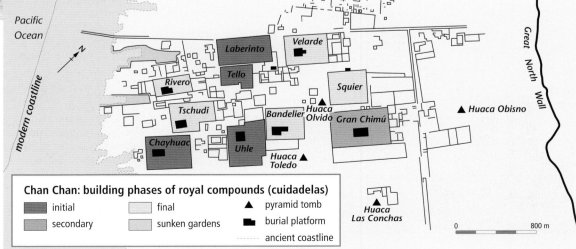

Pacific Ocean

modern coastline

Laberinto

Velarde

Tello

Rivero

Squier

Tschudi

Huaca
Bandelier Olvido Gran Chimú

Chayhuac

Uhle

Huaca
Toledo

Great North Wall

▲ Huaca Obisno

Huaca
Las Conchas

Chan Chan: building phases of royal compounds (cuidadelas)

■ initial	▨ final	▲ pyramid tomb
▨ secondary	▨ sunken gardens	■ burial platform
		---- ancient coastline

0   800 m

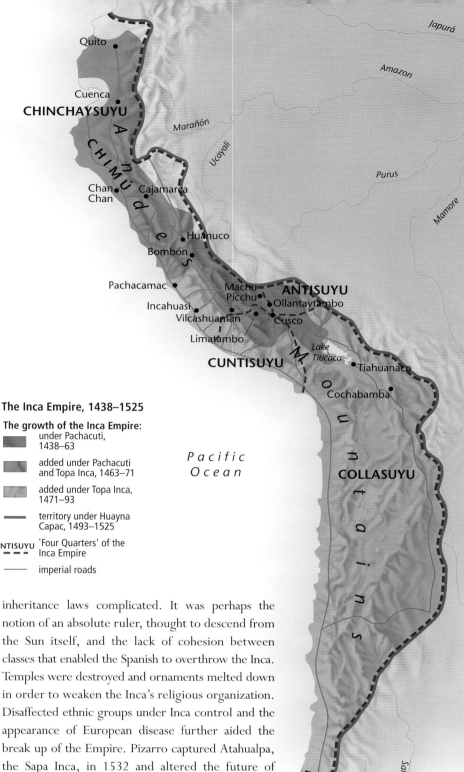

The Inca Empire, 1438–1525

The growth of the Inca Empire:

- under Pachacuti, 1438–63
- added under Pachacuti and Topa Inca, 1463–71
- added under Topa Inca, 1471–93
- territory under Huayna Capac, 1493–1525
- ANTISUYU 'Four Quarters' of the Inca Empire
- imperial roads

herds. These collectives, based upon kinship ties, were called *ayllus*. Ayllus had a founding ancestor and several lineages divided into two 'moieties'. Women traced their kinship through the female line and men through the male line. These divisions were not confined to rural communities but were also present at Cusco. Inca nobility was divided between two royal lineages, *hanan* and *hurin*. Social hierarchy was pyramid-like, with the Sapa Inca at the apex, absolute ruler in political, religious and military matters. Rulership became hereditary and

inheritance laws complicated. It was perhaps the notion of an absolute ruler, thought to descend from the Sun itself, and the lack of cohesion between classes that enabled the Spanish to overthrow the Inca. Temples were destroyed and ornaments melted down in order to weaken the Inca's religious organization. Disaffected ethnic groups under Inca control and the appearance of European disease further aided the break up of the Empire. Pizarro captured Atahualpa, the Sapa Inca, in 1532 and altered the future of Andean socio-political systems irrevocably.

The Inca called their land Tahuantinsuyu, 'Land of the Four Quarters'. Each part had a different name (map above). Dual or quadrilateral divisions were integral to the Inca universe and this is how they perceived the empire, with Cusco at the centre. Through an efficient infrastructure, the Inca managed to hold together a vast and varied state – 40,000 kilometres of interconnecting highways, causeways and suspension bridges criss-crossed the empire, used by messengers and officials.

Sacsahuaman is an Inca fortress that was built on a hilltop overlooking Cusco (left). The walls were a feat of architectural and engineering achievement. Some of the tightly fitted polygonal blocks weigh 100 tons. Excavations at Sacsahuaman have revealed a system of stone channels and drains that suggest water manipulation.

Bibliography

PART ONE–THE BASIS OF CIVILIZATION AND GENERAL WORKS

J.B. Bury, S.A. Cook and F.E. Adcock (eds): *Cambridge Ancient History* Cambridge, 1982 (2nd ed.)
J.T. Hooker (ed.): *Reading the Past* Berkeley, 1990
D.L. Nichols and T.H. Charlton (eds): *The Archaeology of City-States* Washington DC, 1997
A. Southall: *The City in Time and Space* Cambridge, 1998

PART TWO–AGE OF BRONZE c. 3000–1000 BC

B. Allchin and F.R. Allchin: *Origins of a Civilization: the Prehistory and Early Archaeology of South Asia* New Delhi, 1997
F.R. Allchin, with contributions from G. Erdosy, R.A.E. Coningham, D.K. Chakrabarti and B. Allchin: *The Archaeology of Early Historic South Asia: the Emergence of Cities and States* Cambridge, 1995
R.W. Bagley: 'A Shang City in Sichuan Province' in *Orientations* November 1990
J. Bottero, E. Cassin, J. Vercoutter (eds): *The Near East: the Early Civilizations* London, 1967
D.K. Chakrabarti: *India – an Archaeological History: Palaeolithic Beginnings to Early Historic Foundations* New Delhi, 1999
J.D. Clark (ed.): *Cambridge History of Africa* Vol. 1, Cambridge, 1982
O.T.P.K. Dickinson: *The Aegean Bronze Age* Cambridge, 1994
W. Fon (ed.): *The Great Bronze Age of China* New York, 1980
J.M. Kenoyer: *Ancient cities of the Indus Valley Civilization* Karachi, 1998
A.T.L. Kuhrt: *The Ancient Near East c. 3000–330 BC* Vol. 1, London, 1995
B.B. Lal and S.P. Gupta (ed.): *Frontiers of the Indus Civilization* New Delhi, 1984
J.G. McQueen: *The Hittites and their Contemporaries in Asia Minor* London, 1986
G.L. Possehl: *Indus Age: the Beginnings* Philadelphia, 1999
G.L. Possehl: *The Transformation of the Indus Civilization* Man and Environment 24 (2): pp. 3–33 (reprinted from *Journal of World Prehistory* 11(4): pp. 425–472), 1999
J. Rawson: *Chinese Bronzes: Art and Ritual* London, 1987
J. Rawson: *Chinese Jade from the Neolithic to the Qing* London, 1995
J. Rawson (ed.): *Mysteries of Ancient China* London, 1996
J.G. Shaffer: 'The Indo-Aryan Invasions: Cultural Myth and Archaeological Reality' in J.R. Lukacs (ed.) *The People of South Asia* New York and London, 1984
E. Vermeule: *Greece in the Bronze Age* Chicago, 1964

PART THREE–AGE OF IDEAS c. 1000–300 BC

F.R. Allchin, with contributions from G. Erdosy, R.A.E. Coningham, D.K. Chakrabarti and B. Allchin: *The Archaeology of Early Historic South Asia: the Emergence of Cities and States* Cambridge, 1995
J.A. Brinkman: *A History of post-Kassite Babylonia, 1158–722 BC* Rome, 1968
L. Bruit Zaidman and P. Schmitt Pantel: *Religion in the Ancient Greek City* Cambridge, 1992
J.M. Camp: *The Athenian Agora: Excavations in the Heart of Classical Athens* London, 1986
D.K. Chakrabarti: *The Archaeology of Ancient Indian Cities* Delhi, 1995
W. Chan (comp. and trans.): *A Source Book in Chinese Philosophy* Princeton NJ, 1963
T.J. Cornell: *The Beginnings of Rome: Italy and Rome from the Bronze Age to the Punic Wars (c. 1000–264 BC)* London, 1995
M. Dandamaev: *Political History of the Achaemenids* Leiden, 1990
J.K. Davies: *Democracy and Classical Greece* London, 1993
G. Erdosy: *Urbanisation in Early Historic India* Oxford, 1988
M.I. Finley: *Ancient Sicily to the Arab Conquest* London, 1979
R.R. Holloway: *The Archaeology of Ancient Sicily* London, 1991
R.R. Holloway: *The Archaeology of Early Rome and Latium* London, 1994
S. Hornblower: *The Greek World, 479–323 BC* London, 1999
A.T.L. Kuhrt: *The Ancient Near East c. 3000–330 BC* Vol. 2, London, 1995

M. Lal: *Settlement History and the Rise of Civilisation in the Ganga-Yamuna Doab from 1500 BC–300 AD* Delhi, 1984
S. Moscati (ed.): *The Phoenicians* New York, 1999
O. Murray: *Early Greece* London, 1993
R.G. Osborne: *Greece in the Making, 1200–479 BC* London, 1996
G. Pugliese Caratelli (ed.): *The Western Greeks* London, 1996
J. Rawson: *Western Zhou Ritual Bronzes in the Arthur M. Sackler Collections* 2 vols, Cambridge, Mass. and London, 1990
H.W.F. Saggs: *The Might that was Assyria* London, 1984
B. Scharz: *The World of Thought in Ancient China* Cambridge, Mass., 1985
R. Sharma: *Material Culture and Social Formations in Ancient India* Delhi, 1983
E. Shaughnessy: *Sources of Western Zhou History: Inscribed Bronze Vessels* Berkley, 1991
A.M. Snodgrass: *Archaic Greece: the Age of Experiment* London, 1980
J. So: *Eastern Zhou: Ritual Bronzes from the Arthur M. Sackler Collections* Washington DC, 1995
D. Stockton: *The Classical Athenian Democracy* Oxford, 1990
R. Temple: *The Genius of China: 3000 years of Science, Discovery and Invention* New York, 1986
M. Torelli (ed.): *The Etruscans* London, 2001
A. Waley: *The Book of Songs* New York, 1960
A. Waley: *Three Ways of Thought in Ancient China* London, 1946
M. Wood: *In the Footsteps of Alexander the Great* London, 1998
L. Xueqin: *Eastern Zhou and Qin Civilization* New Haven and London, 1985

PART FOUR–AGE OF EMPIRES c. 300 BC–AD 250

M. Alram and D.E. Klimburg-Salter: *Coins, Art and Chronology, Essays on the pre-Islamic History of the Indo-Iranian Borderlands* Vienna, 1999
H. Bechert: *The Dating of the Historical Buddha* Gottingen, 1991
S. Chien: *Records of the Historians* (selections and trans. Y. Hsienyi and G. Yang), Beijing
A. Cotterell: *The First Emperor of China* New York, 1981
E. Errington and J. Cribb: *The Crossroads of Asia, Transformation in Image and Symbol* Cambridge, 1992
P.L. Gupta and T.R. Hardaker: *Ancient Indian Silver Punchmarked Coins of the Magadha-Maurya Karshapana Series* Nasik, 1985
E. Lamotte: *History of Indian Buddhism* Louvain, 1988
L. Ledderose and A. Schlombs: *Jenseits des Grossen Mauer, der Erste Kaiser von China und seine Terrakotta-Armee* Munich 1990
L. Ledderose: *Ten Thousand Things: Module and Mass Production in Chinese Art* Princeton, 1999
M. Loewe: *Crisis and Conflict in Han China, 104 BC–AD 9* London, 1974
M. Loewe: *Ways to Paradise: the Chinese Quest for Immortality* London, 1979
M. Pirazzoli t'Serstevens: *The Han Dynasty* New York, 1982
J. Rosenfield: *The Dynastic Arts of the Kushans* Berkeley, 1967
N. Sims-Williams and J. Cribb: 'A Bactrian Inscription of Kanishka the Great' in *Silk Road Art and Archaeology* Vol. 4, Kamakura, 1995/6
R. Thapar: *Asoka and the Decline of the Mauryas* Dehli, 1997 (revised ed.)
M. Willis: *Buddhist Reliquaries from Ancient India* London, 2000

PART FIVE–AGE OF TRANSFORMATION c. AD 250–750

C.E. Bosworth: *The Islamic Dynasties* Edinburgh, 1967
P. Brown: *The World of Late Antiquity, from Marcus Aurelius to Muhammad* London, 1971
J.O. Caswell: *Written and Unwritten: a New History of the Buddhist Caves at Yungang* Vancouver, 1988
B.D. Chattopadhaya: *The Making of Early Medieval India* Delhi, 1994
K. Ch'en: *The Chinese Transformation of Buddhism* Princeton, 1973
G. Connah: 'The Benefits of Isolation: the Ethiopian Highlands' in *African Civilizations* pp. 67–96, Cambridge,

Melbourne, New York, 1995 (reprint)
D. Devahuti: *Harsha: A Political Study* Delhi, 1998 (3rd ed.)
J. Elsner: *Imperial Rome and Christian Triumph: the Art of the Roman Empire AD 100–450* Oxford, 1998
R. Ettinghausen and O. Grabar: *The Art and Architecture of Islam 650–1250* London and New Haven, 1994
L. Guanzhong (trans. M. Roberts): *Three Kingdoms: a Historical Novel* 3 vols 1991, Berkeley and Oxford
G. Herrmann: *Monuments of Merv* London, 1999
W. Hung: 'Buddhist Elements in Early Chinese Art' in *Artibus Asiae* 47/3–4, pp. 263–316 New York, 1987
H. Kennedy: *The Prophet and the Age of the Caliphates, the Islamic Near East from the Sixth to the Eleventh Century* London and New York, 1986
Y.M. Kobishchanov: *Axum* (ed. J.W. Michels, trans. L.T. Kapitanoff) Pennsylvania, 1979
S. Little (ed.): *Taoism and the Arts of China* Chicago, 2000
S.K. MacIntosh (ed.): *Beyond Chiefdoms: Pathways to Complexity in Africa* Cambridge, 1999
The Metropolitan Museum of Art: *Al-Andalus*: catalogue of an exhibition at the Metropolitan Museum, New York and the Alhambra, Granada. New York, 1992
S. Munro-Hay: *Aksum: an African Civilization of Late Antiquity* Edinburgh, 1991
S. Munro-Hay: *Catalogue of the Aksumite Coins in the British Museum* London, 1999
K.A.N. Nilakanta Sastri: *A History of South India* Delhi, 1955
D. Nivison and A. Wright (eds): *Confucianism in Action* Stanford, 1959
A. Paludan: *The Chinese Spirit Road: the Classical Tradition of Tomb Statuary* New Haven and London, 1991
D.W. Phillipson: *Ancient Ethiopia* London, 1998
J. Schacht (ed.): *The Legacy of Islam* Oxford, 1974
R.S. Tripathi: *A History of Kanauj to the Moslem Conquest* Delhi, 1937
H. Welch and A. Seidel: *Facets of Taoism* New Haven, 1979
R. Whitfield and A. Farrer: *Caves of the Thousand Buddhas* London, 1990
F. Yu-lan: *A History of Chinese Philosophy* (trans. D. Bodde) Princeton, 1983
E. Zurcher: *The Buddhist Conquest of China* 2 vols, Leiden, 1972

PART SIX: ANCIENT CIVILIZATIONS OF THE NEW WORLD

R.E.W. Adams (ed.): *The Origins of Maya Civilization* Albuquerque, 1977
E. Baquedano: *Aztec* Dorling Kindersley, 1993
E. Benson and B. de la Fuente (eds): *Olmec Art of Ancient Mexico* Washington, 1996
K. Berrin and E. Pasztory: *Teotihuacan: Art from the City of the Gods* San Francisco, 1993
E. Blanton et al.: *Ancient Oaxaca* Cambridge, 1999
K.O. Bruhns: *Ancient South America: Cambridge World Archaeology* Cambridge, 1994
R.L. Burger: *Chavin and the Origins of Andean Civilisation* London, 1995
B. Caven: *The Punic Wars* New York, 1992
M. Coe: *America's First Civilization: Discovering the Olmecs* New York, 1968
M. Coe: *The Maya* London, 1993 (5th ed.)
M. Crawford: *The Roman Republic* London, 1992
N. Davies: *The Toltecs Until the Fall of Tula* Norman, 1977
R.A. Diehl: *Tula: The Toltec Capital of Ancient Mexico* London, 1983
K. Flannery and J. Marcus (eds): *The Cloud People* New York, 1983
R.W. Keatinge (ed.): *Peruvian Prehistory* Cambridge, 1988
R. Lane Fox: *Pagans and Christians* Harmondsworth, 1973
C. McEwan (ed.): *Precolumbian Gold, Technology, Style and Iconography* London, 2000
M.E. Moseley: *The Incas and their Ancestors* London, 1993
G. Shipley: *The Greek World after Alexander, 323–30 BC* London, 2000
M.E. Smith: *The Aztecs* Oxford, 1998

Glossary

A

AKHENATEN (1352–1336 BC)

A king of the Egyptian Eighteenth Dynasty. He relocated the main governmental and ritual centre of Egypt to the virgin site of Tell el-Amarna (Akhetaten). Akhenaten is considered to be an exceptional monarch in Egyptian history for a number of reasons. He chose to withdraw from traditional Egyptian royal religious practice by articulating his kingship exclusively through his relationship with the Aten (see below). Scholars have wondered whether the actions of this ruler should be considered as an early attempt to express a monotheistic practice. Furthermore, his wife, Nefertiti appears to have undertaken a formative role within the Aten cult. The artistic production of this period is also unusual, in that the visual representations of the individual took on a more naturalistic style.

AKSUMITE INSCRIPTIONS

These were written in Greek and Ge`ez (Ethiopic). Inscriptions in Ge`ez employ either the South Arabian or Ge`ez script. This latter is known in two forms: one unvocalized (indicating consonants only) and the other vocalized (indicating vowels), a development which probably occurred during the reign of Ezana in the mid-fourth century AD. The epigraphic texts, relating the details of military campaigns, are formulaic in style and propagandist in tone. Ezana's inscriptions provide corroboratory evidence of the conversion to Christianity, with earlier examples invoking the pre-Christian gods of Aksum and later ones invoking the Lord of Heaven and the Holy Trinity.

AMORITE

A Mesopotamian collective designation for a number of pastoral groups of peoples based in the Syrian desert and who first appear in the textual record at the end of the third millennium BC as specialist groups in the army of the Empire of Agade. They are prominent in Mesopotamia during the poorly understood time of the fall of the Third Dynasty of Ur and the beginning of the Old Babylonian Period (c. 2000 BC). Here, rulers with Amorite names are attested as controlling cities from the Levant to south Mesopotamia. This evidence is exclusively genealogical and it is unknown how the Amorites came to form such a substantial population group at this time.

ANYANG

City in Henan province near the border of Hebei province in central China. Scientific excavation at the Bronze Age sites at Anyang was first carried out from 1928–1937 and established that Anyang, or Yin, became the last capital of the Shang dynasty. The revealed ruins of buildings and tombs, including that of Fu Hao, have yielded thousands of objects which provide information about the daily life of the Shang ruling class and its religion, economic activities, warfare, government and diplomatic relations.

ARIANS

Many of the barbarians who crossed into the Roman empire in the fifth century AD and who fought for and against the Roman army were Christians. Most, however, were not Catholics, but Arians. This meant that they had a different view of the relationship between Christ and God, claiming that God, as father, was superior to Christ, the son, just as in human life a son had to be subservient to his father. God the father was 'True God', and Christ's divinity was the result of his being of similar substance to the father (the Greek term was *homoiousios*) but not the same substance (*homoousios*). These apparently minor doctrinal differences were an ongoing cause of tension in the later Roman empire, and the rejection of Arianism is still visible in the wording of the Nicene creed.

ASCETICISM

A word meaning broadly, 'self-mastery'. It took various forms. St Antony pioneered a hermetical form in which the monk would isolate himself from human company, often living on the desert fringes. Gradually, coenobitic rules and institutions developed so that monks could live in settled communities. These forms of Egyptian monasticism were emulated in the West. In Gaul, Martin of Tours was influential in developing monasticism, while Jerome exercised similar influence in Rome. In the West, community monasticism was more practical and popular than hermetical. Monastic foundations were often initially very small but exercised considerable influence. The reputation of monks was such that monastic figures were sometimes selected for episcopal office.

ATEN

Within the Egyptian cosmic order, the winged sun disc Aten originally had a number of symbolic functions. In the reign of Akhenaten, its visual and textual depictions took on a more specific ritual meaning. Unlike other Egyptian deities, the Aten did not take an anthropomorphic form. It is the only Egyptian deity to appear with its name in a cartouche. It appears to be the only deity with which the king Akhenaten chose to associate himself. After the reign of Akhenaten, the Aten returned to the role which it had played previously as a representation of the sun disc.

ATHENIAN EMPIRE

Modern term for the alliance between Athens and many Greek states in the period 478–404 BC. It is also known in its early stages as the Delian League. Although the Athenians gained a reputation for being harsh leaders, in particular because of the way they dealt with cities which tried to leave the alliance, it is likely that most members of the alliance benefited from membership. When the Spartans became unpopular in the early fourth century BC many of the former members of the 'empire' joined a new alliance (in 378 BC).

AUGUSTUS (63 BC–AD 14) is generally regarded as the first Roman emperor. Born C. Octavius, he was adopted by his great uncle Julius Caesar and, as a consequence, became C. Julius Caesar Octavianus. In 44 BC Octavian led the popular movement against those who had assassinated Caesar and subsequently founded a triumvirate with Antony and Lepidus which ruled the empire with dictatorial powers. This alliance fell apart and civil war resulted. After the death of Antony in 30 BC, Octavian returned to Rome in triumph and was granted the title Augustus. He now styled himself Imperator Caesar Augustus. He remained the dominant figure in Roman politics and on his death was able to bequeath his position to his stepson Tiberius.

B

BABYLONIAN CHRONICLES A series of now fragmentary historiographical texts which cover the period from the mid-eighth century BC to the Hellenistic Period. They were composed in Akkadian in Babylonia and provide a remarkably objective year by year account of the historical affairs that affected the Babylonian state. Most of the preserved texts come in copies from periods later than the matters that they discuss. This fact provides an interesting insight into the way in which the Babylonians remembered their own history.

BRONZES Objects made from an alloy of copper and tin, first produced in China from around 1700 BC. The Middle East produced bronzes considerably earlier, using the lost wax method, but the Chinese created their own technique for casting bronzes by pouring molten bronze into pottery moulds. Bronze containers were used to conduct sacrificial ceremonies and offerings to the ancestors. Weapons, including halberds, knives and chariot fittings, also used bronze. Many bronzes are decorated with a design of a monster mask, called 'taotie' in Chinese, although this term was not used before the Eastern Zhou period.

BUDDHIST GROTTOES The 53 cliff shrines at Yungang, near the Northern Wei capital, Datong, are the earliest stone-carved caves in China; most of the 51,000 surviving stone figures date from between AD 453 and 494 and were built under royal patronage. The style reflects influences from traditions brought into China along the so-called Silk Route. The many colossal Buddha figures in these caves typify the early Indian-influenced style of Buddhist art. The caves at Longmen, near Luoyang, were mainly built between AD 495 and 535, after the Northern Wei moved south from Datong, but they continued into the seventh century AD. There are more than 1,300 caves, several pagodas and many inscriptions. The art here represents one of the high points of Chinese Buddhist artistic expression.

 C

CENTURION Centurions commanded about 80 infantrymen and performed a key role in the Roman army. They disciplined the troops, distributed tasks and privileges, and liaised with senior commanders. Centurions would either rise through the ranks or, if of aristocratic origin, be direct appointees. In some provinces, centurions were sent out into the countryside as peacekeepers, bringing Rome's power to the smaller towns and villages of the empire.

CHACMOOL Mesoamerican life-size stone figure in reclining position, legs flexed, head turned to one side. They are usually found at entrances to temples as sacrificial stones or to contain offerings.

CHAKRAVARTIN A term in Sanskrit, the classical language of ancient India, referring to an ideal king or sovereign, especially one who ruled large portions of the Indian subcontinent. The earliest references to Chakravartins or 'wheel-turning monarchs' are in early Buddhist literature and the first representations appear in relief sculpture from the second century BC. The Chakravartin is associated with a number of emblems which served as idealized props of state: the royal elephant, the throne, the treasury, the royal minister, the queen and the 'house-holder'. The house-holder represented landed estates, food production and tax revenues. The Chakravartin was an important ideal but political realities meant that imperial states tended to last for only relatively short periods.

CHRONOLOGICAL DIVISIONS

Archaeologists in the 19th century divided prehistory into three broad periods, the Stone Age, Bronze Age and Iron Age. The Stone and Bronze Ages were divided further into Early, Middle and Late periods. Subsequent discoveries have led to additional terms (e.g. Copper Age, Chalcolithic Age) being used. The terms refer to the materials used for making tools, and the absolute dates associated with them vary in different areas. Aegean archaeologists still divide the Bronze Age into Early, Middle and Late, referring to Minoan (Crete), Helladic (Mainland) and Cycladic (Islands) cultures. These periods are divided further into I, II and III, and even these may be divided into A, B and C, so that the eruption of Thera in 1628 BC is associated with pottery classified as LM (Late Minoan) IA. In the Near East, where there is much more documentary evidence from the third and second millennia BC, this kind of terminology is used less.

CIRCUS FACTIONS The Roman circus had been divided into four factions: the red, whites, blues and greens, but by the Byzantine period we mainly hear of the blues and the greens. These two groups became major institutions within Byzantine cities, running not only teams of charioteers but also theatre groups. The factions attracted political and sometimes imperial sponsorship and the games were important important social and political events at which the crowds could voice opinions about matters other than sport. These acclamations were often recorded and sometimes inscribed at the theatre, especially if in praise of a local aristocrat.

CITY-STATE Term originally applied to the Greek communities which emerged early in the first millennium BC, and commonly used about renaissance Italy. It refers to an area with an urban centre and surrounding territory. City-states were small but autonomous units: there were possibly as many as 750 city-states in the Greek world in the period c. 800-300 BC. The word has been adopted by archaeologists and historians to describe communities elsewhere in the Mediterranean and even further afield, although how far it is applicable to civilizations beyond the Mediterranean is a matter of debate.

CLEISTHENES Leading Athenian who was considered the founder of Athenian democracy through his reforms of 508/7 BC. The reforms made *demes* (villages) the basic political unit of Athens, and organized these into ten tribes (the basic military unit). They also increased the use of the lot for appointment to political offices, and created the annually elected position of General (there were ten, one elected by each tribe). All political decisions were taken at meetings of the Assembly, open to all (male) citizens, and the business of the assembly was prepared by a council of 500 men appointed annually by lot from the ten tribes.

COATEPANTLI A wall with sculptured snakes, usually built to divide the sacred from the profane spaces in Mesoamerica. They are found in the Post-Classic period (c. AD 900–1500).

THE CONVERSION TO CHRISTIANITY: THE STORY OF FRUMENTIUS AND AEDESIUS The Latin writer Rufinus recorded an account of Aksum's conversion to Christianity in the mid-fourth century AD. It concerns the capture of two boys, Frumentius and Aedesius, who became servants to the Aksumite king. At his death the old king left an infant son for whom Frumentius and the queen-mother acted as regents. Meanwhile, Frumentius sought out Christian merchants and promoted the new religion. When the young king, usually identified as Ezana, came of age, Frumentius travelled to Alexandria where he was consecrated as the first bishop of Ethiopia. He is remembered there today as Abba Salama, the Father of Peace.

CTESIPHON Capital of the Parthians and Sasanians. It was located on the river Tigris about 35 kilometres south of Baghdad in modern Iraq. This was at a strategic junction of routes along the Tigris or Euphrates towards the Roman Empire or Persian Gulf, or along the Diyala river towards western Iran. The city has not been excavated apart from some villas decorated with stuccoes. A short distance away lay the royal city of Aspanabr, at which stands the largest surviving vault known as the Taq-i Kisra. This was probably the main audience hall of Khusrau I's palace that was constructed with the help of Byzantine craftsmen. On the opposite riverbank was the city known as 'The City of Ardashir', where excavations have revealed carefully planned areas of housing separated by asphalt roads.

CUNEIFORM Near Eastern writing system. Cuneiform a Latin term meaning 'wedge shaped'. The script was used to render a number of Mesopotamian, Iranian, Anatolian and Levantine languages. It first appeared in the Uruk period (4000–2900 BC) and continued in use up to the first century AD. It in found in monumental form on reliefs or stelae and in the documentation of daily life. The cuneiform script has an extensive number of syllabic values, which were not all used at any given time. Often scholars are able to classify textual evidence by period and genre on the basis of the range of signs with which a document is composed.

DIVISION OF GREEK HISTORY Greek history has traditionally been divided into three periods, marked by key events. *Archaic*, from 776 BC (the traditional date for the first Olympic Games) to 479 BC (the end of the Persian invasion of Greece under Xerxes); *Classical*, from 479 to 323 BC (the death of Alexander the Great); and *Hellenistic*, from 323 to 30 BC (the death of Cleopatra, the last Greco-Macedonian ruler of an independent kingdom). The tripartite division has its origin in 18th-century categorization of Greek sculpture, but was then used more generally. Although art historians would no longer support the rigid distinctions the terms imply, used flexibly this remains a useful way of distinguishing between the principal phases of Greek history.

DYNASTY A term which conventionally describes a line of rulers who belong to a single family. However, this term can sometimes be used to classify rulers who are associated through their affinity to a particular city or a distinct ethnic group. In the case of Egypt, our main source for understanding the classification of rulers into dynasties is the account of the Egyptian scholar Manetho, written in the third century BC, who divided the rulers of Egypt into 30 dynasties. The reality behind his designation of individual rulers into a dynastic scheme is often unclear. Contemporary evidence often reveals that these individuals were not always members of the same family. What is important, however, is that the principle by which Manetho grouped together rulers into dynasties is also evident in an earlier Egyptian document of the New Kingdom (1550–1069 BC) known as the Turin Canon.

FORUM The formal centre of a Roman city. At Rome, the Imperial period saw the massive extension of central facilities. Julius Caesar built a new forum adjacent to the traditional (Roman) forum. Augustus refurbished the Roman forum and built the Augustan forum which was dominated by a temple to Mars. Vespasian and his sons built the now lost Forum of Peace and Nerva completed the Forum Transitorium between the Forum of Peace and the older fora. Trajan's Forum completed the development of the imperial fora and contained libraries, a huge basilica and Trajan's column.

GOTHS The Goths were divided into two federations, the Visigoths and the Ostrogoths. The Visigoths were established in Spain while the Ostrogoths came to control Italy. The tribes appear to have been loose groupings of warriors with few clearly defined ethnic characteristics. The kings were originally leaders of war-bands. During the war in Italy with Byzantium the Ostrogoths were led by Totila. The defeat of the Goths at Busta Gallorum (AD 552) led to the death of about 6,000 men and effectively ended Gothic power in the peninsula.

THE GRAND CANAL The Sui emperor Yangdi (AD 604–17), following on the work begun by his father, Wendi, had by AD 618 built 1,250 miles of canals linking the entire country except Sichuan, and provided an effective system of transport across Central China, from the southern Yangzi valley to the northern Beijing area. This was a powerful, unifying factor of inestimable military and economic value, but its cost was exorbitant and contributed to the eventual downfall of this dynasty.

GREAT PERSECUTIONS Although Christians in the Roman Empire had been intermittently persecuted since the mid-first century AD, the third century saw systematic persecution. In some places, registers were kept of those who sacrificed to the emperor. Since Christians were unable to do this, they immediately became enemies of the state. Although many were martyred as a result, some went into hiding and others escaped the requirement by paying for certificates. Some, however, sacrificed and, at the end of persecutions, the Church leaders had considerable difficulties deciding how to treat the lapsed. Prominent individuals were forced to explain their behaviour during these years.

THE GREAT WALL Called the 'wall of ten thousand li' by the Chinese. The earliest sections of the wall were built by the various warring states as a defence against the mounted nomads from the west. Qin Shi Huangdi (221–210 BC) ordered these sections to be joined up and set a line of fortresses along the empire's western and northern borders. The wall, as seen today, is a Ming dynasty (AD 1368–1644) reconstruction.

GREEK LYRIC POETRY Personal poetry written in the period after c. 650 BC. It was written by members of the elite in Greek cities, women (e.g. Sappho) as well as men, probably for performance among like-minded friends. Although it survives only in fragments, Lyric poetry and the related genres of Elegiac and Iambic poetry can provide valuable evidence for the social and political attitudes of the poets and their circles in an otherwise poorly documented period.

H

HELOTS The population of Messenia, conquered by the Spartans in the seventh century BC and enserfed. There were also Laconian helots, whose origins are uncertain. They had to give a proportion of their crops to their Spartan overlords, who ritually declared war on them every year. Fear of helot revolts had a considerable effect on Spartan foreign policy. The Messenian helots were liberated by the Thebans when they invaded the Peloponnese in 369 BC.

HERODOTUS (c. 484–424 BC) First Greek historian, known in antiquity as 'the Father of History'. His *Histories* tells the story of Xerxes's invasion of Greece in 480–479 BC, and are prefaced by a long account of the 'great and wonderful achievements of the Greeks and barbarians', which includes discussions of the history, geography and social organization of all the lands that the Achaemenid Persians came in contact with, from northwest Africa to India, and from Ethiopia to central Asia. Although elements of it cannot be relied upon, the *Histories* is an invaluable source of information about the Mediterranean and the Near East in the period c. 750–480 BC. Herodotus has sometimes been caricatured as a credulous story-teller, but his work shows the influence of contemporary Greek scientific thought as well as a great interest in and understanding of Greek and non-Greek religious practices.

HIEROGLYPHIC Hieroglyphic is the Greek term for this writing system and it means sacred writings. Hieroglyphic scripts are attested in Egypt from the Late Pre-Dynastic Period (late fourth millennium BC) to the Roman Period. Hieroglyphic scripts were used in ancient Egypt to convey the Egyptian language in monumental form. Hence, it is found on reliefs and on stelae. Day-to-day documentation was written in the cursive script, Hieratic. Elsewhere in the Ancient Near East, a hieroglyphic script was used to render the Anatolian language known as Luwian. This was a monumental script of the Hittite Empire which was normally used in documents concerned with ritual. Subsequently, it became the exclusive

script of the Neo-Hittite states of southern Turkey and northern Syria (c. 1200–700 BC).

HIJRA From the Arabic, meaning 'flight' or 'migration'. It specifically refers to the migration of Muhammad with his supporters from Mecca to Medina on 16 July AD 622 which marks the beginning of the Islamic era and the start of the Islamic calendar.

HIUAN-TSANG Chinese Buddhist monk who visited India between AD 630 and 643. He travelled from China to Kabul, covering a distance of 3,000 miles along a treacherous route north of the Gobi desert. After arriving in India, he visited nearly every kingdom, reporting on the state of Buddhist monasteries and social conditions. He was received by Harsa with great honour. Hiuan-Tsang's detailed records of his travels recorded in his *Si-yu-Ki*, or *Records of the Western Lands*, have become a valuable source for scholars in reconstructing the political and social history of India during the seventh century AD.

HURRIAN The language of the Bronze Age kingdom of Mitanni. It is an Indo-European language and has some similarities with the language of Urartu, although neither language is fully understood, and the similarities do not imply any significant continuity between the two civilizations.

HYKSOS Rulers of the Fifteenth dynasty in Egypt (c. 1648–1540 BC). Their capital city was Tell el-Daba' (Avaris). These kings are notable within the Second Intermediate Period for their Asiatic associations recorded in both the textual record and in the archaeological remains from Avaris. However, recent scholarship has noted that the Levantine influences which are attested are a consequence of a much longer process of acculturation, which currently can be traced from the Twelfth Dynasty into the New Kingdom. Despite unflattering references in later New Kingdom literature, the archaeological record confirms that the Hyksos continued to support traditional Egyptian concepts of society. Furthermore, the Hyksos are thought to have made a number of technological advances including developments in the fields of bronze-working and transportation.

INTERMEDIATE PERIOD A traditional classification of the periods of Egyptian history when the two lands of Upper and Lower Egypt were not under the control of one king. Scholars have isolated three Intermediate Periods in Egyptian history. The absence of direct central control resulted in a variety of inter-regional political situations of fluctuating geographical extent and varying time spans. The breakdown in central control known as the First Intermediate Period (2181–2023 BC) was not the result of factors external to Egypt itself and lasted for only around 100 years. The Second Intermediate Period (c. 1720–1550 BC) was a longer period of fragmented rule for much of which kings of foreign origin, the Hyksos, controlled a large part of Egypt. The Third Intermediate Period lasted for 400 years (1069–664 BC) and included both a period when Egypt was directly ruled by the Nubian-based Napatan dynasty, and periods of fragmented rule by a series of Libyan dynasts who had previously been incorporated into the Egyptian state. In turn, it was one of the groups of Libyan dynasts, the Saïtes, who went on to reunite Upper and Lower Egypt in the 26th Dynasty (644–525 BC).

JOHN CHRYSOSTOM (c. AD 354–407) an extremely influential bishop of Constantinople (AD 398–403) and, prior to his elevation, an important preacher at Antioch. His preaching appears to have been extremely intense, to the extent that an attack on an empress led to John's removal from Constantinople. John, however, rallied popular support and forced a return to the city. At Antioch, one of his greatest oratorical feats was a series of sermons preached to the population following a riot in which statues of the imperial family were damaged, an act of treason for which the population expected dire consequences.

JULIAN Roman Emperor (AD 361–363). Julian was on the fringes of the imperial family throughout much of his youth. Although educated as a Christian, he developed an interest in pagan philosophy. He was elevated to the position of deputy emperor by Constantius II and sent to Gaul to represent imperial interests while Constantius campaigned against the Persians. After victories against Germanic invaders, Julian was declared emperor. Civil war loomed, but then Constantius died. Julian's conservative reform programme antagonized many at court and offended the Christians. In AD 363, he relaunched an offensive against the Persians and was there killed, an event the Christians took as a sign of divine favour.

JULIUS CAESAR Caius Julius Caesar (100–44 BC) came from an old but not prominent family. He was a political ally of M. Licinius Crassus, one of the two most powerful men in Rome in the period after 70 BC. The other was Pompey (see below), and after Crassus's death in 53 BC, conflict between Caesar and Pompey became inevitable. Caesar had been consul in 59 BC, and spent the following decade conquering Gaul. His return to Italy at the head of his army led to civil war, in which he was victorious. He was given far-reaching powers as Dictator, and instituted a series of constitutional reforms and a major building programme. He was assassinated on 15 March 44 BC.

KINGDOM A traditional classification of the periods of Egyptian history when the two lands of Upper and Lower Egypt were under the direct control of one king. Scholars have distinguished three Kingdoms in Egyptian history: the Old Kingdom (c. 2686–2181 BC), the Middle Kingdom (2023–c. 1720 BC) and the New Kingdom (1550–1069 BC).

LABOUR TAX Also called *Mit'a* by the Inca. This is a tax owed by all inhabitants, male and female, to the state and paid for in labour. Agriculture, mining and textile weaving were all products of taxation.

Women and men were required to spin, weave and produce cloth and cord. Major public works, such as religious and administrative buildings, irrigation, land reclamation, terracing and road systems were constructed using labour tax from able-bodied males. It is estimated that 30,000 men laboured to build the Inca fort of Sacsahuaman.

LAW CODE Cuneiform texts written for Mesopotamian and Hittite kings. The earliest preserved example comes from the reign of King Shulgi of the Third Dynasty of Ur (2094–2047 BC). The most famous example is that of King Hammurabi (1792–1750 BC) from the Old Babylonian period. There is keen scholarly debate about the actual purpose of the prescriptive legal statements which are detailed in the codes. Opinions range from viewing the statements as an example of a royal ideology which bears little resemblance to juridical reality to a more sympathetic consideration of the texts as a representation of the day-to-day function of at least some judicial processes.

MESOAMERICA A geographical and cultural region which includes Mexico (except the northern third), Guatemala, Belize, El Salvador, westernmost Honduras and a very small part of Nicaragua.

MYSTERY CULTS Religious cults open only to initiates. Some were major state-sponsored cults like the Eleusinian Mysteries in honour of Demeter and Kore (Persephone), which were controlled by Athens and had thousands of initiates each year, including some Roman emperors. Others were smaller and might be viewed with suspicion by the authorities. Some cults appear to have offered promises of special privileges to initiates after death. Orpheus, who, according to myth, had visited the underworld and returned, was associated with a number of such cults. Under the Roman empire, mystery cults, including those of Isis and Mithras, were popular, and similarities were noted between such cults and early Christianity.

NEBUCHADNEZZAR II
(604–562 BC) A long lived and highly successful king of the Neo-Babylonian period. His active military campaigning in the Levant down to the border with Egypt is narrated both in the Babylonian Chronicles and in the Hebrew Bible. Nebuchadnezzar II was the ruler responsible for the two Babylonian sieges of Jerusalem and the deportations of the Jewish populations to Babylonia. His is also recognized for his magnificent works of reconstruction in Babylonia, most particularly his legendary efforts in the city of Babylon itself.

NOME A regional administrative unit of Egypt under the control of a local governor (nomarch). Egypt was separated into the two lands of Upper and Lower Egypt. Upper Egypt was divided into 22 nomes, extending along the Nile from Aswan to just south of the city of Memphis. Lower Egypt was divided into 20 nomes encompassing Memphis to the south and the Delta region to the north. The principle of drawing together villages, towns and royal estates within an overarching administrative framework was in existence in the Old Kingdom and continued to function into the Roman period. The level of autonomy of a nomarch within the Egyptian state was a factor dependant upon the immediate levels of central governmental control and, correspondingly, the location of the capital of the nome was not necessarily associated with one fixed place throughout the whole of Egyptian history.

ORACLE BONES Animal bones and tortoise shells which were used for divining the future during the Shang Dynasty (1550–1050 BC). The Chinese term is *Jiaguwan*, shell and bone writing. Originally they were dug up by farmers in the area around Anyang in Henan province. They were thought to be 'dragon' bones and used as medicine. In 1899 two Chinese scholars recognized the scratches on them as ancient writing. The point of a heated bronze tool would be applied to the bones and shells until

hairline cracks appeared in them, and the ways the cracks were formed were believed to provide positive or negative answers to the questions asked, which diviners then interpreted. More than 100,000 oracle bones have been excavated in the area around Anyang and about 1,500 distinct marks have been deciphered.

PANHELLENISM The idea of a shared Greek identity. Although the autonomous city-state (see above) was the basic form of political organization in much of the Greek world, it was recognized that Greeks shared certain elements in common, in particular language and religious practices. Major festivals, where participants gathered from all over the Greek world, reinforced this idea, as did the experience of invasion by the Persians in the early fifth century AD. In the fourth century AD Panhellenism became a political slogan, and Philip and Alexander of Macedon presented their invasion of the Persian empire in part as a Panhellenic venture.

PELOPONNESIAN WAR War fought between the Athenians and their allies, and the Spartans and their allies in 431–404 BC. It falls into two periods, the Archidamian War (431–421 BC) and the Ionian or Decelean War (412–404 BC), separated by an uneasy peace. It is described by Thucydides, a contemporary, but his account breaks off in 411 BC. About a quarter of his work actually describes the Athenian expedition to Sicily which took place during the period of peace. There were other periods of conflict between the same powers (e.g. the so-called First Peloponnesian War of 462–446 BC and the Corinthian War of 394–387 BC) and the designation of the conflicts of 431–404 BC as a single, distinct war is arguably inappropriate.

POMPEY At the age of 23 Gnaeus Pompeius Magnus (106–48 BC) raised a private army to aid Sulla (see below) in his civil war against Marius. In the next few years he campaigned in Sicily and Spain, and mopped up the remnants of the slave army of Spartacus. In 70 BC he

was elected consul, despite being below the minimum age and having held none of the lower magistracies on the *Cursus Honorum* (see page 103). His fellow consul was M. Licinius Crassus, and rivalry between the two men carried on until Crassus's death in Parthia in 53 BC. Although he was a skilful general, Pompey seems to have preferred life in Rome, where he was responsible for a number of public buildings. After losing in a civil war to Crassus's former political ally Julius Caesar (see above), he was assassinated in Egypt on 28 September 48 BC.

PRAETORIAN PREFECT The Emperor Augustus established the praetorian guard in Rome in the late first century BC. It provided the emperor with a military capability within Italy. There were normally two prefects of the guard who shared responsibilities, but the office became one of the most politically sensitive in Rome. On the murder of the emperor Gaius (AD 41), Claudius, his successor, retreated to the praetorian camp and used the threat of the praetorians to force the senate to accept him as emperor. The later Vespasian made his son, Titus, prefect of the guard so that his security and that of Rome was in the hands of his most trusted associate.

PROCOPIUS One of the last great Classical historians, following literary models which stretched back to Thucydides in the fifth century BC. Writing in the sixth century AD, under the powerful emperor Justinian (AD 527–565, Procopius provides a narrative account of Justinian's wars, including the reconquest of Italy and Africa. In a further account, Procopius celebrated the buildings built under Justinian's sponsorship. These works of praise contrast sharply with his most famous work, the *Anecdota* or *Secret History*, which contains an extended literary assault on the demon king Justinian and his queen Theodora, blending Christian and pagan traditions of invective in a potent and altogether unparalleled mix.

Q

QURAN From the Arabic, meaning 'recitation'. Refers to the Holy book of

Islam containing the revelations of Muhammad which Muslims believe were a direct communication from Allah.

R

RAJAMANDALA Literally 'the circle of kings', which in Indian political theory denoted the ever-shifting arrangement of the world's kings. Integral to all of the ancient and medieval manuals on Indian politics, the theory of the rajamandala conceived of the array of regional kingdoms as an expression of a contested and shifting hierarchy where contiguous kings were encouraged to antagonize their neighbours and set up alliances with kings once removed from them.

THE RIG VEDA A collection of 1,017 Sanskrit hymns compiled in c. 1800 BC, thought to have reached their final form by c. 1500 BC. Transmitted in the form of divine revelations, their primary interest is ritual in nature. However they are also useful for providing an insight into the cultural world of the Indo-Aryan speaking society reflected in these verses. References to agriculture are limited, but the cultivation of barley appears to have supplemented a semi-nomadic, semi-pastoral lifestyle based on the domestication of cattle and horses. Later additions were made during the 'Late Vedic period' in c. 1000 BC.

ROMAN COLONIES Communities settled by the Romans on conquered land. These were of two main types: Latin colonies, whose inhabitants were not considered full Roman citizens; and citizen colonies. The former tended to be larger, with several thousand settlers, while the latter, which were usually established as a form of garrison, had around 500 inhabitants. Colonization was a means of spreading and maintaining Roman influence through Italy. Towards the end of the second century BC colonies began to be established overseas, and increasingly colonies were used to settle veteran soldiers at the end of military campaigns.

ROMANITAS In the west of the later Roman empire, the elites celebrated their Romanitas – their 'Romanness' of culture. In so doing, they showed allegiance to the values of Rome, an allegiance which survived the fall of the city itself. In the fourth and fifth centuries AD, the poets and orators of Gaul entertained the imperial court with their finely worked speeches in praise of the various imperial figures and their poems, often reworking Classical themes. This learning was preserved and placed at the disposal of the new barbarian rulers of the west.

RULER CULT AND IMPERIAL CULT

The worship of Hellenistic kings and Roman emperors as gods. This practice began shortly before 300 BC, when Greek cities began to address the kings who controlled their destinies as gods, and to create priesthoods and temples in their honour. Worship expressed the gulf between the powers of the kings and the cities, and was a way for cities to acknowledge their dependence on the kings. The practice was carried on by Roman emperors, although at first at least Roman citizens were not expected to pay cult to the emperor. In Rome itself temples were sometimes built to the *numen* (godhead) of dead emperors. The polytheistic religious systems of the ancient world were easily able to incorporate developments of this kind.

SAMANTA A term which originally meant 'lord of the marches' or 'border king', during the post-Gupta period in India it gradually came to denote any underlord offering fealty or tribute to an imperial king. The samanta was often incorporated into an imperial polity through military conquest and was re-established on his throne in return for tribute and military assistance.

SARGON OF AGADE
(2340–2284 BC) The founder of the south Mesopotamian dynasty of Agade in the late third millennium BC. The actual contemporary evidence for the Empire of Agade is slight. However, the fame of the Agade kings was perpetuated through the re-copying of their inscriptions in the Old Babylonian Period. Subsequently, epic literary works such as the *Sargon Birth Legend* were created, copied and revised into the Hellenistic Period. The character and deeds of Sargon of Agade appear to have been of continuous fascination to later Mesopotamian society.

SATRAPY A regional administrative unit of the Achaemenid Persian empire (c. 550–330 BC) under the control of a local governor (satrap) who was appointed by the king. However, within such a large territory there was considerable regional diversity in the operation of the satrapal system. In general, each satrapy had a capital city with a palace from which the satrap conducted his affairs. Administrative centres were often located in the traditional capital of the conquered states, for example, Memphis in Egypt and Babylon in Babylonia. The satrapal centres were the hub from which all regional bureaucratic affairs were conducted and the conduit through which inter-regional concerns were directed under the authority of the king.

SCRIBE A traditional professional class in the Ancient Near East who undertook the administration and publication of most public and private documentation. Scribes were trained in schools and much of the documentary record of the region is preserved in school exercise copies. The scribal profession was not exclusively male. For example, the Neo-Assyrian queens had female scribes at their court to conduct their administrative affairs.

SEA PEOPLE The term Sea People is a translation of an Egyptian collective designation for a multiplicity of named peoples who on two occasions impinged upon the territory of the Egyptian state and who are recorded in the inscriptions of the New Kingdom rulers Merneptah (1213–1204 BC) and Rameses III (1184–1152 BC). Scholars have tried to explain this information by examining it in the light of wider population changes within the Aegean World, Anatolia and the Levant. The issue is whether the movement of population groups such as the Sea People was a cause or an effect of the collapse of the Late Bronze Age imperial system. This question, however, is vexed by an absence of evidence to support either position.

SENATE The principal council of the city of Rome. The Senate was composed of ex-magistrates, who remained members for life. It had 300 members before Sulla's reforms in 81 BC, and 600 afterwards, although the numbers crept up to around 1,000 in the Roman Imperial period. Although it had no legislative powers the Senate was the most influential body in the Roman republic, because of its continuity – in contrast to the annually changing magistrates – and because it contained most of the richest and most powerful citizens. Until the last years of the republic it was rare for magistrates to act without first consulting the Senate. Under the empire authority passed to the emperor, but until the late third century AD the Senate had the role of formally bestowing powers on a new emperor.

SEVEN KINGS OF ROME Believed by Roman tradition to have ruled the city for the first two-and-a-half centuries of its existence. The last three kings may have been historical figures, although probably not kings in any usual sense of the word. The traditional list, with reign dates, is: Romulus (753–715 BC); Numa Pompilius (715–672 BC); Tullus Hostilius (672–640 BC); Ancus Marcius (640–616 BC); Tarquinius Priscus (616–578 BC); Servius Tullius (578–534 BC); Tarquinius Superbus (534–509 BC).

SEVEN WONDERS OF THE ANCIENT WORLD Seven major works of engineering and art. The idea of compiling a collection of descriptions of 'wonders' goes back to Callimachus of Cyrene, Librarian of the Museum at Alexandria, but the canonical list of seven is probably medieval in origin. The seven (with the appropriate pages of this atlas) are: the Great Pyramid of Khufu, c. 2600–2500 BC (page 26); the Hanging Gardens of Babylon, c. 604–562 BC (page 86); the Temple of Artemis at Ephesus, c. 550 BC (page 68); the Statue of Zeus at Olympia, c. 450 BC (page 74); the Mausoleum at Halicarnassus, 350 BC (page 70); the Colossus of Rhodes, 282 BC (page 104); the Pharos of Alexandria, c. 290–270 BC (page 106).

SHIJING The Book of Poetry or Song. Includes 305 poems dated between c. 1000 and c. 600 BC. It is traditionally said to have been collected by Confucius and, along with *The Book of History,* is one of the Five Classics. Many works are folk songs or religious works but later interpretations of the text imputed political implications in nearly all the poems. The texts were discussed in such terms in the imperial examination. Scholars and officials would know much of the text by heart.

SHUJING *The Book of History*, one of the Five Classics of the Confucian Canon. Parts of it at least date back to the 22nd century BC and it was one of the classics destroyed by Qin Shi Huangdi. It was restored in the Han Dynasty by scholars who had memorized the text. The text describes the reigns of the mythical emperors Yao and Shun, then the Xia, Shang and early years of the Zhou dynasties. Sima Qian used it as a source in writing his *Shiji*. The accounts of the Shang Dynasty were sceptically received by historians until the oracle bone discoveries corroborated much of the text.

SILK ROUTE There were several routes between China and the West. The term 'silk route' was coined by the German historian von Richthofen in the 1870s to apply to the routes which ran west from China to Syria in the Middle East and onwards to Rome. It was, though, a generic term for many routes, both overland and by sea, and silk was but one of the many commodities carried over it. The Silk Route began to be plied in earnest during the Han Dynasty, after the explorer Zhang Qian reported back to the emperor the willingness of the peoples of central Asia to trade with China.

SIMA QIAN A court historian during the Han Dynasty who compiled the *Shiji* (Records of the Historian). The first official history of China, it traced developments from the time of the legendary Yellow Emperor to Sima Qian's own day. His father had been Grand Historian before him and began the history, which Sima Qian completed using documents stored in the imperial archives. It contains 130 chapters and is a compilation of all documents available to

him recording Chinese tradition and legends. This history was reworked and expanded by Ban Biao (AD 3–54) as 'The History of the Former Han Dynasty' and this set a pattern of dynastic histories which was continued until the end of the empire in 1911.

SIR ALEXANDER CUNNINGHAM (1814–1893) Cunningham was the first Director General of the Archaeological Survey of India (1861–1865, 1870–1885) and the first person to excavate an Indus Civilization site, Harappa, in 1875. His designation of the principal areas at Harappa (A-B, C, D and E) is still used today. Cunningham was responsible for laying the foundations for field archaeology in south Asia and recorded a number of sites from a variety of periods.

SIR JOHN HUBERT MARSHALL (1876–1958) Marshall was Director General of the Archaeological Survey of India from 1902 to 1928. His principal interest lay in the influence which the classical Greeks had on the subcontinent, which he fulfilled through research at the sites of Taxila and Charsada. However, whilst comparing material from Harappa and Mohenjo-Daro in 1924, he realized that these geographically distinct sites were part of a much larger phenomenon. He termed this the 'Indus Civilisation'. Excavations began under his supervision at Mohenjo-Daro in 1925 and ended in 1931. The published results laid down the foundations for the definition of the Indus Civilization, which was debated by scholars thereafter.

SOCIAL WAR War fought between Rome and its Italian allies in 91–87 BC. It arose largely from Italian resentment at receiving inferior treatment when compared with Roman citizens. Although the Italians were defeated, it suited the interests of a number of Romans to propose extensions of full citizenship to Italian communities, and only a few years after the war all the allies had been made Roman citizens.

STELAE Free-standing commemorative stone monuments which were commissioned by rulers and members of the ruling elite in the Ancient Near East. Stelae were normally inscribed with text noting the purpose behind their existence and images were carved into them. They are disseminated both in the centres of ancient civilization and within the broader landscape. This phenomenon is clearly illustrated by the Babylonian stelae known as *kudurru*. These monuments pertained to the issuing of land grants. They were placed in temples as a record of the motivations behind the donations and also functioned as actual boundary markers.

SULLA L. Cornelius Sulla (138–78 BC) was elected consul in 88 BC and given command of the war against Mithridates of Pontus by the Roman Senate, only to have the command transferred to his rival, Caius Marius, by a popular assembly. Sulla's response was to march on Rome, expel his political enemies and reverse the decision. After his victory against Mithridates he again used his army to force his way into Rome. There he massacred his enemies. Appointed Dictator in 81 BC he reorganized many aspects of Roman legal and political practice before retiring in 79 BC.

THEODORA Theodora, who died in AD 548, is an enigmatic figure, though clearly powerful within the court of her husband Justinian. Before marrying Justinian, she had a career on the stage, allegedly (according to Procopius) performing lewd acts. She later took an interest in saving the morals of actresses and prostitutes, establishing religious institutions for their protection. She is also said to have taken an interest in religious policy, apparently taking a different line to her spouse on the Christological disputes which divided the church after the council of Chalcedon. She also seems to have been particularly influential in Egypt, where she exercized protection over certain communities.

THREE KINGDOMS PERIOD A period following the break-up of the Chinese Empire at the end of the Eastern Han when civil war disrupted China and three kingdoms, Wei, Shu and Wu dominated

the country. This period generated a cycle of folk tales that formed the basis for the epic historical novel 'Romance of the Three Kingdoms' (*Sanguo yanyi*), attributed to Luo Guangzhong (c. AD 1330–1400). This is considered one of the four great novels in China and many of its episodes are still performed in Beijing Opera. It describes the conflict between Shu and Wei, culminating in battle in which the southerners defeat Cao Cao of Wei.

TIGLATH-PILESER I (1114–1076 BC)
A king of the later Middle Assyrian Empire. He had to campaign vigorously against the Aramaean population groups who were encroaching into Mesopotamian territory at this time. He is also renowned for his development of the traditional Mesopotamian royal building inscriptions into a genre which included a chronological account of military campaigns. This literary reshaping became the standard format by which the achievements of all Assyrian kings were narrated. These 'annals' are the framework upon which our historical understanding of the later Middle Assyrian and Neo-Assyrian periods is based.

TRIUMPH A triumph was awarded to a victorious general at the conclusion of a particularly successful campaign. These normally followed an acclamation by the troops and a senatorial decision to reward the general. The general and at least some of his troops would parade through the streets of Rome carrying depictions of his campaigns and displaying the captured property and people. The general himself would be driven through the city in a chariot, dressed in imitation of God. The procession culminated at the temple of Jupiter Optimus Maximus where sacrifices were offered.

TYRANNY Autocratic rule by an individual over a Greek city-state. Tyrants emerge in the seventh and sixth centuries BC in Greece, and although most disappeared before the end of the sixth century BC, tyrants were supported by the Persians in the cities they controlled in Asia Minor until the end of the Ionian revolt in 499 BC. In Sicily a

number of cities were controlled by tyrants until the middle of the fifth century BC, and at Syracuse tyranny re-emerged at the end of that century, lasting well into the fourth. Although tyrants gained a bad reputation, partly reflecting the propaganda of those who succeeded them, and partly as a result of the writings of political theorists in the fourth century BC, they could only have maintained their positions with the support of the bulk of the population of their cities.

TZOMPANTLI Mesoamerican skull rack. Large wooden racks were often placed near temples and used to display skulls of the victims.

VERTICALITY AND HORIZONTALITY
The way ecological resources were distributed was critical in influencing the development of Andean cultures. In the lowlands, the same type of ecology might stretch over a vast area. Societies separated by thousands of kilometres would share the same basic crops and wild resources. These are homogenous, detached resources. Horizontality refers to the direction in which goods were moved. In the Amazon lowlands, products were moved by watercraft along the river systems, in the west, along the coast by sea. In the highlands, ecological zones were stacked one above the other. Over a distance of 100 km as the crow flies, inhabitants of the Andes can move from lowland tropical forests to snow-capped peaks. The movement of products vertically is more difficult.

WRITING SYSTEMS There are several different ways of representing languages in written form. The main distinction is between logographic and phonographic symbols. Logograms are semantic symbols, signs that stand for words and ideas. Some logograms, known as pictograms, are pictures of what they represent, while others may be indirect symbols, such as the Egyptian hieroglyphic symbol for 'ruler', which is a shepherd's crook. Phonograms represent sounds – either individual letters (alphabets), or syllables (syllabaries). Several early writing systems, including Egyptian Hieroglyphics and Mayan glyphs, used symbols both logographically and phonographically. Mesopotamian Cuneiform developed from a pictographic system into a stylized set of symbols which could be inscribed on damp clay with a stick or reed. It was subsequently used as a syllabic system for writing a number of languages.

XI'AN A city which today is the capital of Shaanxi province in western China. Its origin goes back to Neolithic times but it has served as the capital of 12 dynasties over about 2,000 years. It was the capital of the Western Zhou, Qin (at Xianyang), Western Han, Sui and Tang dynasties. It was historically called Chang'an, city of everlasting peace, and by the time of the Tang Dynasty was the largest city in the world, with an area of 80 square kilometres and a population of one million inside the city, which was laid out on a grid system.

ZHANG QIAN (died c. 114 BC) A Han Dynasty general during the reign of Wudi (141–87 BC), who in 139 BC took a military force to the western regions to negotiate an alliance with the Yuezhi tribe against their common enemy, the Xiongnu, and seek out the famous horses of Ferghana. However, he was captured

and held captive for ten years. After escaping he continued his travels and returned to China in 126 BC with alfalfa and grapes and the news that the western regions were anxious to trade with the Han Empire, especially for silk. He made a second trip from 119–115 BC to the horse-breeding peoples of Central Asia.

ZHUANG ZHOU (c. 369–286 BC)
After Laozi, the most important thinker in the Daoist tradition was Zhuang Zhou. *Dao* means way, path or road and in Daoist thought represents the fundamental principle that pervades the universe and everything in it. Since all things are constantly moving and changing, the wise person knows how to yield and flow with the *dao*, by doing nothing, *wu wei*. As a way of life, it was an appealing contrast to the strict moral and social emphasis of Confucianism. Zhuang Zhou was a contemporary of Mengzi, the second-most important Confucian thinker c. 372–289 BC and his writings are collectively known as the *Zhuangzi*.

ZIGGURAT A series of superimposed platforms found within the temple complexes of cities in Mesopotamia. Although similar in shape to Egyptian step pyramids they differed in function. Ziggurats were constructed of solid brickwork and had a temple on the top.

The earliest example comes from the reign of Ur-Nammu of the Third Dynasty of Ur (2112–c. 2095 BC). The physical arrangement of these structures can be seen in the archaeological record to remain relatively constant throughout Mesopotamian history. Like most other features of Mesopotamian monumental architecture, ziggurats were normally painted. The detail of their appearance and function, however, has to be gleaned from depictions upon objects such as seals, representations contained in reliefs and the textual record.

ZOROASTRIANISM Zoroastrianism was the official Sasanian state religion. Fire worship became mainstream and coronation fires were consecrated in the king's name. A large number of fire-temples have been identified on survey in southern Iran. Fire altars, often flanked by attendants, were depicted on the reverse side of Sasanian coins and on central Asian ossuaries. Zoroastrian belief that the earth should not be contaminated prevented the orthodox from being buried until the flesh had been removed through exposure: reused jars or specially made ossuaries were therefore used to bury these remains. However, despite Zoroastrianism being the state religion there were sizeable Christian and Jewish populations plus smaller Buddhist, Manichaean and other religious communities.

Index

Picture Credits

Cover Robert Harding Picture Library **16** Werner Forman Archive, British Museum, London **18** American Museum of Natural History Library/Craig Chesek **18–19** AKG London/Henning Bock **20–21** Scala, Florence **22** Robert Harding Picture Library **23–28** Scala, Florence **29** Werner Forman Archive, Christie's, London **30–31** Scala, Florence **32** (*top*) Scala, Florence (*bottom left*) British Museum (*bottom right*) Ancient Art & Architecture Collection/© R. Sheridan **33** Ancient Art & Architecture Collection/© R. Sheridan **34–35** Scala, Florence **36** AKG London/Erich Lessing **37** The Art Archive/Musée du Louvre, Paris **38** (*top*) Robert Harding Picture Library (*bottom*) Ancient Art & Architecture Collection **39** (*top*) Robert Harding Picture Library (*bottom*) Robert Harding Picture Library/© P. Koch **41** (*top*) Archaeological Museum of Thebes (*bottom*) British Museum **42–43** Scala, Florence **44** Ancient Art & Architecture Collection/© Mary Jelliffe **45** The Art Archive/Jacqueline Hyde **46** (*left*) Ancient Art & Architecture Collection (*right*) Ancient Art & Architecture Collection/© John P. Stevens **47** (*top*) Scala, Florence (*Osiris*) Ancient Art & Architecture Collection/© Mary Jelliffe (*Thoth and Isis*) Werner Forman Archive, Fitzwilliam Museum, Cambridge (*Anubis*) Ancient Art & Architecture Collection/R. Sheridan (*Horus*) Ancient Art & Architecture Collection/© Mary Jelliffe (*Hathor*) The Art Archive/Dagli Orti **49** (*left*) Michael Holford (*right*) Hirmer Fotoarchiv, München **50** AKG London/Erich Lessing **51** (*top*) AKG London/Erich Lessing (*bottom*) Ancient Art & Architecture Collection/© R. Sheridan **52** (*top*) The Art Archive **54–55** British Museum **56** Art Exhibitions China **57** (*top*) Art Exhibitions China (*bottom*) British Museum **58** Scala, Florence **61** (*left*) Ischia, Museo Archeologico di Pitecusa (*right*) Cagliari Museo Archeologico Nazionale **62–65** Scala, Florence **66–67** Archivo PubbliAerFoto/Aerocentro Varesino – Italy **69** The Bridgeman Art Library, London/Peter Willi **70** (*left*) Ancient Art & Architecture Collection/© R Sheridan (*right*) Ancient Art & Architecture Collection/© Mike Andrews **71** Scala, Florence **72** (*left*) AKG London/John Hios (*right*) Ancient Art & Architecture Collection/© R. Sheridan **73** Ancient Art & Architecture Collection/© Mike Andrews **74–75** Scala, Florence **76** The Art Archive/Egyptian Museum, Cairo **77** (*top*) Werner Forman Archive, The Egyptian Museum, Cairo (*bottom*) The Art Archive, The Egyptian Museum, Cairo/Dagli Orti **78** Ursula Verhoeven **79** National Archaeological Museum of Athens, Egyptian Collection **80** Bildarchiv Preußischer Kulturbesitz, Berlin **81** British Museum **82** AKG London/Erich Lessing **82–83** Ancient Art & Architecture Collection/© R. Sheridan **83** (*top*) Werner Forman Archive (*bottom*) Ashmolean Museum, Oxford **84–85** AKG London/Erich Lessing **86** (*top*) British Museum (*bottom*) Werner Forman Archive, State Museum, Berlin **87–89** Scala, Florence **90** (*top*) The Art Archive/Dagli Orti (*bottom*) Mary Evans Picture Library **91** The Art Archive/Dagli Orti **92** (*top*) Werner Forman Archive, Graeco-Roman Museum, Alexandria, Egypt **92–93** Scala, Florence **93** (*top*) British Museum (*bottom*) Ancient Art & Architecture Collection/© R. Sheridan **94** AKG London/Jean-Louis Nou **95** Robert Harding **96** Art Exhibitions China **97** British Museum **98** Robert Harding Picture Library **100** AKG London/Erich Lessing **100–101** Scala, Florence **102** (*both*) Scala, Florence **104** (*top*) Michael Crawford **105** (*all*) British Museum **107** (*top and bottom left*) Ancient Art & Architecture Collection/© R. Sheridan (*bottom right*) Ancient Art & Architecture Collection/© John P. Stevens **109** (*top left and right*) Werner Forman Archive (*bottom*) Werner Forman Archive, Sudan Archaeological Museum, Khartoum **110** Ancient Art & Architecture Collection/© R. Sheridan **111** AKG London/Erich Lessing **112** Ancient Art & Architecture Collection/© R. Sheridan **113–115** Scala, Florence **116–117** AKG London/Erich Lessing **117** Werner Forman Archive, National Museum, Damascus **118–120** British Museum **121** Joe Cribb **122** (*top*) British Museum (*bottom*) Ancient Art & Architecture Collection/©Allan Eaton **124** (*both*) Shaanxi Provincial Cultural Relics Bureau **126** Art Exhibitions China **127** (*top*) British Museum (*bottom right*) Shaanxi Provincial Cultural Relics Bureau **128** British Museum **130–131** Scala, Florence **132** (*top*) Michael Holford (*bottom*) Ancient Art & Architecture Collection/© R. Sheridan **134–135** Scala, Florence **136** Ancient Art & Architecture Collection/© R. Sheridan **137–139** Scala, Florence **141** (*top left and right*) British Museum (*bottom*) St John Simpson **142** Werner Forman Archive **143** (*all*) British Museum **144** Werner Forman Archive, Musée Bardo, Algiers **145** Roderick J. McIntosh **146** Michael Willis **147** British Museum **148** Robert Harding Picture Library/© A. Kennet **149** Robert Harding Picture Library **150–153** British Museum **154** Werner Forman Archive, Topkapi Palace Library, Istanbul **155** (*top*) AKG London (*bottom*) Werner Forman Archive, Mrs Bashir Mohammed Collection, London **156** Robert Harding Picture Library **157** (*top*) Ancient Art and Architecture Collection/© R. Sheridan (*middle*) Robert Harding Picture Library/Adam Woolfitt (*bottom*) Ancient Art & Architecture Collection/© R. Sheridan **158** Werner Forman Archive, British Museum, London **160–163** Elizabeth Baquedano **164** (*top*) Lawrence E. Desmond (*bottom*) Elizabeth Baquedano **165–167** Elizabeth Baquedano **168** (*top*) South American Pictures/Tony Morrison (*bottom*) South American Pictures/Chris Sharp **169** South American Pictures/Tony Morrison **170** (*left*) South American Pictures/Tony Morrison (*right*) South American Pictures/Kimball Morrison **170–171** South American Pictures/Tony Morrison **171–173** South American Pictures/Tony Morrison